A reporter with *60 Minutes*, Ross Coulthart is one of Australia's leading investigative journalists. Winner of a Logie and five Walkley journalism awards including the Gold Walkley, Ross is also the author of the magnificent *The Lost Diggers*. Like Charles Bean, Ross Coulthart studied law and has covered conflicts in hostile war zones such as East Timor, Iraq and Afghanistan. He has always admired Bean's courage and scrupulous honesty, and now he examines the real story of the man who was one of Australia's earliest embedded war reporters.

Charles BEAN

ROSS COULTHART

HarperCollins*Publishers*

HarperCollins*Publishers*

First published in Australia in 2014
This edition published in 2015
by HarperCollins*Publishers* Australia Pty Limited
ABN 36 009 913 517
harpercollins.com.au

HarperCollins*Publishers*
Level 13, 201 Elizabeth Street, Sydney NSW 2000, Australia
Unit D1, 63 Apollo Drive, Rosedale, Auckland 0632, New Zealand
A 53, Sector 57, Noida, UP, India
1 London Bridge Street, London SE1 9GF, United Kingdom
2 Bloor Street East, 20th floor, Toronto, Ontario M4W 1A8, Canada
195 Broadway, New York NY 10007, USA

National Library of Australia Cataloguing-in-Publication data:

Coulthart, Ross, author.
Charles Bean / Ross Coulthart.
ISBN 978 0 7322 9788 6 (paperback)
ISBN 978 1 4607 0052 5 (ebook)
Includes bibliographical references and index.
Bean, C. E. W. (Charles Edwin Woodrow), 1879-1968.
War correspondents – Australia – Biography.
World War, 1914-1918 – Journalists – Biography.
Historians – Australia – Biography.
070.4333092

Cover design by Sam Williams
Front cover images: Australian infantry wounded at a first-aid post near Zonnebeke Railway Station, in the Passchendaele Area, Belgium, 1917, composite image by Frank Hurley courtesy of the Australian War Memorial (E01202A); Charles Bean visiting the frontline trenches held by the 39th Battalion at Houplines, France, December 1916, courtesy of the Australian War Memorial (E00087)
Back cover image: Charles Bean watching the Australian advance at Martinpuich, France, February 1917, courtesy of the Australian War Memorial (E00246)
Index by Michael Wyatt
Typeset in Bembo Std by Kirby Jones
Printed and bound in Australia by Griffin Press
The papers used by HarperCollins in the manufacture of this book are a natural, recyclable product made from wood grown in sustainable plantation forests. The fibre source and manufacturing processes meet recognised international environmental standards, and carry certification.

For Dugald Grist

1960–2012

A fine gentleman, a great storyteller and a true friend

Contents

AUTHOR'S NOTE

Afghanistan, 2010. I am sitting in an American forward operating base ten kilometres south of Kandahar, watching a mortar team set up. We have been awake all night, following a United States infantry combat patrol search unsuccessfully for insurgents trying to smuggle weapons into the city. A week into this embed with the Americans, we are worried that we have no story worth telling, because there have been no clashes with the Taliban anywhere in this area for weeks.

In the heat of the day, I watch the sweating mortar team lob a shell into the tube; we are told it is being zeroed in on empty farmland a kilometre distant to test targeting. It launches with a bang and far in the distance we hear a muffled thud as it lands. There is a pause, then a flustered American officer rushes up and we are curtly informed that filming is over. Something is going on, but it is hours before we learn that the mortar crew has accidentally killed a local Afghan child who strayed onto the bombing range. Our pleas for an escort to cover this tragedy are declined; we are totally dependent on the Americans for information and we would need their security protection to approach the now no-doubt furious local villagers. It is made very clear to us that we would compromise our continued access to the

American unit if we keep on pushing to report the civilian death. Next morning, we decide we have to abandon the embed, hiring our own private security to travel from the American base back through Kandahar in soft-skinned civilian cars. It is a confronting reminder of the risks for a non-embedded correspondent. As we pass through the local village on our tense journey out, the cold, angry, stares of the Afghan locals underline just how difficult it is to safely cover this war without military protection.

As a journalist who has embedded with Australian and American military units in East Timor, Iraq and Afghanistan, and who has also operated in conflict zones independently, I have long been intrigued by the unique position that Charles Bean found himself in in 1915: the incredible access and relative journalistic freedom he enjoyed in Gallipoli and on the Western Front has no equivalent today. He spoke to frontline commanders in their headquarters and then often ventured unsupervised onto the battlefield frontlines to see for himself what was going on, a privilege few if any reporters have enjoyed since. It gave Bean an extraordinary understanding of the course of the war and the failure of tactics employed by the commanders. Bean also promoted the view in his writing that Australia's very sense of itself as a nation was moulded by the experiences of its men under fire – that they went to war for the British Empire and came home with a new sense of Australian identity and a distinct national pride in what they had achieved on the battlefield. Bean's admiration for Australia's volunteer army was intense, and personal; so many of the officers he befriended and admired were to fall during those long grinding years of war. He crafted a powerful legend about the Anzacs that endures today.

Australian journalists do not often write about the generally difficult relationship between the media and the Australian military, but it is a fraught one. While journalists on the whole have a deep respect and affection for the Australian digger, there is now an inculcated cultural distrust of the media in Australia's defence force command that all too often discourages journalists from even attempting embedded coverage. This has meant that Australia's recent engagements in remote war zones like Iraq and Afghanistan have often been inadequately reported. That is what makes Bean's reports so special and relevant today, because he saw the diggers fighting right at the frontlines, something few if any journalists are allowed to do now. These days, the reality on the ground is all too often exactly as we experienced with the Americans in Kandahar: despite promises of access and assistance, the military only helps the press tell the story it wants the public to hear.

It is a measure of Bean's honesty as a chronicler of Australia's role in the First World War that he chose to leave his detailed wartime diaries almost entirely uncensored. He also went to great pains to ensure the diary record was corrected when he realised he had made an error in the fog of war, or where he changed his opinion. His candour has allowed this author to compare what Charles Bean was really seeing on the ground in the Dardanelles and the Western Front with what he reported in his news stories and, eventually, in his postwar official history.

So how did Australia's pre-eminent war correspondent and official historian Charles Bean fare when in 1914 he found himself cast from obscurity onto the national stage as the chronicler of Australia's military involvement in the First World War? How accurate an account of the real war did

Bean give in his wartime journalism and then his postwar official history, and what were the stories he didn't tell? And how faithful to the reality of what he actually witnessed is the legend he crafted about the diggers? This book attempts to answer those questions.

Ross Coulthart

INTRODUCTION

If people really knew, the war would be stopped tomorrow.
But of course they don't – and can't know.
BRITISH PRIME MINISTER LLOYD GEORGE, 1917

On a hot, dusty late afternoon in early May of 1915, an Australian brigadier general, James McCay, squats in a shallow ditch on a gentle slope overlooking the Turkish town of Krithia. As he watches, no doubt with mounting despair, dutiful lines of young Australian men are literally cut to pieces by Turkish machine guns and artillery right in front of him. Huddled at his side is a lanky bespectacled man dressed in a uniform designed to resemble the classic Norfolk officer's jacket, who might pass for one of McCay's subordinates but for the battered black notebook and pen he grasps, along with a telescope and camera case.

Despite his strong personal misgivings, McCay has been ordered with just half an hour's warning to launch this insane attack on open ground in broad daylight. Before the war McCay was a prominent Melbourne lawyer, and served as both a Victorian and federal member of Parliament and even minister for defence. A contrarian thinker for his times, he was an early champion of women's suffrage who once described war as an anachronism and even opposed the deployment of Victorian troops to the Boer War.[1] Now his sound reasons for scepticism about this impossible full-frontal attack are being underlined with the blood and cries of the men of his 2nd Australian Infantry Brigade.

But for the efforts of the man crouched beside McCay, the debacle of Krithia and its command blunders may well have stayed hidden forever on the battlefield. That man is Charles Edwin Woodrow Bean, Australia's official war correspondent throughout the First World War. Not only is his news account of the battle of Krithia a classic piece of war reporting, this unlikely hero – a lofty redhead nicknamed 'Captain Carrot' by the troops – is also about to demonstrate reckless bravery on the Turkish field. Bean has spotted a terribly wounded Allied soldier trying desperately to crawl back under withering fire, just a few metres in front of where Bean and the surviving Australian command are sheltering with British Lancashire Fusiliers troops in what will become known as Tommies' Trench. It is a measure of Bean's humility that while he records what he did that day in his personal diary, there will be no mention of it in the monumental twelve-volume official history of the First World War.[2] Under heavy fire, and against the orders of McCay sitting right beside him, Charles Bean runs out to bring the wounded soldier to safety:

> … one could see that men had been knocked out – a good few of them. There was one chap I could see wounded about 20 yards to my right front – he was moving. I thought he would probably be hit again if he stayed out there, but the prospect of getting out and helping him in was not nice. However, I thought, if one gets into these positions in the firing line one

> must accept the consequences. I waited a bit and presently the youngster rolled over and began to painfully crawl in. One couldn't stay any longer, so I nipped out of the trench and ran out to him and helped him back.[3]

When Bean gets back to the trench, McCay tells him: 'Look here Bean, if you do any more of these damn fool actions I'll send you straight back to H.Q. I've power to you know.' Bean's personal diary records that '[a] few minutes later, [McCay] was doing the dam' fool action himself up on the parapet'.[4] What follows is one of those breathtaking moments in warfare that leave one saddened by the folly of it all, but humbled by the sentiment and the sacrifice. Bean's extraordinary account is one of the classics of Australians at arms. The brigadier general, realising his assault is losing momentum as hundreds of troops shelter in the same ditch from the concentrated Turkish fire, soon turns to Bean and says: 'Well, Bean, I suppose this is where I have to do the damned heroic act.'[5] Bean watches on, astonished, as McCay leaps up onto the side of the shallow trench in the direct line of fire and, looking down on the hundreds of Australians and British troops lying along its length, yells:

> 'Now then Australians – which of you men are Australians? Come on Australians!' The men jumped up – I suppose about 100 in this lot.
>
> 'Come along Australians,' they called – 'Come on Australians.'
>
> They picked themselves up, many with their rifles at the charge, and scrambled over the trench, over the Tommies' heads, into a very heavy fire. The fire really

> was very heavy by now. It was knocking spurts of dust off the parapet into everyone's face … But the Australians went on like a whirlwind.[6]
>
> I heard one chap say: 'Come on chaps. We've got to get it sometime. We can't stay here always!'; and that was the spirit – that, and the feeling that being Australians they must get on. It was very fine to watch, and it was great to watch them as they went, absolutely unaffected by the bullets. I never saw one man whose manner was changed by them, except in that moment when they got up and faced them and rushed over the trench; then their faces were set, their eyebrows bent and they looked into it for a moment as men would into a dazzling flame – I never saw so many determined faces at once.[7]

McCay, who is shot in the thigh during the battle and sent to hospital in Cairo, will later write home to Australia that his rallying shout was in effect a call to the Australian boys to 'come and die … but they came with a laugh and a cheer'.[8] Bean's account, run at length in Australian newspapers, is stirring stuff:

> I have never read of anything finer in history than the way in which this disciplined, seasoned, trained Australian infantry went. They reckoned those bullets no more than if they were a summer shower. One youngster walked steadily into that storm with his entrenching spade held in his left hand a little in front of his face, and to one side, while he looked from under shelter of it exactly as a man looks round his umbrella when walking in the rain down

> a city street … There was an infinitely small pause as they started ahead in tense attitudes and very grim-set faces grasping their rifles and glaring into the unknown. I have seen men stand exactly so in battle pictures, and I wondered if men ever looked so in reality. Well the artists are not all wrong. The men stood there for a barely perceptible space and then with shouts of 'Come along Australians' swept like a hurricane across the deadly heath in front … The moment they left the trench, they began to fall – one here, another there – not thickly, but steadily.[9]

★ ★ ★

The Battle for Krithia was utterly futile. It achieved nothing, and it cost the Australians more than 1000 casualties – half of their number in this one charge – and it was all for naught. Krithia was never taken.

Charles Bean was conflicted in his role as a war correspondent because both the military and even his editors back home in Australia expected him to be a cheerleader for the war effort, that he should overlook the many mistakes made by its commanders that had sent far too many good men to needless deaths. Bean's postwar official history was his effort to correct the wartime historical record that had been blighted by the jingoistic journalism of most of the wartime correspondents. In his history Bean endeavoured to truthfully write what he saw more often than not, no matter who of the top brass it offended. Granted, he did send first drafts of his chapters to some senior commanders but he didn't always accept their suggested changes. So, during the battle at Krithia, he meticulously recorded for posterity, and eventual inclusion in his official history, the decisions made at command headquarters. His postwar history (but not his journalism during the war) notes how, immediately before the battle, some of the advisors to the British commander-in-chief of the Allied attack, General Sir Ian Hamilton, were telling Hamilton the force had done all it could, that further attack was hopeless.[10] Objections had also earlier been raised about the whole notion of such a full-frontal attack in daylight, and even Hamilton had said he preferred to 'cross the danger zone by night and overthrow the enemy in the grey dawn'.[11] But the British commander at Cape Helles from where the attack was launched, Lieutenant-General Aylmer Hunter-Weston – to become infamous as 'the Butcher of Helles' – pigheadedly opposed a night operation. When Hunter-Weston ordered the Krithia attack to resume that day at 5.30pm, he had ignored the frantic concerns of even his own subordinates that this could lead to the complete 'destruction of his force'.[12] We know all of this because of Charles Bean, and what Bean subsequently wrote in his official history was unprecedented for the criticisms he was prepared to make of the command failures that allowed it to happen, although he did exculpate McCay. He criticised Hamilton for his self-serving decision to push on with the Krithia attack regardless when even his own advisers were telling him the situation was hopeless: 'That failure he was unwilling yet to admit.'[13] What Bean went to pains to record was that simply because a British general did not want to admit his attack on Krithia was doomed, he had ordered a pointless, near-suicidal attack by the Australians and New Zealanders. It is a measure of just how committed Bean was to his craft that he walked into battle with the Australians. It was a technique of firsthand observation he would employ at considerable peril throughout the war, unlike many of his professional colleagues who stayed well behind the lines.

Charles Bean's writing was undoubtedly one of the sparks for Australia's nascent nationalism in the early twentieth century. It was Bean who witnessed the rallying cry for 'Australians' to charge at Krithia, men who – until the mateship of battle – had more likely thought of themselves as British. Despite this significance, Bean's huge contribution to Australian history is relatively unknown even today. Public antipathy about the First World War in the decades after it ended possibly played a large part in this – there was strong and bitter feeling even among some of the men who were there that the war had only served British imperial interests, and this feeling intensified during the austerity of the 1930s Depression. There was also a suspicion that writing like Bean's journalism or his official history glorified the savage reality of the war, and there was an overwhelming public sentiment that people just wanted to forget and put the misery and suffering of war behind them. Indeed Bean was torn throughout his career by his fundamental obligation as a journalist and his role as Australia's official correspondent, and eventually as the country's official historian, where there was inevitable pressure from the military brass to present a rose-tinted critique of their role in the war. There would always be tension between what Bean saw as his sacred responsibility to tell the truth about the war and the pressure he and every other correspondent clearly felt to wave the flag for readers back home and boost the war effort. While other correspondents frequently dashed off often fictionalised tosh on their typewriters, Bean's strain to meticulously record the truth as he saw it sometimes meant his reportage was less colourful than his more imaginative Fleet Street colleagues.

The evidence from Bean's own diaries and letters suggests that he made a decision in 1917 to move away from his correspondent's role and focus on his postwar official history, in part because he knew it was impossible to tell his readers the truth under the then censorship constraints, and the jingoism of his editors meant a more candid report would probably not be given a run anyway. Charles Bean did not want to be a 'star' news reporter if that meant compromising the truth. His densely detailed multi-volume official history – which he devoted most of his adult life to researching, writing and updating – sold well during his lifetime but its great historical importance has really only begun to be fully appreciated with the renaissance of public interest in the First World War in the last few decades since Bean's death.

In the near century since Bean wrote the news articles, diaries and notebooks that, together with official records, formed the basis of his epic *Official History of Australia in the War of 1914–1918*, he has more recently been widely eulogised as a fearless and ground-breaking war correspondent. In a recent speech by a defence minister, Bean was described as having 'bravely and unflinchingly told the truth about war'.[14] But the facts also show that like all journalists operating in a war zone, and despite having the best of intentions, Charles Bean did not always tell the whole story of what he saw. He had to make constant compromises about what he could write, not always because of legitimate operational security concerns but because he did not want to jeopardise his access to the ongoing news stories he was writing as a journalist. Bean was also compromised by his own class and social prejudices, which in hindsight can seem quite xenophobic and blinkered but were commonly held in his day. He was one of the first journalists to cover a conflict as what is today termed an embedded correspondent, and the experiences he witnessed and how he reported them are as relevant now as they were a century ago.

Much has been made of the fact that when he came to write his official history, Charles Bean extracted the Australian government's agreement that he would suffer no censorship of it, and that was the case. But Bean's history was written after the war, and there is good reason to question why Bean chose, particularly during the war, but also in part after the war, not to report to his readers much of the incompetence and bungling by Allied senior command that he witnessed. Charles Bean's wartime reports mythologised the Australian soldier, and fired the notion that the Anzacs achieved something nation-defining on the shores of Gallipoli and the battlefields of Western Europe, and Bean also found himself under extraordinary pressure to conform to a tradition of war correspondents who were generally expected to boost the war effort. One of his much-hailed British contemporaries, Philip Gibbs, penned a nauseatingly positive account of the Allies' disastrous first day on the Somme with the deceitful line: 'And, so, after the first day of battle, we may say: It is on balance a good day for Britain and France.'[15] But Gibbs subsequently had the decency to admit the dirty secret of war correspondence: 'We identified ourselves absolutely with the armies in the field … There was no need of censorship of our despatches. We were our own censors.'[16] British Prime Minister Lloyd George later admitted that when he heard Gibbs' more truthful private account of the disastrous British battle losses he had witnessed, Lloyd George realised that if the public was actually told the truth about what was really happening they would never support the war:

> I listened last night … to the most impressive and moving description from him of what the war in the West really means, that I have heard. Even an audience of hardened politicians and journalists was strongly affected. If people really knew, the war would be stopped tomorrow. But of course they don't know and can't know. The correspondents don't write and the censorship would not pass the truth.[17]

There is a lot of evidence in Bean's favour to show that he did as good a job as he was allowed to do. He was extraordinarily brave and was recommended for decorations for the risks he took to rescue wounded soldiers under fire. Bean was also a victim of unjustified official censorship in his dispatches during the war, and the key to Charles Bean is that the inner turmoil he felt about the truths he could not tell during the war was resolved, most of the time, by detailing what really happened in his diaries and notebooks, as deliberate research for his postwar history. Repeatedly throughout Bean's reportage, there are traces of the journalistic compromises he made to avoid clashing with the commanders who gave him such unhindered access to the frontlines. If Bean had one significant flaw it was his overzealous, albeit laudable, desire to see Australia's role and sacrifice in the war properly acknowledged, which sometimes made Bean selectively blind to the failings of the Australian commanders he inevitably became close to as he followed them from Gallipoli through the key battles of the Western Front. This blind spot is clear even in what he wrote in the *Official History of Australia in the War*.

Bean realised very early in his time as a correspondent that there were all too many truths and realities about this war that would never escape the censor's pencil. During the same battle of Krithia where he risked his life in Tommies' Trench with McCay, Bean's private diary recorded details of horrific suffering that were a long way from his news story portraying soldiers advancing as if in a summer shower:

> I saw one poor devil, out of the hundreds who were lying there, trying to get back to cover. I asked if I could help him – he was hit through the leg, high up and was crawling. We went some way together, limping – he in great pain, when he fell saying 'Oh God – oh Christ – oh it's awful'. He had been hit a second time through same leg or other leg. I asked if he could still come on. 'Oh no – no, I can't,' he said. The plateau was very exposed, so I simply dragged him by both legs, he consented, into the nearest thing to a dimple in the ground that I could find – got hold of two packs and put them round him and left him … I don't fancy he can have lived – poor chap.[18]

The news journalism that Charles Bean produced at the time on the Krithia operation did not convey to his Australian readers the full tragedy and squandering of life that it truly represented. Bean's subsequent article says of the same battle that, after one advance, the Australians came through 'without a man hurt', but acknowledges 'of course some must have suffered'.[19] But his diary records how

Brigadier General McCay had privately acknowledged to him that the Krithia assault was a pointless waste because the task set for the Australian troops was 'impossible'.[20] None of this made it into Bean's frontline reportage because it would have been censored even if he had tried to write it; the commanders took the view that anything that undermined public morale and support for the war should be censored.

But even after the war ended Bean chose not to air McCay's damning admission in his official history. Bean was perhaps conflicted by his own concerns about McCay's leadership on the day, realising that part of the blame for the disaster must lie with McCay for not questioning the daylight attack more aggressively with his commanders. These doubts Bean expressed privately in a 1927 letter about McCay's 'excitability and of the foolish extravagance which robbed him of the respect of the men he led'.[21] He also described McCay in his private diary in 1918 as 'wildly unpopular throughout the AIF'.[22] Bean's official history did eventually record that some of McCay's own men believed he was responsible for the heavy casualties at Krithia because they felt he should have insisted more strongly on a night attack.[23] But, as he did so often with the Australian commanders in his history, Charles Bean spared McCay by not repeating his harsher private criticisms:

> In each of the Anzac brigades one ill result was a growing conviction that they had been needlessly sacrificed; in the case of the 2nd Brigade, the blame quickly, but quite wrongly, settled upon McCay. He had, it is true, driven his troops hard, and perhaps too swiftly for good order; in personally directing almost every company he had put needless pressure upon

> eager men. These things lost him the popularity which his great personal bravery might have gained. But the plan of attack was not his. He but vigorously carried out his part of the plans for the Second Battle of Krithia, which, limiting themselves almost to the routine of an Aldershot field-day, in three days expended an army in merely approaching the enemy.[24]

Bean's actual journalism was often highly sanitised of his private harsher criticisms. His May 1915 dispatch of McCay's heroics at Krithia for Australian and British newspapers reads like an Empire-era boy's own annual, glorifying the bravery of the Australians but ignoring completely the command failures that sent so many fine soldiers to a forlorn, unnecessary, and often agonising death:

> I have seen many troops at work during the last week [but] I never saw anything approaching the swiftness or the dash of that advance ... They were in high spirits, laughing and yarning over all sorts of things – what the people in Australia were thinking, the incidents of the day, of the landing, every sort of topic except the charge they had just made.[25]

It may be a controversial view, given the low stock in which journalists are generally held today, but it would be unthinkable for a contemporary journalist not to attempt to aggressively report on how such a classic failure in military command had caused the unnecessary deaths of so many young soldiers, irrespective of the military censorship that would seek to suppress it. Judged by the journalistic standards of his day, however, Bean was considerably less jingoistic and much more committed to the truth than most of his colleagues. In truth, just as embedded correspondents in conflicts across the globe do today, Bean compromised on what he told his Australian readers. As a journalist he never once acknowledged what he wrote privately in his diaries of 'the utter hopeless wastefulness of this whole war'.[26] It was Charles Bean who glorified the Anzac soldier as demonstrating 'reckless valour in a good cause',[27] but he made little or, more often than not, no acknowledgement of the hundreds of Australians whom history records deserted their posts and refused to waste their lives on a British imperial command strategy of bloody attrition. His detractors, like historian Charles Manning Clark, believed writing such as his was jingoistic, making Australia 'a prisoner of her past'.[28] Bean has been accused of generalising from the personal stories of extraordinary individual soldiers to fit his mythological image of the digger as somehow superhuman.

During the war, Bean knew he needed to stay onside with the sources he was cultivating, and this coloured his reportage. He was a contemporary of the same English public school as Allied generals Haig and Birdwood, and he was heavily influenced by his later childhood and early adult years in England. Bean's notions of the heroic Australian stockman were formed in the prewar years when he finally returned to Australia and befriended writers such as A.B. 'Banjo' Paterson. Bean also notoriously allowed anti-Semitism to colour his impressions of the man who turned out to be Australia's most effective general, Sir John Monash (a failing he acknowledged much later in his life). And the notion he pushed in his writing of a unique democratic kinship between Australian officers and their men in battle was soon dispelled postwar when Bean came to distrust the unions and the socialist/communist movement in Australia. As one academic analysis has ventured about two former prime ministers of Australia, 'Keating quotes Manning Clark but never Charles Bean, and Howard quotes Bean but never Clark.'[29]

Despite these flaws, what is special about Charles Bean is that he generally lived by a credo of truth and honesty that few other correspondents of his generation heeded. More a chronicler than a journalist, Bean made it his role to visit every battle scene as close as possible to the moment it happened, and often during a battle. He soon realised the folly of waiting behind the lines to be spoon fed the day's events by propaganda officers from military intelligence at command HQ. He strived to get firsthand accounts of battles from the men who had just fought in them – and that is what set him apart from his peers. Charles Bean was driven by a strong desire to ensure the sacrifice of so many young soldiers whom he knew, deeply admired and all too often watched die or suffer grievous wounds was not for nothing. His determination to record the feats of the Australian fighting soldier was to culminate in not only one of the most extraordinary official war histories ever written but also in the conception and creation of one of the world's great war memorials.

One

PLAY UP AND PLAY THE GAME!

Without the Empire we should be tossed like a cork in the cross current of world politics. It is at once our sword and our shield.

BILLY HUGHES, AUSTRALIAN PRIME MINISTER 1915–23

English supremacy should last until the end of time because it means universal freedom, universal liberty, emancipation from everything degrading.

ALEXANDER MACKENZIE, CANADIAN PRIME MINISTER 1873–78

It was a very different time, the era into which Charles Edwin Woodrow Bean was born in Bathurst, country New South Wales, on 18 November 1879. Just three years earlier, Queen Victoria had been declared Empress of India, a meaningless title crafted by the then British prime minister, Benjamin Disraeli, as an act of craven flattery to his monarch, but significant for the fact that it was the moment England first acknowledged itself as an empire – Victoria was queen of an imperial empire that had painted a swathe of British pink right across the world map.

Despite their distance from 'home', the respectable citizenry of Bathurst saw themselves as British to their bootstraps. In the books and newspapers that young Charles read, and the social circles that his parents moved in, the British Empire was still seen as mythically great, and it was truly the white man's burden to keep order, peace and good government among the citizens, colonists, heathens and natives across England's territories. To be British was to be superior and, above all, to be inculcated with a strong sense of duty and responsibility.

'We are called upon to rule [the colonies], as far as we do rule them, not for our glory but their happiness,' the English novelist Anthony Trollope wrote in 1873, credulously extolling the virtues of British colonisation.[1] For generations of privileged young Englishmen, aside from family, the primary place where most of them were indoctrinated with the sense of imperial duty and obligation that saw them sent off as officers and bureaucrats to run the Empire was the English public school system. Confusingly named (and so known because anyone could apply, regardless of where they lived or their religion), these privately run establishments exploded in popularity in Victorian England, first with Thomas Arnold's Rugby school and then a plethora of establishments servicing the British elite. They imbued students with notions of muscular Christianity and a competitive sporting spirit, which produced fine fodder for the military and the colonial service. Charles Bean's father, Edwin, devoted his life in Australia to emulating the best qualities of the British public school system from which he came, with Thomas Arnold's public school humanitarian ideals as his guide, and this was a huge formative influence on the young Charles.

Edwin was indeed to be a constant benevolent and moral influence throughout his son's life. In a short biography

Charles Bean wrote for his new wife in 1924 when he was threatened with ill health, Charles went to great pains to ensure she and future biographers knew how important his father had been to him, crediting Edwin with much of his early learning.[2] There was always a firm culture of diary and record keeping in the Bean family; when Edwin went on a visit to New Zealand in 1885 he kept a fastidious diary of everything he saw from the moment he left Bathurst and boarded a steamship across the Tasman, including a lovely description of the Blue Mountains: 'Soon we approach the ranges that stand back from the plain like wild things gazing suspiciously at man's civilization.'[3] Diary keeping was a habit he clearly passed on to his son, whose meticulous notebooks and diaries were to eventually provide the backbone of the official war history. Charles' mother, Lucy, was no slouch either, in August 1886 beginning a small diary for 'Charlie Bean' when he was nearly seven years old, which he treasured and later added to throughout his life.

Edwin Bean arrived in Australia from England in 1874 when he was 22, having not scored highly enough in either his Oxford University results or Indian civil service examinations to secure a place in the colonial service that would have allowed him to follow in his own father's footsteps. John Bean was a surgeon in the East India Company and a surgeon major in the British Army in India, where Edwin was born in 1851. As was the custom of the day, Edwin was sent back to England at the age of six to board at Somerset College in Bath and then to the newly opened Clifton College in Bristol, one of the original 26 British public schools. Clifton, which also featured prominently in his son Charles's life, is resonant with the history of that era of imperial England. Its cricket ground, known as 'The Close', is where Sir Henry Newbolt based his preposterously blood-soaked ode 'Vitaï Lampada' (which translates as 'They pass on the torch of life'):

> There's a breathless hush in the Close to-night –
> Ten to make and the match to win –
> A bumping pitch and a blinding light,
> An hour to play and the last man in.
> And it's not for the sake of a ribboned coat,
> Or the selfish hope of a season's fame,
> But his captain's hand on his shoulder smote
> 'Play up! play up! and play the game!'
>
> The sand of the desert is sodden red, –
> Red with the wreck of a square that broke; –
> The Gatling's jammed and the colonel dead,
> And the regiment blind with dust and smoke.
> The river of death has brimmed his banks,
> And England's far, and Honour a name,
> But the voice of a schoolboy rallies the ranks:
> 'Play up! play up! and play the game!'[4]

To this day, boys at Clifton remove their hats as they walk through a solemn memorial arch in the school grounds dedicated to the teachers and pupils who died in both world wars. It is not difficult to understand the crushing sense of imperial duty that both Bean father and son felt as alumni of Clifton.

After arriving in New South Wales, the young Edwin took a job at Sydney Grammar School as a teacher of classics before marrying Lucy Butler, the daughter of a well-known Tasmanian legal family, in 1877. They first lived at

'Stowell' in Ocean Street, Woollahra, and then moved to Bathurst in January 1878 when Edwin took up the position of headmaster at the recently established All Saints' College. It was a busy time for the young newlyweds, and for Lucy, who was pregnant when the couple arrived in Bathurst, it would have been a terrible strain arriving in the sweltering and dusty country town at the height of an Australian summer. As well as getting the house ready for a new baby, she was also the housemother for the students.

Lucy and Edwin's first child, Madeline Jessie, was born on 4 May 1878. It is likely that Edwin and Lucy took their baby daughter for a Christmas visit with the Butlers in Hobart and, tragically, during this visit eight-month-old Madeline Bean became ill with meningitis. The young couple did not get to return to Bathurst with their baby daughter, the *Hobart Mercury* newspaper death notice grimly recording her passing on 8 January 1879.

About ten months later on 18 November 1879, Charles Edwin Woodrow Bean was born at the family's residence at All Saints' College, Bathurst. Having lost her firstborn, Lucy Bean was understandably anxious at times during Charles's early life, particularly when he suffered a fever at fourteen months that was very similar to the symptoms of little Madeline's fatal illness –almost exactly two years since her death; the threat to infants from diseases such as meningitis in this era without antibiotics was very real. There were to be two more sons, John (also known as Jack) in 1881 and Montague (called Monty and later Tig) in 1884.

Edwin's appointment as headmaster at All Saints' was a risky move for the young couple because the fledgling school's future depended wholly on his ability to attract students, but it was a welcome country change after Sydney.

Bathurst was a large town then, built on the 1850s gold-mining boom, and as one of the richer towns of country New South Wales it already had a Catholic school, St Stanislaus' College. All Saints' was the Church of England's pitch for the hearts and minds of Bathurst's Anglican congregation, founded with the support of Bishop Marsden, a fellow former Trinity College graduate with Edwin Bean. Marsden's grandfather was the legendary Reverend Samuel Marsden, who is perhaps unkindly remembered as the 'flogging parson', well known for his intense dislike of Irish Catholics and his aggressive introduction of Christianity to the New Zealand Maori. His namesake grandson was reportedly a more conciliatory character, and he no doubt appointed Edwin Bean because he knew the school needed an energetic leader to convince the local landed gentry to send their sons to this new church school. The headmaster did not disappoint: it was Edwin Bean's eleven years as headmaster that transformed the school into a highly respected institution.

Lucy Bean's diary intimates a warm and loving family life: 'The getting out of your cots in the morning, (you, Charlie always first awake) after morning kiss to sleepy Father and Mother, the scamper down the passage in your little flannel combinations to the nursery.'[5] She describes an idyllic life in Bathurst for Charles and his brothers of outdoor games – football, cricket, horses, digging in the garden and swinging on a horizontal bar. Early on, Jack told 'Chas', as he called his older brother, that he should be a war correspondent because that was the job that suited him.[6] As a teenage schoolboy Charles was intensely interested in the British forces; he subscribed to *Army and Navy*, an illustrated service magazine. According to Jack, 'Charlie knew the tonnage and gunnage of the various ships of war to a nicety and the meaning and make-up of the various naval flags.'[7] Charles also loved sketching, even drawing in his hymnbooks during church.

As Bean later recounted in a personal history for his future wife, Effie, it was a matter of great pride in the family that a fictionalised account of an incident involving Bean's uncle, Henry Woodrow, was featured in the famous 1857 novel *Tom Brown's School Days* by socialist reformer Thomas Hughes.[8] In the book, the implausibly decent hero, Tom, here based on Woodrow, stands up for a younger lad who is being bullied by a senior school brute for kneeling beside his dormitory bed to say his evening prayers. The book is set at the famous Rugby public school at the time when the real-life Thomas Arnold was headmaster and it presents an idealised view of English public school life, young gentlemen triumphing over cads and bullies and developing into adult men of good character and selflessness with a hefty dose of Christian morality. Arnold's views were to become a constant guide throughout Bean's private and public life and they undoubtedly had a huge influence on his notions of Australian mateship and selflessness. This idea of moral character in leadership dominated Charles Bean's thinking through his life, especially his idealised war accounts of Australian officers selflessly leading their men into battle.

Three young boys born in just five years no doubt kept Lucy Bean busy, and because she also had enormous obligations helping Edwin run All Saints' the family hired nannies and governesses. Lucy Bean's diary remembered Charles's nanny, Esther Johns – 'Kind old Nursie' – with great affection; she had taught him how to recite the alphabet backwards at the age of three and a half. At the age of about five or six years old, Bean began at the new preparatory school his father had created at All Saints'. He won a book prize for his schoolwork – *The Golden Treasury of Oxford Verse* – and it is an indication of his archivist tendencies that decades later Bean still had the no doubt slightly battered book of verse and loaned it to his work colleague Arthur Bazley, for his children.

Bathurst was a railway hub and farming service town, as it is today, with a rich history of convicts and bushrangers that no doubt fired the imagination of young Charles and his brothers. A huge part of Edwin Bean's job was to tour the local farms touting for students, particularly when the first state-run school was proposed for Bathurst as a result of the 1880 education reforms, which saw the state assume responsibility for public education, and All Saints' enrolment numbers came under considerable pressure. It also took a heavy toll on Edwin Bean's health, and a propitious bequest from his father in 1882 made it possible for him and Lucy to take a break, returning to England in early 1883 to sort out his estate, leaving the boys with their nanny.

Charles loved the community of school life at All Saints'. The boarders who attended became extended members of the Bean family and, as he later told his wife, Effie, one of his great pleasures right through his life was to read the school magazine, *The Bathurstian*, to catch up on school happenings and the latest updates on old boys with whom he shared so many happy school years. It was also at Bathurst that Bean began a lifelong love of cricket.

One of the most intriguing characters in Charles Bean's life at this time was Arthur Wilberforce Jose, the son of an English merchant who came to Australia when the family's fortune was lost. Only 22 when he was appointed as a master at All Saints', Jose had met Edwin in Hobart when the Beans were visiting Lucy's family. Descended from Spaniards who settled in Cornwall, he was briefly a student at Oxford but, after the loss of the family money, he knocked back the offer of a dull clerical position in Bristol to 'go bush' travelling Australia – a proto-British backpacker. By the time he met Edwin while tutoring in Hobart, Jose had lived rough across Victoria and Tasmania, picking fruit, working as a fencing contractor and hacking lumber for the railways. Like so many backpackers of today, Jose had a huge love of Australia, especially the bush, and he filled young Charles's head with perhaps his first sense of pride in being distinctively Australian and not just of Mother England. Jose went on from Bathurst to an illustrious career on a path not dissimilar to Charles's own, studying at the bar then becoming a writer. One of his books, *The Growth of the Empire*[9], first published in 1900, lauded the British Empire and championed the White Australia policy, and in 1899 Jose went to South Africa as a war correspondent. The two were to stay friends throughout their lives and also worked professionally together when in 1920 Jose was hired by Bean to write the official history of the Australian navy's role in the First World War.

Charles Bean did not write as much about his mother's influence as he did of Edwin's guidance, but much later in his life he acknowledged just how important a mother's role was: 'Each young Australian in his life passes through two great schools of character. The first is his home. The second is his school, college, or apprenticeship. The greatest factor in all education (in spite of all other set ideas about it) is the home, and beyond question a boy or girl's greatest educator is their mother.'[10] In the diary she kept for her son, Lucy set out the seeds of Charles Bean's moral code, an Anglican morality and a strong conviction that her son commit himself to an honourable life where he told the truth without fear or favour: 'I do not want to see you a rich man, or a man holding a leading position, so much as to see you a good, charitable man.'[11]

But money was a constant worry for Lucy and Edwin as All Saints' enrolments came under pressure after the establishment of a state high school in Bathurst. Edwin had campaigned against the education reforms which brought in the state schools, arguing instead for a scheme of subsidies and scholarships to private schools, and his fears were well-founded: enrolments at All Saints' were going backwards by 1886. Edwin began an aggressive marketing strategy, visiting the families of prospective All Saints' students in the local area, and in the end his persistence won the day – the new Bathurst high school was eventually closed. By the end of 1889 Edwin Bean had managed to triple enrolments at All Saints' but, exhausted from overwork, he and Lucy decided to take the family on an extended break back to England. Edwin had the money to travel because he had prudently purchased a substantial number of shares in the massive Illawarra coal deposits near Wollongong which by the 1890s were returning a healthy income on his investment. It seems very likely that Edwin Bean was not just tired but had suffered a nervous breakdown at this time, for his plan was to take the next two years to rest in Europe with his wife and family.

In early 1889 the Bean family, including nanny Esther Johns, left Bathurst for England, and, as fate would have it, Edwin and Lucy would not return to Australia for more than two decades. They sailed on the P&O steamer *Valetta*, a journey that delighted the nine-year-old Charles Bean, who loved playing with the younger children on the ship. As Charles would later acknowledge to his wife Effie, it was in England where he and his brother got the bulk of their education: 'When we left to go back to England, I was fairly well on, but not in any way a marvel of learning or industry.'[12]

Charles and his family were devoted Anglophiles even before they left Australia, but the time he would spend as an older child and then a young man in England formed him for much of his early life and career. The boy who arrived on the dockside in England in 1889 unquestioningly thought of himself as British, thrilled by her imperial might and notions of British racial superiority and purity. Despite this, what is intriguing about Charles Bean is how his personal life story tracks the very origins of Australian nationalism. Over the following decades, his own growing sense of Australian self-identity would transform so much of what he and all Australians had once so passionately believed.

Two

TO SET THE CAUSE ABOVE RENOWN

England expects every man to do his duty

NELSON'S SIGNAL

A century ago, it was still possible to visit an old battlefield thirteen kilometres south of Brussels and find the gruesome relics of war, the bones and bullets and shredded kit from one of the most epic massed cavalry charges and infantry confrontations in military history. In much the same way that antipodeans travel to Gallipoli today, during the latter part of the nineteenth century, when Charles Bean and his family spent nearly two years travelling to and from the Continent, a popular part of the grand tour was to visit the battlefield of Waterloo, the small Belgian town near where French emperor Napoleon was brought to his knees by an Allied coalition dominated by British and Prussian soldiers in June 1815. Every English boy of the era learned in school of the stoic Allied infantry and dashing cavalrymen holding off and finally breaking the French attack, the essence of British sangfroid and stoicism. A measure of true English grit could be demonstrated in the legendary anecdote from the battle featuring the Earl of Uxbridge and the Duke of Wellington, when the earl was hit with a cannonball and the two gentlemen's exchange reportedly ran thus:

The earl: By God, sir, I've lost my leg!
The duke: By God, sir, so you have!

Edwin Bean was an enthusiastic student of British military feats of arms, and after the family's arrival in England in 1889 he used recently acquired funds (from a decision to sell shares in All Saints' school and a bequest from his father) to take a well-earned rest, which eventually took the family to lodgings very near Waterloo. For the first couple of months the family had stayed with Charles's Aunt Betty in London's West Kensington, but Edwin was now able to afford to take a house for the summer in Oxford and to rent another house in Brussels for the winter. For much of the summer of 1889, Edwin taught his two elder school-age sons at home himself, Charles later recalling how much he loved the intense study of Euclid and geometry under his father's tutelage. Afternoons were always reserved for the boys to enjoy a game of cricket with their father, or the trio would head off to row at Oxford. But what most excited the young Charles was to be on the Belgian battlefield of Waterloo during the winter with his father – what better way to broaden the minds of his young sons than to stride the historic ground for days on end, scouring the landscape features for key moments in that epic clash. The battle was even in the family history: in 1815, Charles's great-grandfather, Dr Cornelius Butler, was given the honour of reading the news of the victory at Waterloo to the townsfolk of Brentwood, where he was a doctor for much of his life and warden at the Brentwood School.

Charles and his father particularly enjoyed roaming the battlefield with the aid of an account of the battle entitled *A Voice from Waterloo*, written by former cavalry sergeant major Edward Cotton of the 7th British Hussars, who had fought in the battle.[1] Cotton had cannily set up a hotel on the battle site, offering fine British ales and London porter beer to the visiting tourists. His hotel museum exhibited many gruesome relics from the battlefield that no doubt awed young master Bean, including 'a pair of Napoleon's silver spurs' and 'a dragoon's saddle-bags with blood stains still visible'.[2] Sergeant Major Cotton's firsthand account of the battle likely sowed seeds in Bean's mind that a quarter of a century later would be harvested when he had to decide how to write his accounts of Australia's First World War battles. Cotton's blow-by-blow forensic account of the battle of Waterloo was refreshing for its candour, admitting enemy success and Allied error and command failure where each was due, an antidote to the traditionally hagiographic official battle histories of the time. Cotton wrote in his preface: 'One of my objects in writing, is to correct opinions which have gone forth, and which are greatly at variance with facts: opinions so erroneous as to warrant the remark of [French] General Jomini, that "Never was a battle so confusedly described as that of Waterloo."' The pages of *A Voice from Waterloo* also carried a truism from United States' president John Adams that Charles Bean was to hold with for the rest of his career: 'Facts are stubborn things.'[3] Another history of the battle of Waterloo by H.T. Siborne also later influenced Bean's *Official History of Australia in the War of 1914–1918* and, as historian Denis Winter has recorded, inspired Bean's use of thumbnail sketch maps of key battle scenes.[4]

While in Brussels a French governess educated the boys, who became fluent in her language. The family kept up this civilised lifestyle between Oxford and Brussels over the next two years before Edwin Bean's financial security was hit by the 1890s depression that followed the collapse and closure of many Australian banks, his investments all massively declining in value and forcing him to seek employment.

Brentwood School has sat since 1558 in a huge pocket of prime Essex countryside on the northeast outskirts of the city of London. Two years after Edwin Bean and his family arrived in England his reputation as a headmaster still preceded him, and he was invited to apply to be the headmaster of the respected British public school. It helped too that Edwin's grandfather, Dr Cornelius Butler (no relation to Lucy), had been warden there, and that his father, Sergeant Major John Bean of the East India Company, was an illustrious old boy.

The family moved to Brentwood School in April 1891; with just 42 boys enrolled, there was huge pressure on Edwin to turn the school's dire financial position around. Charles Bean was rightly proud of what his father was to achieve over the next 21 years as headmaster, and he was also proud that although he and his brothers were the headmaster's sons, they were treated like any other boarder – in fact, his father was particularly strict with them, and 'never for a moment did any boy accuse us of being favoured'.[5] Edwin quickly made a tremendous impact, implementing the ideas of his idol, Rugby school headmaster Thomas Arnold; Charles recorded how the tone, which had been 'snobbish, not very good or keen' became 'splendid and gentlemanly. The boys began to love this school.'[6]

Brentwood was historically one of the English grammar schools endowed by act of Parliament with a charitable bequest to ensure the free instruction of all the boys of the town of Brentwood without discrimination. But a parliamentary inquiry had sniffily opined just two decades before Edwin Bean's arrival as headmaster that there was 'concern that the communication of learning of the lower kind in the school has the tendency and effect of reducing the institution from a grammar school to one of a different and inferior species'.[7] Like so many English public schools of the time, the newfound status and snobbery among the Victorian elite meant there was pressure to lift the fees of Brentwood to a level that would scare off the riff-raff. For Edwin Bean, it was a huge challenge to have to pander to the vanities of the richer parents who could keep the school afloat while also adhering to the moral principles he held dear to ensure that the school remained faithful to its charitable charter. The poorer boys who came to Brentwood from the town under this charter were all too often victims of bullying in the school because they lacked the right clothes or books. So principled and moral a man was Edwin Bean that he often paid for these items out of his own pocket, on occasion running into serious debt as a consequence.

For fourteen-year-old Charles Bean, his move three years later in 1894 to Bristol's Clifton College, his father's old school, must have been an overwhelming experience, for he now found himself in one of the nurseries of British imperial power and the profession of arms. While the school was only 30 years old, when the Bean family made the financial stretch to send their eldest son to Clifton, the wealth and vanity of Victorian England was reflected in its majestic architecture; the chapel's stained-glass windows and vaulted ceilings are breathtaking. Charles was there just seven years on from Queen Victoria's 1887 golden jubilee, and the art and statuary in the school celebrated the peak of British imperialism and the notion of soldier scholars.

Clifton has always prided itself on its martial tradition, and a disproportionate number of its young men had, by the time Charles arrived, shed blood or lost their lives on the battlefields of colonial England. An extraordinary 578 boys of Bean's generation of Cliftonites, one in four, would go on to die in the First World War in an army led by a Clifton old boy, Commander-in-Chief Sir Douglas Haig, while another old boy, Lieutenant General William Birdwood, commanded Australian and New Zealand forces on Gallipoli. Clifton College produced an astonishing 23 major generals and 52 brigadier generals for the conflict that was to become Charles Bean's obsession, and the social networks and attitudes with which he was imbued during his time there are crucial to an understanding of him.

In 1908, Clifton old boy Sir Henry Newbolt published a poem 'Clifton Chapel' dedicated to the school's chapel that became an unwittingly prescient and eerie dirge to the carnage that was to come:

> ... To set the cause above renown,
> To love the game beyond the prize,
> To honour, while you strike him down,
> The foe that comes with fearless eyes;
> To count the life of battle good,
> And dear the land that gave you birth,
> And dearer yet the brotherhood
> That binds the brave of all the earth ...[8]

That message of selfless sacrifice, of soldiery as a noble cause – the heroic virtue of being that man who died young far away but a soldier, and for his country[9] – was hammered into Bean and every other student at Clifton.

Charles boarded in the house run by one of Edwin's old friends from the school, assistant master E.N.P. Moor. Charles was known by the boys and the masters as the 'Rum 'Un' because of his Australian accent, but he recalled the ribbing soon stopped so he figured he must have finally lost the twang: 'some of the English boys in their turn pulled my leg gently by inviting me to "baowl them out". In spite of this we soon became practically English boys.'[10] Bean's fanatical love of cricket broke the ice – it probably helped that the first five test Ashes series between England and Australia ran during the year he arrived at Clifton, and that Australia lost. (English dominance of the game was only brought to heel after Dr W.G. Grace's successful 2–1 winning captaincy in 1896. There was an Ashes clash of its own at Clifton, for Bean was never quite good enough to make the First Eleven team, and the boy who narrowly beat him into it was W.G. Grace's son.)

Not long into his first year, Charles Bean found himself sharing rooms with a fellow student who became his close friend, Thoby Stephen. Thoby was the brother of a woman who was to become one of England's greatest novelists, Virginia Woolf. Until his untimely death, Thoby and his sister Virginia's sharp intelligence and precocious sociability ensured the Stephen family home was a magnet for many of the cultural and literary luminaries of the time, culminating in the formation of what was to become known as the Bloomsbury Group. Their father, Leslie Stephen, was a literary critic whose first wife, Harriet, was the daughter of another great English novelist, William Makepeace Thackeray, so writing was in the family blood and this no doubt enthused the bookish young Charles Bean. Nicknamed 'the Goth' by his friends, the lanky Thoby enjoyed the extraordinary social networks of the privileged upper middle classes of Victorian society and he took his new Australian friend into this entrancing world.

Charles played a lot of cricket at Clifton but on his own admission was not as good as he would like to have been, failing to win his colours because he was 'too nervous in the field – I dreaded missing catches'.[11] His grades also suffered in his first few months sharing a study with Thoby Stephen, the Clifton archives recording a less than glowing academic report. While some comments were 'satisfactory' and 'shows promise', the record sheet also includes 'Working well but rather childish in mind' and 'Very feeble, poor health, seems to have no mind', 'work very poor'.[12] His disappointed father sent him a stern missive: 'One thing would grieve me more and that would be to think that you had lived immorally as well as idly – but that, I trust, I need not fear. But remember that you must live a life of duty. If your new study life produces results like this to think that you had.[13]

Edwin need not have worried; Charles eventually did very well as a student at Clifton. He picked up a small two-year scholarship of 25 pounds in 1895. Bean told Effie he was lazy but developed a writing style that was an act of rebellion against some of the ponderous academic philosophers he was compelled to read at Clifton and later at Oxford: 'I determined never if possible to write a sentence which could not be understood by say a housemaid of average intelligence. I came to loathe the use of long words.'[14] It was a maxim he held to throughout his career.

Bean loved literature and the classics at Clifton, and all the way through school he and Thoby Stephen were good-naturedly competitive, Bean saying of his friend that he 'was a great deal quicker and cleverer than I'.[15] In his senior year Charles was surprised to be appointed as the head of the house they shared. It bothered him that he only came seventh in the school academically because his father had been second as well as head of his school house.[16] Bean acknowledged the influence Clifton had on him much later in his life: 'I owe an enormous debt to Clifton. My four and a half years there altered my whole outlook on life.'[17]

As both Charles and his brother Jack neared the end of their schooling, with Jack keen to study medicine at Cambridge, it was a looming worry for Edwin how he was going to be able to pay for both boys' university tuition. (Monty was to go on to study to be an electrical engineer, at University College in London.) Relief came in 1896 when Charles applied for and eventually won the coveted Essex Scholarship to study classics at Oxford University, which guaranteed him one hundred pounds a year for five years. He parted ways with good friend Thoby Stephen who went on to Cambridge, only for Thoby to die tragically young from typhoid eight years later while on holiday in Greece.

In 1899, the second Boer War began between British forces and those of the Transvaal and the Orange Free State, shattering a truce secured with the Transvaal in 1881. Many Clifton old boys were fighting for the British forces in this latest conflict – a fight largely to do with British imperial designs on Transvaal's recently discovered massive Witswatersrand gold find – and Charles Bean was no doubt caught up in the fervour of the moment, seriously considering commission as an officer in the British Army

Engineers early in his time at Oxford. Bean's father advised he would support him but: 'I think one ought to feel a distinct "call" for that profession as the soldier's is a hard life and there is much self-sacrifice in it and of course, much risk. I might be able to help you with £100 a year but no more.'[18] As Edwin intimated, an officer in the British Army at the time was expected to meet many of his own costs, and in the end Charles abandoned the idea. He did however join the Oxford University battalion's officer training corps.

Bean lost many friends who served in the Boer War; his private papers show he kept a list of old Cliftonians who died in service over the next four years. But while he supported the British campaign, it was not without criticism. An early glimmer of Bean's principles on openness and full disclosure on military affairs can be seen in a letter he wrote to *The Pall Mall Gazette* in October 1901 during the Boer War. That year a courageous British philanthropist named Emily Hobhouse had been able to inveigle her way past the British military guards to expose the shameful conditions inside the British concentration camps built to house Boer families, where hundreds of children, women and elderly folk were dying every month because of appalling nutrition and disease. Her revelations in public meetings back in London generated outrage. Charles Bean wrote to the *Gazette* criticising its editorial efforts to play down the disgraceful conditions in the camps, his comments showing a moral conviction about truth that was to pervade his attitude towards writing for the next sixty years: 'I do not think that any good cause can be harmed by the publication of the truth, though only harm can come from its suppression.'[19]

It is clear that during his time at Oxford, Bean was as vexed as any young adult over his future career. His mother's side had a long history of lawyers so in 1900, in conjunction with his university studies, he also began legal studies at the Inner Temple in London, the professional training association for barristers in England and Wales, but it is clear that from the start his heart was never really in it because he was soon looking for alternatives. Afflicted with appendicitis and pneumonia in the later stages of his Bachelor of Arts classics degree at Oxford, he gained only second-class honours in 1902. Sitting his civil service examinations in July 1902 in an attempt to get a job in South Africa or India, just as his father had attempted decades earlier, he failed to score high enough marks. Out of 145 candidates he came 118th in one application for a clerkship; possibly he was not actually well enough to sit some papers because he was recorded as having scored zero out of 500 in his Roman law exam and no marks in his English law. He also went on to gain a lacklustre Oxford Bachelor of Civil Law degree with third-class honours in 1904, and while he stayed in the law for the next few years, it was clearly his career choice only by default. None of these results fairly represented Bean's academic capabilities; Bean's Oxford tutors felt his illness that year had seriously affected his results, one of them writing that Bean's work during the classics degree had put him in line for first-class honours. As Bean told his wife, Effie, he only really studied the Oxford law degree because he thought it might be useful as a stepping stone to tutoring or some other profession, but a third-class honours degree was nothing to write home about. Bean's later letter to his wife boasted, not too persuasively in light of his actual results, that he found examinations very easy: 'From the time I was a small boy I always knew what the examiners wanted; I could always, on a minimum of work, pass a good examination.'[20]

Clearly this whole period was a very trying time for Charles because his brothers, Jack and Monty, were both excelling in their studies: Jack was studying medicine at Cambridge and Monty was on his way to becoming an engineer. As the eldest son, Charles was under not inconsiderable pressure to do his duty and make some sort of a living while he worked out what career to pursue. After a brief stint as tutor to a young Scots lad in Teneriffe on the Canary Islands, to get away from the chilly English winter, in 1904 Charles and his father decided it would be best for him to return to Australia to try his hand as a barrister at the Sydney bar. Through his father's old connections he also had the offer of some work at Sydney Grammar School teaching Greek for a few hours a week. But it seems Charles soon realised he was not cut out for teaching: 'I was always in difficulties there for though I read and wrote Greek well I was always hopeless at Greek grammar, and it did not take the class long to find this out.'[21]

Things also did not go as planned with hopes to break into the bar. Bean took space at Wigram Chambers in Phillip Street but struggled to get briefs in those early months, so a family friend helped him get a job as a judge's associate. His judge, Justice William Owen of the Supreme Court, was soon overseeing a Royal Commission into the administration of the New South Wales Department of Lands and Bean was sent off on circuit with other judges for part of that period. He toured the countryside around Wagga Wagga and Deniliquin during 1906 with two other judges, and in 1907 he also went on circuit with Justice Owen to Newcastle and Tamworth. It was an opportunity to reacquaint himself with the Australian bush but, as Bean later told Effie: 'One saw thus a good deal of the country – perhaps the worst side of it.'[22]

Bean had time on his hands in the job, and he was beginning to recognise within himself a calling to write. Even before he started as a judge's associate he had started penning articles for the Sydney *Evening News* newspaper, edited at the time by A.B 'Banjo' Paterson, an old boy from Sydney Grammar where Charles's father, Edwin Bean, had made such a favourable impression as a devoted teacher. By this time Banjo Paterson was already famous for his writing: he had penned the bush ballad 'Waltzing Matilda' and the best-selling poetry book *The Man from Snowy River and Other Verses*. Paterson had also studied and practised as a lawyer and served as a war correspondent for *The Sydney Morning Herald* during the Boer War, and the two men became good friends. It is also likely Paterson imbued Charles Bean with his own romantic view of the Australian outback and its men and women on the land.

For Bean, the job as Justice Owen's associate was a colourful journalistic introduction to the rough and tumble politics and corruption of backwoods colonial New South Wales, because the Royal Commission was exposing tales of political intrigue that Banjo Paterson would no doubt have enjoyed offering his *Evening News* readers. The New South Wales minister for lands under scrutiny in the commission hearings was a heavy-drinking, hard-gambling but generally much-respected Irish Catholic lawyer named William Patrick – Paddy – Crick. The severe drought of 1901 had decimated the far western divisions of New South Wales's outback farmland, and Paddy Crick adopted a liberal policy of granting leases to pastoralists whose leases had already expired to help them through the bad times. Justice Owen's Royal Commission investigations revealed that in doing so Crick had ignored the recommendations of his bureaucrats and there were suspicions that Crick had been paid bribes for his largesse. In the end the commission could not prove Crick was corrupt but he was forced to resign his seat and formally expelled from the Parliament. Working so closely with the judge, Bean would certainly have had a privileged insight into an investigation that revealed much about the politics of the day. To Bean's credit, he did not draw on any of this inside knowledge in his initial forays into newspaper journalism, showing a discretion that was to later make him such a trusted intimate of military commanders in war.

Instead, one of Bean's first major pieces of journalism in Australia was an analysis piece about the significance of Japan's then imminent naval clash with imperial Russia. A month before his piece appeared in *The Sydney Morning Herald* the Japanese had defeated the Russian Army in Manchuria at the Battle of Mukden, forcing the Russians into a humiliating retreat and leaving 90,000 of their soldiers dead on the battlefield. But, as Bean wrote in late April 1905, a massive Russian battleship armada was now headed on an epic 33,000-kilometre rescue bid to relieve its forces via the Russian port of Vladivostok, and Japan faced a serious threat. The coming clash was to be the first test of the huge new battleships that the British navy had also begun building in response to perceived rising German militarism. Bean wrote that 'it will, in all probability, be the most important sea-fight since the days of Nelson … The great modern battleship – in fact, the whole genus of armoured ships – is still an unknown quantity … It is of vast importance to the British people that the modern battleship should emerge from the struggle vindicated.'[23] At the time no armoured ship had yet been sunk at sea by gunfire and Bean accurately predicted that a key factor in the coming battle would be Japan's use of small torpedo boats to counter the numerical superiority of the Russian fleet. He was proven right. In the epic Battle of Tsushima Strait on 27–28 May, the Russian fleet was obliterated. For the loss of just three Japanese torpedo boats and 116 sailors, the Russians in turn lost eight massive battleships – the pride of their fleet – and more than 5000 men.

By the end of 1906, Charles Bean probably quite rightly felt that he was in a legal backwater working as an associate for a judge who was now very close to retirement: 'It was a pleasant life but promised nothing.'[24] He decided to return to Wigram Chambers in Phillip Street, where he had first taken space as a barrister shortly after arriving in Sydney. But he struggled with shyness and the anxiety of the public performance of thinking and speaking on his feet as a barrister. He tried to overcome his fears at Sydney College of the Arts debating evenings but, as he later admitted, he did not have the 'nerves of iron' needed for the bar: 'You have to be ready for sudden home thrusts, which are sometimes fair and sometimes not, and I never felt sure that I should keep my head: I was more afraid of it than of missing those catches at Clifton, and this fear would have hampered me horribly.'[25] More practically, he was also not getting any clients: 'I was too nervous for success at the bar; I was a nervous, self-conscious speaker, very liable to break down, or anyway to do injustice to my subject through extreme nervousness. I knew that I could get work as a schoolmaster, but my school discipline was not good. I was too soft with the boys – or, rather, too anxious to please & be popular with them. Father always said that was a fatal weakness in any schoolmaster … I was not cut out, as Father was, for a teacher, & I loved writing.'[26]

While working for Justice Owen, Charles Bean had found time to write a book, *Impressions of a New Chum*, which included his fresh-eyed observations of turn-of-the-century Australia and illustrated with his own drawings. The book was never published but *The Sydney Morning Herald* ran selected extracts from it during June and July of 1907, Bean using the title 'Australia by C.W.B'. He handled the rejection by publishers Angus & Robertson with characteristic good-natured self-deprecation: 'It was a rather crude & somewhat priggish production, and I was afterwards exceedingly glad that it was so firmly rejected, though it was written with enthusiasm & meant well.'[27] Bean was right; his writing was mawkishly romantic about the 'ideal Australian' and probably sounded naïve to the average Sydney reader.

One of his published *Herald* articles also launched into a fervent defence of the White Australia policy, which had its origins in the 1850s when fears of oriental hordes taking over Australia were fanned by competition on the goldfields between British and Chinese miners. The population of New South Wales was only 200,000 in 1851, but after gold was discovered nearly 50,000 Chinese immigrated to the Australian colonies over the next twenty years. When Australia became a federation in 1901, laws were passed to restrict non-European immigration to Australia. Whilst indubitably a racist and unjustifiable policy by today's standards, public support for the White Australia laws was overwhelming at the turn of last century, and it was a socially acceptable and perhaps even mainstream view for a man of Bean's status and class to express. Ever sensitive to criticism from 'home', Australians were smarting from attacks in the British press about the discriminatory immigration laws and

Bean wrote another piece that ran in the London *Spectator* that was also uncompromisingly prejudiced, stating that 'living together, the Western demoralizes the Eastern, and vice versa'.[28]

Bean enjoyed the experience of seeing his articles published in the *Herald* so much that he decided to attempt a move into fulltime journalism. He first went to Banjo Paterson for advice about getting into the business, who prudently advised him that newspapering was a 'poor job' but that if Bean was serious he should go and speak to James Fairfax, a senior director of John Fairfax and Sons, owners of *The Sydney Morning Herald*. Fairfax was another old boy of Sydney Grammar who remembered Bean's father with affection, and he gave Bean sage advice: 'He told me that there were no openings for writers of special articles or leaders; that if I joined the staff of the Herald I must begin at the beginning and work my way up; but that if I was prepared to do that, he saw no reason why I should not get on quickly.'[29] Bean spent the next four months learning the required shorthand and was finally hired as a junior reporter on the *Herald* in January 1908 on a paltry four pounds a week. Of his own admission it was very difficult at first for him to be covering the law courts he had been striding as an aspiring barrister just months earlier as a junior reporter. But he soon found 'the fellowship among pressmen so good, & the men in the *Herald* & *Telegraph* & other offices so unselfish & helpful, that the strangeness of the start gradually wore off & I spent one of the happiest times of my life in the old *Herald* office. It was a big family … All the old *Herald* men were loyal friends, too, of old Sir James Fairfax; & when I got to know him, some years later, I too grew most fond of him.'[30]

Charles Bean was to take his apprenticeship in journalism very seriously. For the first time in his life he loved his work, and honed his word craft:

> I always looked upon the reader as a fish to be hooked if possible in the first sentence and then 'played' (or kept tight on the hook) until the article was finished … if you put in one uninteresting sentence, he would wriggle off and dash away to some other article … I can generally see the flaw in a false argument and have a pretty good sense of where the right and wrong lie. It is these two faculties which made me the right sort of person to take up journalism … this and a sense of duty which Father and Clifton gave me have carried me through.[31]

It was during this time as a journalist covering the strikes on the wharves and visiting Sydney Trades Hall that Bean befriended William 'Billy' Hughes, later to become the federal Labor Party parliamentary leader and a long-time trade union organiser. Theirs was a friendship that was to help Bean considerably throughout the First World War after Hughes became wartime prime minister of Australia in 1915. Hughes, born in London of Welsh parents, had migrated to Australia as a young man. His canny intelligence helped him quickly progress from jobs in labouring and as a cook to becoming a tough union organiser and one of the sharpest politicians of his day. After success working for the Amalgamated Shearers' Union during the 1880s, Hughes was elected to the New South Wales Parliament in the seat of Sydney-Lang in 1894, an electorate that covered the wharf district of Darling

Harbour. By the time Hughes and Bean met, the MP had become a barrister as well as the first national president of the powerful Waterside Workers' Federation. He had also become a federal MP in the first ever national election in 1901 under the new Australian Federation. At the turn of last century the working wharves in Hughes's electorate were a constant source of news to journalists and, as the wharfies' union boss, Billy was the man to go to whenever there was one of the many disputes on the docks. The working conditions for wharf workers in those days were arduous and often horrifically dangerous; men were forced to walk the 'Hungry Mile' docksides in Sydney (and the 'Wailing Wall' in Melbourne) to offer their services as day labourers for poor wages. The battle for better working conditions on the wharves, and the broader battle for workers' rights across the economy, was to play a big role in launching Billy Hughes's Labor Party into office.

When Charles Bean met Billy Hughes, the new union was just beginning to fire up its eventually successful campaign for better terms and conditions for its workers, and Billy Hughes was a rich source of copy; Bean was a frequent visitor to Hughes's home at Gore Hill. Bean was now working so hard on the *Herald* that, as his father had done, he came close to a breakdown. In July 1908 Bean took an epic outback journey to Broken Hill by train and coach, reporting on the two rival routes for the proposed railway to the ore-rich outback town 1100 kilometres west of Sydney. 'It was my first view of the West and I was intensely interested in the people, the country, the grasses, the animals, the trees and the life.'[32]

On his return from the outback Bean was assigned to cover the 'Great White Fleet', the nickname for a massive

United States Navy battle fleet that was touring the globe from December 1907 to February 1909 in a brazen display of America's new wealth and military power. The US president, Theodore Roosevelt, had decided to flex American military muscle, and the sixteen enormous white battleships that made up the fleet were awing the world. Bean was thrilled to be sent to Auckland on HMS *Powerful*, the Royal Navy's flagship in Australia's naval squadron, to cover the visit there; his demonstrated expertise reporting the Japanese navy clash with Russia had stood him in good stead, *Herald* editor Archie Whyte telling him 'you may like it, you speak the language'.[33] Bean spent many hours talking with navy officers in the wardroom of HMS *Powerful* as she steamed towards New Zealand, and this experience made him aware of an opening for him to write on naval and military affairs. He was proud of what he had achieved in such a short time: 'I was by then one of the recognised descriptive writers of the *Herald*.'[34]

Bean thought that publishing a book would help his journalistic reputation so he wrote about his experience on HMS *Powerful* and called it *With the Flagship in the South*. Again he could not find a publisher so he spent a substantial 100 pounds on printing it himself, only making 50 pounds in sales. He dedicated the book to his mother and father: 'To the most capable man and the most gracious woman he is ever likely to know. This book is affectionately dedicated by their son.'[35] It was an unabashedly imperialist tome, singing the praises of the Royal Navy, but what is intriguing is how much Charles Bean and the navy officers on whom he based the book's opinions clearly saw war with Germany as a strong possibility, even in 1909:

> Whether that battle is imminent, none can say. Plenty, who will never fight it, are doing their best to make it so. Those who are bringing this Empire and Germany into war – if ever they do – think that it will go easy for the Empire. Those who will fight it, officers and men too, are not in the least given over to that very foolish mistake. The Navy knows that the German is a magnificent sailor in magnificent ships; and the war would be desperate.[36]

It also carried excellent drawings and watercolours done by Bean himself, a skill he had learned as a young lad walking the battlefield of Waterloo with his father, and one that would help him enormously when he came to describe the battlefields of Gallipoli and the Western Front. The book's frontispiece was Bean's imagining of a future Australian navy, for which he made a strong argument in his book. Self-publishing may have left Bean out of pocket, but in its wake he was offered jobs by the rival *Argus* and *Daily Telegraph* newspapers, and as a consequence he won a pay rise from the *Herald* to nine pounds a week.

In 1910 Bean wrote another book called *On the Wool Track* that this time was successfully published, eventually becoming a best-seller.[37] It was reprinted in Australia twice and also published in London and America, catching the public's imagination because so few Australians had actually seen the country's outback interior. It came out of another journalistic assignment when he was instructed to report on the country's wool industry, then a major part of the Australian economy. Bean later admitted that he initially 'thought it a dull subject', but as he travelled across the central west and then down towards the Darling River, he settled on a narrative thread for his articles that actually dared to make the subject of wool interesting.[38] He told readers in the preface to the US edition that his story was about the people behind the industry: 'The writer … has tried to show what life on the back stations really is for the men and women who work there … The wool industry turns out wool and meat and tallow and glue and cold cream and many other things. But the most important things it turns out are men.'[39]

For the first time in his writing, Bean was beginning to speak with a genuinely Australian voice, delighting in weaving tales of the tribulations and trials of the people of the outback around what would otherwise have been a worthy but dry-as-dust analysis of the wool business. He admired the self-sacrifice and plain hard work of the men and women he met on his travels; writing about bushfires, he was struck by the fact that everyone in the district volunteered to help a neighbour fight the blaze on his property:

> They fought and galloped for 48 hours continuously as a matter of fellowship, thrashing the flames until they were blacker than sweeps; rushing in upon the few for a few moments and then retiring choked and breathless. Their clothes were burned. Their hair was singed from their faces and their hands. Their eyes and throats were swollen and sore … and most of these men would wonder why anyone would bother to tell about it. For though it is fighting as hard as [the battle of] Dargai Heights there is nothing in it that is out of the day's work in the bush.[40]

When Bean later wrote about the feats of the Australian men who became the soldiers of Gallipoli and the Western

Front, he was heavily influenced by the memories of his time in the outback. In 1910 he was already thinking of what good soldiers the Australian bush labourer would make, approvingly quoting British military commander Lord Kitchener, who had visited Melbourne that year and said that as soldiers, Australians were the equal if not the superior of any people he knew.[41]

In hindsight, if there was one weakness in Bean's journalism at this time it was his blind jingoism for imperial Britain; Bean clearly saw himself as essentially British. In *On the Wool Track*, after having eulogised the unique qualities of the Australian working man, he curiously felt the need to refer back to the motherland and wave the flag for British racial purity: 'Such qualities as Australians have are, of course, only drawn from the British race, because the people of Australia is as purely British as the people of Great Britain.'[42]

In 1911 Bean wrote another book based on his outback experiences after journeying down the Darling River in a steamboat on another journalistic assignment, this time for the weekly *Sydney Mail* newspaper.[43] Some of his observations about Australia's relationship with its outback in *The Dreadnought of the Darling* are as perceptive and relevant today as they were back then:

> The Australian, one hundred to two hundred years hence, will still live with the consciousness that, if he only goes far enough back over the hills and across the plains he comes in the end to the mysterious half desert country where men have to live the lives of strong men. And the life of that mysterious country will affect the Australian imagination much as the life of the sea has affected that of the English.[44]

He was clearly much taken with the selfless mateship of the men he had met in the outback and, with the threat of war with Germany looming, he used his book to answer the question of whether Australia would help Mother England if so. His tub-thumpingly imperialist (and accurate) prophecy was that England would find 'in the younger land, existing in quite unsuspected quarters, a thousand times deeper and more effective than the showy protestations which sometimes appropriate the title of "imperialism", the quality of sticking – whatever may come and whatever may be the end of it – to an old mate'.[45]

It is difficult to escape the sense in these early books about Australia that Bean was often torn by an internal conflict, that his nascent attempts to define a unique Australian national identity were hampered by his inability to see it through anything other than his pro-British prism and hard-held views on white racial superiority. His 1913 book, *Flagships Three*, ostensibly about warships and Australia's need for its own navy, betrayed Bean's sensitivity about the fact that even in his beloved London there was public condemnation of the White Australia policy. He repeated the case he had made in the *Spectator* years earlier, that:

> for the good of either Australia or England, a western and an Oriental race cannot live together in Australia … the probability of an Oriental invasion, peaceful or warlike is enormous, and justifies urgent measures … right or wrong, the resolve of Australians to keep their country white is of an intensity undreamed of in England … Australians, knowing this, believing a fierce racial war, due to a policy of which England disapproves, to be ahead of them,

> and determined to fight it at any cost, 'harbour no illusions' as to England's supporting them in it. That this doubt [exists] does immense harm to the cause of Empire in Australia, and is deliberately made use of by separatists.[46]

Bean argued that the English only had experience of 'Orientals' from history books or from those visiting England, and that in imperial India the English lived 'over the head' of native India. 'A narrow Western aristocracy, of splendid intellect and character, rules, for its great good a race which you do not believe capable of ruling itself. The rulers live absolutely apart. They would be highly shocked if their womenfolk had any intimacy with natives … Well the Australian sees a deal of the oriental.'[47] Such were the attitudes of the time.

It is important to acknowledge Bean's prewar views on race not because he should be judged by today's standards for his racist views but because of how dramatically his attitudes were to change over the following decades; and the story of why that happened is as much a story of Australia as it is about Bean the man. As Bean went on in his writing to more clearly define what it meant to be Australian, he admitted much later in his life that he was wrong on race: 'We must, for example, adjust ourselves to the truth that the possibility of our maintaining a claim to racial superiority has passed beyond recall. We have to be taught, if necessary at school, that our past attitude towards foreigners and strangers is a sign of old-world ignorance.'[48]

In April 1910, Charles Bean's prolific and quality copy earned him the plum job on the paper as *The Sydney Morning Herald*'s London correspondent. Before he left

Australia he wrote a long feature for the newspaper marking the death of King Edward VII. While at Oxford, Bean hadjoined the Oxford University battalion of the Oxfordshire Light Infantry. His 4000-word article, 'The Last Great Passing by One Who Was There', recounted his battalion's role in the Windsor Castle funeral proceedings for Queen Victoria some nine years beforehand. The article is full of adulatory prose, including a gushing description of the royal coffin:

> It was something more precious than anything in the world just then. And somewhere in the centre of this precious little spotless white burden was another thing, much smaller still, a tiny something which sparkled and flashed and coruscated with the cold crisp gleam of diamonds under the cold sky. It was the Crown of England. But just then one could not help somehow imagining that this tiny scintillating core of the whole great spectacle was the sign of the pure transparent soul of the great woman that lay beneath.[49]

Soon afterwards, Bean left for England. His father was still headmaster of Brentwood School and Edwin and Lucy welcomed him back into their London home in early 1911. For the next two and a half years, Bean's output from the London bureau was prodigious. He was also able to witness firsthand the formation of the Australian navy. Two cruisers, HMAS *Sydney* and HMAS *Melbourne*, were being built in the United Kingdom as well as the battle cruiser HMAS *Australia*, one of the great ships around which he focused *Flagships Three*, which he wrote while in England.

Charles had hoped to stay in England as the *Herald*'s correspondent because his father, Edwin, was unwell, but the paper wanted him back in Sydney and so he returned in late 1913 for what was to be an unfulfilling time as a leader writer. It was a promotion for him in newspaper terms, but it was a tedious desk job for Bean after his years in Europe. He liked getting out amongst it, interviewing people, absorbing information and telling stories; his private papers reveal he was restlessly musing on other book ideas to keep himself busy. One unlikely assignment in early 1914 saved him from boredom when he was asked to report on the work of the South Australian Railways Standing Committee, a dull brief in theory but the trip gave him the excuse to travel the length of the Murray–Darling river system. The thirteen articles he wrote traced his journey down river from Queensland through the Snowy Mountains, the Macquarie Marshes and the Darling Lakes system. It was another of Bean's epic journeys into the outback interior of Australia. Within weeks of his return from that journey, Charles Bean's life would be changed forever by events on the other side of the planet.

Three

THE PLAIN, UNVARNISHED TRUTH

If the truth were told from the outset, there would be no reason and no will for war.

ARTHUR PONSONBY, BRITISH POLITICIAN, 1928

In the corner of a grand old museum building in Vienna, Austria, tourists still queue to get a glimpse of a battered limousine, a Gräf & Stift Double Phaeton, in which the heir to the Austro-Hungarian throne, Archduke Franz Ferdinand, and his wife were assassinated by fanatical Serbian nationalist terrorist Gavrilo Princip on 28 June 1914; among the gruesome relics on view is a bloodied jacket worn by Franz Ferdinand. One of the bodyguards standing on the running board on the day of the assassination later told how the archduke was heard to mutter 'It's nothing' as the bullet that had pierced his heart drained his life away. The archduke's dying words could not, of course, have been more wrong: his murder was to unleash the most grotesque and apocalyptic human carnage the world had ever seen.

Exactly one month later the Austro-Hungarian Empire fired the first shots as it declared war on Serbia in response to the assassination. The mobilisation of the Austro-Hungarian Army tripped a domino series of treaty obligations that were to suck most of the great powers of Europe into the conflict. France, bound by treaty to Russia, found itself at war against Germany and Austria-Hungary. The Germans miscalculated, assuming Britain would stay neutral if they went to war with France, and within weeks Germany had invaded Belgium, aiming for Paris. But by 4 August 1914, Britain and soon after its empire, including Australia, had also entered the war.

On the other side of the world in the offices of *The Sydney Morning Herald*, Charles Bean had been writing editorials on the mounting Balkan crisis and then the outbreak of war. Bean was appalled by the huge civilian casualties during the German advance through Belgium – we know now that at least 6500 died – but, while the evidence suggests the Germans did commit some appalling mass killings of civilians, what whipped anti-German hysteria across the Empire to a fever pitch were reports of widespread specific sadistic atrocities and war crimes committed by the German Army; the *Herald* and other Australian newspapers loudly decried these atrocities. The extent of the crimes the Germans committed in Belgium is still the subject of some debate; as Phillip Knightley has written in *The First Casualty*, his exposé of war correspondence journalism: 'The Germans were portrayed as only slightly better than the hordes of Genghis Khan, rapers of nuns, mutilators of children and destroyers of civilization. Once the commitment to war had been made, an overwhelming majority of the nation's political and intellectual leaders joined this propaganda campaign.'[1] While more recent analysis[2] suggests that the Germans did commit war crimes in Belgium, because some civilians fought their invaders, a number of the more lurid atrocity allegations, including the wide-scale lopping-off of hands as a punishment, were never substantiated after the war.

Knightley claims that too many of these German atrocity stories could in fact be traced to a discreet arm of the British Foreign Office that secretly funded a French press bureau with 25 million gold francs from secret service funds to spew out atrocity stories, so many of them that they were published under a general headline – *'Les Atrocities Allemandes'*. In Australia, *The Sydney Morning Herald* published many such stories in the last half of 1914 that had also appeared in the British press, their authenticity later to be seriously questioned postwar:

> Appalling has been the price paid by Liege for its ever-memorable stand against the barbarian … A girl of 17 was outraged in such terrible fashion, she is now in hospital … At Liege a party of German brutes were billeted at the house of a grey-haired old woman … one of them extended his arm as if to shake hands with her, but at the same moment as she put out her hand, another German, standing beside her, raised his sword and deliberately hacked off the poor old woman's hand at the wrist … One woman, the wife of a miner who has escaped from Mons with her child said the Germans' … first care was to block up the shafts of mines in which a number of miners were working. Ill-fated men have been buried alive in the workings at other mines.[3]

The story of the elderly woman was just one of a genre of severed-hand stories that could not be substantiated during or after the war. The French minister in charge of censorship of the press admitted in the 1920s that he had attempted and failed to find evidence for one story that hysterically circulated at the beginning of the war, that two scientists had witnessed a hundred children whose hands had been cut off by the Germans. The *Herald*'s claim that miners were buried alive was also subsequently strongly denied by the general secretary of the Belgian miners' union.[4] That did not stop atrocity stories like these from being published, so the fierce outrage they inflamed across Australia continued, as did the flood of volunteers wanting to sign up for the fight. Sadly, there was no need to fabricate such allegations against the Germans because the evidence is overwhelming that they did engage in mass killings in Belgium.

Bean was 34 years old as Australia's engagement in the war loomed. He had considered enlisting as a soldier as his brother Jack had already done, but a family friend and commander of the 26th Infantry Regiment, Colonel Henry MacLaurin, sent a message saying 'not yet'.[5] (MacLaurin was later shot by a sniper at Gallipoli.) Charles Bean was hankering for the opportunity to follow in the footsteps of his old friend Banjo Paterson as a war correspondent and he now seized the chance.

In August 1914 Bean wrote to the defence minister, Senator Edward Millen (a former journalist with *The Central Australian and Bourke Telegraph* newspaper), seeking approval for him to accompany the Australian forces as an eyewitness. The minister replied that Bean's application would be considered if the chance arose to send a press correspondent. On the same day that Bean received the response from the minister, the Australian government was cabled by the British Army to inform it that each

Commonwealth dominion would be allowed to have one correspondent accompany its expeditionary force. But rather than appoint Bean, the minister chose to invite newspapers from Sydney and Melbourne – *The Sydney Morning Herald* and *Daily Telegraph*, the Melbourne *Argus* and *The Age* – to recommend a journalist. They respectively nominated Banjo Paterson and Phillip Schuler, the latter being the son of Gottlieb Schuler, the editor of the Melbourne *Age* newspaper.

However a federal election on 5 September 1914 saw a change of government, with the Labor Party winning power under Andrew Fisher. George Pearce, the new defence minister, opted to go with the original British proposal for just one official correspondent to represent Australia and suggested the Australian Journalists' Association hold a ballot of its members to make the selection. Charles Bean won by a whisker over Keith Murdoch, who was then the chief Melbourne-based political correspondent for the Sydney *Sun* newspaper. Murdoch was a formidable adversary: he had many national political contacts from his time as the parliamentary correspondent for the Melbourne *Age*, but he was gracious in his good wishes to Bean.

As it transpired, Bean would not be the sole Australian correspondent covering the First World War as two other appointments were confirmed by the outgoing Liberal government before it left office after the September 1914 election: Phillip Schuler for the Melbourne *Age* and Charles Smith for *The Argus*.[6] Both men eventually based themselves at the Australian base in the Egyptian port of Alexandria, writing stories based on the official dispatches and on interviews with the wounded. (Not being designated 'official' correspondents, Schuler and Smith were not allowed to accompany the AIF at the Gallipoli landings, but in July 1915 they were given permission to visit the Gallipoli peninsula.) There was clearly profound disappointment in the Australian press that Bean's deployment as official correspondent would be the extent of the media presence with the Australian forces and *The Sydney Morning Herald* put some pressure of its own on the government in an article in early October 1914. The London-by-lined opinion piece took the time to lament 'the final supersession of the war correspondent' and gave the clear expectation that the job of a correspondent such as Bean would be to wave the flag about the bravery of troops to readers back home.[7] This was only one of the vexing issues with which Bean would now have to learn to grapple for, even more than today, the role of a war correspondent at the turn of last century was a controversial one. The motivation for the British government decision to allow an official correspondent was made clear in early 1915 when it selected Royal librarian Sir John Fortescue to write what it clearly expected would be a propagandist war history for the public.[8] Fortescue was told that the British Army wanted a series of volumes like those written by British conservative politician and journalist Leo Amery, who had written a multi-volume series on the 'deeds of valour' of the British Army in the Boer War.

As a young man, Bean no doubt thrilled to stories from the so-called golden age of war correspondence, a time between the American Civil War and the beginning of the First World War when newspaper journalism boomed. British education reforms in the 1870s had made it possible for every child to learn to read and the number of newspapers doubled between 1880 and 1900. It was a hugely profitable time in the newspaper business, allowing proprietors the money to dispatch their correspondents to far-flung corners of the globe where imperial Britain was having its latest clash with the local indigenes. For a brief few decades, before the military realised the efficacy of censorship during the Boer War, there was an extraordinary freedom for journalists to report whatever they wanted from a conflict zone. Phillip Knightley has written that the military establishment was very slow to realise the power of the media in moulding public opinion, and how the new technology of the telegraph had opened up opportunities in news coverage:

> … for the first time it was both physically and financially possible for a newspaper to carry its own correspondent's report of a battle within days, instead of weeks or months, of its conclusion. Also it was clear to the editors and proprietors of the popular press that public demand for these reports was immense – providing they were written mainly as narratives of adventure without too much political comment or moralizing to interrupt the narrative.[9]

The one British commander who first realised the risks of letting war correspondents tell the truth about what was really going on in a combat zone was Sir Herbert Kitchener (later to become Lord Kitchener) during his campaign in the Sudan against the Muslim dervishes. Kitchener, who would become the British secretary of state for war during the First World War, treated journalists with undisguised disdain, limiting their telegraph communications rights and giving them no help or information. During the Boer

War he was notorious for his censorship and outright dislike of journalists, on one occasion yelling at a group of correspondents: 'Get out of my way you drunken swabs.'[10]

War was good for sales; in America, media proprietor William Randolph Hearst used war to boost circulation in his competition with Joseph Pulitzer for dominance of the New York newspaper market. One story, which may be apocryphal, highlighted Hearst's desire to get the United States into the Cuban battle for independence from Spain during the 1890s. As Knightley tells it, Hearst's reluctant correspondent was an artist, Frederic Remington, who on arrival in Cuba telegraphed his boss: 'EVERYTHING IS QUIET. THERE IS NO TROUBLE HERE. THERE WILL BE NO WAR. I WISH TO RETURN.' Hearst is said to have replied: 'PLEASE REMAIN. YOU FURNISH PICTURES. I WILL FURNISH WAR.'[11]

At the outbreak of the First World War, Lord Kitchener, in his new role as British secretary of state for war, oversaw extraordinary censorship rules imposed on the British media under the *Defence of the Realm Act*. An extremely draconian piece of legislation, it gave the government sweeping powers to promote the war effort and to suppress dissent: 'No person shall by word of mouth or in writing spread reports likely to cause disaffection or alarm among any of His Majesty's forces or among the civilian population.'[12]

When British journalist Philip Gibbs began reporting from Belgium and France in the face of the German advance, Lord Kitchener put out orders for his arrest as an unauthorised correspondent. Finally captured at Le Havre, Gibbs was told he would be put against a wall and shot if he returned to France. This blatant attempt to gag independent reporting aroused criticism in Fleet Street and the United

States. The German military was allowing American reporters access to its frontlines, and several American correspondents had written articles debunking some of the more sensational British media claims of German atrocities in Belgium. The British cabinet began to realise that despite Kitchener's strong distaste for the press, it had to permit some war correspondents – hence the approach to Australia and other dominions for correspondents.

Accepting his appointment as official correspondent, Bean went to Melbourne to meet Major General William Bridges, the officer placed in command of the soon to be deployed Australian force. The founding commander of The Royal Military College at Duntroon, Australia's officer training school, Bridges was born a Scotsman with sound imperial connections who had served as Australia's representative on the Imperial General Staff in London. Lord Kitchener had recommended him for the Duntroon job and, as Bean learned, Bridges was an officer in the Kitchener tradition, savvy enough not to play to the press. Bridges' staff officer, Lieutenant Colonel Cyril Brudenell White, would become one of Charles Bean's closest friends. In Melbourne Bean was briefed on the terms under which he would be employed as an official correspondent. As he explained years later in his official history, he was graded as a captain but remained a civilian 'deliberately, on the advice of Birdwood and White, who held that he should be free of their control as regards his work, and able to express an independent opinion – whether adverse to themselves or not – upon any matter concerning the Australian force, subject only to the rules of censorship.'[13] The one basic rule was that no message should be despatched except through the censor.

He also met with Senator George Pearce, the defence minister, whose office was based in Melbourne's Victoria Barracks. It was in the course of this initial conversation with the minister that the idea was first floated with Bean that he should write an official history of the war as well as his press reports. In the quaint tradition of British army officer entitlements, Bean was also given a personal servant – or batman – as well as army rations and a horse. At the suggestion of one of Bean's journalist colleagues, an eighteen-year-old clerk named Arthur Bazley from *The Argus* newspaper would take the batman role. Like almost all young men at the time, Bazley had served several years in the cadets and was very keen to join the AIF. The war was actually declared on Bazley's eighteenth birthday, the youngest possible age for enlistment, and so, with Bean's cautious approval, Arthur Bazley falsified his age as nineteen to ensure there was no problem. It was the beginning of an extraordinary association between the two men, who would become great friends through peril and peacetime; Arthur Bazley was to work closely with Bean as his assistant in the field and afterwards on the official history for two decades.

Charles Bean's salary was to be funded by a levy on the newspapers that ran his stories, but this would eventually change to a fixed yearly subscription based on the size of the city in which the newspaper was published. He described his directive as official correspondent as to 'satisfy the poignant anxiety of Australians for news of their men, their daily life, their behaviour in action, their peculiar Australian interests', and his duties after the war to write 'an account of the Australian part in it for a permanent record for schools and libraries'.[14]

Whether Australia would contribute troops to the war effort was never in question, it was just an issue of how much. The government's first commitment was to put Australia's new navy under the direct control of the British Royal Navy. Then, within days of the outbreak of war, Australia agreed to supply an expeditionary force, initially 20,000 and then 33,000 men. Tens of thousands were rushing to join up in a swell of patriotic fervour. The Empire's bugles had called and the politicians had pledged all of Australia's resources to the war effort, Labor opposition leader Andrew Fisher having vowed during the 1914 election campaign that 'Australians will stand beside our own … to our last man and our last shilling'.[15] The war news from Europe was grim: both the French and British were taking a hammering. The British Expeditionary Force had been forced into a humiliating retreat at Mons in Belgium and the German advance into France was only halted at the Battle of the Marne near Paris in early September. Shortly after joining the war, Australian troops defeated German forces holding communication stations in a chain of German colonies across the Pacific, including New Guinea.

But all eyes and public concern was focused on the grim situation in Europe, and the Australian Imperial Force (AIF) was readied. On 21 October 1914, after weeks of preparations with the AIF staff at Victoria Barracks, Bean found himself farewelling his mother before travelling with his father to Port Melbourne. His initial entry in his number-one black diary, the first of hundreds he would fill with his distinctive longhand observations over the next four years, recorded the date of the AIF's departure as Trafalgar Day, the anniversary of the British admiral Horatio Nelson's victory over the Spanish and French fleets at Trafalgar in 1805. The departure of Australia's first troops from Melbourne now unleashed a similar swell of British imperial pride as tens of thousands of citizens flocked to the port to farewell their sons and husbands; it was a day charged with emotion. It must have been an emotional day for the Bean family, too, because while Monty would stay in Australia to work as an engineer, the two elder sons, Charles and his brother Jack, now a medical officer with the 3rd Battalion, were leaving for an unknown theatre of war on a foreign shore. But if he felt moved by the moment, Bean did not confide his feelings to his diary.

Bean had no real inkling of the extraordinary journey he was about to undertake, and indeed his journalistic colleagues were sceptical, telling him not to expect to see Australian troops fighting at all. Charles Bean's editor at *The Sydney Morning Herald* doubted he would be allowed to report anywhere near the actual battlefields where Australians were to be deployed, telling him he was foolish to take up the position because Australian troops would never be used at the frontlines. As Bean later proudly recounted after the war to his new wife, Effie, both prophecies would prove to be far from the truth: 'I obtained a chance such as no journalist in this war, or probably any other, has had of going absolutely where I liked … without any restrictions so long as I was with our own troops.'[16]

Bean was on board the passenger liner HMAT *Orvieto*, the flagship transport for the AIF, with General Bridges, Lieutenant Colonel Brudenell White and the rest of the staff from the 1st Division. The 42-day journey first to Albany, Western Australia, and then across the Indian Ocean was an opportune time for him to befriend its officers in the mess, including Tasmanian orchardist and Boer War British Army veteran Major John Gellibrand, who would become another great friend to Bean. One of the rare Australian officers with British Army combat experience, Gellibrand was the quartermaster general who would eventually be responsible for ensuring the division kept up its supply lines on Gallipoli. Bean sometimes took himself away from his books to enjoy a dose of shipboard life, once fighting a boxing bout that he studiously recorded in his diary: 'Assistant purser asked me to box him at 7am. Did so, & found he knew something about it. 3 rounds, got banged in the nose and also knocked down.'[17]

It must have been an emotional time for everyone in the now massive convoy as it gathered in King George Sound off Albany during October 1914. As *Melbourne* guarded the entrance to the port, there was feverish activity as ships were loaded, orders given and troops boarded. The government now also belatedly began imposing strict censorship on the letters sent home by the men, although Bean's diary noted that several newspapers had already rashly reported on the composition of the convoy and the names of the ships. Australia's defence chiefs knew there was a serious risk of an attack on the convoy and it was vital that news of its movements now be suppressed. There was a German fleet in the Pacific and the German raider SMS *Emden* was known to be somewhere in the Indian Ocean. There would be strict bans on vessels displaying lights during the voyage but, as Bean commented, there was so much smoke as the dozens of vessels steamed up that their presence was a giveaway. 'If the *Emden* keeps up her energy she might manage a fine coup by sighting our smoke before our cruisers see her … we're off now in a really huge hazardous experiment.'[18]

On Sunday, 1 November 1914, the 28-ship convoy began its departure. It would have been an impressive sight as the

1st Australian Division ships steamed out through the heads. For all too many of the Australian volunteers on board, that receding glimpse of Albany would also be the last time they would set eyes on Australia. Everyone expected the convoy was headed for England but the next day Bean made a prescient observation in his diary, noting that England and Russia had also just declared war on Turkey: 'Shall we be stopped in Egypt?'[19]

Bean the naval buff was beside himself with delight as he carefully recorded the escort vessels from Britain, New Zealand, Australia and Japan, the latter on the side of the Allies in this war; the gigantic 148-metre-long Japanese battleship *Ibuki* was the lead escort. On 8 November, Bean noted that Captain Silver of HMAS *Melbourne* had said that the most dangerous time for the convoy would be as it passed the Cocos Islands, so the next evening he slept on the deck in the balmy tropical heat 'in case anything would be seen of the Emden'.[20] In fact the *Emden* unwittingly cut across the convoy's path 30 kilometres ahead during the night of 9 November;[21] Bean woke that next morning to hear the news that an unknown warship had been sighted ahead and its radio messages intercepted. His diary notes capture the spiralling rumour mill on board as officers and men scrambled to find out what was happening: 'At breakfast a rumour was going around the table. "If it were true they wouldn't let it out," said someone … By the end of breakfast I heard that a warship had been sighted on the other side of the Cocos.'[22] Everyone on board watched as HMAS *Sydney* peeled off from the convoy to close with the enemy vessel 80 kilometres over the horizon.

A couple of hours later the news broke that HMAS *Sydney* was now fighting the German light cruiser *Emden*;

for Bean, it was his first opportunity to write about Australian soldiers in combat: 'Just over the horizon someone was being done to death, in the midst of crashing steel work, burning decks, sudden flashes of flame. We ought to see something of it any moment … About 11.15 we heard the fight was practically over. The enemy had been stopped before she even came within sight of us. "Enemy run ashore to save sinking," said the message.'[23] Later in the afternoon: 'The message had come through at last. *Emden* beached and done for … So it was the *Emden*. Her business had been finished in about 25 minutes that morning – done whilst we waited. After all her long career sinking ship after ship in the Indian Ocean, bombarding Madras, raiding Penang, she had wandered down here probably to meet her collier under the lee of one of these coral islands.'[24]

HMAS *Sydney* was carrying a large number of prisoners from the *Emden*, and as it moved through the convoy after the battle it requested that there be no cheering from other ships in consideration to the 135 German wounded on board, a chivalrous act by the Australians that would soon seem incongruous in light of the brutal fighting at Gallipoli or on the Western Front. The *Emden* captain, Karl von Müller, was also now speaking frankly to his captors about what he would have done if he had stumbled upon the convoy that night: '"We should certainly have sunk six ships and probably 12 before your escort could have come along and prevented us" … He said he didn't want much to meet us because there would not have been space in any ship to have taken on board the men from the ships that had been sunk.'[25] Catastrophe had been a whisker away for the Australian force.

As the convoy continued on its way across the Indian Ocean, plans were afoot for the troops not to be sent to England as they had expected. *Emden*'s prisoners were transferred at Colombo in mid-November and the convoy continued, with mounting rumours that the final destination would be Egypt. Charles Bean was also getting into the rhythm of his new obligations as a correspondent and future official historian (as had been raised in his meeting with defence minister Pearce); the sinking of the *Emden* had underlined the huge historical significance of the job he was undertaking and Bean was beginning to plan how to record what he witnessed.

> I have decided to make this diary my chief personal record of the war. A classification of items under subjects – such as I generally make – is not suitable for this job – not yet at any rate. The diary has drawbacks; but, after all, where the events are mainly historical, and later events put the nose of earlier events out of joint, the diary form is useful. Generally I have had to describe and explain merely a state of affairs, which have already become facts – the wool trade; the life in the bush, or on the rivers. Here it is a series of new facts every day. There are strong points against a diary. It is not always easy to find from it the facts you want when you are writing up some particular subject.[26]

It was not until 28 November that Bean finally learned of the decision to land and train the Australians in Egypt. This was the strongest hint yet that fighting with Turkey might be the AIF's first objective. Imperial Germany had spent years fanning revolutionary nationalist and liberation groups in

Egypt to cause mischief with the British, and the threat of an attack by Germany's ally Turkey on the strategic Suez Canal was very real. One month after departing Albany, the *Orvieto* entered the canal, making its way towards Port Said and then to the Mediterranean port of Alexandria. Indian colonial troops on the banks cheered the passing troopships when they realised it was the Australians, while the British officers commanding them signalled 'Good luck to you boys'.[27]

Bean arrived in Alexandria on 3 December 1914, watching on as a 'native' policeman savagely beat an over-enthusiastic local Arab hawker with a horsewhip on the dock. For all the Australians the sights of Egypt were confronting, and it reinforced the prejudices Bean held at the time about the need to bully the 'natives' to get things done: 'It seems almost the only way of dealing with the rabble here. They have no restraint and no morality of our sort; and although they have considerable virtues of their own you are apt to get disaster when people with their morality meet with people of our morality unless the two are kept apart by a hard and fast division.'[28]

The Australians and New Zealanders finally got off their ships at Alexandria and were boarded on a train south to Cairo. From the railway station the Australians were cheered by British troops and watched by bemused Egyptians as they passed. Bean took a patronising view of the British regulars: 'They are Lancashire territorials, little fellows, often scarcely more than English schoolboys with pink cheeks and blue eyes … although they are infants beside our men, they are turning into good smart little soldiers.'[29]

For the thousands of young Australians it was an extraordinary thrill to find themselves marching fifteen kilometres through Cairo on a night lit by a full moon towards the ruins of the Pyramids, including the Great

Pyramid of Khufu (then known as Cheops) at Giza, one of the seven wonders of the ancient world. It was a monument built to see a pharaoh through to the afterlife left by a mighty civilisation nearly 5000 years earlier and a site visited by other occupation armies, including Napoleon; now this was to be the backdrop for the Australian 1st Division training camp at Mena. On their first night the Australians simply wrapped themselves in woollen blankets and lay down on the desert sand to sleep. The Light Horse Brigade was based nearby at Maadi and the New Zealanders were camped across the city, a few kilometres northeast. For weeks thousands of troops rolled into Mena from Alexandria and the camps gradually became feverish with activity; there would be constant drilling and training for war for the next four months.

Almost as soon as he arrived in Mena, Bean was asked to attend a ceremony that underlined Britain's fragile and often unpopular hold on this strategically vital colony. Following the declaration of war, England declared Egypt a protectorate, having no faith in the country's nominal ruler, the Khedive Abbas Helmi II who was perceived as an ally of the Ottoman Empire, so the British engineered a tidy bloodless coup where the Khedive's uncle, Hussein Kamel Pasha, became sultan. On 18 December 1914, Bean and several other correspondents, including Phillip Schuler from the Melbourne *Age,* attended the new sultan's inauguration, donning the best ceremonial clothing they could find, including – absurdly for the desert climate, but required dress at the time – top hats, morning coats and gloves.

One of Bean's earliest pieces of writing in Egypt was a pamphlet for the troops entitled 'What to Know in Egypt – A Guide for Australasian Soldiers'. It warned of the dangers of immorality and vice in the seedier parts of Cairo, including its notoriously unsanitary brothels. 'Cairo has made a name in the world as a hotbed of both gonorrhoea and syphilis. There is a reason for this. Egypt is not a country under the full control of its Government … if a man will not steer altogether clear of the risk by exercising a little restraint, his only sane course is to provide himself with certain prophylactics beforehand to lessen his chance of disastrous result[30] … Men must be careful to avoid any attempts at familiarity with native women; because if they are respectable they will get into trouble, and if they are not venereal disease will probably be contracted.'[31]

But it soon became apparent to the Australian commanders that many of their soldiers were not reading his advice. On New Year's Day 1915, Bean wrote with concern in his diary about how hundreds of soldiers were absent without leave in Cairo, singling out for special criticism Australian veterans of the Second Boer War of 1899–1902 in South Africa.

> But when all is said and done, the chief cause of trouble is the tone amongst a certain section of old South African soldiers, and men who have been through the Imperial service. I have noticed this myself and I have heard it on every side; so much so that if one sees a chap in trouble now, drunk or brought up a prisoner, or if one sees a dirty untidy soldier going without his belt in town in a crumpled field service cap (which looks sloppy and is against orders) one looks automatically for the South African ribbon.[32]

Bean's reporting on the Australian discipline problems in Cairo was to teach him a very important lesson early on about the perils of writing what he saw as the uncensored truth for the Australian public. Throughout the war, virulent venereal diseases, especially the syphilis being contracted by the troops in Cairo brothels, was an extremely serious morale and health issue for the imperial commanders, and often an extreme source of embarrassment for the men who contracted it. The worst form of the disease was largely incurable, and in this pre-antibiotic era the usual therapy was months of hospital treatment and bed rest – young soldiers out of action because of a grubby sexual coupling in a Cairo back alley. Postwar the dreadful legacy of syphilis in servicemen left many of them infertile, or for those who did bear children their offspring were all too often blinded and suffering other birth deformities as a result of the lingering disease. Bean was echoing the concerns of senior commanders when he diarised his concerns that a few experienced men were leading the young fellows astray:

> They say these old hard heads often make the best soldiers – I don't believe it. I daresay they fight well. But their influence on the young fellows with them, and on the general tone of the army, far more than counterbalances that. Some of our commanding officers have had boys come to them – bright decent youngsters who in Australia would have been ashamed to do or think of the things, or go near the places, into which they have been led here – the youngsters have come to them almost in tears bitterly ashamed and half horrified with themselves. I don't mean that Australians are squeamish but there are clean debauches and unclean debauches and Cairo is

> the home of all that is filthy and beastly if you like to go and look for it.[33]

Throughout the war there would always be a tension between the Australian and British commanders regarding the relatively lenient Australian attitude to disciplining its wholly volunteer servicemen. Because the Australians were not a conscription army, the Australian government would refuse to allow the British Army to carry out death sentences imposed on her soldiers in the First World War, but many so sentenced were thrown into the brig to serve a death sentence commuted to life in prison. In that first Christmas abroad there was an understandable view among the troops that the pleasures of Cairo's bars and brothels should be enjoyed while they still could, and many of the Australian officers and non-commissioned officers took a lenient view to their men being absent without leave, much to the concern of the British command – whose views Bean echoed.

> I don't think these chaps who stay out all night (and sometimes don't come back all day) realise how their crime might be treated. It's all very well whilst we have our own commanders who understand us. But someday that may change – and some man will wake up with a shock in the guardroom to realise that he is on active service & that the punishment to which he is liable for his prank is death.[34]

In early January 1915, Bean was summonsed by General Bridges to the Mena camp. The general detailed a letter from the British commander of the Australia Corps, Major General William Birdwood, raising his concerns about

Australian indiscipline. 'From what he said, I take it that he would not take it amiss if I sent a letter and a wire to give people in Australia some idea of how things are.'[35]

And so he did; Bean sent home both a wire and a letter describing the bad behaviour of some of the Australian troops based at the Mena camp on the outskirts of Cairo. A widely published article carrying the by-line 'Captain Bean, Australian Press Representative with the Troops' blazed the scandalous headline 'Australia's Fair Fame, Wasters In The Force, Some Not Fit To Be Soldiers'. Bean did not pull his punches. He told readers that Australia was getting a bad name among the other forces because of the drinking, debauchery and errant behaviour of some soldiers: 'The truth is that there are a certain number of men among those who were accepted for service abroad who are not fit to be sent abroad to represent Australia.'[36] He estimated that about one or two per cent of soldiers were to blame for the bad behaviour and he, perhaps unwisely, voiced his private opinion, sheeting much of this blame to Boer War veterans:

> There is in the Australian ranks a proportion of men who are uncontrolled, slovenly, and in some cases what few Australians can be accused of being – dirty. In a certain number of cases, it is noticeable that these men are wearing the South African ribbon. Possibly they are the men who since returning from the war have never had any settled occupation, and who were therefore the first to enlist when recruiting for the present force was begun; or it may be that the discipline in the South African campaign was very much slacker than that required of troops before they will be permitted to go to the front in the present class of warfare.[37]

Bean repeated the assertion in his article that these experienced men were leading the younger soldiers astray: 'They are losing Australia her good name in the outside world, and those Australians who happen to be living in Cairo or in touch with the world outside the camps have the mortification of looking on while day by day the reputation of Australia slowly vanishes before the actions of a handful of rowdies who do not really represent the country.'[38]

General Bridges had decided the most effective way of disciplining the wayward Australian troops would be to send them home in shame, with paperwork explaining just why they were being returned, publishable at the whim of the government; (about 130 disciplinary cases were sent home at this time). This proved to be a very effective sanction, but for the soldiers camped in Egypt the threat that they could be publicly vilified and shamed back home in Australia was intolerable and, in their view, wowserish. In his stern news story, under the subheading 'Weeding out wasters', Bean wrote that 'a percentage will probably find their way back home from here, the reason for whose return has been that they have damaged their country's reputation, and a few of them have been got rid of as the best means of preserving it'.[39]

If an article like this was written today the response online and in social media would be instant, but a century ago it was a slow but eventually incendiary burn as the story filtered back to the troops from Australia. The response it generated in Australia was extraordinary: concerned parents, sweethearts, wives and relatives read the widely published article and wrote to the Egypt-based soldiers about it, often enclosing clippings. Lieutenant Colonel Harold 'Pompey'

Elliott, commander of the 7th Battalion AIF at Mena, was furious to hear of Bean's claims about the South African veterans leading the younger men astray; having served in the Boer War for three years and earning a Distinguished Conduct Medal, Pompey had re-enlisted in the army after a distinguished legal career. Clearly not realising that the story had been published at the behest of senior commanders, he attempted to call what he saw as Bean's bluff on the South African comments by asking Brigadier General McCay for statistics on the men implicated to test the veracity of Bean's claims, only to be summoned to General Bridges' office to be rebuked for getting involved.[40]

Bean, still not fully aware of just how angry soldiers were with his comments, learned of Pompey Elliott's move against him. Still very angry, Pompey wrote a letter home to the former mayor of Essendon, Fred Henderson, later published in the *Essendon Gazette*:

> Captain Bean stated the cases of misconduct were confined to about one or two per cent. Judging from my own Battalion, and I would not say it is better or worse than any other battalion in the division in this respect, this is exaggerated ... the root of the trouble lies in the fact that these men had given way to drink. In extenuation of their conduct, I desire to point out that practically all the misconduct occurred during the Christmas festivities, when even at home, a certain amount of insobriety is tolerated.[41]

As Elliott wrote to his wife, Kate, the anger towards Charles Bean was intense: 'Some of the men were very angry and wanted to catch Mr Bean and tar and feather him. It was a great pity it was ever sent.'[42] But because of the delays in the post it was not until early March 1915 that Bean realised the brewing sentiment against him. He was shocked by the angry reaction and suggested he had been taken out of context by certain papers, blaming the Sydney *Sunday Times*, which had lifted Bean's article from the Melbourne papers and appears to have given it a dose of journalistic 'stick'. A poem, which savagely painted Bean as an uptight wowser, was also published in the *Egyptian Mail* (and ended up in some local newspapers in Australia as well):

> To our critic
> from an Australian soldier in Egypt.
>
> Ain't you got no blanky savvy,
> Have yer got no better use,
> Than to fling back home yer inky
> Products of yer pen's abuse?

The poem attacked Bean, suggesting he was playing to the home crowd by slurring the reputation of all the Australians:

> Do yer thinks they likes yer better
> For yer tales of drink and shame?
> Do yer think they'll praise yer action
> In defamin' our fair name? …
>
> Do yer think ye'r Gawd Almighty.
> 'Cos yer wears a captain's stars?
> Thinks us blokes is dirt beneath yer,
> Men of low degrees, and bars?[43]

Bean now suffered abuse and threats as he went about the Mena camp and he had genuinely good cause to fear for his own safety. As he was now learning, it could be a tough and isolating job being a journalist who tells the 'truth', and it would no doubt have been highly concerning for him that many of the very same 1st Division men and officers he would need to help him write his journalism and official history were treating him with contempt before the fighting had even begun. He could hardly resile from what he had written because, as his own diary makes clear, he did believe the Australians were responsible for the worst of the drunken and rowdy behaviour in Cairo. So he now imprudently tried to make amends with a further dispatch on the subject ambiguously headlined 'Troops in Egypt. Unjustified criticisms', explaining his original article had been taken out of context:

> An article in which I stated that the Australian troops were not responsible for certain rowdiness in Cairo some months ago, but that it was due solely to a small percentage of unsuitable men, seems to have been so twisted and misquoted by a certain newspaper (or newspapers) as to appear to be an attack on the Australian troops in Egypt. That is exactly opposite to what was written by me or intended. Readers of my articles and cable messages know that the condition of the Australian force in Egypt, the way in which it has carried through its strenuous and tiring training, and the condition in which it is emerging from it are such as would make Australians, if they could only see it, very

> proud indeed. The newspaper article alluded to also contains sweeping criticisms on the whole of the officers, who were never mentioned in my article, and the criticisms are quite unjustified. Such offences as took place were military offences. Nothing else occurred which does not happen in Australia and other cities every day. The newspaper article referred to omits the fact which I was careful to state, and which it is immensely important not to omit that all the men returned to Australia are not unsuitable, but that a large proportion consists of men whose health has broken down often through hard work and exposure, and who are bitterly disappointed at not being able to go on.[44]

But this story merely resulted in another harsh poem from the camp entitled 'On our critic's apologies':

> So you crayfished, Mr Critic
> From your journalistic stand;
> In an impolitic manner
> You have surely shown your hand.
>
> Seems you were not sure when writing,
> Of your subject or your theme,
> In your milk and water scrawling
> You neglected all the cream …
>
> Will your 'pardon me's' bring solace,
> Or dispel the haunting dread?
> Your apologies bring respite
> For the bitter things you said? …

Will they build and mend the remnants
Of a father's shattered pride;
Will it soothe the wounded honour
Of the absent soldier's bride?

For our loved ones, wives and mothers,
All have felt the poisoned dart
Of your journalistic venom
With your subtle, cruel art …

So just train your pen and send home
Just the plain, unvarnished truth,
And you'll gain the firmest friendship
Of Australia's bravest youth.[45]

Bean was stung by these criticisms and the whole affair clearly rattled him as he mentions it several times in his diary entries. He was deeply concerned about the antipathy towards him from many soldiers of the 1st Division; he knew well he would need their cooperation to do his job: 'I could apply to be attached to the 2nd Division – which doesn't feel the same way – but I'm not going to. The 1st Australian one is the one I've been with and I'm not going to criticise them and run away.'[46]

He mused that he might not have written the article had he known it would be 'so hopelessly misunderstood'. But Bean was also defiant and dogmatically determined that his job was to tell the people of Australia 'the truth':

> When things go wrong – and they looked like going very wrong at Christmas time – my job is to see that at any rate the blame is put on the right people and

> that the innocent don't get a bad name for what they didn't do. When things go right I have to try and see that the Australian people knows the right people to get the credit. If they want someone to feed them on soft pap, only to tell them good and pleasant things whatever happens, then I am not the man for the job. … I have told no-one except Jack [Bean's brother] … that the General asked me to write this article.[47]

Decades later in his final book, *Two Men I Knew*, Bean admitted that the feeling against him was so strong among some of the South African veterans that 1st Division commanders blocked him meeting them to explain his stories:

> Garbled accounts of my letter caused great resentment among the troops, the upshot of which was that senior officers among the veterans of the South African War invited me to explain it to a meeting to be held in the form of a 'social' in the camp. I urged Colonel White to use his influence with Bridges to let the meeting take place, but at the last moment the general forbade it. Long afterwards, I learnt that, unknown to the organizers of the meeting, a few hard heads had decided to waylay and deal with me as I walked down to it.[48]

From the Mena camp, Singleton soldier Fred Newling wrote to his mother that the Bean 'wasters' article was pasted up on the walls of all the men's rooms around the camp; he also told her it was lucky for Bean that the general had stopped Bean's attempt to hold a meeting to explain himself:

'I think it was a very wise thing to do or Captain Bean would have had something to write home about.'[49]

For Bean, the vociferous response to his articles on the wasters was a big lesson. He had written the unadulterated truth when he knew he had the support and encouragement of the AIF commanders, but he chose to keep secret the fact that Bridges had asked him to write it. 'I am not telling anyone that the General asked me to write the article because I wanted to write it and I believe that it has done good; and secondly it would make him unpopular and it is far better that I should be unpopular than he.'[50]

One consequence of Bean's writing about the Australian indiscipline in Egypt was that it sharpened his perception of the character differences between Australian soldiers and other fighting men in the British Empire forces, although the indiscipline of many Australian servicemen would be an issue that Bean sometimes found difficult to acknowledge from here on. He had learned that the Australians stood up for themselves and had a rough egalitarian sense that, as volunteers, they would not be looked down upon by a mere captain journalist. Bean was also beginning to lose his British-is-best bias, taking a pride in the AIF men in Egypt and in what Australia's deployment represented for this relatively new nation; and that is probably most of all why he found the Australian indiscipline offensive:

> ... I could not help noticing that what people in Cairo said was true – the Australians were responsible for most of it. There were rowdy noisy British territorials and rowdy drunken N[ew] Zealanders, but my own observation was that the Australians

> were easily the most noticeable and the most frequent offenders were Australians. I think we have to admit that our force contains more bad hats than the others, and I think also that the average Australian is certainly a harder liver. He does do bad things – at least things that the rest of the world considers as really bad; but it is equally true that he has extraordinarily good points – more, I should say than the English soldiers here and than the N[ew] Zealanders. If he is unrestrained he is also extraordinarily generous and openhearted. He is not in the least colourless or negative – you don't often meet an Australian who is without a character. He often has strong positive vices but he often has strong positive virtues also ...[51]

Writing the story had very nearly jeopardised his relationship with the men whose wartime feats he would now be trying to tell. The whole episode had underlined the dilemma he faced as what we would term today an embedded military correspondent: what Bean had learned was that he should not be writing articles at the request of military commanders as he had done here. All credit to Bean though that when he did come under considerable pressure to withdraw his claims about the 'waster' Australians, he did not resile from his obligation as correspondent to tell the truth about what he saw.

> I think the Australian will have to rely on the good things he does to wipe out the bad ones; and I think the sum will come out on the right side when it is all totted up. That is my great comfort when I wonder how I shall ever manage to write up an honest

history of this campaign. I fully expect the men of this force will do things when the real day comes which will make the true history of this war possible to be written.[52]

The real test of Bean's journalism would come later when the truth required him to voice criticisms of that same Australian command.

Four

THE MOST INTERESTING OPERATION IN THE WAR

Through a Churchill's excess of imagination, a layman's ignorance of artillery, and the fatal power of a young enthusiasm to convince older and more cautious brains, the tragedy of Gallipoli was born.

CHARLES BEAN

As the Australians trained in Egypt, the Allied forces facing the Germans in Western Europe were taking a hammering. The German Army had swept through neutral Belgium and into France but was now stalled in a gruesome trench war stalemate with defending British and French forces, facing a long defensive line running from Lorraine in the south right through France up to the Belgian coast. After British forces failed disastrously in an offensive at the Battle of Loos in September 1915, British commander Field Marshal Sir John French would be dismissed and replaced by General Sir Douglas Haig. Haig and his general staff command were zealous 'Westerners', rigidly opposed to any schemes that took the war effort away from Europe's Western Front. They passionately believed the war could not be won until Germany was defeated in that arena, and Haig believed the only way to do that was by employing sufficient force to 'wear down the enemy and cause him to use up his Reserves'. Haig's plan when that was achieved was to then 'throw in a mass of troops (at some point where the enemy has shown himself to be weak) to break through and win victory'.[1]

But there was another faction in the British government despairing at the awful losses in Europe. They were dubbed the 'Easterners', a group of British politicians who believed it was wrong to be pouring all resources into breaking the Germans on the Western Front and that it was vital that an eastern front be opened up on the German Empire. From his office at the end of the London Mall, First Lord of the Admiralty Winston Churchill was one of the Easterner strategy's chief proponents. He had his eyes on a golden prize, the Dardanelles strait, a 61-kilometre-long sea passage just over one kilometre wide at its narrowest point that was controlled by the Turkish, and now German-Allied, Ottoman Empire. On one side of the strait was Europe, represented by the Gallipoli peninsula, and on the other, the beginning of mainland Asia. In the official history, Bean described the rationale as follows:

> The forcing of the Dardanelles and the capture of Constantinople would enable munitions to go to Russia and Russian grain and oil to come out. It would shut out Germany from the east, would put Turkey out of the war, and would prevent Bulgaria from joining the enemy. It would possibly cause Bulgaria, Roumania, and Greece to join the Allies.[2]

That, at least, was the plan at the start. Once ground troops were committed, the dénouement was to prove a miserable failure that would cost Churchill his Admiralty job and Britain, France, Australia, New Zealand and India tens of thousands of lives.

During the first few months of 1915, Churchill and his commanders were plotting the fate of the Australians and New Zealanders training in Egypt 3500 kilometres distant. Eight years earlier a Royal Navy study had concluded that a purely naval attack on the strait was a folly, and that such an operation should only be undertaken as a combined army ground attack and naval bombardment. But Churchill, believing in the indomitable might of the Royal Navy, had impetuously demanded a plan from his commanders for a naval-only attack, and this was presented to the British Government's War Council in mid-January. Despite the strong opposition of some in the navy command, the plan was formally approved. Crucially, as military historian Robin Prior has noted, the ships to be used in the naval attack were not the newest in the fleet and were considered dispensable:

> A group of old battleships was to attempt to blast their way through the Dardanelles to Constantinople. If operations in the Straits prospered, well and good; if they did not, all seemed to agree that the ships could sail away. This might make a slight dent in British prestige, but it could then be emphasized that these ships were in the second or third rank, as could the probing nature of the attack.[3]

In the end, the new super-dreadnought battleship HMS *Queen Elizabeth*, with huge 15-inch guns, was added to the contingent and on 19 February a combined British and French fleet began a series of naval bombardments of the outer Turkish fortresses at the mouth of the Dardanelles. The attacks continued over several weeks until a final onslaught on 18 March but the bombardments failed to achieve their objectives and there was no hope of pushing through to Constantinople. So ended 'one of the most poorly thought out operations of the war'.[4] The Royal Navy's failure to seize the Dardanelles underlined to everyone that a ground attack would be needed in support of any naval attack.

Across in Cairo, Charles Bean was fighting his own battle with the British military command to be allowed to accompany the AIF on what seemed an imminent fight. As official correspondent for Australia, he was one of three such appointees across the Commonwealth (the other two being from Canada and New Zealand). He had fully expected to be allowed to accompany the Australian divisions into battle but in early February 1915 received the depressing news from General Birdwood's office that he would be treated no differently from any other of the journalists following the war: 'if it is true, it is simply thick-headed because there are clearly only three other journalists in my position in the British Empire.'[5]

To add to his pain, the British secretary of state for war, Lord Kitchener, had resumed his traditional opprobrium of war correspondents; Bean was advised that Kitchener had asked for all communiqués to be wired to him before publication. Not only did this mean they would be published in London first, if at all, but also Bean was told he would not get to see copies of his articles.

> I simply can't do the job the Australian Government sent me here for. As my work could not by any possible flight of imagination be considered as doing the least vestige of harm to the minutest military interest, I don't mean to accept the position without, if necessary, a reference to the Australian Government. I have to get the story of the war for them for subsequent publication and I can't possibly do that without seeing something or hearing something more than I am at present allowed to do under these restrictions.[6]

Just how close the fighting was coming to Cairo was brought home in mid-February when Bean, on an inspection tour with Australian commanders, saw his first dead bodies of enemy soldiers; they were Turks who had been killed in a skirmish with Australian troops as they attempted to cross the Suez Canal on pontoons. 'It gave me a bit of a shock at Toussoum to see, after we had entered the canal, some Indian soldiers about 200 yards behind us, dragging something from the canal and piling it – one, two, three I think there were – on the bank. Dead Turks.'[7] It was the subject of fierce speculation in Cairo why the British had not deployed their huge reserves of men in Egypt to chase and rout the Turkish forces as they fled back over the desert; Bean learned that the British had ordered there be no attack as the Turks retreated. 'They are almost wild about it on the canal,' he wrote in his diary.[8] The British order was probably the result of failed diplomatic efforts by Britain to woo the Turks back to the Allied side, a strategy the British foreign secretary, Sir Edward Grey, had hoped might work before Churchill's planned Dardanelles bombardment later that month.

On 28 February the Australian 3rd Infantry Brigade was to be moved out of Egypt to an undisclosed location. The speculation among the ranks was that it would be to Syria, then under Turkish Ottoman Empire control, or the Dardanelles. Bean was being kept in the dark as much as anyone else in Cairo, conjecturing on the AIF's sudden rush to purchase fly whisks, mosquito nets and tropical helmets. Efforts were being made on Bean's behalf to get a commitment from the Australian government on whether he should be allowed to accompany the Australian troops into battle but, by mid-March a clearly frustrated Bean was being told that all press correspondents would still be confined to Cairo:

> That means the British Government or War Office is determined to treat me as any other Press Correspondent and of course it is a slight to Australia. Though I don't suppose they realise it, that the man the Australian Government chose to send with their force to give some sort of account of it should be treated by the War Office as if they couldn't see any difference between him and the correspondent of any English newspaper. They make a big difference in the case of their own Eyewitness.[9]

Britain had at this stage accredited five official correspondents to cover the war, Philip Gibbs, Percival Phillips, William Beach Thomas, Henry Perry Robinson and Herbert Russell.

At Lieutenant Colonel White's suggestion Charles Bean sent a wire to the Australian high commissioner in London, the former prime minister Sir George Reid. It was Reid who had persuaded Lord Kitchener to train the Australian troops in Egypt because of fears the European winter would damage their health; he clearly had some influence in Whitehall. Bean's wire entreated Reid's support to get War Office consent for Bean to go with the troops on condition he wrote nothing until authorised.[10]

While he waited for a decision, Bean travelled with his brother Jack, now the medical officer with the Australian 3rd Battalion, down to the famed Valley of the Kings at Luxor on the Nile, translating the Roman graffiti left on statues there thousands of years earlier; it was a happy break for the brothers before they went off to war. On the train on their way back to Cairo, a group of New Zealand soldiers opened a picnic basket containing what they claimed was an ancient mummy's head, hand and pieces of its painted wooden case; they had bought the lot for one shilling and sixpence.

Finally, at the end of March, Bean was able to travel to Alexandria to meet General Sir Ian Hamilton, the British commander who would lead the Allied attack on Gallipoli. An intellectual, kind and courageous man, Hamilton had been recommended for the Victoria Cross twice during his military service in the First Boer War. He came to Cairo from a fairly backseat role as commander in charge of land defences in England and, probably because of his age – he was 62 in 1915 – he was never given a Western Front command. He was also a keen writer himself, publishing some 83 works in eight languages during his lifetime, and perhaps this predisposed him to Charles Bean because the meeting between the journalist and the general went very well.

> He told me that he believed a pressman could do the necessary press work in war better than an eyewitness. There are points a pressman would notice of great

> interest to the public and perfectly harmless which [an] eyewitness is apt to miss. He thought that as we had this Eastern show in English hands the government would let the people have a little more information – or rather would give the journalist a little more scope.[11]

Hamilton also encouraged Bean to start keeping fastidious notes for his proposed official history and promised to help him with it however he could. But Bean left Alexandria with no firm guarantees from the general about his desire to accompany the Australians into battle – that decision was still to be made by the curmudgeonly Lord Kitchener in Whitehall. A move into battle was clearly in the wind for, on 1 April 1915, the word went around that all leave was stopped: 'One knew of course what that meant. We – or rather – they, the Division, were off.'[12]

The very next day was Good Friday, and because most of the preparations for the division's departure were already in hand, about a quarter of its soldiers were given day leave. What followed late that afternoon was the notorious 'Battle of the Wassa', when around 2000 troops were either spectators or took part in rioting and the burning and wrecking of many buildings in the Wagh el-Birket red-light district of Cairo. There were a lot of pent-up feelings about 'The Birka', not only because of the high rates of venereal disease among the Australian and New Zealand troops but also because of the perceived high propensity to theft and dishonesty among the Birka locals. What happened was on a scale far worse than had been seen before in Cairo. Bean blamed the Kiwis for starting the trouble:

> Some New Zealanders who had picked up certain diseases in a particular street near Shepheard's Hotel seem to have made up their minds to go in and pay the house back for what they got there. About five o'clock this plan first began to have visible results. Mattresses and bedding were probably torn up inside the house or houses first but the first the public knew was when this debris began to be piled into a bonfire in the street.[13]

Many of the soldiers were very drunk by this stage from liquor sold in the street, and some in the crowd tried to stop a Light Horse Regiment officer from arresting a number of the rioters, Bean recording that the 'officer of the picket was hit heavily on the hand by a big New Zealander who was holding a staircase'.[14]

Charles Bean's initial diary recollections mitigate blame for the riots on the Australians – he suggests they just followed the police posse to watch the fun – but there can be little doubt that the Australians were in part responsible for what happened, and Bean eventually acknowledged this in his official history. Things got so badly out of control, according to one witness account noted by Bean, that when military police arrived they were ordered to fire at the crowd if it did not disperse, and even when the MPs did so there was no response. That young soldier witness told Bean how onlookers were shot by the MPs, one possibly fatally: '"I looked and saw that the man behind me had fallen at my feet. I picked him up. He seemed to me to have been shot through the heart. All the others were wounded in the legs as far as I could see. The Police must have fired low."'[15]

Perhaps Bean was chastened from the blowback over his wasters article a few months earlier, for despite the Wassa riot being far more serious than the events that prompted Bean's strong December story, it appears no story on it by Bean was published in the Australian papers at the time – so an incident of appalling indiscipline by Australian troops overseas was effectively suppressed from the media until accounts of it began to appear in letters home that were eventually published. Yet Bean's own personal diary account details how soldiers were actually shot in this riot, perhaps even mortally. Even after the war, despite the severity and shame of this episode, the sole mention of this extensive and destructive riot in Bean's official history was confined to a single sentence that clearly sought to play the whole event down: 'In the whirl of preparation, the riot which occurred in Cairo on Good Friday, the day after the order for the move – a disturbance of which the tradition still clings in Egypt – passed almost unnoticed by the staff of the two divisions.'[16] There is a footnote from that sole mention of the riot in the official history that, curiously, leads the reader to another lengthy footnote account of the Cairo riot in a separate chapter of the history. There Bean also plays down the incident, describing it as differing very little from an Oxford or Cambridge university 'rag'. Perhaps because the division was moving out the next day Bean was distracted by the urgency of an army imminently on the move, but more likely he made a deliberate decision to douse it down. Within weeks Bean would be in a battle zone with these men and he needed them onside.

Next day was a solemn one for Charles Bean and his brother when Captain Jack Bean's 3rd Battalion was given orders to prepare for the move out. The sobering news came that heavy fighting was expected wherever they would be landing and casualties were predicted to be as high as 30 per cent. 'These fellows are just the men to carry it out. Whatever they can do they can certainly fight.'[17] As Charles watched on, his brother inspected men whom he had assessed, because of sickness or injury, as lacking the strength to fight. There was such a patriotic fervour among the troops about the imminent battle that none wanted to miss the 'fun' by being deemed unfit for duty: 'the men were so bitterly disappointed. One or two who had been sent for were not there. He knew they were dodging him.'[18]

All afternoon and into the evening, Charles helped his brother pack his bags and medical stores. He knew it was possibly the last time they would ever see each other; Jack's chances of being killed were as high as every other soldier's. As Jack rode off on his horse past the flickering rubbish fires that evening, Charles recorded in his diary how a sympathetic officer reassured him with the words: 'I don't say it because you're his brother but I've never met a kinder man in my life than our old doctor. If anyone needs him nothing is ever too much trouble for him.'[19]

By 6 April 1915, the 18,000 troops with the Australian 1st Division had mostly departed and the once teeming Maadi and Mena camps were nearly deserted. Bean was reduced to forlornly packing his bags in the hope that he might finally get an answer from British command on whether he would be allowed to travel with the division. He moved into the Continental Hotel in Cairo with the Australian base depot and organised for all his spare kit and diaries to be stowed, but there really was not much for him to do until he got an answer on his future. He sent another wire to Sir George Reid, the London high commissioner, lamenting the pity if the Australian eyewitness could not be present when the Australians went into battle.

On Thursday 8 April, Bean was summonsed by the 1st Division commander, General Bridges, and told that he should send another wire to Sir George Reid demanding an answer within 24 hours. The general also told him that he would at the very least be coming with the division as a staff officer who would not write anything unless authorised: 'I took it of course that this was the arrangement all along suggested, that I should write nothing until authorised. I sent the wire off at once.'[20] Later that day, Lieutenant Colonel White showed Bean a message from the War Office confirming this arrangement. Bean was elated:

> It means that I shall eventually be able to give the Australian people an account of one of the most interesting events in history from a position closer than that of any observer who has been allowed to write his impressions in the present war. White and the General have got me this privilege – it's a great reward for all the restraint one has imposed on oneself to have got their confidence to this extent and it is very handsome of them to have supported me like this.[21]

Charles Bean did not record what it was in which he had shown 'restraint', but it was presumably a reference to his having heeded the military request that nothing he wrote be sent for publication until it had been cleared by the censor.

On 9 April Bean arrived by early morning train in Alexandria, where the 1st Division troops had already been loaded; he made his way onto the 14,000-tonne prewar Atlantic Ocean passenger liner SS *Minnewaska*. The harbour was a jumble of French, British and Australian ships, all loading and preparing for the move. Bean reported to the headquarters of the Allied Mediterranean Expeditionary Force (MEF) and was eventually referred to the 1st Division's staff intelligence officer, Major Thomas Blamey, who made him sign an undertaking as a press correspondent: '"I hereby guarantee not to communicate anything to the press until I receive definite sanction" … all that remained was for me to get "definite sanction" as soon as the War Office considered it absolutely safe, whenever that might be.'[22]

When the *Minnewaska* lifted anchor the next morning and headed out of Alexandria harbour, Charles Bean found himself sharing bunks in the command headquarters of what was then Australia's biggest-ever overseas military deployment. He overheard the captain discuss how he had opened his sealed orders and confirmed the division really was on its way to the Dardanelles as everyone had long expected. It was to be an extraordinary event in history, a huge amphibious landing designed to turn the course of the war.

> I had a yarn with Col White and he tells me he thinks it is an extraordinary compliment the Australian troops are being chosen to make the present attempt on the Dardanelles … They wouldn't send us unless they thought we were competent he said. As for me, I am in luck if ever any pressman was. This is perhaps the most interesting operation in the war – one of the most interesting in history; a business of this sort on this scale has never before been attempted. And I am nearer to it than any journalist has been to the actual firing line since the beginning of the war.[23]

At the Sunday service, General Birdwood addressed the troops on board, telling them that they had all been given a very big task – to turn the German flank. For the first time the troops were told that they were to land at the Dardanelles and would be facing not only Turks but German soldiers as well. Birdwood said he had complete confidence that they would do all that the honour of Australia and England demanded of them.

Two days later on 12 April 1915, the *Minnewaska* arrived in Mudros harbour on the Greek island of Lemnos. Bean was immediately fascinated by the array of British naval power gathered for the imminent invasion, the super-dreadnought *Queen Elizabeth* among them. While there, Bean watched a rehearsal of what would eventually be the Gallipoli landing; it made him realise the immense risk in the undertaking. The plan was for the Australians to clamber ashore, no doubt under heavy fire, from landing boats, each carrying just 38 men. For the first time the enormity of what the Australians were about to undertake struck Bean: the line of boats coming to shore would be sitting ducks for Turkish artillery fire and snipers. Just one shrapnel shell exploding over an open hull would shred every man inside before they got to Turkish soil.

Six days before the Gallipoli landing, Bean learned that British press correspondents had now been sanctioned by the British command to join the troops and write for English papers about the imminent attack. The Australian command, assuming Bean would be given the same permission, sent him across to the British Royal Mail steamer *Arcadian* where the British general staff was based under Sir Ian Hamilton. A letter from Major Blamey recommended Bean to the British command as loyal and discreet, asking that he be given the same privileges as the British press.

Bean learned from one of the intelligence officers on the *Arcadian* that a journalist named William Maxwell of the London *Daily Mail* was on board the ship to act as censor, that renowned war correspondent Ellis Ashmead-Bartlett would be writing for a number of London papers, and that another journalist would be writing dispatches for the Reuters news agency. But Bean was devastated by the bureaucratic and rude British staff officer's response:

> He said he was rather surprised Blamey had asked I should have the same facilities as the English pressmen because it was perfectly understood that I had only come on condition that I was to write nothing at all. I corrected him: the order I had received was 'Nothing at all until sanctioned' and I had supposed that when arrangements were made sanctioning English pressmen they would also sanction me … He said … they had no reason to suppose sanction would ever be given.[24]

Bean was clearly infuriated; he was even kept waiting while the British staff went off for their lunch. When he finally returned to the *Minnewaska* he wrote: 'I must say I breathe again to be back amongst Australian manners after these experiences of the English official.'[25]

On 23 April, just two days before the landing, at the urging of Australian commanders, British commander Sir Ian Hamilton intervened on Bean's behalf, sending a cable to the War Office in London asking if Bean could be allowed to represent the colonial press. By this time Mudros harbour was full of one of the greatest naval armadas ever assembled – hundreds of boats teeming with men and supplies; by day, dozens of local Greek lighters moving between the giant warships offered fresh fruit and other supplies to eager troops. For Bean, it was a major exercise to make his way across the harbour on the local Greek 'bumboats' to get to the *Arcadian*'s British command headquarters, but when he finally got there he was delighted with the *Daily Mail* journalist turned censor William Maxwell, who greeted him warmly. The two men discussed how Bean's press reports would be censored and then Bean went to see the telegraph operator manager who would actually be sending them. Sending telegrams was formidably expensive, and Bean was able to reassure the manager that his messages would be short, normally less than a thousand words, whereas the British newspapermen were expecting to send dispatches of up to 6000 words. Bean knew he would have a battle on his hands persuading papermen back home to pay the likely prohibitive costs of these telegraph messages: 'When I saw the Sydney proprietors they objected to spending any money on cables at all.'[26]

As Bean was travelling back across the harbour he realised the invasion force troopships were beginning to move out, so he hurried back to the *Minnewaska*; the departure for the Dardanelles was now imminent. That evening, sailing towards the battle zone, the troops on board remained jovial and friendly, but there was a realisation that this was finally the eve of their going into action. Bean shared a bottle of wine with Major Thomas Blamey, the two men incongruously discussing Gilbert and Sullivan opera, no doubt to take their minds off the next day's violence. After dinner, as Bean watched officers of the 1st Division try on their battle kit in the ship's lounge, he was approached by Lieutenant Colonel White and shown the actual orders for the Gallipoli landing, a measure of the extraordinary relationship the two men had developed that White felt he could entrust Bean with this secret information. Bean enthused, 'Colonel White is the ideal staff officer. He never forgets anything. Everyone on this divisional staff knows his value. He is too modest to push himself. He would not know how to do it … it would be just a tragedy if anything happened to him.'[27] It was a solemn moment as Bean watched White transfer across that same evening to the *Prince of Wales*, the ship that would carry him and the rest of the 1st Division staff command to Gallipoli, lugging a swag as remaining officers from the division wished him well. Bean was to stay on board and only follow the invasion force once it was consolidated in the attack zone. As he watched both White and Blamey depart, Bean no doubt wondered if he would see either man alive again.

Just before he left, Blamey had quietly told Bean that this night would not be the landing; that was to happen two days hence on Sunday, 25 April. As Bean returned to the *Minnewaska*'s now nearly empty staff room, the ship's remaining officers were being told to remove the coloured brassards on their uniforms in case their status drew enemy fire. Bean knew he would raise Turkish suspicions if he was ever captured in his unconventional uniform, and the day's events had given him good cause to dwell on his own mortality: 'It's best to conform with all the rules, otherwise the chance of a non-combatant being shot if captured is pretty good. I don't possess a pistol or any arms of any sort.'[28]

Early on the morning of 24 April, Bean woke to feel the ship turning and went up on deck to watch the great fleet of troopships depart for the 110-kilometre journey to the Dardanelles. Two birds flew overhead, one wit quipping they were 'the doves of peace'. Bean listened on as Australian men from one battalion, following on with him in the *Minnewaska*, were reminded of the rules to be heeded when they were transferred to the landing boats at Gallipoli: 'No talking in the boats. No one to stand up. Men to be clear of the beach as soon as possible … the attack is tomorrow morning for certain.'[29]

The invasion plan was a bold one, calling for the Australian 3rd Infantry Brigade to land north of a place called Gaba Tepe on the Aegean coast and to then fight their way across the Gallipoli peninsula, cutting off the Turkish troops. The attack plan also called for French troops to make a diversionary landing across the strait on the Turkish mainland at Kum Kale and to then join the British 29th Division back on the Gallipoli peninsula at Helles. The idea was that a successful attack would then free up the Dardanelles strait, allowing the British navy to pass through and seize Constantinople. But the delays meant the Turks knew well that the Allies were on their way and they had spent weeks reinforcing their defences and men.

Bean watched on during the day as the Australian troops yarned and joked on deck. He knew that as he landed on the beach at Gaba Tepe with the headquarters staff tomorrow he would be 'in a devil of a funk' as it was likely they would all be under severe rifle and shellfire.

> One sometimes is inclined to think of the utter hopeless wastefulness of this whole war … Of course some people have been a little thoughtful tonight because we know what a tremendous job it is, this assault on a strong fortress. But the Australian troops and officers are pleased with the compliment that has been paid

> them … It's a great gamble the whole thing really – a lot of bits of metal in the air and just a chance whether you stop one or let it pass. A lot of men at one end of a machine throwing things into space with a deadly swiftness without the least idea what is going to be the effect of each discharge: It may mean a tragedy in some little cottage home in Tasmania or in an English country house; it may kill or wound or take out an eye or take off a leg. And a lot of Australians – boys who began life on the Murray or in a backyard in Wagga or Bourke or Surry Hills will be left lying in Turkey.[30]

All through that final night, Bean made methodical entries in his diary, noting scraps of conversation between soldiers and recording the unlit ship's glide through the darkness past the Greek islands until the looming silhouette of the Turkish mainland appeared. His normally tidy copperplate writing is erratic – perhaps with the excitement, as well as the fact that he was writing in near darkness. Well past 4am, he noted that it was 'the time when our 3rd Brigade ought to be rushing out of their boats somewhere up the slope of those grey hills ahead. There is no sign yet of action … It is still too dark to see what I am writing. But the dawn is slowly growing.'[31]

At 4.38am, Bean heard the distant sound of firing. 'I catch faintly on a gust off the shore a distant knocking, as if someone had held up a small wooden box and knocked the inside of it with a pencil … there is no mistaking it whatever. It is the first time I heard the sound but I have no doubt on earth of what it is. It is the distant echo of rifle firing – first a few shots, then heavy and continuous.'[32] Nearly twenty minutes later Bean heard artillery fire and he could see the flashes from the Turkish fortifications at Gaba Tepe, from where the Turks were firing shrapnel 400 metres ahead: 'a bang, the whirr of a shower of pellets sprayed as if from a watering can, the whip-up of another circle of sea below and another white fleecy cloud slowly floating overhead. The wondering crowd on the promenade deck says to itself "So that is shrapnel".'[33]

The British warships ahead returned fire, to the cheers of the troops on board. Bean's ship passed between the constantly firing warships towards its berth, still a long way from shore. A small overturned rowing boat drifted past the *Minnewaska*, the first and only sign anyone had yet seen of the death and dying that lay ahead. Then the landing cove came into view; to Bean's eyes the multitude of small boats close to the beach seemed to be scattered erratically about the bay: 'Why are they going so many ways, digging out for all they are worth. Has the landing been beaten off? Is this the remnant?'[34]

At 5am the troops on board headed to the mess for their final breakfast before being taken into the beach to join the attack. Shells were falling very near the ship but men had to eat, and the troops knew this might be their last decent meal for days, but Bean was so wound up he could scarcely think of it. After a rushed cup of tea and bowl of porridge, Bean was back on deck watching the destroyers firing closer into shore: 'Still that rattle rattle all along the hillside. It doesn't sound as if our men have got far. The ships are roaring huge broadsides now. Huge buffets of guns.'[35]

At 6.45am the infantry from Bean's ship began climbing down rope ladders to the destroyer that would take them closer into shore. He watched as his brother Jack's ship discharged its last men onto the destroyer below them –

'Old Jock is in that lot'. Then someone spotted men standing on the skyline of the Gallipoli peninsula – were they Turks or Australians? Bean judged, correctly, that they were the latter. 'There was no mistaking that casual gait – it was a sure sign throughout the war. They were Australians.'[36] He also watched as wounded men were loaded back on board, grimly noting rumours coming back from those tending them that the first two boats onto the beach had lost half of their men to Turkish machine guns. (Bean later acknowledged this was wrong, and that the severe losses were in fact suffered by the 2nd Brigade, which came in later). A second destroyer came alongside with more wounded, its decks slippery with blood.

At 9.20am it was finally time for Charles Bean to begin the move to shore and go to war; he donned his overcoat, slung his packs over the side to a waiting destroyer and then climbed down the rope ladder to its deck. He waved goodbye to his batman, Arthur Bazley, on *Minnewaska*'s deck – he was to follow with the rest of their kit if and when the landing was established. As his destroyer moved closer in to land, Bean watched battery fire from the Turkish guns falling around the battleship HMS *Prince of Wales* and close to *Minnewaska* behind him, taking photographs on his camera and hurriedly writing details into his notebook (Bean admits he did add extra details to his diary later). A couple of hundred metres from shore, they transferred to rowboats and began to move inshore.

> The sight of hills as we got in closer … made one realise what our men had really done. I remember someone saying the map ought to have been made more precipitous and that it didn't really give any

> idea of how steep the hills actually were … The place is like a sandslope on a huge scale, raw sandslopes and precipices alternating with steep slopes covered with low scrub … The boat grounded in at two feet of water. We jumped out … waded to the beach and stood on Turkish soil.[37]

High above Bean towered a steep scrubby slope rising about 100 metres to the skyline. The boatloads of troops arriving on the beach were speedily marched off into action. They were the lucky ones who had made it ashore, making their way past drifting remnants of shattered boats and lines of corpses on the beach. It dawned on the commanding officers, now checking their maps and looking at the terrain, that the navy had landed them on the wrong section of coastline, one and a half kilometres north of the planned landing spot near Gaba Tepe; as Bean later recorded in his official history, one senior officer said at the time that those first few hours onshore proved to be 'a terrible muddle'.[38] It meant that the target objectives in the original plan were now a kilometre or so northeast from what was being called Anzac Cove, and Australian officers were pushing their men up a steep escarpment to reach the hills they had been ordered to seize.

Bean followed the divisional headquarters staff to a narrow gully where General Bridges had based himself, the sand around it peppered with shrapnel marks. Wounded men lay on the beach waiting to be evacuated, and further to the north of the beach Bean soberly noted the bodies of about 30 dead Australians, covered with overcoats and blankets. For the first time he also noted the distinct sound of the whizzing bullets passing overhead, mistaking them at first for insects: 'It was so feeble, that sound, and so spent it was quite comforting. One had expected something much more businesslike.'[39]

As Bean watched on, the impetuous 2nd Brigade commander, Brigadier General James McCay, never one to be restrained in pushing his men into battle, came across members of one battalion retreating to the beach, and the brigadier let fly with abuse: '"You bloody cowards. You bloody curs – get up – what are you doing here; for God's sake, remember you are Australians."'[40] Bean went looking for his brother Jack's 3rd Battalion dressing station, climbing along trench lines filled with Australians and New Zealanders on the slopes. He could not find his brother but when he returned to the 1st Division headquarters around dinnertime on that first day he heard the upsetting news from Lieutenant Colonel White that his brother had been evacuated, the only medical officer wounded that day. Reassured that the injuries were not too serious, Bean now concentrated on keeping himself alive in the showers of shrapnel, artillery rounds and rifle bullets. Following the lead of every other soldier, he began to dig himself in.

> The man in the dugout next door strongly objected – I don't know who it was. 'What do you want to keep awake with that damned digging for?' he asked. 'Haven't you got any bloody consideration?' I thought that was a bit humorous – a chap who was safely cuddled up in his dugout objecting to me making one on a night like this.[41]

Bean's diaries during the first 48 hours on Gallipoli are understandably a bit of a mess and, as he later acknowledged in a scribbled side note, much of what he wrote was compiled from jotted notes during the day that he then wrote up at night:

> If I am plugged and anyone gets this diary they'll probably think that I was either tight or very unnerved when I wrote it. The fact was it was written by night when no candles were to be had and I had to do as best I could in the moonlight. On some nights the sky was clear and one could see fairly well. On others, I simply had to place the lines by guesswork and many of them are written over one another.[42]

In those first few days Bean was subsisting on chocolate, biscuits and water, walking around the battlefield all day long and then writing up his observations at night. He was reasonably safe inside his dugout but the regular patter of shrapnel hitting a huge pile of kerosene tins just outside was a reminder of the suffering being endured by the men in the trenches up above. A few days after the landing, Bean joked in his diary that they considered themselves old soldiers because they had become used to the rifle and shellfire.

On the first night at Gallipoli, Australian commanders were concerned that the Turks had successfully repelled the Allied invasion and there were recommendations made by senior officers that all troops be withdrawn, perhaps even that same night. Colonel Brudenell White (appointed a Colonel in June 1915) admitted to Bean in 1916 that he had advised General Bridges to withdraw from Anzac Cove soon after the landing. '[W]e knew the Anzac landing had failed and as it had not succeeded the right thing was to get out of it and use the troops where they could be effective,' White told him.[43] Bean had picked up the rumours as he talked with officers at the divisional headquarters late on that first evening:

> … clearly something was in the wind. In a minute or two I heard what it was – some question as to whether we were to hold on or to embark at once … The General had gone somewhere – I don't know where – but one understood that the decision would be brought back by him … I heard a message being read out from the General's dugout for sending to all the units out on the ridges. 'Sir Ian Hamilton hopes that they will dig … and that the morning will find them securely dug in where they are'.[44]

Later, Bean managed to get details of just how close it came to an entire evacuation of Gallipoli on that first night. It must have been sobering for the eyewitness official correspondent to be on enemy territory taking notes recording the views of Allied generals that their own brigades were saying they could not hold on. Things were very grim indeed that initial evening at Anzac and evacuation was only abandoned because it was logistically impossible: when British commander General Birdwood asked the Royal Navy if it had enough vessels to effect an immediate evacuation that night, the answer was no. But Bean recorded that orders were still given to all transports to have their boats inshore so as to be ready to re-embark, and that if there had been enough boats there to effect a withdrawal then that might have indeed happened. Most experienced officers were opposed to any immediate evacuation because they knew it would lead to panic and probably massive loss of life.

But none of this near catastrophe was to find its way into Charles Bean's news reporting. Wartime censorship meant it was impossible for Bean to tell his Australian readers of just how confused the landing at Gallipoli had been and how dire the situation now was for the Allied forces there. His first press story on the landing, finally published in mid-May in Australia, made no mention of the navy's failure to land troops at the right objective, nor did it mention the 1st Division command's deliberations on whether to withdraw. But Bean's press account did deftly hint that things had not quite gone according to plan:

> The Third Brigade went over the hills with such dash that within three quarters of an hour of landing some had charged over three successive ridges. Each ridge was higher than the last, and each party that reached the top went over it with wild cheers. Since that day the Turks have never attempted to face our bayonets. The officers led magnificently, but of course, nothing like an accurate control of the attack was possible. Subordinate leaders had been trained at Mena to act on their own responsibility, and the benefit of this was enormously apparent in this attack. Companies and platoons, little crowds of 50 to 200 men, were landed wherever the boats took them. Their leaders had a general idea of where they were intended to go, and once landed, each subordinate commander made his way there by what seemed to him to be the shortest road. The consequence was that the Third Brigade reached its advanced line in a medley of small fractions inextricably mixed.[45]

A shrewd reader back in Australia might have been able to read between the lines, for as best he could within the constraints of strict censorship, Bean was inferring that the day was chaotic. It must have been terribly frustrating for Bean the journalist to not be able to tell his audience what was really going on. Bean was uniquely placed with his insights from the divisional command to tell his readers how precarious a situation the Allied forces faced, but instead censorship constraints meant that much of his report focused (albeit deservedly) on the heroism and sacrifice of the individual men and officers. Bean acknowledged, as he told the story of the heroic loss of one Australian officer, that the toll had been high:

> Australia has lost many of her best officers in this way. The toll has been really heavy, but the British theory is that you cannot lead men from the rear, at any rate, in an attack of this sort. It would be absurd to pretend that the life of an officer like that one was wasted. No one knows how long his example will live on amongst men. There were others, whom I will mention later on when the casualties have all reached Australia, who died fighting like tigers, some who fully knew they would die. One was sometimes inclined to think this sort of leading useless, but none who heard the men talking next day could doubt its value. 'By God! Our officers were splendid,' one Australian told me. Wherever I went I heard the same opinion expressed.[46]

That first Bean story from Gallipoli also reassured readers that he would have published reports from there earlier if he had been able to obtain leave from the British Admiralty, for in an act of bastardry the British had kept a gag on Bean's reporting until his first story was finally allowed to be sent through the censor on 3 May. It must have been a bitter disappointment for Bean that the British held him to his promise that he not publish any report from Gallipoli until he was authorised to do so, yet they allowed their own press correspondents to file stories; it meant he was scooped on perhaps the biggest story of his career by British war correspondent Ellis Ashmead-Bartlett, whose breathless report of the Gallipoli landing was the first to be published in Australian newspapers. Ashmead-Bartlett only got to Anzac at 9.30pm, a full twelve hours behind Bean, who had waded ashore that morning with the Australian 1st Division. The British *Daily Telegraph* correspondent was then arrested as a spy because of his unusual civilian clothing before he was finally released and allowed to collect information for his report. But this did not hinder the former British Army Second Boer War veteran from offering his Australian readers a thrilling firsthand account of the plucky Anzacs giving Johnny Turk a taste of cold steel.

> The Australians rose to the occasion. They did not wait for orders, or for the boats to reach the beach, but sprang into the sea, formed a sort of rough line, and rushed at the enemy's trenches. Their magazines were not charged, so they just went in with the cold steel, and it was over in a minute for the Turks in the first trench had been either bayoneted or had run away … Then this race of athletes proceeded to scale the cliffs, without responding to the enemy's fire. They lost some men, but did not worry. In less than a quarter of an

> hour the Turks had been hurled out of their second position, all either bayoneted or fled … For 15 mortal hours the Australians and New Zealanders occupied the heights under an incessant shellfire, and without the moral and material support of a single gun from the shore. They were subjected the whole time to violent counter-attacks from a brave enemy, skilfully led, and with snipers deliberately picking off every officer who endeavoured to give the command or to lead his men. No finer feat has happened in this war than this sudden landing in the dark, and the storming of the heights, and, above all, the holding on whilst the reinforcements were landing. These raw colonial troops, in these desperate hours, proved worthy to fight side by side with the heroes of the battles of Mons, the Aisne, Ypres, and Neuve-Chapelle.[47]

There is no doubting that Ashmead-Bartlett's colourful reporting thrilled Australian newspaper bosses and their readers alike but, because he was not on the ground at the time, his story was inaccurate and grossly misleading in its impact, leading readers to believe the warrior Anzacs were well on the way to securing victory against their weaker Turkish foes. Events though would prove Ashmead-Bartlett to be one of the more honourable correspondents, determined to get the truth about Gallipoli told. He was to soon become furious at how all his reports from Gallipoli were so heavily censored by Captain Maxwell, who as Phillip Knightley's *The First Casualty* details, would allow:

> no criticism of the conduct of the operation, no indication of set-backs or delays, and no mention of

> casualty figures; finally, he refused to give permission for any of Ashmead-Bartlett's messages to be transmitted until [commanding General] Hamilton's own official cables had reached London. This meant that, at a time when there was more interest in the fighting in France, Ashmead-Bartlett's Gallipoli dispatches, days late and heavily censored, often failed to appear in print.[48]

The reality on the ground was very different from what both Bean and Ashmead-Bartlett presented in their news stories. There can be no doubt of the extraordinary heroism of many Australians and New Zealanders on this now mythical day, but there were also numerous soldiers who made the arguably rational decision to keep their heads down and avoid getting shot in what history has since acknowledged as an ill-conceived attack on strong Turkish defences. Both in his diary notes and his final official history, Charles Bean admitted there was what he termed 'stragglers' on the beach on the first day of the Gallipoli landing.

> Of course the beach was fearfully congested. As the night went on a great number of these stragglers were organised into parties to carry water, ammunition, and food, up to the lines. I have heard their number put at anything from 600 to 1,000. They, many of them, came down with wounded men. This is an offence in war, but few realised it at this early stage. The helping down of wounded did not really begin until about 4 or 5. Then it began to reach fair proportions – 6 men came down with one wounded officer. It is very easy to persuade yourself that you are

> really doing a charitable soldierly action in helping a wounded soldier to the rear. In later actions this has been chiefly done by the wounded themselves – one wounded man helping another – the men now realise that it is not right to leave the firing line. They were raw soldiers on that first day. However straggling did reach serious proportions – although there was every excuse for it – many, as I say, going down to the beach because it was the only place to get instructions what to do. Many men were legitimately there – sent down for water or ammunition …[49]

In another mention of the stragglers, Bean acknowledged that soldiers pointedly refused to move when ordered: 'Ramsay was sent along this first night to collect stragglers on the beach … He got a number who were lying down on the beach at the south end. Dead fagged. Bullets were whistling over. Some absolutely refused to move. Said they were crook.'[50]

Bean's acknowledgement of the Australian stragglers was to unwittingly play a part in unleashing a major postwar scandal that was labelled by a Sydney newspaper as 'the vilest libel of the war' when British Army official historian Cecil Aspinall-Oglander attempted to write about the Australian stragglers on that first day. Ultimately he was attacked for his candour, but Aspinall-Oglander kept letters and accounts from British officers that supported his original version of the landing – an account that was damning of the Australians.[51] Bean's own official history account of the first day at Gallipoli was published in 1921, and when Aspinall-Oglander's draft British official history was sent to Australia six years later to get feedback from the AIF commanders who were there, the stragglers story became a touchstone for the angry Australian perception that Britain had consistently understated Australia's military prowess throughout the war. Aspinall-Oglander's draft history controversially suggested that just 'when a well-coordinated attack could scarcely have failed to beat down the Turkish opposition and to carry the line to its objective on the highest points of the range there was confusion among the Australians'.[52]

The British historian also wrote how reinforcements were delayed and that command broke down in the frontline, hindering a coordinated attack. Alistair Thomson's analysis of the controversy describes how Aspinall-Oglander's draft painted an extremely unflattering picture of the Australians, writing that towards the end of the daylight 'the "severe strain to young and unhurried troops in their first day of battle" was beginning to tell. "For many the breaking point had now been passed, and numbers of unwounded men were filtering back to the beach" in an "endless stream" so that the gullies in the rear were choked with stragglers and men who had lost their way.'[53]

Aspinall-Oglander pushed the line in his draft history that the presence of the Australian stragglers was actually one of the main factors which persuaded the senior command staff at Anzac Cove that things were so critical they recommended evacuation on the first day. This was a very 'long bow' argument: he was in essence suggesting that Gallipoli was a defeat because of Australian cowardice, a calumnious and almost certainly unfair attack on the Australians. Bean argued with the British Army's historical section about this draft conclusion, suggesting that the Australian commanders making this evacuation recommendation had not yet come to realise the quality of their soldiers. He also enlisted the support of the Australian defence department, asking for the British to give full consideration to the Australian government's views. As Bean's diary account had noted, many men were legitimately on the beach because that is where they got their orders, and there was great confusion in that first day caused chiefly by the failure of the British navy to land troops on the right beach in the first place. However Aspinall-Oglander stuck to his guns and insisted that:

> though I yield to no-one in my admiration for what Australians did on 25th April, I have found that unless one does point to confusion in the rear, one is doing less than justice to the superlatively brave men in front who, but for that confusion, would have been strongly reinforced and must have been able to deal with the comparatively small numbers of Turks who were opposing them and who were in equal straits.[54]

When the story was leaked to the Australian press it was banner headlined in Sydney's *Daily Guardian* on 7 October 1927 as the 'vilest libel of the war'. Fleet Street also picked up on the notion that the Australians had gilded a false Gallipoli myth, claiming that the Anzac story as told to millions of schoolchildren by that time in the 1920s actually ignored the many shirkers who had herded on the beach while an adventurous few Australians actually did the fighting. It was an inflammatory allegation and eventually the head of the British Army's historical section, Brigadier General James Edmonds, intervened and ordered the British draft history to be modified to appease understandable Australian outrage. Aspinall-Oglander clearly resented the changes and retained in his personal papers the criticisms of the British officers who saw the Gallipoli landing as a tragic shambles.

On 26 April, the day after the landing, Bean ran into the commander of Australian and New Zealand troops on Gallipoli, General Birdwood, who was clearly rattled by the setbacks of the previous day. '"First there was the mistake of landing us a mile and a half north of where we should have landed," he said, "in this ghastly country. And then there's this enormous line. The troops very gallantly took an enormous extent of country against 500 well entrenched Turks." He was confident they'd hold it.'[55]

Everyone was expecting a massive Turkish counterattack, and there was no certainty that the Allied forces would be able to withhold it if they did, but none came. The Allies now held a slender beachhead; they had landed two divisions but the companies and battalions were dug-in across the slopes above Anzac in erratic and shallow trench lines. Bean began doing what became his routine on Gallipoli, tracking alone along the gullies, paths and communication saps towards the frontlines to see what he could. His technique was to attempt to reconstruct the battles that had taken place by interviewing in groups as many as possible of the individual soldiers that had fought in different parts of a conflict. It was exhausting and extremely detailed work, but his idea was that by piecing together all of these individual accounts he could build up a general picture of the battle. The freedom Bean enjoyed inside the Australian lines, effectively as an embedded journalist observer, was extraordinary, far beyond what any journalist could expect in any frontline military embed today. He was allowed to roam, and even given helpful tips by Major Blamey about how to navigate safely up to the 3rd Brigade headquarters on a higher ridge.

On his way up there, Bean again noticed numerous 'stragglers' keeping under cover: 'Men who had collected there as a comfortable position having nowhere else to go – and no one to see that they went there – that is the straggler's frame of mind. They were collected afterwards ...'[56] He also noted in his diary that the packs belonging to dead soldiers had been opened and plundered; this was another unpleasant observation about the behaviour of some troops that censorship would almost certainly have forbidden Bean from telling his readers: 'I saw these same packs opened and everything of solid use taken but singlets, pants, shirts, photos, letters lying all over the roadside. I supposed the officer whose company or platoon they belonged to was dead. A stronger police organization could stop a very great deal of irregularity of this sort ...'[57] The 3rd Brigade had been through some horrendous fighting and when Bean dropped in on the headquarters trench a thick hail of bullets was flying overhead. He was able for the first time to actually watch Australian soldiers in combat but he also witnessed troops walking away from the frontline battle.

> You didn't notice the men hit – you noticed them limping or rolling back wounded. I saw one man – wounded or unwounded I don't know, for the surface of that hill was very hot – rolling over and over and over through the scrub until he reached a hollow ... I saw a most curious sight there – some of the men in the first lines came back fairly fast – others in the lines going up passed them going straight by them as you might pass a man in the street, taking not

> the slightest notice of them, one going up and the other coming back, almost brushing one another as a steamer might pass another steamer at sea. Evidently the man going forward had enough determination to say to himself – 'My job is to go forward and I'm going forward whatever the other chap does.'[58]

Another unflattering portrait of the Australians that was not recorded in either Bean's war journalism or his postwar history was the desperate efforts of officers just behind the 3rd Brigade frontline headquarters to persuade Australians to get back into the fight: 'They had most of them been coaxing stragglers up into reserve … They were most of them dead tired and would sit down every 20 yards or so and now and then one would refuse to go any further. It was no good being rough with them. They simply had to be handled.'[59]

Bean was still with the 3rd Brigade the next morning as the Turks launched a strong counterattack. The Australians were so close to their enemies in the trenches opposite that they could actually hear the Turkish officers yelling at their soldiers to urge them on into the fight: 'They came on pretty thick. Our men pumped lead into them, standing up so that they showed over the crest of the hill and handing their rifles back to be refilled. When the Turks were getting near our men fixed bayonets and the men on the rear slope of the hill prepared to charge but the Turks did not come on.'[60]

The situation was very desperate for the 3rd Brigade at times and it was a major issue for the commanders that the troops on occasion refused to fight, including the New Zealanders:

> At one time a New Zealand battalion was there which Colonel Owen asked to come up. They would not come and their officers (so Colonel Owen told me) would not bring them. He sent Lamb back to see what he could do and Lamb brought them up himself. He did this continually for two days. He was wounded twice … 'If it had not been for Lamb,' said Colonel Owen, 'I don't think we could have held on.'[61]

Bean also recorded a claim that never made it into his news stories on the battle which appears to suggest that some Australian troops, who mistakenly shot at other Australian units believing them to be the enemy, were then themselves deliberately shot at in retaliation. His diary notes do not make it clear if the retaliating Australians knew they were firing on Australians, but the inference seems to be that they did: 'The man picked out one of the Australians and dropped him. The others retired.'[62]

However as time went on, Bean learned to be more sceptical of such claims made to him by frontline soldiers, because he soon realised that many accounts from battles that he was assured were correct were in fact totally false. He continued to make fastidious notes during the day in the trenches with the troops and would write up his diary at night whenever he could. He was increasingly careful with the information he received from soldiers, even if it presented as firsthand information, and especially if a soldier was wounded. On one return to camp he wrote about how he came across Major Brown from the 3rd Battalion, who had been injured during the fighting and clearly badly affected by the shock of what he had just experienced.

> He told me a long story. 'It was a sniper, I'm sure, that hit me the third time – I think he was beside me in the trench – the bullet seemed to come past from that way – I'll swear they were in the trench on both sides of us – they're brave by cripes, they are, much braver than we are. You could see the German officers in green uniforms with their swords at the carry walking up and down the line prodding the soldiers with them to make them get on.' A few minutes later he told me that they saw little or no sign of German officers. That made me think (although old B. was a man whose account one would trust against that of a hundred others), this must be some sort of hallucination. I had just tumbled to it when Blamey as I walked away said quietly 'Bean, I suppose you know it's not wise to take seriously what a man says when he's in a condition like that ... I meant to warn you.' I had already grasped it ...[63]

It was exceptionally difficult for Bean to piece together the truth of what he was hearing of the fighting raging across the wide front at Gallipoli when he could not possibly cover the entire frontline firsthand, not even within the 1st Division. On one occasion, which underlined just how much the confusing 'fog of war' made Bean's task a difficult one, a clearly very shaken Colonel John Monash told Bean that his Australian 4th Brigade troops had come under fire from an Allied artillery battery, detailing very specific accounts of how much was fired and from where. But Bean accepted the assurances of White that Monash was wrong.

In those first few days at Gallipoli, one officer whom Bean singled out for praise was the commander of the Australian

2nd Battalion, Lieutenant Colonel George Braund. On the first day of the landing, Braund had led his men up the precipitous narrow tracks to the junction of Russell's Top and Walker's Ridge, and by 27 April he was desperately holding on against a determined Turkish attack. Bean's official history paints Braund as a courageous officer: 'the gallant Braund with his two companies of the 2nd Australian Infantry Battalion and a remnant of New Zealanders from The Nek held on …'[64] On 27 April, Lieutenant Colonel William Malone, of the New Zealand Wellington Battalion, was ordered to support Braund's men, however his diary notes leave an altogether much more unflattering picture of Braund and his men than Bean ever acknowledged.

> Arrived at the foot of the ridge, found [New Zealand commanding] General Walker, and heard a roar for reinforcements coming down the hill. Irresponsible men. Australian privates, passing the word for 'reinforcements at the double'. General Walker told us at once to send a [New Zealand] company up … So away they went … Some of the best soldier men in the world. They were being sent to chaos and slaughter, nay murder.[65]

Later that morning Malone took his remaining companies up the same ridge, after yet more appeals from the Australians for reinforcements. On the way he passed 'scores of Australians unwounded lying all along the track'. He climbed up to where Lieutenant Colonel Braund was commanding and demanded to know why he was calling for New Zealand reinforcements when he had left many of his own men down the ridge.

> He didn't know and knew nothing. Had no defensive position, no plan, nothing but a murderous notion, that the only thing to do was to plunge troops out of the neck of the ridge into the jungle beyond. There Turks of whom very few were seen by any of my officers, were lying down shooting down all the bits of track that led from the ridge outwards, having range marks fixed and dropping our men wholesale ... Colonel Braund came along and ordered the [New Zealand] platoon commander to go on and plunge into the jungle further and further. On their protesting, he claimed as senior officer their obedience to his order and so on and on they went, and got slaughtered.[66]

By Malone's diary account he forced Braund to get all his straggling Australian troops sent up to the frontline and to shift his own headquarters forward. On one occasion when he was returning to Russell's Top from a meeting at the brigade headquarters he ran into a lot of Australians 'tearing down the track yelling "fix bayonets, the Turks are coming"'.[67] Expecting a massive Turkish counterattack, Malone set up his own men in a defensive position and waited for the attack, but it never came. So next time when Braund asked Malone for even more reinforcements, the New Zealander refused.

> He then said as I would send him no more reinforcements he would have to retire to his first position. I told him he never ought to have left it.[68]

The allegations Malone makes in his diary about the Australians are astonishing because they contradict entirely

Bean's portrayal of Braund as a 'clear-headed and tenacious commander' and that of his men as gallant defenders against a determined attack.[69] Instead, this New Zealand commander was actually reduced to throwing stones at Braund's Australian troops, and kicking them in the behind, to try to force them into the fight. When he confronted Braund, the Australian 'said the truth was, he feared that if he didn't go on his men would run away. I said that was no reason to sacrifice aimlessly my men.'[70]

Because of the Australian plea for reinforcements, Malone's battalion of about 450 men had suffered what he believed was needless casualties, 45 dead and 150 wounded in the first hour of combat. The New Zealander was clearly livid with Braund, peppering his diary with vitriol directed at the Australian commander. Malone actually insisted that the Australians be withdrawn the next day, telling General Walker that he would rather see them gone because the Australians were:

> a source of weakness. All night long they kept up a blaze of rifle fire, into the dark at the Turks who they could not see and thus drew fire. The Turks knowing where we were. I tried to stop them but it was useless. About 1am Col Braund came to me for more ammunition. I refused to give it to him telling him he was wasting enough and only telling the Turks that he was scared. He insisted and said responsibility on me. I sat tight and told him to go and see General Walker as without his order I absolutely refused to give him any more ammunition. At 6am the Australians left. It was an enormous relief to see the last of them. I believe they are spasmodically brave and probably the best of

> them had been killed or wounded. They have been I venture to think badly handled and trained officers in most cases no good. I am thinking of asking for a Court Martial on Col Braund. It makes me mad when I think of my grand men being sacrificed by his incapacity and folly.[71]

The transcripts of Malone's diary held in New Zealand's National Library record one additional handwritten footnote attributed to a New Zealand machine-gun officer named Captain J.A. Wallingford. He said that when Lieutenant Colonel Braund asked Malone for more ammunition, Lieutenant Colonel Malone colourfully told him, 'Go to hell and fight it out with the bayonet.'[72]

In the end Malone did not go ahead with his plan to court-martial Braund, probably because a week later Braund was killed by one of his own sentries as he took a shortcut through the scrub to his trenches. The New Zealand commander's strident criticisms of Braund are mentioned nowhere in Bean's diary notes during the war so it seems he may not have known about them when he wrote his official history, and therein lies the limitations of being Australia's official eyewitness: like every journalist, Charles Bean was only ever as sharp as his sources. One can only assume that Bean's friendly sources in the Australian 1st Division headquarters were not rushing to disabuse him of his romantic notions about Anzac comradeship in battle, even when they vetted his draft history postwar; the Anzac myth was allowed to go to the printer untainted. It is unlikely Bean would have been as effusive in his account of the comradeship in combat between the New Zealanders and the Australians at Russell's Top if he had known the full story, because his history uses the story of Braund's 2nd Battalion to begin to weave the definitive Anzac myth on Gallipoli, writing lyrically about the mutual respect and admiration between the New Zealanders and the Australians that was forged on those bloody hills:

> Braund ... had shown every quality of a really great leader ... The feeling of the New Zealand Infantry, as Braund and his battalion left them, was one of warm and affectionate admiration. Day and night Australians and New Zealanders had fought together on that hilltop. In this fierce test each saw in the other a brother's qualities. As brothers they had died; their bodies lay mingled in the same narrow trenches; as brothers they were buried. It was noticeable that such small jealousies as had existed between Australians and New Zealanders in Cairo vanished completely from this hour. Three days of genuine trial had established a friendship which centuries will not destroy.[73]

Months later, on 8 August 1915, New Zealand's Lieutenant Colonel William Malone was also killed, shortly after leading the capture of the Turkish positions on Chunuk Bair at Gallipoli. He had led his men in frantic bayonet charges against the Turkish defenders, finally seizing the position, but only after Malone had characteristically defied his Allied commanders by refusing to send his Wellington Battalion into a futile charge on the objective in daylight: 'I'm not going to send them over to commit suicide.'[74] He and his men seized Chunuk Bair at dawn the next morning, and that very same evening Malone was killed – possibly by friendly artillery fire. Of the 760 men who followed him into the attack on Chunuk Bair, an appalling toll of 690 of them were killed or wounded; Malone is one of 310 New Zealanders who died in that battle with no known grave. Sadly, their sacrifice was all in vain – Chunuk Bair fell to the Turks two days later while it was being defended by British troops. It is as well that Malone did not survive to see the squandering of the lives of so many of the young men in his battalion; he is remembered as a forthright commander who always spoke his mind.

Five

COME ON AUSTRALIANS

That will blood the pups.

Attributed to British Lieutenant General Aylmer Hunter-Weston at the Third Battle of Krithia, after sending the Scottish 52nd (Lowland) Division into battle with insufficient artillery support

Nothing better illustrates the callous desperation, ruthlessness, and utter folly of the fighting at Krithia, further down the Gallipoli peninsula from Anzac Cove, than the action that won 2nd Lieutenant George Moor his Victoria Cross in June 1915. Born in St Kilda, Melbourne, Moor had enlisted in the British Hampshire Regiment at the start of the war and was posted to the the British 2nd Battalion prior to the operations at the Dardanelles, landing near Cape Helles at Gallipoli on 25 April 1915. The Turks put up a formidable fight and Moor's battalion was one of several that suffered heavy casualties on the beach.

Undeterred, the British planned to capture the town of Krithia and the nearby hill of Achi Baba, but weeks later in early June the battle had become a forlorn and bloody stalemate. Lieutenant Moor and his men found themselves fighting the Third Battle of Krithia – the third attempt to wrest this strategic point from the Turks – and as Moor watched on his battalion was now turning and running, fleeing from the enemy. His Victoria Cross citation only hints at what Moor did next:

> When a detachment of a battalion on his left, which had lost all its officers, was rapidly retiring before a heavy Turkish attack, 2nd Lieutenant Moor immediately grasping the danger to the remainder of the line, dashed back some two hundred yards, stemmed the retirement, led back the men, and recaptured the lost trench. This young officer who only joined the Army in October, 1914, by his personal bravery and presence of mind saved a dangerous situation.[1]

There can be no doubting eighteen-year-old Moor's heroism, but the British citation typically sanitised what he had really done, for Moor's VC was awarded, in part, for shooting his own men. When Moor ran back behind the hundreds of fleeing British troops and pulled his service pistol on his own soldiers, the Hampshire Regiment's official history records that he shot at least two of them before the British retreat was turned.[2] It is a measure of just how awful and desperate the fighting was at Cape Helles that an officer was given the highest award for gallantry after he had shot his own fleeing soldiers. As the British 29th Division's commander General Henry de Lisle is perhaps apocryphally attributed as having said of Moor, he shot 'the leading four men and the remainder came to their senses'.[3]

Earlier, in the First Battle of Krithia on the day of the landing, the British had suffered shocking losses as they landed at the aptly named Cape Helles. The repeated hopeless attempts since to take the position had only served to underline its strategic importance in the mind of British commander Sir Ian Hamilton. Everything else at Gallipoli, including the Australian and New Zealand landing at Anzac Cove, was seen as a subsidiary operation to the main prize at Cape Helles. In early May, a clearly somewhat peeved Charles Bean noted in his diary that the British were taking the 2nd brigades of Australia and New Zealand away from Anzac Cove to Cape Helles to assist in that attack.

> One is inclined to wonder why he doesn't push through here. Still, I suppose Birdwood must have been consulted. He's taking the 2nd Brigade and one other. One can't help a natural disappointment in finding our show turned into a sideshow.[4]

By early May 1915, in just a couple of weeks of fighting, the Australian 1st Division had lost nearly 5000 men killed or wounded, 40 per cent of its strength. But Bean was still a believer that the Anzacs could win the day: 'One's natural wish is that they would give us our Light Horse, give us our reinforcements, and then let us push through.'[5] But, recognising that things at Anzac Cove were now at something of a trench-war stalemate, Bean asked for permission to follow the 2nd Brigade down to Cape Helles where they were being sent as reinforcements. It was meant to be a covert departure late on the evening of 5 May, but instead the Turks watched on early the following dawn as the thousands of Australian troops boarded the boats to move further down the peninsula. Bean lamented the grievous planning failure that had allowed this to happen, for it surely alerted the Turks that reinforcements were coming to Cape Helles and that Anzac Cove had reduced its defences by thousands of troops.

After landing down the coast at Cape Helles there were a desultory few days when weak French attacks were beaten back by the Turks. Bean's postwar official history records the truth about what happened over the next few days at Cape Helles, that he would almost certainly not have been able to tell his readers in the news stories he was to write from there: that the Allied army assembled was woefully under-gunned with its artillery and it only had 48,000 rounds for its field guns and 1800 for its field howitzers. As Bean recorded, it was 'a store which later in the war would have been consumed in a single minor assault'.[6]

Because of his limited artillery, British commander General Hamilton actually preferred to use what Bean's official history carefully described as a 'well-recognised' strategy to neutralise the Turkish machine guns: a night advance over the wide plains towards Krithia. '"It would be good tactics",' Bean recorded the general as saying, '"to cross the danger zone by night and overthrow the enemy in the grey dawn."'[7] But Bean's official history records the commander of the British 29th Division, Lieutenant General Sir Aylmer Gould Hunter-Weston, who had to carry out the attack, was opposed to a night assault because it was too easy for units to lose direction and contact – and even to mistakenly engage each other – in darkness. Bean did say later in the official history what he could not say in his wartime journalism, just what a catastrophic blunder it was for the senior General Ian Hamilton to then make the decision to bow to the opinion of his subordinate Hunter-Weston: 'the Commander-in-Chief lacked either the perception or the crude strength to overrule him'.[8]

Sadly for the Australian and New Zealand troops, Hunter-Weston was one of the less capable First World War generals, tagged by commander General Haig as a 'rank amateur'. Nicknamed pejoratively as 'Hunter-Bunter', he is remembered in one account as 'one of the Great War's spectacular incompetents'.[9] His own men later referred to him as the Butcher of Helles. Some military historians are less harsh in their assessment.

So it was that in broad daylight, late in the afternoon of Saturday, 8 May, the New Zealanders and Australians were suddenly sent into the killing maw in an irrational and poorly planned attack. Without any prior warning, the Anzacs were told to line up and advance across an open plain towards a ridge four kilometres away behind the village of Krithia. As the Australian commanders knew, it was an impossible objective in the face of the entrenched Turkish defences, the flat terrain, and their harrowing artillery barrages. The Australian commanders were also given just 25 minutes to get organised, and to ensure all the orders were sent out through the battalions; there was not even time for a reconnoitre. Bean records in his official history one absurd detail, how just before the attack a call came in from the commander-in-chief's headquarters asking if the Australians had any military bands and regimental colour flags with them in order to put on a display that would encourage the watching French troops.[10] It was sensibly ignored.

So peremptory was the order to attack that some companies only found out they were going into battle scant minutes before the advance. At 5.20 in the late afternoon, Bean walked with the command headquarters staff as they started the move towards their objective, the signallers following behind unrolling a long cable for the commander to stay in telephone contact. 'The ground we had to advance over was a shallow ridge rather like the back of your hand, sloping away very gradually on all sides to the two creeks which bordered it … It was covered with very low scrub, not higher than your ankles or shins and there was not a wrinkle in its surface, not a dimple large enough to hide a wounded man in.'[11]

In a surreal moment, Bean found himself walking with the brigade commander, Colonel James McCay (temporarily appointed as a brigadier general in August 1914, a promotion made permanent in October 1915), at the very head of the massive attack: 'I can't say I exactly expected to lead the advance however there we were. We advanced steadily up the open heath in fighting column … As we came out the bullets began to whizz past fairly thickly … We were walking fast but not running. No-one paid any attention at all to bullets … You could not hear the bullets whizz. It was a bit of a relief to that extent. But I was never in the midst of such an uproar. Bang Bang Bang Bang … It was as if the universe was a tin-lined packing case and squads of giants with sledgehammers were banging both ends of it.'[12]

It was during this advance that Colonel McCay, Bean and the command headquarters staff came across the trench filled with Australian and British Lancashire Fusilier troops sheltering from the Turkish enfilading machine-gun fire now sweeping across the plain in front of them. McCay jumped up onto the parapet to spur his men on to the fight into a hail of bullets, a stirring tale that thrilled Bean's Australian readers in a newspaper report published a few weeks later on 28 May 1915:

> Then the Brigadier who had so far led the charge himself jumped up on the parapet. 'Now then, On Australians', he said waving his periscope ... The men gathered themselves up and shouting 'On Australians, Come on Australians'. They swept over that parapet like a whirlwind and out across the deadly plateau. A perfect storm of bullets met them.[13]

Bean's private diary however records a markedly different account of Colonel McCay's heroism and a very different impression about the response of his soldiers; for it was not just his periscope he was waving to urge his troops on – in his other hand he held a revolver with which he was threatening a reluctant Australian soldier:

> I saw him with his revolver in his hands. He had just been talking to some chap in the trench some 10 yards to my left. I heard afterwards it was a Sergeant and McCay threatened to shoot him if he didn't get out damned quick.[14]

Bean had the same dilemma at Krithia as at Anzac Cove: he knew that a news story telling the ghastly reality of Gallipoli would never be tolerated. Reporting a detail such as Colonel McCay forcing men out of the trenches at gunpoint into an almost suicidal attack at Krithia would have been deleted by the censor's blue pencil. As he did throughout the war, Bean chose again to see the very best in Australia's troops and to overlook their failings, for clearly the bulk of them did act heroically and willingly walked into that hail of Turkish bullets without needing to be cajoled at gunpoint. This is some of what he told his readers he saw:

> They reckoned those bullets no more than if they were a summer shower. One youngster walked steadily into that storm with his entrenching spade held in his left hand a little in front of his face … while he looked from under shelter of it exactly as a man looked round his umbrella when walking in the rain down a city street.[15]

In another newspaper report Bean's account of the Krithia charge was absurdly triumphalist about the battle, assuring readers no man had faltered and that shrapnel did little actual harm.

> Sometimes when shrapnel burst in front of them, you would see some youngster defend his forehead with his elbow and come through dust clouds almost blinded but I never noticed one man falter and curiously enough I believe that the shrapnel did little actual harm. It must have hit some men of course but I saw none fall. Never could there be a better object lesson of the maxim that the best way to avoid shrapnel is by going forward.[16]

At best these news reports from Bean were misleading; to be faithful to his journalistic tenet of truth, he should not have implied to his wartime readers that advancing into Krithia's artillery and machine-gun fire was as innocuous as walking down George Street. To also say he saw 'none fall' from shrapnel at Krithia was not correct, as his own diary and notebooks record him witnessing numerous casualties. Perhaps the censor or the regional newspaper editor who published Bean's story embellished it (as sometimes happened), or perhaps on this one occasion Bean was caught up in the gloriously terrible sight of such selfless men rushing into almost certain death, and he was telling his newspaper readers what they wanted to hear: that they had sacrificed gallantly. The truth was that almost every man who heeded McCay's instructions to advance was soon killed or wounded, as then Brigadier General Gordon Bennett, of the Australian 2nd Brigade, admitted well over a decade after the war: 'The men who at McCay's urging dashed forward were met by a screaming hurricane of bullets. They advanced by short dashes, crouched to avoid the hail of lead with shovels and packs held before them like shields. Shovels and packs provided no protection against high velocity bullets and the line quickly melted away.'[17] Bean's official history did later acknowledge that the troops were dropping very fast at this time and that, after minutes of Turkish machine-gun fire, 'the lines were very thin. Men were dropping at every rush.'[18]

By 6.30pm, a little more than an hour after the attack had begun, the 2nd Brigade advance had been brought to a bloody halt; before them the entrenched Turkish positions in front of Krithia were now visible but still over 360 metres distant. Almost all the Australian officers and NCOs had been hit; across the plain in front were strewn the khaki-clad bodies of 1056 dead and wounded. McCay sat in the Tommies' Trench headquarters calling for more reinforcements to come forward 'or the day would be lost', and then, losing his patience, he strode out towards the frontline with his staff to see for himself what had happened. He soon realised, as one of his staff was shot dead through the heart beside him, that the situation was desperate and hopeless; the attack had been a futile failure. Later back at

Tommies' Trench, as Bean spoke to Major Cass, one of the senior Australian officers, already wounded in the chest, Cass was again shot right in front of him: 'He fell and as he lay on the ground was hit again on the shoulder. He lay there from 6 to 11 before he could be brought in. Stretchers were so short that night.'[19] When some French infantrymen came into the trench where Bean was sitting, he and an Australian officer tried to encourage them to advance out into the heavy fire: 'Hastie and I went along to them and tried to explain in French – "Il faut avancer avec Australiens … avant avec Australiens" he said. But they nodded and lay still.'[20]

Later that night, when darkness fell, Bean went out with the brigadier across the battlefield, lighting matches over dead faces in a sombre search for McCay's fallen officers, men Bean had come to know in the previous days. All night the cries and sobs of the wounded could be heard on the battlefield, many of them shot through the stomach or intestines, an excruciatingly painful injury that few would survive. Once, when injured men called for a stretcher-bearer close to the trench, Bean noted in his diary the insensitive comments of one messenger who had just come up to the line and yelled back: '"You won't see them tonight my boy. They're rarer than gold. You won't get them along here." It was an idiotic thing to say. "You might let us think we will," said one of the wounded men, feebly.'[21] Bean did what he could for them, going back to fetch water, and reassuring the injured men, falsely, that the stretcher-bearers would be along soon. His diary records: 'It was most unlikely but it was the one thing they clung on to … It made you simply mad to think of the dull, stupid cruel bungling that was mismanaging the medical arrangements.

The men in the firing line would gladly have gone without a day's rations if only the carts could have been used in carrying the wounded down from the dressing station to the beach.'[22]

Bean was typically humble about his extraordinary act of courage in going out into that killing zone and rescuing a couple of these wounded men under fire before darkness fell. 'I have no right to the credit of the lowest simplest soldiers, and I am not as brave as most of them.'[23] He was chastened by the futility of the sacrifice of the Australian soldiers and their officers who had fallen that day, and perhaps for the first time his diary implicitly accepted that there was every likelihood he would not survive the war. Charles Bean never saw anything he did as anywhere near the sacrifice he saw of Australian troops in battle. He was also realising for the first time just how incompetent and callous the British Army could be: 'Once the wounded leave our hands there seems to be the same general muddle which is the one thing that impresses with almost everything this British staff has done as far as we have seen it. Everything is late – nothing up to time – no evidence of brains that I've seen.'[24]

The attack was the closest Bean the journalist had come yet to dying and indeed it was a miracle he survived. His courage and empathy for the troops did not go unnoticed, and the story of his bravery circulated among the trenches back at Anzac Cove and even back in Australia. In late July a letter praising Bean from Signaller Dave Benson of Perth was published in *The Sydney Morning Herald*: 'Captain Bean carried water to the trenches and helped the wounded back all through the night. He is an honour to Australian journalists.'[25]

The assault on Krithia, a frontal attack in broad daylight, had cost the lives of far too many young men for absolutely no strategic gain. But back in Australia, newspaper readers would be told a very different story by an unnamed 'special correspondent' for the Melbourne *Age* newspaper; although Bean filed for *The Age*, this was definitely not an article penned by him. It falsely stated, under the headline, 'The attack on Krithia – a gallant charge', and in another headline, in an Adelaide paper, 'Taking of Krithia. Gallant Australian Charge. Commanding Officers' bravery', that:

> The village is now in our hands and in taking it the Australian troops played a glorious part with the New Zealanders. It is the story of a charge sustained over the whole front for 1,000 metres in the face of a withering fire of shell and bullets … On the night of the 9th or 10th in a grand final charge, the Allies entered the village. The details have not yet reached me but the sacrifice was great and the cost to be reckoned more than even that of the first days of fighting.[26]

The giveaway to this deceitful story was that it was tagged as written from Lemnos, the Greek island where the main Allied base for the Dardanelles was located. Clearly the British command had overconfidently expected the 2nd Brigade attack on Krithia to be a grand success, and the appalling lie in this article, suggesting it had been taken, had been telegraphed back to Australia before the real story became known. It was not the first time a blatantly untrue story had been planted in Australasian newspapers during the conflict, and it would not be the last.

On 11 May 1915, the order came for the Anzacs to be pulled out of Cape Helles and returned to Anzac Cove. Bean recorded another observation in his notebook that he never reported in either his journalism or his official history. The Butcher of Helles, Lieutenant General Hunter-Weston, the commander who had insisted on a suicidal daylight attack at Krithia, now walked out of his headquarters tent and confronted the tired troops coming out of the battle, looking for a place to camp:

> [He] told them he despised them. If he had any troops he could put in their place to do the same thing this battle would be won.[27]

There is little doubt that the feeling from his men was mutually contemptuous.

Six

THE DESTINIES OF EMPIRES

I don't order you to fight, I order you to die. In the time it takes us to die, other troops and commanders can come and take our places.

MUSTAFA KEMAL, TURKISH COMMANDER AT GALLIPOLI[1]

They had all been warned on their way up Monash Gully that it was wide open to sniper fire. 'Be careful here. Run across here,' Australian soldiers told their 1st Division commander, General William Bridges, and his staff officers as he clambered along the gully towards a frontline headquarters. Each time Bridges and his officers had left a gap between each man, and that morning the general had paused near a dressing station run by a soldier named Thompson. It was Charles Bean who later recorded how Bridges had lit a cigarette as he waited for Lieutenant Colonel White to catch up with him.

> 'Well White, time to be moving on.'
>
> Thompson said: 'Be careful of this next bit sir. We've had several men hit.'
>
> The General went on and the last Colonel White saw of him was his long legs disappearing in the scrub.

'I don't know quite how it happened,' Colonel White said, 'but Casey and I were standing there waiting to follow at intervals when on a sudden there was a commotion in the air. Someone hit.'[2]

Just before he came ashore at Anzac Cove on his return from Cape Helles on 17 May, Charles Bean heard the shocking news that the Australian 1st Division commander General Bridges had been shot by a sniper near the frontline. When Major Blamey met him at the dock, Bean learned that the wound was bad and 'there was very little hope for him'.[3] Lieutenant Colonel White had been there when the general was hit: '"The General used to be very daring," he said. He exposed himself without any care for bullets and when the rest of the staff took cover he would chaff them: "What are you getting down there for White," he would ask.'[4] Bridges lingered on for several days on a hospital ship but he knew he was dying: 'The wound had become gangrenous through failure of the blood supply and the enormous loss of blood also had affected him. He said to Colonel Ryan, who dressed him, just before Ryan left: "Well anyhow, I have commanded an Australian division for nine months."'[5]

The general was initially buried at Alexandria (before his body was returned to Australia in June). At about the same time Bean attended the beach burial of another officer, Major William Stuart. Grappling with these two deaths, a lyrical Bean was moved to introspection about the hundreds of soldiers now buried on Gallipoli: 'They have left those troubles and they are in the poppy fields and the daisies with the blue Dardanelles below them.'[6] He also recalled some of the humorous stories told about Bridges: 'General

Bridges used to have a guard, by the name, Bill, when they went around the trenches. Bill was from Sydney and in one of the trenches he met a Sydney friend. "Allo Bill," he said, "Who's yer prisoners?" Another batch of men saw the three Generals [Walker, Bridges, Birdwood] coming along: "Say Jim," he was heard to say to one of his chums – "better put a guard over the biscuits; here's three bloody Generals."'[7]

It was a wiser and more pragmatic Charles Bean who returned to the 1st Division Anzac headquarters after Krithia; the Turks and the Australians had become locked into a trench war stalemate and Australia's official eyewitness was now questioning what the entire operation was trying to achieve. Writing in his diary of the attack at Krithia, he said the Australians had done the work 'which very few of the troops down there could do – that is, advancing straight upon the enemy in the face of a very heavy fire. And what is it all for? Ian Hamilton sends letters to our army corps telling them that they are doing magnificent work … He may be right – we are holding up a big number of Turks here. But the position is that whilst we are doing so and sending them every help and going short in artillery, aeroplanes and gun ammunition … they [the British at Krithia] are not pushing on apparently because they can't push on. The fact is that while most of the material for pushing on is down there, most of the personnel which could push on is up here … I don't know enough about it to say whether we could push through here.'[8]

Late on the evening of 17 May, a telegraph message was sent through to the 1st Division signal office that looked like the Turks had somehow tapped into the Allied telegraph system: 'We will put you into the sea tomorrow, you Australia basta[r]ds. Big guns we will give you. We will give you mines you Australia bastards.'[9] As Bean records in his official history, years later it was uncovered as a hoax from someone inside the Australian lines, but at the time it was taken very seriously as an indication of an impending massive Turkish attack.[10] A British aeroplane flew over Turkish lines the next day and reported a large number of reinforcements being landed. By complete fluke the hoax was right: an attack was imminent. Across on the Turkish side that night of 18 May, 42,000 infantry soldiers were being readied for a massive assault the next morning. All during the preceding day barely a shot had been fired from the Turkish trenches, then at 5pm the Turks unleashed their largest artillery bombardment ever on the Allied invasion force. Had the Turks attacked just a week earlier then the Anzac brigades would still have been at Cape Helles and a much weaker force would have had to fight to rebuff the Turkish attack but by the night of 18 May the returned 1st Light Horse, 2nd Infantry and New Zealand Mounted Rifles brigades had been brought in to reinforce the line.

When the Turks did finally attack at dawn the next morning, the Australians were ready for them; it was a slaughter and the Turkish bodies piled high in front of the Australian lines. Out of the 42,000 Turks who attacked, 10,000 became casualties and nearly 3000 were killed in action or died of wounds. In the aftermath, Bean noticed that the massive number of dead and suffering Turks lying in front of them had changed the attitude of the Australians towards them: 'They are quite friendly with the Turk; anxious to get in the wounded if they can – give them cigarettes.'[11]

Many of the dead Turkish soldiers scattered on the battlefield had horrific head injuries: 'frightful wounds in the head, half the head blown away. I saw one head wound like a star or a pane of broken glass.'[12] For many weeks Bean had been hearing stories from the army doctors and soldiers that the size of many of the wounds suffered by Australian soldiers at Gallipoli could only have been caused by illegal 'dumdum' or expanding bullets fired from the Turkish side. However, what they were actually seeing for the first time was not dumdum rounds but the awful consequences of modern killing technology, the effect of high-velocity full metal jacket projectiles or shrapnel on human flesh and bone. The British censors had effectively encouraged this misleading speculation by not censoring the troops who wrote home stating this alleged war crime as a fact, and many of these letters were now being published in metropolitan newspapers including that of Bean's former employer *The Sydney Morning Herald*. One private told his parents:

> The Turks were using dum-dum poisoned bullets, also copper and brass bullets, which poison the wounds. They disregarded all rules of warfare and made the battle of Sunday last a fearful hell of hells. I don't think things could be worse. The conditions were awful and the sights heartbreaking to witness. I can assure you that none of us wounded have any desire to again witness such awful slaughter.[13]

It seems that so long as soldiers directed their opprobrium and allegations at their Turkish enemy, the censor would turn a blind eye to the letter's veracity. So Bean was concerned to learn that a plethora of monstrous claims of torture, mutilation and other war crimes were being levelled at the Turks through letters published in the daily papers. Another soldier's letter ran: 'I could make your hair stand on end if I told you some of the barbarous methods adopted by the Turks on some of our unfortunate wounded who were overtaken and tortured.'[14]

But there was also a more sinister propaganda war being played as part of a deliberate strategy run by British military intelligence. A report filed by news agency Reuters from Cairo on 3 May ran in *The Singleton Argus* and numerous other newspapers in June, quoting an unnamed wounded soldier's story of the treachery of a German officer:

> The officer had been seriously wounded and had been attended to in a very considerate manner by an Australian Red Cross soldier who dressed his wounds. The gratitude shown by the German officer was to draw his revolver and shoot the Australian soldier in the back as he walked off to assist his wounded comrade. I felt very bad indeed but the sight of such a ghastly outrage put new life into me. I crawled along the ground slowly and summoning all my strength, put an end to the life of the German with my bayonet.[15]

Inevitably, such stories were given great prominence in many Australian newspapers throughout the war and, especially when the letters were published, the public belief that they were true became very strong. The New South Wales Mitchell Library still holds a battered scrapbook in its archives of such news clippings including many soldiers' letters to the newspapers detailing a compendium of alleged Turkish crimes. There are letters and articles referring to the same story of a medic being shot in the back, all sourced to an anonymous soldier, suggestive perhaps of a deliberate propaganda campaign similar to that which was run out of the British Ministry of Information from London throughout the war, for there is no doubt that deliberate official lies alleging Turkish and German atrocities were sown in Australian newspapers. In fact, as Phillip Knightley's *The First Casualty* reveals, Reuters news agency, whose graphic atrocity story was run in *The Singleton Argus*, had secretly placed its entire resources at the disposal of the Allied propaganda cause throughout the war.[16] Many of the staff recruited to the government's Ministry of Information propaganda agency were drawn from the offices of top Fleet Street newspapers. Knightley writes, 'They were not hampered by what Dr Johnson termed "needless scrupulosity", they had a feeling for words and moods, and they knew that the public was not convinced by logic but seduced by stories.'[17]

Many letters and articles were published which described Germans wearing British or Australian uniforms coming into Gallipoli trenches and saying, in perfect English, 'Pass the word along to cease fire.' Other letters reported that someone called out, 'Every man for himself, make back for the beach.' Again, these were also attributed to a cunning enemy: 'Some Turks are nearly white and can speak good English.'[18]

There were many letters published in the Sydney papers from an anonymous soldier who was by-lined 'Trooper Bluegum'. He was actually an officer with the 6th Light Horse Regiment, Lieutenant (later Major) Oliver Hogue, the son of a former New South Wales education minister and current editor of the Sydney

Evening News.[19] As 'Trooper Bluegum', Hogue frequently described Turkish atrocities and the 'treachery' of both the Turks and the Germans at Gallipoli who, he claimed, were 'in our trenches, in our uniforms, calling out "Cease fire you fools, you are firing on your own men" and "Cease fire – stretcher bearers coming" ... but on the stretchers were machine guns'.[20] Another published soldier's letter said there were 'interpreters in every regiment and many have been found out to be spies'. Yet another claimed an Australian soldier with one battalion who was known to be an excellent sniper kept going out ahead by himself to 'snipe', but it turned out he was sniping Australians; he was 'Australian born but with German parents'. Almost all of these stories were baseless, and in late May Bean began writing stories rebutting the claims. He had previously believed he had seen 'dumdum' bullets on the battlefield, rounds designed to expand or fragment on impact, illegal under the 1899 Hague Convention.[21] But the injuries suffered by the Turks in the 19 May attacks had convinced him the bulk of these ghastly open and jagged wounds were not caused by expanding bullets. On 29 May, under a subheading entitled 'Baseless atrocity stories', Bean wrote how stories of explosive bullets were 'quite without foundation – due to men misunderstanding the curious double-crack of the [Turkish soldier's] Mauser rifle'.

> Our wounded in the enemy's hands are said to be well-cared for. A few stories of atrocities are current, and may reach Australia. I can only say that the principal one which I have tested, proved wholly untrue. Some dum-dum bullets have been picked up but the stories of explosive bullets are quite without

foundation … some of the wounds are terrible and I would put them down to expanding bullets had I not seen wounds quite as terrible in the heads of Turks.[22]

Bean conceded in another article that there must have been some isolated atrocities committed by the Turks, as sadly happens in every war, but he went on to say that the Turkish soldier was a very 'maligned person who certainly does not compare with the German in frightfulness, if the tales of the German are true … It is necessary to receive very guardedly stories told by men concerning the action in which they have been wounded or of any action in which the nerve strain has been very severe … I know that many of the stories that have been somewhat loosely told in Alexandria and elsewhere about Gaba Tepe and what happened there are not true.'[23]

Charles Bean also described the Turks as a brave and courteous enemy, superior to the German soldier. One widely circulated claim that had inflamed outrage at Anzac Cove and back in Australia was that the mutilated body of a former Australian member of Parliament had been found by his mates on the battlefield during the first day of fighting. Bean wrote that 'Australian readers must be warned against accepting seriously such stories … These stories may greatly distress people in Australia and so far as anyone on the spot knows there is not the least element of truth in any of them … this brave man's body was found where he fell, absolutely intact except for the wound that killed him.'[24]

In another article Bean took a swipe at the blatant propaganda being pumped out of Allied command in Lemnos: 'It must be remembered that it is impossible to obtain quickly news that Australians really want …

Australians will by now have realised that cable messages from Greek islands, which are generally the earliest to arrive, are seldom true. Mr Ashmead-Bartlett's cable messages are, needless to say, thoroughly reliable.'[25]

But as the saying goes, if you tell a lie big enough, eventually the people come to believe it; Charles Bean had not reckoned on the ferocity of a propaganda myth now so powerfully believed back home in Australia. His dismissiveness of the Turkish atrocities was savaged the next month in an article mischievously sourced largely to the second-hand claims of 'Trooper Bluegum'. The story, headlined 'Turkish fiends exposed. Captain Bean's defence refuted. Overwhelming evidence of enemy's barbarous methods', disparaged Bean:

> It will be remembered that it was Captain Bean who made certain statements concerning the sobriety and general conduct of the Australian troops in Egypt, that led to a quite improper impression being gained of the bearing of our troops and the manner in which they were upholding the honor of their country in a strange land. It would now appear that our official representative has made another unfortunate blunder in attempting to whitewash an enemy to whose native talent in the matter of cruelty has been added the cultivated frightfulness of his Hun ally.[26]

The story was a rehashed Sunday paper 'beat-up' of all the previously published letters of Australian soldiers alleging atrocities, presenting no new substantive evidence to support the primary claim that dumdum expanding bullets were being used by the Turks. Sadly for Bean, he became the focus of a Sydney tabloid's fury anyway, and its editors even had a cruel dig at him for not filing the first report from Gallipoli. 'Where was Captain Bean when the Australians landed on Gallipoli? We had to rely on the work of a British journalist to give us the first story – and the best.'[27]

There was one weakness in Bean's defence of the Turks that he did not acknowledge to his readers as his own first Gallipoli story had also reported the false claims of Australian soldiers being tricked into ceasing fire: 'The Turks are well trained in German methods and orders have certainly been given to the men in trenches by strangers. Possibly in scrub near a trench there is one who gives an order in perfect English and it is passed along the trench. I have seen personally, one clear example of this.'[28] Bean did acknowledge after the war that the claims of Turkish trickery were wrong, and he explained how this had happened. In a 1937 speech he gave to the Australian English Association entitled 'Furphy – war historian', Bean cited the Turkish trickery as one example of a false rumour (or a 'furphy') that began after the first day of the Gallipoli landing.[29] One story that circulated said the Turkish troops had cleverly tricked the Australian and New Zealand troops by calling out as they approached 'Indian troops' and 'Indian troops on the left, don't fire'. Bean said that he had investigated this rumour and discovered that the Anzacs did indeed hear these cries but that in fact they came from their own troops. The Anzacs saw dark-skinned soldiers in khaki (who were actually Turks) but, having heard that the 29th Indian Brigade was to take part in the action, took them to be Indian troops and called out as such. 'The Anzacs didn't fire and the Turkish troops were able to get around their flank and fire on them, causing much injury,' Bean explained. When he published his book *Gallipoli Mission* in 1948, Bean wrote again about this alleged Turkish ruse and acknowledged a Turkish commander, Major Zeki Bey, had adamantly denied it: 'Zeki Bey, however, when I told him the story looked so incredulous that it was clear not only that he had never heard of it, but that he felt – as I had long done – that such a ruse was beyond the capacity of Turkish infantry to carry out.'[30] Bean did not acknowledge he had made such a claim himself in his writing during the war.

In his official history, Charles Bean again explained how a lot of these false rumours had started at Gallipoli, suggesting most or all of the shouts were actually from Australian troops and not the Turks at all.

> There is no question that, in the fighting near The Nek, owing to the report that Indians were fighting on the left, the Turks had constantly been mistaken for Indians. It was afterwards firmly believed that these messages had been spread in the Australian line by some Turkish or German officer creeping close enough to do so, or by an agent in the Australian lines themselves. The Syrian interpreters, and even the Zion Mule Corps, came under the suspicion, and steps were actually taken temporarily to withdraw them. But it is more than doubtful if any one of these 'spy messages' was really started from a hostile source. It is one of the ordinary effects of battle strain that men attribute to their enemies an almost superhuman cunning … It is only possible to say definitely that, in every case in which a 'spy message' could be traced by the Australian Staff,

whether in Gallipoli or in France, it proved to have been an innocent mistake.[31]

Postwar, Bean refuted an inaccurate story he again had had a hand in creating, a reflection perhaps of the 'fog of war' and his then relative inexperience as a war reporter at the time because it involved another misconception he had included in one of his first reports from Gallipoli. In a story entitled, 'Gallipoli. Fight in the hills. The first day. Men that went beyond', Bean reported claims that on that first day Australian soldiers went well past their original objectives. He wrote of men who 'may have formed one of the many small parties which must have got away into the ridges out beyond the rest of our line and never returned'.[32] Later in the article he writes of 'these parties of men, parties large and small, who pushed on into the country far beyond our present line, the country belonging to the enemy'. But in an interview with *The Sydney Morning Herald* in 1941 to mark the finishing of his final volume of the official history, Bean cited the claims about the 'men who went beyond' as one example of a falsity he had been able to refute.[33] He talked of how 'the legend that the Anzac went miles inland at the landing on Gallipoli in an indiscriminate rush was without foundation. As a matter of fact, none went beyond their objective.'[34]

Charles Bean was learning that journalism is truly the first rough draft of history and that, almost inevitably, journalists will get things wrong; this is especially so in the complex and constantly changing environment of a war zone where so many men's recollections are, as he acknowledged, affected by stress and injury. Bean would have been mortified to think he had made false claims in his news reports and it is quite likely that he did not notice his own relatively minor errors of fact in his journalism when he came to write his postwar official history, in which he corrected the historical record.

As for the outrageous tale of the German officer shooting the Australian medic in the back after he had tended the German's wounds, Bean was undeterred by his tabloid critics and did his own investigations into that rumour, still circulating towards the end of 1915. 'Most of these stories have in the weaving of them perhaps some single thread of truth,' Bean wrote in a December newspaper article. He then recounted that an ambulance man had told him how the rumour had started.

> It is a fact that in the early days one of our stretcher-bearers was bending over a wounded Turkish infantryman and had taken out his knife and was beginning to slit away some of the man's clothes to get at his wounds, when the Turk grabbed the knife from him and stabbed at him twice with it. The Turk obviously was under the impression that he was about to be disembowelled. I daresay they had been told we were in the habit of dissecting our helpless enemies and he was going to fight for his life. The thing was so obvious that the stretcher-bearer, who was not seriously hurt, managed to calm his patient down and went on dressing him.[35]

In late May Bean noted in his diary that a Private Simpson from the 3rd Field Ambulance had started using a donkey to help carry wounded soldiers down from the line. 'It struck him that it would be useful to bring down from the firing line men with wounds in the leg – we have seen in Egypt what these donkeys can do. He went off and camped with this donkey amongst the Indians and all day and half the night he made continual trips to and from the firing line with it. He put a red cross brassard around its forehead and any time of the day you might meet him coming down the gully … He became fatalistic. If they were going to hit him, they would whatever his precautions.'[36]

His subsequent newspaper story, praising the selfless work of Private John Simpson Kirkpatrick and his donkey, and how the soldier had died helping wounded men to safety, was hugely popular back in Australia and remains one of the enduring legends of Gallipoli:

> Everybody knew the man with the donkeys and everybody knew that if ever a man deserved honour in this war it was he … You cannot hurry a donkey very much, however close the shells may burst and he absolutely came to disregard bullets and shrapnel … When the shells were so hot that many others thought it wiser to duck for cover as they passed the man with the donkey calmly went his way as if nothing more serious than a summer shower was happening … He was coming down the gully on this morning of May 10th after the attack, clearing some of our three or four hundred wounded – the Turks lost twice that many thousand – when he passed the water-guard where he generally took his breakfast. It happened this morning that the breakfast was not ready. 'Never mind,' he said to the engineers there, 'Get me a good dinner when I come back'. But he never came back. He and his two patients were nearing the end of the journey when he was

> shot through the heart, and both of his wounded men were wounded again ... The commander of this section of the line told me the man with the donkey had been worth a hundred men to him.[37]

Bean's report was a warmly told human-interest story, personalising the stoic sacrifice of Simpson, but it also went on to make the point that other stretcher-bearers had died in similar ways; in his report he also honoured a battlefield surgeon with the 5th Battalion, Captain Mathieson, who died after weeks of extraordinarily courageous acts helping wounded men from the battlefield. But it was the legend of Simpson and his donkey that caught the public's imagination. Schoolchildren were given texts of his story, and Simpson is immortalised in books, plays, movies, banknotes and even statues to this day. In recent years there was even a push on for Simpson to be awarded a posthumous Victoria Cross for his bravery, however an inquiry tasked to review his suitability in 2013 decided that Simpson's valour could not be distinguished from numerous acts of bravery shown by other stretcher-bearers, which was, after all, the original point Bean had made. It also demolished a series of lies that had grown around the Simpson legend, falsities that were not the fault of Bean's original story but were often deliberate inventions by lesser journalists who had taken the story – and run with it. They suggested that Simpson had rescued hundreds of men, many under fire in no-man's-land. Careful investigations revealed that eyewitnesses who gave stirring firsthand accounts of Simpson's rescue of men from the frontline under fire could not possibly be correct.

One of the journalists who had exaggerated Simpson's story was Ernest Buley, who dedicated a chapter to it in a book called *Glorious Deeds of Australasians in the Great War.*[38] As *The Sydney Morning Herald* reported in 2013, Buley was the first journalist to write concocted accounts of Simpson dashing into no-man's-land to rescue wounded men.[39] Investigations revealed Buley was in fact a 'scurrilous gutter press journalist' and a convicted fraudster who had also anonymously written another blatantly propagandist tome called *The Real Kaiser.* Bean would have been mortified that his original story had been so corrupted.

The truth is that Charles Bean had an almost obsessive attention to accuracy and his writing was often replete with unnecessary detail, which on occasion made him the butt of jokes from his journalistic colleagues on the peninsula. In one huge 3000-word article, Bean went into encyclopaedic detail about the sound made by every different shell and bullet on Gallipoli, describing one gun's distinctive squeak and another shrapnel shell's donkey bray.[40] The British correspondent on Gallipoli Ellis Ashmead-Bartlett is often quoted as having said, 'Oh – Bean – I think he almost counts the bullets.'[41] As Bean sportingly admitted when he later wrote Ashmead-Bartlett's obituary in 1931 (the soldier-correspondent had died prematurely at the age of 50), this was a truer statement than Bartlett realised: 'On some nights at Anzac in an endeavour to see if one could reach a standard by which to measure the amount of disturbance as compared with that on other nights, I used to note down the number of rifle shots on an average in a minute.'[42]

So many potential news stories are mentioned in Bean's diary during his time on Gallipoli that never made it into print during the war. He never wrote a newspaper story about the Allied command's failure to provide sufficient stretcher-bearers and medical assistance at Krithia, where so many young Australians had been terribly wounded and had likely died because their evacuation from the battlefield was so delayed. Another similar story of medical treatment failures at the hospitals in Egypt was written by his *Age* colleague Phillip Schuler, generating huge concern back home in Australia.

On Bean's return from Cape Helles, his mounting concerns that Anzac Cove was becoming a low priority for the British commanders never made it into the papers. In his diary, with great frustration, he described how the Australians were not allowed to fire artillery at the Turks because their howitzers and field guns were being limited to just a handful of shots per day. 'Batteries now have to watch the Turks digging without being able to fire a shot at them … Before we used to frighten them off this sort of work – but now we can scarcely interfere with them. One of our observers … asked the ships to fire on a good target the other day. The reply was: "Sorry, I've used my 5 shots."'[43]

On reflection, it is highly unlikely Bean would have been allowed by the censors to write such critical stories anyway but, as Phillip Schuler did in Alexandria with his revelations of medical failures, there was nothing stopping Bean from putting critical stories to the censors to at least try to get them published. Without question, both of these criticisms that he privately voiced, and many more in Bean's diary, would be entirely legitimate news stories in today's media, and clearly some of the soldiers on Gallipoli felt there were critical stories that should have been told by Bean at the time, and were frustrated with him for not doing so. For example, by July 1915 health and hygiene at Gallipoli were becoming major concerns; every day 200 of the 25,000 Australian soldiers there were being sent away sick to hospitals in Lemnos and Alexandria. Bean noted concerns that the men evacuated had often soon recovered but that it took up to six weeks to get them back to Anzac Cove. In his notes he acknowledges that it was suggested he write a story about how the division was not being kept up to its full strength:

> I have had it said to me – 'Isn't it your business?' – but it is not. It is strictly against the regulations for me to criticise and I have not been asked by the authorities to do so. My job is to tell the people of Australia all I can about their troops here and I should be sent back if I tried to do anything else … The unofficial correspondents in Cairo and Alex[andria] will take it up and it will be righted through a press agitation and not the official channels – I have no doubt.[44]

These wrongs were not righted by press coverage in Egypt at all, for the correspondents there very likely did not even know about the extent of the problems on Gallipoli. Charles Bean had privileged access to the frontline but he was constrained not just by the regulations of press censorship: he was also facing the realities of being an embedded journalist with the Australian forces. For the reality was that he needed to preserve both his sources and access not only to Anzac Cove but to the private chats he enjoyed with Colonel White or Major Blamey that gave him an understanding of what was really going on. If he had ever dared venture criticism of the Allied command without checking with the censor first then he may indeed have been sent back to Australia in a flash. He may not have fully realised this at the beginning of the war when he accepted the invitation to become official eyewitness correspondent, but his time on Gallipoli had made him realise he was effectively now a journalist with one hand tied behind his back.

Much later in the war, Bean set out for one of his assistants what he perceived to be the duties of the Australian official correspondent. He said the role was 'to give Australia a knowledge of what the men and officers of the force are doing, and what is really happening in the war as far as they are concerned in it consistently with (1) not giving information to the enemy (2) not needlessly distressing their families at home. The rule of the censorship also forbids criticism.'[45] But Bean surely knew that these particular censorship regulations did not absolutely forbid criticism – they just required any correspondent who signed the undertaking to ensure his copy was first vetted by the censor before publication. The so-called war correspondent's declaration undertook that he was 'not to attempt to correspond by any other route or by any other means than that officially sanctioned'. A correspondent also had to promise that for the duration of the war he would not 'impart to anyone military information of a confidential nature … unless first submitted to the Chief Field Censor for censorship and passed for publication by him'.[46]

Prewar British War Office service regulations had also stipulated that licensed war correspondents were to pay a 300 pound surety to follow instructions not to refer to strength, composition or location of forces, movement of troops, casualties, important orders and morale of troops, or to engage in 'criticism and eulogies of a personal nature'. They were also forbidden to cause 'alarm, despondency or unrest amongst the inhabitants of the British Empire or of any Allied power'.[47] If correspondents had heeded such ludicrously tight restrictions, however, nothing would have ever been reported, and it does not appear Bean or other Australian correspondents were asked to sign such an undertaking. But this is very likely to have been the source for the notion held by Bean that his reports were not allowed to criticise at all, derived no doubt from the British command.

In practice, whatever the regulations or undertakings stipulated, it was very likely that any journalist writing a story that was highly critical of the Gallipoli campaign would have been censored. Bean's biggest rival at Gallipoli, Ellis Ashmead-Bartlett, the London *Telegraph*'s correspondent, was only able to get some fairly gentle criticisms past the censor before the British commanders tried to muzzle him. An eminent war correspondent well before he came to cover Gallipoli, Ashmead-Bartlett also had connections, coming from blue-blooded stock back in England; his father had been the civil Lord of the Admiralty. Both he and his son had close affections with Winston Churchill's in-laws: Ellis's father had an affair with Churchill's mother-in-law, and young Ellis had continued the family tradition by falling in love with Churchill's sister-in-law Gwendoline.[48] A swashbuckling adventurer, when he was just sixteen years old Ellis travelled with his father to observe the Turkish Army in the Graeco-Turkish war where both of them were taken prisoner by the Greeks, and he also served as a soldier in the Bedfordshire Regiment in the Second Boer War. While Bean had written his analysis of the Japanese navy from his Sydney desk, Ashmead-Bartlett witnessed the 1904 Russo-Japanese war and other French and Italian campaigns firsthand. Just a few years before the Allies invaded Gallipoli he befriended Turkish commanders at their headquarters during the 1912 Balkan War. Indeed, he probably knew better than most of the English commanders the calibre of the foe the Allies were now facing.

Ashmead-Bartlett's dispatches from Gallipoli, especially his first story – hailing the invading Australians at Gaba Tepe as 'a race of athletes' – had won him considerable praise in England and Australia. But as the weeks went by at Gallipoli he became increasingly disillusioned with the appalling losses of so many men because of what he believed were serious Allied command and logistic blunders. Within a couple of weeks of the landing, Ashmead-Bartlett was flagging to his London readers that the Turkish troops were not going to be the pushover that much of the British command and a mostly compliant media was inferring they would be. He had finished his account of the battle of Krithia on 16 May, saying that the Allied plan to break through to Constantinople was being met by an 'indomitable foe' and that 'extreme patience' would be necessary: 'Our men have done everything mortal man could do.'[49] It was as close as he or Bean ever got in newsprint to saying the campaign was a failure.

Soon after arriving at Gallipoli, Ashmead-Bartlett realised that the worse things went for the Allied invasion force, the more the military tried to crack down on his freedom to report. Censorship was bad from the start; he had been assured he would be allowed to take pictures of the invasion but his undeveloped films were confiscated.

After the tragedy of Krithia he wrote a critical report that he intended for publication by the English press. If the censor gagged it then he figured it would confirm his worst private fears, that 'the military authorities out here were concealing the truth from the authorities at home'.[50]

He submitted this document to both the censor at Imbros and General Hamilton and it was censored in its entirety. Ashmead-Bartlett also made several shrewd observations in his diary that showed he believed a role of official eyewitness, such as Bean's, inevitably involved a serious compromising of a reporter's journalistic independence. He said the Gallipoli commanders:

> realised three things which they never forgave ... Firstly that I had a perfect conception of the extent of our so-called success up to date; secondly, that I knew too much and disapproved of the strategy of the campaign; and thirdly, they saw for the first time that I was not prepared to be an official eyewitness, but was determined to remain an independent one who could not be got at in anyone's interests.[51]

When he lost all his possessions, including his copy of his critical Dardanelles campaign report, in the May 1915 sinking of the navy battleship HMS *Majestic* at Cape Helles, Ashmead-Bartlett returned briefly to England. While there he met with Churchill, Arthur Balfour and other government ministers to convey his grim impressions of the Gallipoli campaign. As Bean later wrote in Ashmead-Bartlett's obituary, these politicians had 'sought [Ashmead-Bartlett's] views explaining that Lord Kitchener told them nothing of the realities of the campaign. He spoke to them freely in his own vein. Kitchener, who also saw him, extracted a promise that he would talk of the campaign to no outsider, except the editor of his paper, *The Daily Telegraph*, whose discretion could be trusted.'[52]

Ashmead-Bartlett was a natural rebel, contemptuous of the self-serving censorship imposed on all the correspondents, and he delighted in pricking the pomposity and exposing the privilege of the Allied commanders to his press colleagues at the Greek Imbros base where he and most of the correspondents, except for Bean and New Zealand's Malcolm Ross, were based. One story he told, Bean noted, was about General Hamilton on the day of the landing at Suvla. Wanting to go across from Imbros to review the troops on the ground, the commander boarded a torpedo boat but unfortunately the boat had a breakdown and the trip was delayed because of these technical problems. Bean recorded, 'They weren't smoothed "... until about 12 o'clock," said Bartlett. "Of course then it was too late, it was getting near time for lunch." G.H.Q. hates him for this style of talking.'[53]

The British command at Gallipoli likely heard from the secretary of state for war, Lord Kitchener, about Ashmead-Bartlett's criticisms of their campaign back in London, and even before he returned to Gallipoli a crackdown began on the correspondents at Anzac Cove. Bean was frustrated with the increasingly over-tight censorship on himself, complaining that one German report was actually more accurate than what he and other official correspondents were allowed to write:

> The [Alexandria newspaper] *Peninsula Press* publishes with great scorn an article in the Berlin *Courier* saying that 'our attack as at present conducted is a fizzle due to the ineffectual bombardment of March 18th, the insufficient size of the landing forces and the failure to embroil Bulgaria against Turkey'. As far as the military operations go it seems to me this statement is literally and absolutely correct ... it's a far better summing up

> of the position than our official reports give. This is the point to which the censorship has reduced us, that the German official accounts are far truer than our own.[54]

He also complained how the censor not only banned information that was militarily sensitive, 'which of course is right', but that the military also blocked publication of any 'truth calculated to depress or alarm the public. That is worse than useless with British people. It is harmful. The one thing to buck them up is to let them know exactly how things are, good or bad.'[55]

In late June, Bean and New Zealand official correspondent Malcolm Ross were given orders by General Hamilton's headquarters that they were to leave Anzac and to base themselves out of the war correspondents' camp at Imbros in Greece. Bean was furious about this prospect and he lobbied both General Birdwood and the new Australian commander, Major General Gordon Legge. In a memorandum to Legge, a clearly fraught Bean made it very clear to the Allied command that, as official eyewitness correspondent, he was prepared to accept curbs on his journalistic freedom back at Anzac Cove; he also indicated his newspaper reporting was secondary to his role as the official historian of the conflict.

> it is quite impossible for me to do at Imbros the work for which my Government appointed me.
>
> 1. The Australian Government in the instructions given me during my interviews with the Minister for Defence attached importance to two points: (a) to having with this distant force a representative who could satisfy the poignant anxiety of Australians for news of their own

> men – their daily life, behaviour in action, their peculiar Australian interest which could only be given by an Australian, and (b) to be special instructions given to me to write after the war the history of the Australian part in the war, as a permanent record for libraries, schools, and the nation generally …
>
> 2. The category of news which my duties require me to obtain has no relation to that required by correspondents responsible to newspapers … I have not attempted to sum up the general trend of the campaign, except in one, or possibly two small references to events already long since published in England. I do not know, I do not want to know, and, needless to say, have not attempted to even remotely touch on any future plans …
>
> 4. The news which I cannot obtain at Imbros is the details as to the life, scenes, bearing of men, scenes that will stir Australian pride … which is what the nation I represent wants to hear.[56]

Bean was always respectful of Ashmead-Bartlett, and perhaps a little in awe of him, despite what he revealed in his obituary of the English correspondent in 1931: that it was possibly not the British high command at all who had wanted to move all the correspondents from Gallipoli but that the decision was the result of lobbying by Ashmead-Bartlett because he felt it was unfair the official correspondents were allowed to stay permanently at Anzac Cove.

> We assumed – and I think we were told in good faith by William Maxwell the censor – that the step was

> necessary in order to keep Bartlett under control. Sir Ian Hamilton's diary of June 25th however says: 'Bartlett ... wants certain changes made and I have agreed'. So it may have been he that pointed out that our privilege of living at Anzac near the front was unfair to other correspondents.[57]

When Ashmead-Bartlett finally returned to Gallipoli in July he found the censorship was even worse, complaining in his diary: 'I thought there were limits to human stupidity but now I know there are none. The censorship has now passed beyond all reason. They won't let you give expression to the mildest opinions on any subjects ... There are now at least four censors all of whom cut up your stuff ... only a few dry crumbs are left for the wretched public. The articles resemble chicken out of which a thick nutritious broth has been extracted.'[58] In contrast, Charles Bean admitted he rarely needed to be censored at all, almost certainly because he chose in his wartime newspaper stories not to criticise how the war was going. He was clearly favoured by General Hamilton because he was told with a bit of a wink and a nod that, despite the new rules, he would be able to visit Anzac Cove as often as he liked, suggesting perhaps that the move to restrict correspondents was to do with restricting Ashmead-Bartlett's access after all. It is probably unfair to judge Bean's willingness to compromise on his journalistic freedoms with today's media standards, for he believed that supporting the military effort should come ahead of his commitment to telling the full truth to his readers; Ashmead-Bartlett clearly took a different view of his journalistic obligations.

Indeed, at times Bean was in danger of sounding like an obedient head boy at Clifton rather than an intrepid war reporter, such as his obvious pleasure in early July 1915 when the chief censor, Captain Maxwell, congratulated him:

> He said he had hardly had to censor my work at all – that it was much the most complete that had been done here. The reason for rounding the rest of us up was in order to round up Ashmead-Bartlett. They weren't at all satisfied with his proceedings and wanted to have him thoroughly under control … Maxwell told me that Ian Hamilton wanted my dispatches published in London … he had never had a correspondent who had given him so little trouble – all of which was very good hearing.[59]

While at Imbros, Bean was briefed by Ashmead-Bartlett on the failure he felt the entire Gallipoli campaign to be and that he had told people back in England exactly how badly things were going. Bean clearly disapproved of such unauthorised candour: 'It seemed to me to be typically and exactly the thing that a War Correspondent ought not to do. But I am bound to say I think he's a competent man, tho[ugh] certainly inaccurate.'[60]

Ashmead-Bartlett certainly had a point: after three months of stoic Allied attacks against the Turks at Gallipoli, the frontline had barely advanced and the 25,000 Allied troops were packed into a space at Anzac Cove of little more than 1.5 square kilometres, disease and dysentery now rampant. The waste of such good men infuriated Ashmead-Bartlett: 'Men are butchered to make a G.C.B. or a K.C.M.G. These cursed letters after their names are apparently all our leaders think about. It is appalling that the destinies of Empires should be entrusted to such small and petty and inhuman minds.'[61]

As Ashmead-Bartlett wrote this in late July 1915, those commanders responsible were planning a breakout. They planned a final massive surprise push from the Anzac perimeter to capture the Sari Bair Ridge to the north. At the same time, the plan called for the British to focus on taking Suvla Bay. As well but some hours earlier, the 1st Australian Division was to attack at the place known as Lone Pine on the right of the Anzac line. This would work as a feint to deceive the Turkish troops as to the direction of the attack and draw them away from the main effort in the north. As it turned out, the offensive was to be both the proving in blood of the Australian and New Zealand troops yet also the final failure that was to confirm Ashmead-Bartlett's grim pessimism.

Seven

SHEER BLOODY MURDER

Men, you have ten minutes to live.

Lieutenant Colonel Alex White, Victorian 8th Light Horse commander, at The Nek, August 1915

They heard and saw the diversionary attacks begin with the shelling at Helles down the coast, plumes of dirt and smoke from the shelling visible from the hills above Anzac Cove. But on the afternoon of 6 August 1915, the men of Australia's 1st Infantry Brigade were focused on the heavily fortified Turkish parapets atop a position known as Lone Pine. If the Turks could be persuaded that the main attack was to the south of Anzac then it was hoped they would move their troops away from the actual main offensive on the Sari Bair Ridge to the north.

At Lone Pine, a hundred metres of relatively flat ground would have to be traversed under heavy machine-gun fire by the Australians before their charge got them to the Turkish trenches. It was a bright and beautifully warm summer afternoon as men crammed into the parapets of the Australian trenches opposite, a position known as the Pimple, and just before 5.30pm the order came to get ready. The distinctively lanky, ginger-headed and bespectacled figure of Charles Bean was probably a curious sight to the soldiers there as he waited with them in frontline trenches, watching, sketching and making meticulous notes of what he heard. Within a few minutes, so many of the young men now clustering around him would be dead, before they even got to the Turkish trenches. Bean's diary records the beginning of the slaughter: '"Five twenty seven – get ready to go over the parapet", said a young officer crouched in the corner of one fire step glancing at his wristwatch … A whistle sounded and was repeated shrilly along the front. In a scatter of falling bags and earth, the young officer and his men scrambled from the bay.'[1]

Bean was puzzled to see those Australians who did survive the terrifying charge across the no-man's-land now gathering in clumps at the enemy's trenches. It was only later that he was given a description of what they found there: instead of a trench they were confronted with a sandy mound that was the solid covered roof of the fortified Turkish trench position, with loopholes through which the Turks could fire at their attackers. The only way to take it was to crawl into the gallery beneath and fight a bloody hand-to-hand fight through every trench.

> Many were killed within a few minutes of entering, since it was easy for a single Turk at bay beyond a bend and warned by a bayonet coming around it, to shoot one man after another. In several places Australians lay dead four or five deep, having been shot in this manner, sometimes with a heap of Turks similarly killed a few yards distant from them.[2]

As the fighting went on at Lone Pine, Bean walked back through the Pimple trenches to hear his brother Jack had again been seriously wounded and was being evacuated. His notes are full of extraordinary details from that day, drawing from the men he met as he made his way through the Australian positions; fighting at Lone Pine was so close, for instance, that the Australians actually had a peephole straight into a Turkish trench. Despite the enormous disadvantage of the reinforced Turkish trenches, on that first night the Australians managed to hold Lone Pine, but for the next few days the Turks would mount several savage counterattacks to try to win it back. Of the 4600 Australians sent into the fight during the Battle of Lone Pine, nearly half of them would be either killed or wounded, the highest casualties of the campaign, while the Turks suffered more than 7000 casualties, killed or wounded. Australian commanders privately called it a disaster; British commander Ian Hamilton lauded it as a 'desperate … fine feat'.[3]

Bean was walking the tracks late that night, still monitoring the various actions, when his luck finally ran out: a stray round struck him in the upper part of his right leg and, feeling blood, he realised he had been shot. After his wound had been patched at a dressing station, he was limping back to his dugout when he heard distant firing at around 4.30am as dawn was breaking. It was the Turkish response to an attack beginning on the narrow ridge called The Nek, which led from the Australian positions at Russell's Top to the Turkish defences above on a hill the Allies had named Baby 700. Two regiments of the Australian 3rd Light Horse Brigade were engaged in one of the most futile and poignant charges of the campaign.

What happened at The Nek has become the focus for everything that went bad at Gallipoli. The preparatory bombardment unfortunately stopped seven minutes earlier than the planned 4.30am charge and this allowed the Turks to reassemble their defences. Then three waves of Light Horsemen, each of 150 men, consecutively stepped up to the parapet, readying for the suicidal dash towards tier after tier of Turkish trenches and then, up the hill known as Baby 700 beyond. The first wave was mown down within half a minute, a small handful of Australians making it to the Turkish trenches and raising their coloured signal flags before they too were mostly slaughtered. The sight of that flag prompted the second wave two minutes later, and again almost all the men were cut down. It has now become legend that the commander of the 10th Light Horse Regiment, Lieutenant Colonel Noel Brazier, tried to have the third wave cancelled because the whole thing was nothing but 'sheer bloody murder', but instead his men were ordered by Allied command to charge with their rifles unloaded and bayonets fixed.[4] The bodies of hundreds of young Australians who died in this command folly lay thickly where they fell on a patch of ground little bigger than a few tennis courts. Incredibly, a fourth wave of troops was also allowed to follow on and it too was annihilated.

Bean's account of this tragedy in the *Official History of Australia in the War* is a credit to his painstaking collection of the facts, telling the story of The Nek in methodical and painfully moving detail and explaining how the catastrophe occurred, while men on a hill opposite were forced to watch helplessly:

> [T]he Australian line start forward across the skyline and then on a sudden grow limp and sink to the

> earth, 'as though', said one eyewitness, 'the men's limbs had become string'. As a matter of fact many had fallen back into the trench wounded before clearing the parapet. Others, when hit when just beyond it, managed at once to crawl back and tumble over the parapet, thus avoiding the certainty of being hit a second and a third time and killed. Practically all the rest lay dead five or six yards from the parapet.[5]

Perhaps the most poignant account in Bean's history is that of West Australian boys from the 10th Light Horse Regiment climbing into their positions on the parapet as the wounded and dead bodies of their Victorian colleagues are brought down beside them.

> Among the Western Australians who occasionally halted to let them pass, every man assumed that death was certain and each in the secret places of his mind debated how he should go to it. Many seem to have silently determined that they would run forward as swiftly as possible since that course was the simplest and most honourable … Mate having said goodbye to mate, the third line took up its position on the fire-step … The 10th went forward to meet death instantly, as the 8th had done … With that regiment went the flower of the youth of Western Australia, sons of the old pioneering families, youngsters – in some cases two and three from the same home – who had flocked to Perth at the outbreak of war.[6]

When Bean's newspaper report on the 7 August offensive was finally published in Australia towards the end of the month, he hailed the seizing of Lone Pine for the gallant effort that it was but made no mention of the huge and wasteful sacrifice of men. A shrewd reader, though, would have picked up from his very last paragraph that things had gone badly for the Light Horse at The Nek: 'We retain none of the trenches attacked in the fight. But for sheer self-sacrifice and heroism this charge of the Australian Light Horse is unsurpassed in history.'[7] Postwar, when Bean was able to tell the full story without censorship in his official history, he did not hold back in his criticisms of British generals Birdwood and Skeen, who had overseen the feint attacks planned in the August offensive. He also for the first time showed he was prepared to severely criticise Australian commanders: 'For the annihilation of line after line at The Nek the local [Australian] command was, however, chiefly responsible. Although at such crises in a great battle firm action must be taken, sometimes regardless of cost, there could be no valid reason for flinging away the later lines after the first had utterly failed.'[8]

Ten minutes before the Victorian 8th Light Horse Regiment went over the top at The Nek in the first wave, its commander, Lieutenant Colonel Alex White, had gone to say goodbye to the brigade major, John Antill, knowing he was about to die. White had been told not to go into the battle, but knowing his men were heading to almost certain death he determined to be the one who would lead them over. 'Men, you have ten minutes to live,' he was reported as having told them (and, again, it was Bean who recorded these poignant details). White's bullet-riddled body was lying just a dozen steps from that trench a few minutes later as the third wave of troops, the West Australian 10th Light Horse Regiment, stepped up to the parapet. It was

Major John Antill back at the headquarters who refused to cancel the attack; he was under Birdwood's inflexible orders to continue, and he believed the sighting of the signal flag in the Turkish trenches meant Australians there desperately needed support. When the third line had gone and failed to cross that murderous strip of ground, Colonel Brazier desperately tried to stop the needless waste of life in the fourth wave and, as Bean records, he 'again referred to … Antill but was ordered to advance'.[9]

What compounded the tragedy of The Nek is that the fourth line of Light Horsemen attacked before it had even been resolved whether they should go over due to a misunderstanding that the charge had been ordered, and they too advanced straight into the Turkish machine guns. By 6am the entire attack had been brought to a bloody standstill; Bean recorded that the fire the Light Horsemen had walked into was the worst any Australian soldier faced in the entire war. John Antill, a New South Welshman, lived until 1937, and his decision to rigidly obey orders was to see him criticised forever by Bean's official history as the officer who sent hundreds of young men to senseless deaths:

> But it seems certain that Antill at headquarters did not make himself aware of the true position, and, apart from the blunder in timing, it is to this that the heavy loss was mainly due. It may also be argued that the gallant White, acting as a sportsman rather than a soldier, by leading forward the first line, deprived his regiment of the control which should have been exercised over its operations … had his protest been added to Brazier's, Antill might have discontinued the attack.[10]

In the high-tech world of modern twenty-first century communications it is inconceivable such command blunder and resulting slaughter could ever be gagged today by censorship rules on the media. A journalist today would never accept it was not his or her obligation to make legitimate criticisms of a failing campaign, but this was a different time with different standards. However, it must be asked whether even in 1915 there was any good operational security reason why the senseless loss of men across the Gallipoli peninsula could not be reported, other than the incalculable damage it would cause to morale and the prestige of the commanding generals. If readers had been allowed to know about the scandal of The Nek, how would they have responded to the squandering of so many young men's lives? Might not the commanders have been compelled to review their logistics and tactics much earlier?

By the end of August it was clear the entire month-long offensive was a debacle. At its start the British had been able to land at Suvla Bay with few losses, but, confused by conflicting orders and geography, they became disorganised and managed only to secure the hills around the beach area. The Turks were able to consolidate in the overlooking hills and stop them from advancing. Meanwhile, almost all the feint attacks that were meant to support the main Sari Bair assault failed to seize their objectives: at Cape Helles a feint by the British 8th Corps ended with heavy losses; at Anzac Cove the New Zealanders had come close but failed to take the peak of Chunuk Bair; and the attack they were supposed to be supporting – the Light Horse Brigade at The Nek – was a catastrophe. An attack on Hill 971 at Anzac Cove

Charles and his brother Jack, taken in London in the early 1890s, when Charles was about twelve. (Courtesy of Anne Carroll and Edward Bean Le Couteur)

Lucy Bean. (C.E.W. Bean Private Collection, Australian War Memorial)

The small diary which Lucy Bean started for Charles in 1886.
(Courtesy of Anne Carroll and Edward Bean Le Couteur)

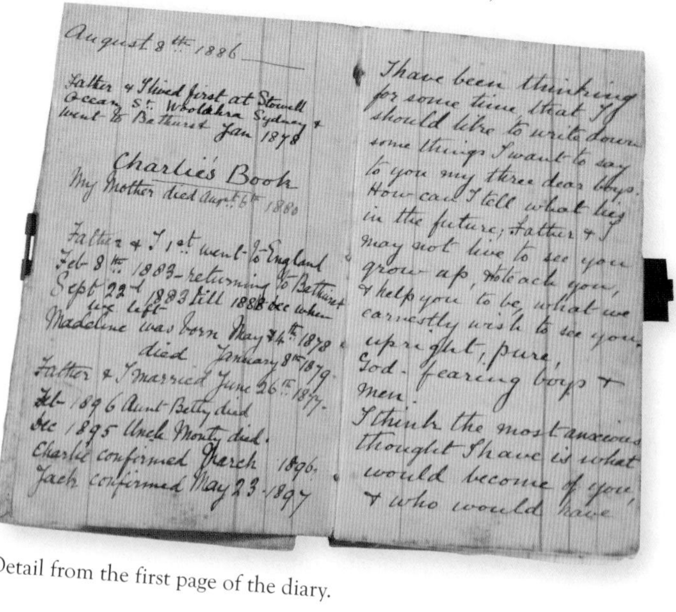
August 8th 1886

Father & I lived first at Stowell Ocean St. Woollahra Sydney & went to Bathurst Jan 1878

Charlie's Book

My Mother died August 6th 1880

Father & I 1st went to England Feb 8th 1883 returning to Bathurst Sept 22nd 1883 till 1888 Dec when we left

Madeline was born May 24th 1878 died January 8th 1879

Father & I married June 26th 1877.

Feb 1896 Aunt Betty died

Dec 1895 Uncle Monty died.

Charlie confirmed March 1896.

Jack confirmed May 23 1897

I have been thinking for some time that I should like to write down some things I want to say to you my three dear boys. How can I tell what lies in the future; Father & I may not live to see you grow up, to teach you, & help you to be, what we earnestly wish to see you upright, pure, God-fearing boys & men!

I think the most anxious thought I have is what would become of you & who would have

Detail from the first page of the diary.

Like father, like son – an Edwin Bean sketch. (C.E.W. Bean Private Collection, Australian War Memorial)

Bean's teenage depiction of a senior British officer underlines his early fascination with the British Army's imperial adventures. (It appears to be a fictional account.) (C.E.W. Bean Private Collection, Australian War Memorial)

A young Charles Bean's watercolour – most probably depicting the Battle of Waterloo. (C.E.W. Bean Private Collection, Australian War Memorial)

Edwin and Lucy Bean with the students and teachers of Brentwood School.
(C.E.W. Bean Private Collection, Australian War Memorial)

Bean in the cricket team during his first year at Clifton.
(C.E.W. Bean Private Collection, Australian War Memorial)

Thoby Stephen photographed in 1898, during his time at Clifton College. Bean kept a copy of this picture in an album and had a framed photograph of Stephen in his study. (Courtesy of Anne Carroll and Edward Bean Le Couteur)

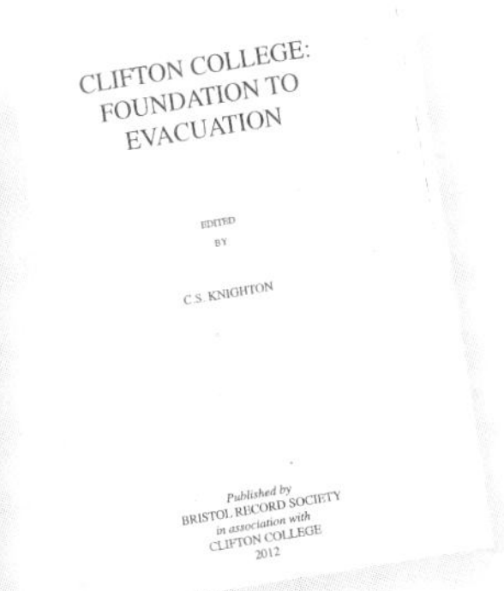

CLIFTON COLLEGE: FOUNDATION TO EVACUATION

EDITED BY

C.S. KNIGHTON

Published by
BRISTOL RECORD SOCIETY
in association with
CLIFTON COLLEGE
2012

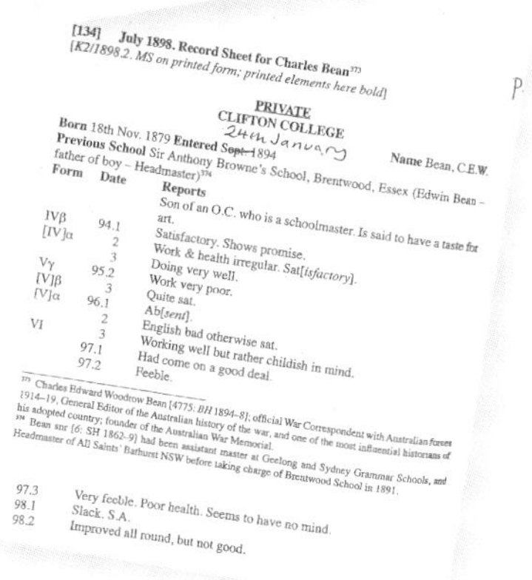

[134] July 1898. Record Sheet for Charles Bean[373]
[K2/1898.2. MS on printed form; printed elements here bold]

P.

PRIVATE
CLIFTON COLLEGE

Born 18th Nov. 1879 **Entered** ~~Sept.~~ 24th January 1894 **Name** Bean, C.E.W.
Previous School Sir Anthony Browne's School, Brentwood, Essex (Edwin Bean – father of boy – Headmaster)[374]

Form **Date** **Reports**

Son of an O.C. who is a schoolmaster. Is said to have a taste for art.
IVβ 94.1
[IV]α 2 Satisfactory. Shows promise.
3 Work & health irregular. Sat[*isfactory*].
Vγ 95.2 Doing very well.
[V]β 3 Work very poor.
[V]α 96.1 Quite sat.
2 Ab[*sent*].
VI 3 English bad otherwise sat.
97.1 Working well but rather childish in mind.
97.2 Had come on a good deal.
Feeble.

[373] Charles Edward Woodrow Bean [4775: *BH* 1894–8]; official War Correspondent with Australian forces 1914–19, General Editor of the Australian history of the war, and one of the most influential historians of his adopted country; founder of the Australian War Memorial.
[374] Bean snr [6: SH 1862–9] had been assistant master at Geelong and Sydney Grammar Schools, and Headmaster of All Saints' Bathurst NSW before taking charge of Brentwood School in 1891.

97.3 Very feeble. Poor health. Seems to have no mind.
98.1 Slack. S.A.
98.2 Improved all round, but not good.

Bean's own rendition of himself as a cricketer.

One of Bean's school reports from Clifton College. (Courtesy of Dr Knighton, archivist, Clifton College)

Bean's house photograph from his final year, when he was made head of the house over Thoby Stephen. Bean is in the middle, seated, wearing a boater. Stephen sits two places to his right, looking decidedly grumpy. (Courtesy of Clifton College)

Monty, Charles and Jack, early 1900s. (Courtesy of Anne Carroll and Edward Bean Le Couteur)

The Brentwood 'old boys' cricket team. Monty is seated first on left, Charles third from left, and Jack fourth from left.

(C.E.W. Bean Private Collection, Australian War Memorial)

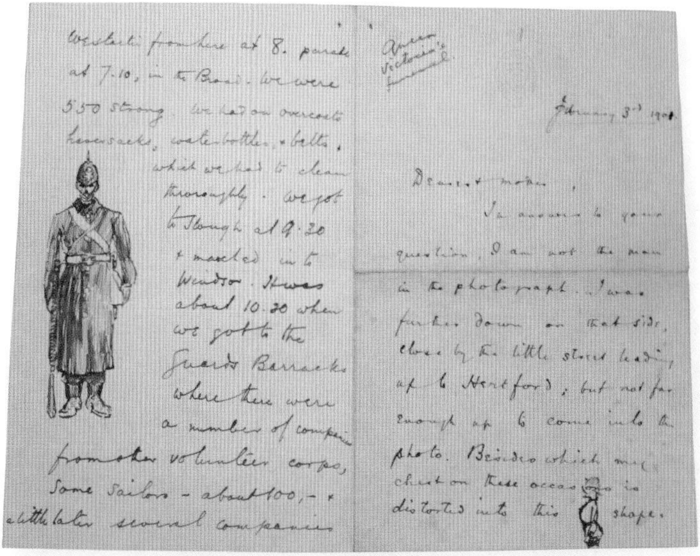

We started from here at 8. parade at 7.10, in the Broad. We were 550 strong. We had on overcoats haversacks, waterbottles, & belts, which we had to clean thoroughly. We got to Slough at 9.20 & marched in to Windsor. It was about 10.20 when we got to the Guards Barracks where there were a number of companies from other volunteer corps, some sailors – about 100, – & a little later several companies

Queen Victoria's funeral

February 3rd 1901.

Dearest mother,

In answer to your question, I am not the man in the photograph. I was further down on that side, close by the little street leading up to Hertford, but not far enough up to come into the photo. Besides which my chest on these occasions is distorted into this shape.

A letter from Bean to his mother describing his Oxford University battalion's participation in the funeral of Queen Victoria, 1901.

(C.E.W. Bean Private Collection, Australian War Memorial)

of Gravelotte. On Wednesday (the battle of Colomby in which the Jägers were foremost) there was a parade, & they marched past – notice the legs! (the parade march on state occasions)

splendid for a march

Here is the march past. The tune was

This is the kind of painting I have been doing lately to

A rare photograph of Bean 'robed' as a barrister, taken around 1905.
(Courtesy of Anne Carroll and Edward Bean Le Couteur)

Bean at Brentwood when he was back in England for *The Sydney Morning Herald* between 1910 and 1913 and, below, with the machine he helped to construct for batting practice.
(C.E.W Bean Private Collection, Australian War Memorial)

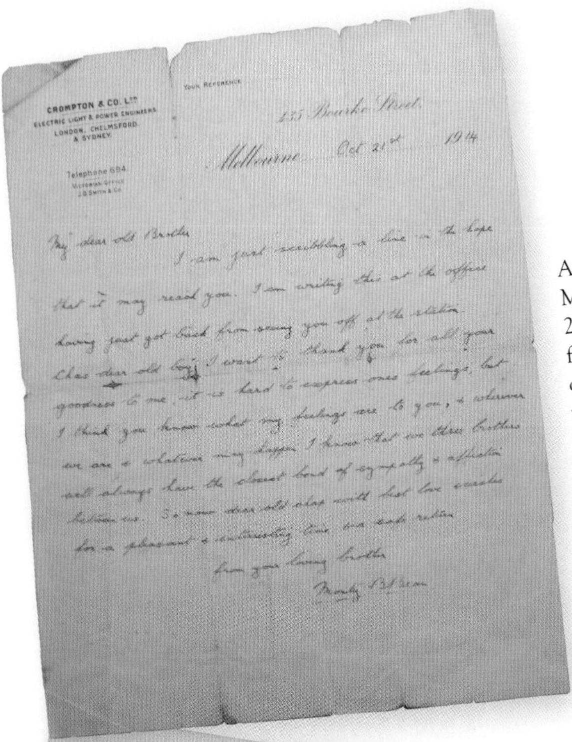

CROMPTON & CO. LTD.
ELECTRIC LIGHT & POWER ENGINEERS
LONDON, CHELMSFORD & SYDNEY.

Telephone 694
VICTORIAN OFFICE J.G. SMITH & CO.

YOUR REFERENCE

435 Bourke Street
Melbourne Oct 21st 1914

My dear old Brother

I am just scribbling a line in the hope that it may reach you. I am writing this at the office having just got back from seeing you off at the station. Chas dear old boy I want to thank you for all your goodness to me, it is hard to express ones feelings, but I think you know what my feelings are to you, & wherever we are & whatever may happen I know that we three brothers will always have the closest bond of sympathy & affection between us. So now dear old chap with best love wishes for a pleasant & interesting time & a safe return

from your loving brother

Monty B. Bean

A letter from Monty Bean, 21 October 1914, farewelling his older brother off to war – and, below, Bean's postcard to his brother from the Suez Canal, dated 24 November of the same year. (C.E.W. Bean Private Collection, Australian War Memorial)

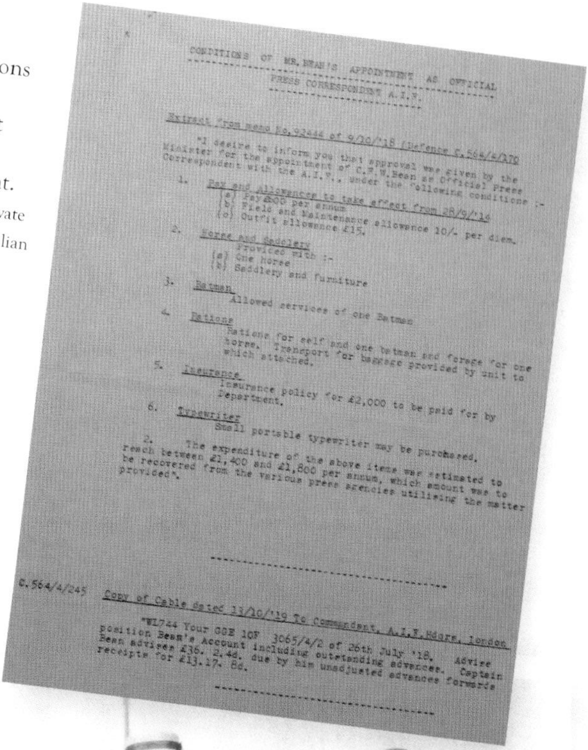

CONDITIONS OF MR. BEAN'S APPOINTMENT AS OFFICIAL
PRESS CORRESPONDENT A.I.F.

Extract from memo No.92444 of 9/10/'18 (Defence C.564/4/270

"I desire to inform you that approval was given by the Minister for the appointment of C.E.W.Bean as Official Press Correspondent with the A.I.F., under the following conditions :-

1. Pay and Allowances to take effect from 28/9/'14
   (a) Pay £600 per annum
   (b) Field and Maintenance allowance 10/- per diem.
   (c) Outfit allowance £15.
2. Horse and Saddlery
   Provided with :-
   (a) One horse
   (b) Saddlery and furniture
3. Batman.
   Allowed services of one Batman
4. Rations
   Rations for self and one batman and forage for one horse. Transport for baggage provided by unit to which attached.
5. Insurance.
   Insurance policy for £2,000 to be paid for by Department.
6. Typewriter
   Small portable typewriter may be purchased.

2. The expenditure of the above items was estimated to reach between £1,400 and £1,800 per annum, which amount was to be recovered from the various press agencies utilising the matter provided".

C.564/4/245 Copy of Cable dated 13/10/'19 To Commandant, A.I.F.Hdqrs, London

"WL744 Your GGE 10F 3065/4/2 of 26th July '18. Advise position Bean's Account including outstanding advances. Captain Bean advises £36. 2.4d. due by him unadjusted advances forwards receipts for £13.17. 8d.

The conditions of Bean's appointment as official correspondent. (C.E.W. Bean Private Collection, Australian War Memorial)

Edwin Bean, Charles Bean, Archie Whyte (editor of *The Age* and the man who championed Bean for official correspondent) and Phillip 'Peter' Schuler, correspondent for *The Age*. Taken in September or October 1914, around the time Bean became official correspondent. (Australian War Memorial)

Bean outside his tent at the Mena Camp near Cairo, 1914 or 1915.
(Australian War Memorial)

Standing on a pyramid on New Year's Day, 1915, overlooking Mena Camp. This photograph was taken by Phillip 'Peter' Schuler.
(Australian War Memorial)

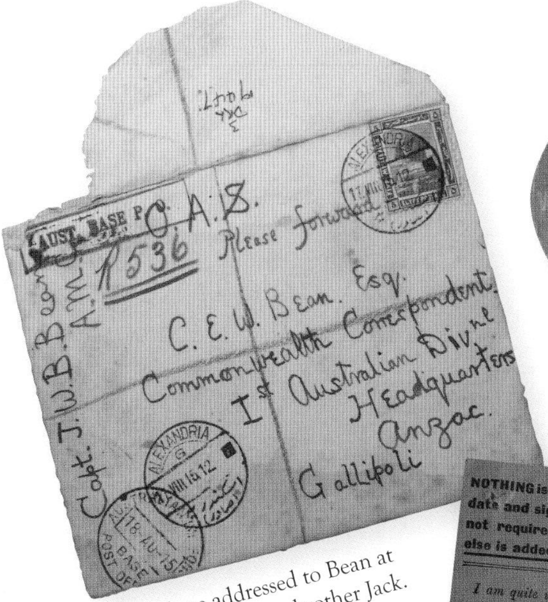

Bean's official 'dog tag'.
(C.E.W. Bean Private Collection, Australian War Memorial)

Envelope addressed to Bean at Gallipoli from his brother Jack.
(C.E.W. Bean Private Collection, Australian War Memorial)

A Field Service Postcard from Bean to his father dated 30 April 1915, five days after the landing at Gallipoli.
(C.E.W. Bean Private Collection, Australian War Memorial)

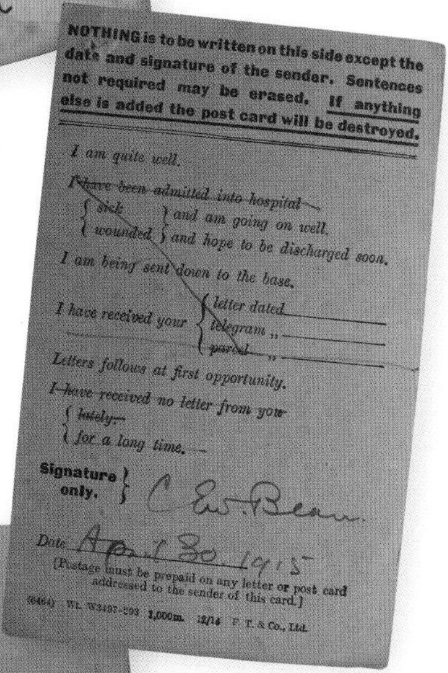

NOTHING is to be written on this side except the date and signature of the sender. Sentences not required may be erased. If anything else is added the post card will be destroyed.

I am quite well.

I have been admitted into hospital
{sick / wounded} and am going on well. / and hope to be discharged soon.

I am being sent down to the base.

I have received your {letter dated / telegram ,, / parcel ,,}

Letters follows at first opportunity.

I have received no letter from you
{lately. / for a long time.}

Signature only. C.E.W. Bean

Date April 30. 1915

[Postage must be prepaid on any letter or post card addressed to the sender of this card.]

(6464) Wt. W3497-293 1,000m. 12/14 F. T. & Co., Ltd.

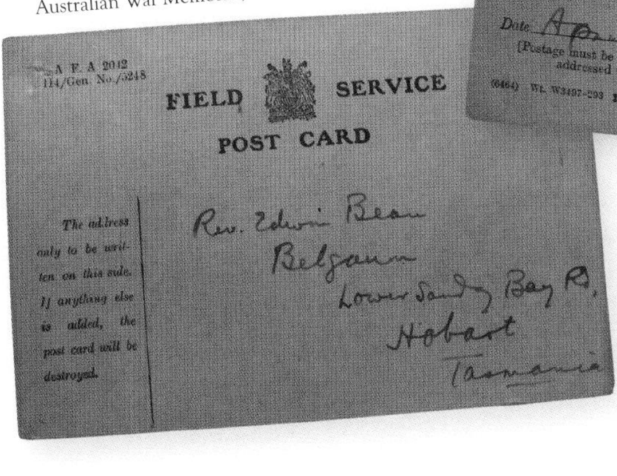

A. F. A. 2042
114/Gen. No./5248

FIELD SERVICE

POST CARD

The address only to be written on this side. If anything else is added, the post card will be destroyed.

Rev. Edwin Bean
Belgaum
Lower Sandy Bay Rd,
Hobart
Tasmania

Bean's cousins outside their dugout on Gallipoli: Arthur Maxwell, 6 feet 5 inches; and Duncan Maxwell, 6 feet 3 inches.
(Australian War Memorial)

Bean and Ashmead-Bartlett taking a break from Gallipoli on the island of Imbros, August 1915.
(Australian War Memorial)

Cyril Brudenell White and Neville Howse, photographed by Bean outside the 1st Divisional Headquarters, White Gully, Gallipoli in August 1915. (Australian War Memorial)

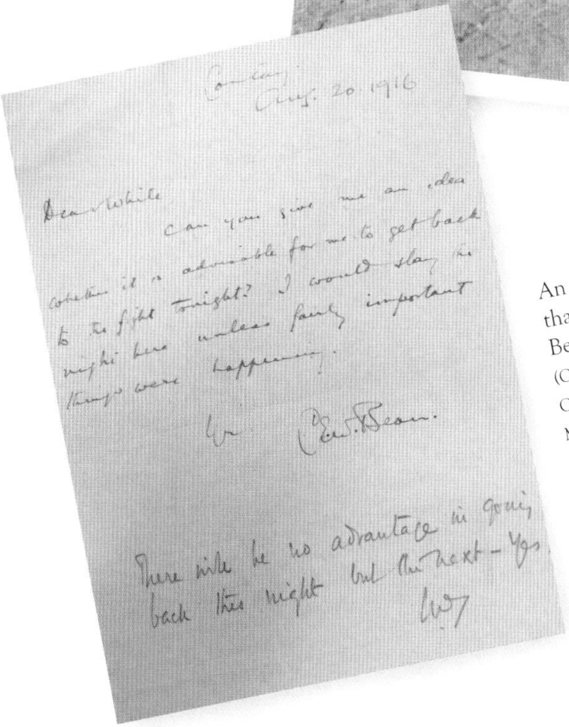

Contay
Aug. 20 1916

Dear White

Can you give me an idea whether it is advisable for me to get back to the fight tonight? I would stay the night here unless fairly important things were happening.

Yrs C.E.W. Bean.

There will be no advantage in going back this night but the next – Yes.

CBW

An example of the notes that passed between Bean and White. (C.E.W. Bean Private Collection, Australian War Memorial)

Bean's sketch of the Battle of Krithia, depicting the revolver in McCay's hand.
(Bean's diary, AWM38 3DRL 606/37/1 p. 50)

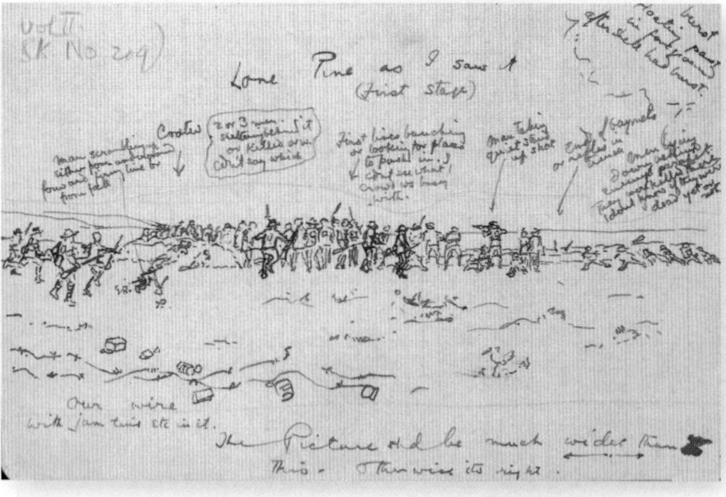

'Lone Pine as I saw it', August 1915. (Bean's diary, AWM38 3DRL 606/37/1 p. 51)

also failed because the Australian and Indian soldiers lost their way during the night, and then the Turks beat off a subsequent attack. Colonel Malone's New Zealanders had done their heroic best to hold out at Chunuk Bair, but when British regiments relieved the position they soon lost the Kiwi gains and were slaughtered in a counterattack. The one bit of good news was the extraordinary Australian achievement at Lone Pine but it was achieved at a horrendous cost, and even that victory was a liability because now the Turks could shell their former position from the Baby 700 hill they held overhead. Lone Pine remained the most dangerous place on Gallipoli until the withdrawal later in the year.

In his diary notes, Bean was scathing about Brigadier General John Monash, who led the Australian 4th Infantry Brigade in a failed assault on a position known as Hill 971:

> Shrapnel was pouring on them going up valley – men were deadly tired, and so Monash did not push on but dug in on the ridge nearer this way ... It seems to me a decision which many weak commanders would make but utterly unjustifiable. That is to say – instead of pushing on in spite of fatigue till he was actually stopped by the enemy[,] he stopped short of his objective without being stopped.[11]

There is no other way to put it: the Turks had routed the Allied invaders, with a few isolated exceptions. Charles Bean's diary shows he knew the Allied commanders had poorly planned the offensive, that the Australians were not always well led, and that the entire August operation was a miserable failure, but he still felt obliged to put his best spin on the shambles in his news report, presumably because he knew it was the only way to get any kind of story past the censor. It was stirring stuff, but one can only imagine how he choked on the celebratory words as he wrote:

> From the whole history of this fierce fighting one thing stands clear – that the force did all that men could do. Our troops were magnificently led and when the full history comes to be written I have not the slightest doubt that it will figure as one of the most glorious episodes in the history of this or any army.[12]

That full history of the August offensive was of course eventually written by Charles Bean a few years after the war, and while he did acknowledge in his official history the exemplary heroics of many of the Australians and New Zealanders across Anzac Cove, he did not cast it as a glorious episode but, truthfully, as the failure that it was. He revealed General Hamilton had asked for 100,000 more troops to achieve the final breakthrough in the Dardanelles that he had so far totally failed to achieve, but in August the general was told the priority was now France and he was refused[13]. Bean wrote that the British government did not appear to understand the extent of the looming catastrophe in the Dardanelles. This realisation came only when Hamilton telegraphed London warning that because of rampant sickness among the troops he only had 50,000 men to defend a length of 21 kilometres, and that he would have to evacuate either Suvla Bay or Anzac Cove. It created a crisis in London about Hamilton's leadership at Gallipoli, and paranoia developed in the British War Cabinet that it was not getting the full story from Lord Kitchener of what was happening there.

Around this time there was also a distinct turn in Bean's private observations about the British, reflecting perhaps the attitude inside the Australian 1st Division headquarters where he was based at Anzac Cove. No longer was he the ardent Anglophile he had been as a younger man, noting the Australian troops' hard-won respect for the New Zealanders and the Gurkhas, and their new contempt for the quality of the British Tommies:

> they (and the NZ men too) do not trust the Tommy ... they have not the slightest confidence in K's [Kitchener's] Army – nor have our officers – nor have I. The truth is that after 100 years of breeding in slums, the British race is not the same, and can't be expected to be the same as in the days of Waterloo. It is breeding one fine class at the expense of all the rest. The only hope is that those puny narrow-chested little men may, if they come out to Australia or NZ or Canada, within two generations breed men again. England herself, unless she does something heroic, cannot hope to.[14]

Bean had elected to stay at Gallipoli despite his bullet wound, and while he recuperated in his dugout at Anzac Cove he reached a very low ebb, weak from dysentery and his healing wound. One of those who came to visit him in early September was the journalist he'd beaten to the job of official correspondent, Keith Murdoch. Asked by the Australian Prime Minister Andrew Fisher to investigate concerns about the AIF's postal service between Gallipoli and Australia, Murdoch had asked General Hamilton for permission to visit Gallipoli. Hamilton had sent the authority from Imbros for Murdoch to travel to Anzac Cove, but it was a decision he would soon come to bitterly regret.

Eight

THE PUBLIC CAN NEVER KNOW IT

... the Government does not need war correspondents – it simply tells the people what it thinks will conduce towards winning the war. If truth is good for the war it tells them truth; if a lie is likely to win the war it tells them lies.

Colonel William Tyrrell, chief of military intelligence, Gallipoli

Charles Bean was still struggling with illness when Keith Murdoch made his short visit to Anzac Cove in early September 1915. Autumn had set in and the weather was increasingly chilly and wet, with icy winds blowing off the Aegean Sea. There was often thick mud and overflowing effluent underfoot, and disease was rife among the Allied army. Like many of the troops, Bean was stricken with diarrhoea and dysentery so was barely able to get up off his dugout camp bed to show the Australian correspondent around. So Murdoch took himself to headquarters to see Major General Harold Walker, the British commander of the Australian 1st Division, and he also climbed up the steep track to tour the now legendary position at Lone Pine. Just before Murdoch left Gallipoli, on his final day on the peninsula,

Bean was well enough to show him around Quinn's Post, the Australian frontline post surrounded on three sides by Turkish positions, a scene of constant fighting and bombing since the landing.

Murdoch travelled to the main Allied headquarters on the Greek island of Imbros, just across from Gallipoli, and found a place to stay at the press correspondents' camp near Hamilton's headquarters. He soon struck up a friendship with the London *Daily Telegraph*'s correspondent, Ellis Ashmead-Bartlett, who was well known on the island for his lavish spending on fine liquor and having his own personal chef. Endowed with great charm and engaging conversation and a magnet for any visitor to the camp, Ashmead-Bartlett was also soon impressing Murdoch with his grim views on the British Army's conduct of the war on the peninsula. As the hours went by, no doubt over more than a few glasses of Ellis's fine claret or champagne, the Australian began to realise there was an extraordinary failure of command at Gallipoli that, because of strict censorship, was not being revealed.

What the experienced war correspondent had strongly impressed on Murdoch was that the entire Dardanelles operation was a fiasco and at serious risk of failing during the coming winter. Ashmead-Bartlett had already crystallised his pessimistic take on the campaign in an earlier newspaper report that was gagged by General Hamilton and his staff, so at the urging of the young Australian he agreed to set out his views again in a letter to British Prime Minister Asquith, which Murdoch agreed to secretly carry to London. Both men knew this was probably a technical breach of the British censorship rules and the standard press correspondent's undertaking, which Murdoch had also signed, but they judged the looming catastrophe too serious to not bring the issue to the attention of the British government. Why, they no doubt reasoned, should the British prime minister of all people not be told about the grim state of the campaign, no matter the military's self-serving attempts to gag the story?

When Murdoch left Imbros for England he had Ashmead-Bartlett's confidential dispatch in his baggage, but someone in the correspondents' camp had betrayed the men. On arriving in Marseilles, Murdoch was detained by military police and told to hand the letter over. To this day no one knows for sure who tipped off General Hamilton's headquarters, but most suspicion falls, probably unfairly, on Henry Nevinson, the *Guardian* correspondent. Nevinson, a highly experienced and respected war correspondent, was also a fierce critic of the heavy censorship on Gallipoli; his own first dispatch on the landing had been blocked for four months for no good reason, so if he was the mole then it would appear to be out of character. Nevinson always denied being the spy and he pointed the blame at a Royal Navy photographer who was in the camp at the time. Bean suggested it was a British Army private called Murray who worked for the censors; the correspondents subsequently ensured he was fired from their Imbros camp.[1]

When Murdoch finally made it back to London in late September he wrote everything he could remember of Ashmead-Bartlett's dispatch down in a letter addressed to Andrew Fisher, the Australian prime minister, and subsequently passed it on to the British cabinet. He did not pull his punches:

> I now write of the unfortunate Dardanelles expedition ... It is undoubtedly one of the most

> terrible chapters in our history. Your fears have been justified. I have not military knowledge to be able to say whether the enterprise ever had a chance of succeeding. Certainly there has been a series of disastrous underestimations ... The first two efforts, those of the fleet alone and of the combined forces in April–May, failed miserably because London expected far too much from floating artillery ... The last great effort, that of August 6–21, was a costly and bloody fiasco because, in addition to wretched staff work, the troops sent were inadequate and of a most uneven quality. That failure has created a situation which even yet has not been seriously faced – i.e: a choice between withdrawal of our armies and hanging on for a fresh offensive after winter.[2]

Murdoch's letter cannot have been a complete revelation especially after Ashmead-Bartlett had personally briefed Asquith on how dire things were there during his earlier visit in June. It did however cause a stir.

Writing in compelling journalese, with a dollop of occasional exaggeration, Murdoch explained why the Dardanelles operation was a complete failure. He frankly told them how 'no serious advance could be made direct inland' from Anzac Cove because of the hilly country that favoured the Turkish defenders, and he correctly pointed out that while Lone Pine had been hailed as a brilliant victory, Australia had lost 2500 men for an advance of some 300 yards (275 metres). He savaged the British commanders for allowing inexperienced soldiers to be landed at Suvla Bay 'without any orders whatsoever' and for their logistics supply failures, which meant there was a serious water shortage for the landing British troops in the summer heat that may have thwarted the securing of a crucial hill position.

> The work of the general staff in Gallipoli has been deplorable … The August 6–10 operations at Suvla left us holding a position which is nothing more than an embarrassment. We are about one mile and a half inland; but we do not hold a single commanding point nor one of real strategic value … Winter is on us and it brings grave danger … Can we keep the armies supplied? … Many mariners and some naval men say no … The new offensive must then be made with a huge army of new troops. Can we get them? Already the complaint in France is that we cannot fill the gaps, that after an advance our thinned ranks must be replenished …[3]

Murdoch also skewered General Hamilton, suggesting he should be recalled because the army had completely lost faith in him. This was possibly Murdoch over-reaching himself, with a lot of help from Ashmead-Bartlett. Before the letter was even sent to Australia, Murdoch showed it to cabinet minister Lloyd George, who immediately insisted it also be shown to Prime Minister Asquith. Before so much as checking the letter's allegations with Kitchener, the prime minister immediately ordered the letter to be printed as a submission for the attention of the Dardanelles Committee, the government body nominally in charge of the campaign. Back at Gallipoli, told of Ashmead-Bartlett's role in trying to smuggle the original letter to Britain, General Hamilton was delighted to be able to move against his nemesis, telling him no doubt with some relish that he had instructions from the War Office to dismiss him from the battle zone forthwith. A still frail Charles Bean admitted in his diary he had initially said 'Lucky Beggar' when he heard the correspondent was leaving, but as it became clear Ashmead-Bartlett was being sent home for breaking the censorship rules Bean was defensive of his friend, though clearly torn about the propriety of what he had done.

> It was a brilliantly written letter – rather overstating the case as Bartlett always does, but a great deal of it was absolutely unanswerable and badly needs understanding[4] … He made one mistake – I think. He ought to have taken the letter home himself … unless he went I don't think the letter could have got through – the censors would not have passed it. So he decided that the object was worth any means[5] … Hamilton received a wire from the War Office telling him that Bartlett must be recalled[6] … I have been as loyal as I could possibly be – have brought myself into constant trouble in Australia by being loyal to military rules; my own Australian staff knows that it can trust me to the uttermost – but this little bounder [the British censor] the British War Office has put over us is trying to put every difficulty he can in my way.[7]

Bean was also wrestling with his private disdain for the work of many of the other correspondents he was working with on Imbros; it was the beginning of his great disillusionment with popular journalism and the dawn of his far greater interest in becoming Australia's official historian. In one diary note he lamented the 'wretched cant' in the newspapers, especially the writing of Ashmead-Bartlett, which – while popular and stirring for his readers – was often loose with the truth and prone to absurdly glorifying the bloody nastiness of warfare, saying:

> that is why I can't write about bayonet charges like some of the correspondents do. Ashmead-Bartlett makes it a little difficult for one by his exaggerations, and yet he's a lover of the truth. He gives the spirit of the thing: but if he were asked: 'Did a shout really go up from a thousand throats that the hill was ours?' he'd have to say 'No it didn't'. Or if they said 'Did the New Zealanders really club their rifles and kill three men at once?' or 'Did the first battle of Anzac really end with the flash of bayonets all along the line, a charge, and the rolling back of the Turkish attack,' he'd have to say 'Well – no, as a matter of fact that didn't occur.' Well I can't write that it occurred if I know it did not, even if by painting it that way I could rouse the blood and make the pulse beat faster – and undoubtedly these men here deserve that people's pulses shall beat for them. But war correspondents have so habitually exaggerated the heroism of battles that people don't realise that the real actions are heroic. If you say 'The line went forward and not one man came back' – that is really a thing that can very seldom be said of any but the most magnificent troops … As a matter of fact everyone who has seen a battle knows that soldiers do very often run away; that soldiers, even Australian soldiers, have sometimes to be threatened with a revolver to make them go on – in individual cases.[8]

Nowhere in Bean's diary notes does he ever admit to feeling overwhelmed by the horror of the carnage he witnessed in his time on Gallipoli. Neither did his family see any signs of emotional trauma from his war experiences later in life, which is surprising in light of what he experienced. Perhaps the closest he came was during this period when he spent more time in the tent provided for him in an olive grove on Imbros, bitterly resenting the misleading populist triumphalism in the dispatches of the other correspondents after months of failures and losses in the peninsula campaign. What seems to have caused Bean the most emotional distress was this 'wretched cant' which he knew misrepresented to the public what was really happening, but it does seem to have been lost on Bean that, because of censorship, he was not telling the full story either. If there was a credo that came to define Charles Bean, this was it:

> There is plenty of heroism in war – it teems with it. But it has been so overwritten that if you write that a man did his job people say: Oh but there's nothing heroic in that! Isn't there? You come here and see the job and understand it and get out of your head the nonsense that is written about it. There is horror and beastliness and cowardice and treachery, over all of which the writer, anxious to please the public, has to throw his cloak – but the man who does his job is a hero. And the actual truth is that though not all Australians, by any means, do their job, there is a bigger proportion of men in the Australian Army that try to do it cheerfully and without the least show of fear, than in any force or army that I have seen in Gallipoli. The man who knows war knows that this is

> magnificent praise. The public can never know it … One has some satisfaction in sticking to the truth in spite of the prejudice against it – the satisfaction of putting up a sort of fight. But I have a suspicion that I've spoilt my chances forever of being some day tolerably well off.[9]

The other absurdity of the British military's censorship rule was its double standard, with letters and photographs sent by soldiers home – or as Bean put it,

> any swindler, or, at any rate, rule-breaker of an officer who gets a film or photo smuggled home past the censor to have it published in the London press – which has perfect impunity in publishing it, in advertising [and] requesting officers in flat defiance of orders to send similar photographs in, and in booming £1000 prizes for them. It censors rigorously all the names of officers and regiments out of my letters – written by one who actually saw them: and allows them to be picked up and forwarded second hand in a bundle of exaggerations and untruths quite uncensored from Cairo.[10]

One London newspaper even published an uncensored soldier's photograph of the new trench periscopes being used with great success on Gallipoli, which was a huge secrecy breach at the time. 'If they would give more attention to censoring facts which assist the enemy and less to censoring facts which may show the public what blunders they have made (or at any rate what danger the country is in) they would be taking at least one step towards winning the war.'[11]

Then Bean received news from the defence department in Melbourne that must have been devastating for him to hear: the proprietors of *The Argus* and *The Age* newspapers had decided to stop using his news stories because they were of 'insufficient interest to them'.[12] It was a slap in the face for the official correspondent, and he angrily rationalised that the two newspapers would probably be happier taking stories from correspondents based out of Cairo because their reports, unhindered by the stringent censorship rules, would arrive in Australia a lot earlier. Bean wrote that *The Argus* preferred its news to come from Reuters rather than the official government correspondent. Yet most of the Reuters stories, he said, were 'wild sensational inventions' (and, as was later revealed, often controlled by the British military) whereas he 'risked my life hundreds of times over on the spot itself in order that they may know that every word is as true as it can be'.[13]

Bean was also beginning to feel the heat about his work from critics in Australia. The *Bulletin* magazine was vicious regarding Bean's copy, mocking his minute-by-minute account of the landing:

> When another man ... would be forging thunderbolts Bean is eternally watchmaking under fire. One of his articles was as precise a specimen of journalistic horology as I have ever seen. It was that formal diary written under fire and timed by a stopwatch of the development of a trench attack. Each paragraph began '3.45', '3.50', '3.57' and so on – and there wasn't a thrill in a column of it ... Such a man could do algebra while Rome was burning ... [D]espite his slickness in getting the news, Bean pants

> bravely along the track with a millstone about his neck and a padlock on his soul.[14]

At the same time, he also clashed with the British intelligence chief at the main Imbros headquarters, Colonel William Tyrrell, clearly a living parody of the Colonel Blimp satire: he suggested to Bean that war correspondents were a 'dying profession'. Bean argued back that the old style of war correspondent was indeed dying, in a clear reference to those who were prepared to corrupt their journalism by telling untruths, riposting that the new generation of correspondent like himself was instead keen to give the public actual news of their troops.

> They can't send away an expedition overseas and then put up with absolute silence about it … It does no harm to any conceivable military interest to tell the people how their sons and brothers live, how they fight, what a battle looks like – and that can be done a thousand times better by a journalist than a staff officer … Tyrrell could not understand this in the least – at any rate he didn't seem to. His point of view was: 'If the people is properly organised the authorities need not tell them anything at all' … Secondly, he had a different ground: 'In a properly organised nation the Government does not need war correspondents – it simply tells the people what it thinks will conduce towards winning the war. If truth is good for the war it tells them truth; if a lie is likely to win the war it tells them lies. At the present moment I believe that the truth would do good … But the regulations tie my hands – you see I can't

> help myself. In any case the one aim the Government and people possess in war time is to win the war and if telling lies to the people will win the war then the authorities should tell lies to them.'[15]

Bean was scandalised by the intelligence chief's views, which is no doubt why he detailed them in his diary for posterity. He felt that men like Tyrrell failed to understand that the way in which a war was won could do more harm than defeat.

> Think, for example, of the enormous damage that you do to a nation's powers in peace if you destroy all the confidence the public has in the Government's official statements (that damage has been done in this war to the credit of the British Government). You may destroy the belief of all the small nations in your nation's honesty or humanity … Therefore I think the nation must have as true an account of the war as military necessity can possibly permit … you can't have the war correspondent running a modern war; but I do think the people of any modern state worth living in will require some sort of information at least partly independent of their generals and general staffs as to what is happening and they are not getting that in this war.[16]

As usual, Ellis Ashmead-Bartlett had the best last word on the issue, when Bean told him about Tyrrell's appalling comments later that day back at the camp: '"He thinks we're dying does he," said Bartlett tonight. "Well I'm glad we're dying game!"'[17]

In London, concern about the leadership of General Hamilton had been brewing for some time and the Murdoch letter underlined the alarm. On 17 October, Bean and the other correspondents at Imbros were shocked to hear that General Hamilton was to be relieved of his command at Gallipoli. 'It came as a bolt from the blue,' Bean wrote.[18] Ashmead-Bartlett of course was not surprised in the slightest; before he left Imbros he had bet one of his fellow correspondents that Hamilton would be gone before the end of September – he lost the ten-pound bet by just a couple of weeks. Bean felt for Hamilton: 'The poor old chap looked to me very haggard, almost broken up,' Bean noted. 'So were some of the staff … I am honestly very sorry to see Hamilton go. He is a gentleman and has always been courteous and considerate to us. The British Army has never believed in him.'[19] Revealingly, Bean privately agreed with the criticism that Hamilton was too weak – 'He has not the strength to command his staff, they command him' – and that when things were at their worst on Gallipoli the commander was incapable of acknowledging his plan had failed. 'The British public certainly was utterly deceived as to the difficulties and the obvious failure.'[20]

As the winter set in at Gallipoli, Bean's growing private contempt for the incompetent British command became obvious; on one occasion he lamented in his notes the fact that there was not enough corrugated iron to provide the men in the trenches with shelter from the rain and snow. Yet, he privately wrote, at the same time as the soldiers were suffering across at Anzac Cove for the lack of just one sheet of iron to cover their trench, the general headquarters on nearby Imbros was using twenty sheets of iron on each of the latrines it had installed for its officers and their batmen.

He did not attempt to write the news story; that would most definitely have been censored.

He and White, the headquarters chief of staff (who had been appointed to the rank of brigadier general in early October), had also become firm friends; one night their conversation turned to a certain telling pride in the distinctiveness of the Australians at Anzac Cove, men with 'strong, lined, individual faces which men get who stand and think by themselves'. They talked about how the British could only get their men to advance by ordering them to do so but that the Australian military ran on the idea of the 'strong independent willed men carrying on the weak one'. Bean confided in his friend that what he had seen of the imperial British Army shambles at Suvla Bay 'is making me a socialist'. White's response: '"It's not making me that," he said, but I'll tell you what I should like to tell the people of Australia, what – if I get the chance I shall tell them some day – and that is that they are right in one main thing: they may be wrong in details but – I'm no politician as you know but I'm sure they're right in this – in giving every man a chance, a good equal chance.'[21] It was significant that two men born and raised in colonial Australia, inculcated in the glorification of imperial England, no longer thought of themselves as wholly English and, because of their experiences at Gallipoli, were both becoming increasingly disdainful of the empire's rulers.

White made an extraordinary admission to Bean about the extent to which he believed Winston Churchill, a member of the War Cabinet until he was forced to resign over the Dardanelles debacle in November 1915, was responsible for the catastrophe at Gallipoli. He said: 'We know that Winston Churchill is responsible for the deaths of at least 25 per cent of the men who have fallen at Gallipoli – almost as directly responsible as if he had shot them. Well what happens to him – a man like that ought to be hanged as surely as any criminal.'[22] It was 40 years before Bean revealed White's angry criticism. In 1957 he described a version of White's comments in his book *Two Men I Knew*, but perhaps because Churchill was still alive at the time he chose not to mention that an Australian general had thought the British cabinet minister was a war criminal, instead carefully saying that 'in White's opinion he was responsible for a great part of the loss of men on Gallipoli "almost as directly as if he shot them"'.[23]

As the winter set in, the talk back in London increasingly focused on whether Allied forces in the Dardanelles should be withdrawn. General Hamilton had believed withdrawal would probably cost the loss of half the entire force and most of the armaments and supplies. His replacement, General Charles Monro, soon realised the imminent likelihood of a Crimean War–style catastrophe if his force stayed on the peninsula during the winter. On 12 November 1915, Bean was given the tip by White that the British secretary of state for war, Lord Kitchener, would be visiting Anzac Cove that day. By now renowned as the poster boy for Britain's volunteer army – his face appeared in almost every train station with the well-known phrase 'Your Country Needs You' – Field Marshal Horatio Herbert Kitchener enjoyed wide praise for his recruiting efforts and was seen as the father of the new British Army. After Kitchener strode ashore and news got around that he was there, Bean noted in his diary that many soldiers came out of their positions to give him a rousing cheer:

> The men would not have cheered many men. They would never have cheered Ian Hamilton like it, for all his kindness and gentle manners. K.[Kitchener] is the sort of man every Australian admires … these men honestly admire him far more than the British do; the British really admire a man who has more display about him, but these men, honestly and quite sincerely, like the absence of display.[24]

Kitchener's visit was to seal a decision that had been brewing in secret for weeks: the evacuation of the entire Allied force from Gallipoli. Bean did not yet know the evacuation was now likely and he was increasingly worried that the Anzac troops, and remaining British troops, would be sacrificed to hold onto the peninsula through the winter months, 'at the cost of the utmost suffering to which our past trials have not been a fleabite by comparison'.[25] He privately railed against the incompetence of the British command – 'The fault happens in this case to be purely and simply the hopeless weakness, want of imagination, and, above all, want of moral courage' – thundering that the British nation had not the brains to make war.[26] Yet publicly, in his journalism, Australians were being assured in his newspaper reports of the 'gallant and unflinching conduct' of the troops, proudly reporting the praise of the King and Kitchener.[27]

It was likely no coincidence that at the same time, attention turned inside the Allied command headquarters to managing the propaganda implications of what would effectively be a retreat from the peninsula. Bean was approached by one of the British Army intelligence officers with the idea that he prepare an 'Anzac Annual', with prizes offered for the best writing and drawings prepared by the Anzacs on Gallipoli. He was to eventually edit this into a publication called *The Anzac Book* and the official correspondent, understanding that he was in the employ of the defence department and not any Australian newspaper, threw himself into the production of an idealised and good-humoured portrayal of stoic and cheery Anzacs on Gallipoli. The book, published in London in 1916 and eventually in Australia, sold extremely well – 100,000 copies were sold in just the first year – and for many of its readers it was the first chance they had to see images and accounts of Gallipoli. It has been suggested the book was shameless propaganda, largely because of Bean's selective editing of anything too critical of the command, but it was not pretending to be anything other than a mostly good-hearted university-style troops' rag, poking fun at the officers and including much laconic Australian humour. The book did actually include some very moving accounts of suffering in battle, the wounded and dead, and images of graves at Gallipoli. An illustrated article detailing an 'Anzac Alphabet' gives the flavour, the letter 'I' taking a dig at the 'Intelligence officer who is said to exist at G.H.Q'. 'R' was 'the Report of the latest success, strictly compiled for the use of the Press', while 'V' was the 'Victory talked of by editors who wish to get rid of importunate creditors'.[28] What was special about the book was it showed the Anzacs, for the first time, truly thinking of themselves as Australians and New Zealanders rather than British.

By late November it was bitterly cold in Bean's Anzac Cove dugout; snow was falling outside and writing was getting more difficult, his diaries showing his longhand scrawl increasingly strained. British troops were freezing to death and even drowning in the trenches at Suvla, and Bean wrote how he had been told by doctors that two men had died from cold in an Anzac Cove gully the previous night.[29] The first details of the future evacuation came to Bean when he went down to Suvla on 14 December and heard that the plan was for both Suvla and Anzac Cove to be deserted; the idea was that the smallest number of possible troops would be left to hold the frontlines and the rest would embark from the beach at nightfall. Bean was alarmed to learn from the crew of HMS *Cornwallis* that this was 'common talk', and when he later asked the Australian 1st Division command whether he could stay just a little longer until the pending evacuation, they were shocked that he knew about the secret plan. A jittery Bean spent the next few days holding his breath that the Turks would not twig to the preparations for withdrawal, all the time keeping a worried eye on the weather and hoping that on the day of embarkation it would be calm enough to actually get the troops off the peninsula – early storms had swept away two piers at the cove, underlining the grim conclusion of the commanders that it just was not going to be possible to keep resupplying Gallipoli through the winter.

News of the impending evacuation was met with mixed reactions among the troops; many felt despondent that, after so much sacrifice by so many in the fighting, the Turks would finally win the day. There was great bitterness too that the bodies of their 6000 dead comrades had to be left behind. But there was also huge relief that the Allies would be getting off the peninsula before the bitterly cold winter. The plan called for one of the greatest deceptions in military history: self-firing guns would be mounted in trenches to convince the Turks that soldiers were in the Anzac positions, while soldiers played cricket in the open to maintain an impression of normality. Then, under the cover of night, the evacuation began on 15 December and continued through to the morning of 20 December, soldiers placing sandbags over boots and boardwalks covered with blankets to muffle stomping feet.

Ironically, after months of catastrophic command failures, the evacuation was to prove the most successful operation of the Dardanelles campaign. During the night of 17 December, Charles Bean was finally evacuated from Gallipoli onto a ship in Anzac Cove. The first thing he did was enjoy a twenty-minute warm bath and then donned clean clothes courtesy of the Royal Navy. His old Clifton school connections helped again – it turned out the captain was the son of the famous cricketer W.G. Grace, whose brother had pipped Bean to the First Eleven at school. As usual, the army propagandists were putting the best possible spin on events at Anzac, and Bean learned there was a story going around that the plucky Australians had refused to leave. He wrote that this wasn't true, but that '[t]he men aren't frightened and there have been lots of volunteers for the last lot – the Die Hards'.[30] The last 36 hours for the Australians on Gallipoli would be, he acknowledged, a 'pure bluff' on the Turks. At 4.15am on 20 December 1915 it was confirmed: the embarkation of the entire Anzac force from the Gallipoli peninsula had been completed. Bean watched from his ship when, around 7am, swarms of Turkish troops ran through the deserted Australian positions.

The story of the evacuation was a rousing one, a logistical and operational success that deserved to be speedily told. But on Boxing Day 1916 at Imbros, Bean learned the censor was to have the last laugh, deciding that, for the moment, no details could be published explaining how the troops were withdrawn. To Bean, '[t]his was like an unexpected shrapnel shell in the pit of the stomach. The dispatch on which I had poured out more care than anything of which I have written here – the only chance one has had of even attempting to rival Bartlett's work (which no man ever censored in this degree)'.[31] The story would eventually be told – a few weeks later even *The Argus* ran Bean's report on the evacuation, despite previously telling the defence department they would no longer be taking his stories – and Australians read for the first time of the withdrawal of their troops from Gallipoli.[32]

'The Dardanelles expedition thus failed to gain the end for which it had been undertaken,' Bean eventually acknowledged in his official history.[33] In his analysis of the campaign he half-heartedly pushed a positive spin, suggesting that the Dardanelles operation had usefully distracted the Turks from advancing on Egypt, but he finally admitted in his official history what the censor had previously forbidden him to say, that the entire operation had been a cataclysmic waste of men and equipment. 'It is difficult to believe that these results alone would have justified so great an expenditure of lives and effort,' was Charles Bean's final measured take on the strategic debacle of Gallipoli.[34]

Bean, more than any other writer, now began the careful crafting of the Gallipoli legend, focusing on the selfless heroism and sacrifice of the thousands of Australians who served there. Perhaps his best and most moving articulation of this came in his *Anzac to Amiens* book, written just after the Allied victory in the Second World War: 'By dawn on December 20th Anzac [Cove] had faded into a dim blue line lost amid other hills on the horizon as the ships took their human freight to Imbros, Lemnos and Egypt. But Anzac stood, and still stands, for reckless valour in a good cause, for enterprise, resourcefulness, fidelity, comradeship, and endurance that will never own defeat.'[35]

Nine

EXAGGERATING SUCCESSES AND MINIMISING REVERSES

When I look at the appalling casualty lists, I sometimes wish it had not been necessary to win so many [great victories].

British politician David Lloyd George

after the Battle of the Somme

Within just a few weeks of leaving Gallipoli, Charles Bean was visiting the frontline trenches of the European Western Front. After the rigours of living in a freezing Gallipoli dugout under incessant artillery and rifle fire, his first impressions were that it was all a bit of a doddle in comparison. With his military pass he was able to catch a boat to Boulogne and was then sped to a beautiful French chateau with moat and tennis court; inside was a massive dining and drawing room with billiard table. 'It was a miserable, blowy, wet day. But what a life compared with the one in Gallipoli,' Bean thrilled.[1] His obvious misconception about the realities of the Western Front would soon be completely shattered.

Inside the chateau he met many of the men who would become his journalistic colleagues and rivals over the next few years. One of them was Philip Gibbs, the London *Daily Chronicle* and *Daily Telegraph* journalist who in 1914 was arrested by the British Army and sent back to London on threat of summary execution if he attempted to return. Now one of the five British official correspondents appointed to cover the war, he had agreed to accept military censorship in order to be allowed back. 'He knows more of the real history of the Battle of Loos – the pitiable true history of it – than almost anyone I've met; but of course neither he nor the others were allowed to write it.'[2] The attack on German positions around the French town of Loos in September was the largest British offensive of 1915 and it ended in defeat for the British and French armies, a story the correspondents were banned from properly telling during the war. It was the first time the British had used poison gas and, coming during the disaster at Gallipoli, the 50,000 British casualties suffered at Loos (compared with 25,000 Germans) were a huge blow to Allied morale. Gibbs gave Bean a private firsthand account:

> They [the British] simply broke and came back in pieces … column after column coming back dejected, hangdog, disgraced – they knew it, almost ready to weep on the mention of the disaster – a beaten ashamed army … It never got into the papers but there was a real row about it.[3]

Another correspondent, Herbert Russell, had worked alongside Bean at Gallipoli and Bean enjoyed answering all his interested questions about the evacuation, while Russell and the other correspondents shared their knowledge of the French and Belgian fighting. The British correspondents were very impressed with one of Bean's rivals on the Western Front, an Australian named Henry Gullett from the Sydney *Daily Telegraph* who had gone out beyond the frontline into no-man's-land one night with a sniper, staying the whole night. Bean was sobered by what he witnessed on a tour of the frontlines around the northern French town of Armentières. It was the effect of German shelling on local civilians and their towns that shocked him most, so different from the Dardanelles, their car pausing as military police moved a dead civilian from a bombed road and then moving through the burning ruins of a devastated village. He was also struck by the proximity of the locals, how the troops could leave a battle and then take tea in a café served by a pretty French mademoiselle; 'Some men will marry French girls,' he noted wryly.[4] It was clear to him there was much more at stake here, how the hatred of the German enemy was much more obvious than at Gallipoli. Bean's news report of his tour reflected his realisation that while the suffering at Gallipoli had been exceptionally hard, the Western Front was an even nastier war, afflicting the local civilians more cruelly. 'The exaggerated effects of shellfire in tons; the heart-rending spectacle of the civilian lying face down in a gutter … young wives and little children standing in open doorways with strain imprinted on every line of their pale faces – we saw none of this on Gallipoli.'[5]

By the end of 1915 the Western Front war was hopelessly stalemated, the German chief of staff Erich von Falkenhayn privately conceding that breaking through the Allied lines might no longer be possible. In February 1916, within a few weeks of Bean's visit, the Germans would try a huge offensive at the Battle of Verdun, but heroic French efforts halted German hopes of a major breakthrough. The

Germans were now planning for a bloody war of attrition, designed to wear down and 'bleed France white'.[6] The mincing machine of Verdun would grind on throughout the year. In March 1916, the Australian Imperial Force (AIF) would begin its move into France, and the swampy ground around Armentières where Bean was touring was where the Australians would be prepared for Western Front trench warfare.

On his return to England in late January 1916, Bean was encouraged by Keith Murdoch to visit Lord Northcliffe, the powerful newspaper baron who owned *The Times*. Born Alfred Harmsworth, Lord Northcliffe was the Rupert Murdoch of his generation and no doubt a great inspiration for Keith Murdoch's eventual rise in the Australian media. Northcliffe loathed Prime Minister Asquith and Lord Kitchener and regularly undermined both of them in his newspapers, using the failure of the Dardanelles campaign to mount a strong attack on the government's war preparedness. In fact it was Northcliffe who had shown Murdoch's Gallipoli letter to Lloyd George. 'It was easy to see there was no will on the Northcliffe papers except his own,' Bean wrote after their meeting at his country home. 'He was full of sneer at our own side for dealing too humanely and too honourably with the Huns.' Bean picked Northcliffe as a 'man who is ignorant – who flies to a judgment'.[7]

Bean was also fascinated with Keith Murdoch, who had cultivated a close friendship with Northcliffe, using his relationship with Australian Prime Minister Billy Hughes to lobby British politicians, military leaders and media barons in Australia's interests. (Hughes had succeeded Andrew Fisher when he resigned as prime minister in October 1915.) To

Bean's Anglophile eyes, one distinctive and admirable quality of the eager young Murdoch was that he was a man who 'made a religion' of being proudly Australian, as distinct, no doubt, from most of the colonial Australians of his generation who were still loyally British to their bootstraps.

> He is wholly Australian and nothing except Australian. I never realised the qualities of this type before but there's a great deal more in it than I was wont to give Murdoch credit for. These young Australians aren't afraid of any other creed and they'll go a long way … They think the world would be better for being Australian and they tell it so whenever they can and the world won't like them for it.[8]

He also heard from Murdoch about how his Gallipoli letter to the Australian prime minister had ended up as a cabinet paper submission to the British government's Dardanelles Committee, playing a part in the dismissal of General Hamilton. Bean privately described Murdoch's letter as one-sided: 'It overstated it. But M [Murdoch] believes in impressing people by overstatement. I don't. His idea is if you don't overstate the case your punch won't go home and you might as well not have spoken.'[9]

Conservative politician Andrew Bonar Law also solicited Bean's views on the Dardanelles and Australia's commitment to the war; he was serving as colonial secretary in the Asquith government but postwar he would become Britain's prime minister. Bean was unimpressed with Law but, revealingly, reassured the politician – without any call for him to do so – that 'I didn't believe there would be any serious criticism <u>during</u> the war from Australia'.[10]

Bean and his batman, Arthur Bazley, had finally left the Dardanelles from Greece on New Year's Day 1916, taking a ship to England on the steamer *Wahine* and holding their breath en route that German submarines did not torpedo them. In wintry London he was able to visit his old school Brentwood, where his former headmaster father, Edwin, and mother, Lucy, were still remembered with great affection, and he also worked on finalising publication of *The Anzac Book* as well as fitting in his brief tour of the frontlines. Within the month he was back on a ship to Egypt to catch up with the Australian forces moved there from Gallipoli to help secure the Suez Canal as everyone now expected the Turks to attack Egypt since their forces were no longer caught up in the defence of the Dardanelles. Bean returned to find the Australian Army going through a massive transformation. Rather than being discouraged by the setback of Gallipoli, the legend of that epic struggle had seized the Australian public's imagination and the number of volunteers had soared. With all these extra troops, the AIF was being remodelled into a massive army of five infantry divisions, based at Tel-el-Kebir on the edge of the desert on the Nile delta fan northeast of Cairo. It was a chance for the men who served in Gallipoli to rest and recuperate, and for the new recruits to be trained up beside them. In his later official history Bean over-generously attributed a large measure of the boost in volunteers to Ashmead-Bartlett's 'magnificent' account of the Anzac Cove landing. (He also took a pot shot at the British censorship that had tried to whip up such public enthusiasm about the war by downplaying disasters, saying 'the policy which had unfortunately been adopted in Britain … of exaggerating successes and minimising reverses was no longer producing universal optimism'.[11])

Australia had truly sacrificed the finest of its youth into the 1st Division that was blooded in Gallipoli; to attract more volunteers, the government soon after in 1916 reduced the requirements for enlistment from a minimum of five feet six inches tall and 34-inch chest between 19 and 38 years to a much less lofty Anzac height of five feet two inches, a 33-inch chest and a wider age range of 18 to 45 years.[12] There was even talk of conscription.

Once again the 1st Division troops played up badly in Egypt, and again Charles Bean chose not to acknowledge the serious crimes they committed in either his news reports or even his official history; he had firmly learned his lesson from his 1915 'wasters' article. He privately recorded how a few 'real bad' Australians dressed up as policemen, faking their badges and regimental insignia, had ridden over to a nearby village and pillaged it. 'The idea was to get women, I am told; they also got whisky and burnt the village or part of it down and got away. It is said they would certainly have been shot if caught … I believe they belonged to the 1st Australian Division.'[13] Bean's subsequent published writing only ever referred broadly to ill-discipline in Cairo and not to this incident, playing the 'rowdiness' down by quoting officers saying it was only a small number of men responsible.[14]

The appalling failures of the British command in the Dardanelles had hardened the view among Australian officers that an army composed of Australians and New Zealanders, separate from the British, would be preferable to having to endure British command again, but the chief of the British Imperial General Staff, General Sir William Robertson, rejected this proposal and the Australian government meekly complied. Instead it was decided to form the Australian and New Zealand divisions into two 'Anzac Corps', but with the British generals William Birdwood and Alexander Godley in command of each. There was a great deal of ill feeling towards the Australians in the British Cairo command, likely much to do with the English upper-class officers' disdain towards the colonial soldiers. 'There is no doubt the British staff here hate the Australians pretty badly – it is the English common people who like us; with the exception of those British officers who have fought with us, the British officer does not generally like us. The Australian doesn't salute him – as a general rule; also he is jealous of the praise we get as soldiers.'[15]

The women of Cairo stirred bachelor Bean's interest at this time but not for reasons of romance, more to do with his disapproval that women should not be allowed to be a distraction in a war zone; he was already planning his ideas for an official history and not going to be diverted. He approved of the 'competent' Australian and New Zealand nurses who wore 'a rather stiff and grey uniform', but he thoroughly disapproved of the Canadian nurses who 'are largely young girls who were not nurses before the war and who wear a very picturesque light blue dress with a very handsome dark blue and red overcoat ornamented with an officer's stars. There's no question which is the most attractive to the officers – naval and military officers swarmed around the Canadian hospitals. Also it seems to me there is no question which is best for war – the Australian government is right and the Canadian government wrong.'[16] Australia's official correspondent had time on his hands in Egypt and his diaries of that time are filled with new accounts from Gallipoli and amusing stories from the mess. He and the other correspondents were camped down near the Suez Canal and the old sentries patrolling near their tents at night mightily amused them with their challenge:

> It's a very quiet 'halt who goes there!' then and when you hear it you know there's a very unreliable finger hooked round that trigger.
>
> 'You take your —— finger off that —— trigger and I'll tell you,' answered a Light Horseman coming through Ryries trenches …
>
> 'Pass friend,' said the sentry.[17]

Finally at the beginning of March 1916 came the news that the Australians were headed to France. The 2nd Division left in the middle of the month, then the 1st Division; Bean finally sailed from Alexandria with I Anzac Corps headquarters staff on HMT *Transylvania* on 30 March. A Tasmanian parson on board who had joined up to fight, Lieutenant Frank Pogson Bethune, was an old friend of Jack Bean from Cambridge, and on the first Sunday morning at sea he delivered a stirring sermon to the men reassuring them of the justness of their cause and to not fear dying in the service. His fervent sermon may seem quaintly naïve today but Bethune summed up what so many of the volunteer soldiers listening no doubt wanted to believe about their grand adventure:

> And what if some of us do cross over to the other side in the course of it? What does that matter? Isn't it just the sort of death that you'd wish to die – going forward with your dear ones behind you and your friends on either side of you and God above you and only the enemy in front? Why when we were boys isn't this exactly the sort of adventure that we longed

> to come upon, to go across the World to fight for the right in many lands. It was almost beyond our hopes that we should ever have the chance of coming upon an adventure like that.[18]

Bean wrote that many of the Australians listening to the sermon were moved by the validation of what it was that had motivated them all to choose to go to war, blinking back the tears in their eyes: 'The soul of the nation was in the upturned face of that crowd.'[19]

There is an interesting postscript to the parson-turned-soldier who delivered this sermon, Lieutenant Bethune, who lived his rousing words through his actions and proved to be a most extraordinary soldier in combat. Two years later in March 1918, when the Germans launched a massive attack along the Western Front, his 3rd Machine Gun Company was defending an area around Ypres known as Buff Bank. Told his position had to be held at all costs and believing his men were being ordered to defend a 'useless death-trap', he typically insisted on carrying out the order himself and issued this extraordinary written command to his men, telling them in essence that their duty was to defend or die:

> Special Orders to No 1 Section 13/3/18
>
> (1) This position will be held, and the Section will remain here until relieved.
>
> (2) The enemy cannot be allowed to interfere with this programme.
>
> (3) If the Section cannot remain here alive, it will remain here dead, but in any case it will remain here.
>
> (4) Should any man through shell-shock or other cause attempt to surrender, he will remain here dead.

(5) Should all guns be blown out, the Section will use Mills grenades and other novelties.

(6) Finally, the position, as stated will be held.

F.P. Bethune Lt

O/c No 1 Section.[20]

Bethune and his men held out against a formidable German attack for eighteen days, and survived; not one of his men was killed in that time. He was awarded the Military Cross for his gallantry and devotion to duty and unofficially, one suspects, for writing perhaps the most spectacularly obdurate written order of the war. (Bethune survived the war, living in Tasmania until his death in 1942.)

Such sentiment as Bethune's aside, the next day there was for Bean a reminder of the bloodshed and carnage that he had already witnessed such good men fall to. The following Monday after Bethune's sermon, General Birdwood approached Bean on the boat and asked if he could think of 'anything special' that the 2nd Brigade had done in the Dardanelles. Bean reminded him that it was McCay's 2nd Brigade that had 'made such a splendid advance in front of Krithia on May 8th'. 'Of course – yes,' Birdwood replied, and he went off to write his speech; the commanding general had actually forgotten about the sacrifice of a third of an entire brigade in one of his key Dardanelles battles.[21] There had been over a thousand casualties in that Krithia attack alone.

On 8 April 1916, Bean finally caught up with the Australians now stationed in French Flanders, the marshy lowlands around the border with Belgium. On a train from Calais, he excitedly spotted Australian troops from his carriage as it rode through Saint-Omer en route to

Hazebrouck. 'After that, outside every farmhouse were Australians, sitting in the garden cooking, gathering round the estaminet, walking through the fields in twos, sometimes a hundred or two on parade outside a barn. The country seemed populated with them.'[22]

The Anzac headquarters was in a small chateau out of town but Bean found a billet in one of the local houses, hearing from the mother of the house how her husband had been lost in battle. He noted the dull thud of the frontline artillery guns nineteen kilometres away, and at night he could see their flashes; they reminded him of the view of Cape Helles from Anzac Cove, now half a world away. He also noted the stories of passing soldiers, including one Scotsman who was excited that Winston Churchill, dumped as a cabinet minister after the Dardanelles debacle, was now a colonel commanding the nearby Royal Scots Fusiliers 6th Battalion. They discussed the shooting of prisoners – did it happen, Bean asked? 'I wouldn't stop it, I don't blame the men,' one soldier told him. 'If you go on firing a machine gun to the last moment you can't expect to get off with your life.' He confided that, during one recent battle, the Scottish Argyll troops 'were lining up the Boche and shooting them – and I wouldn't have interfered'.[23] It was an astonishing claim and a potentially important story that Bean chose to dismiss as a likely exaggeration and never wrote; the British military was keeping a whip hand on access by correspondents to the Western Front, much more than at Gallipoli, and even attempting to get such a story past the censors would no doubt have roused official displeasure. He was beginning to realise just how different this war would be for him to cover as a journalist and historian: not only was there a vast frontline for him to attempt to traverse but the accuracy and power of the German artillery also made it much more dangerous than Gallipoli.

> I don't suppose we can ever again get so close to a battle as we used to be in Gallipoli. The firing line trenches are so drenched with artillery fire after a fight that I suppose the losses there would be 30 per cent – which means that in 3 fights your being hit is practically certain. And as we have to watch every fight and not just one out of 3 or 4 (like a brigade staff) this would be risking one's life to an extent I don't care to do.[24]

He was also operating under much tighter restrictions here than he had at Gallipoli; he was not even allowed to visit the British lines without being closely followed by a press officer, and at this stage of the war he was not permitted to take any photographs at all. When he complained about this the British command instead sent him Ernest Brooks, a British official photographer who Bean had worked with at Gallipoli. 'Really they are the limit,'[25] Bean harrumphed. While he was soon impressed with Brooks's courage in the frontlines, he was angry about his willingness to take faked photographs, 'which the editors will print, doesn't care two-pence whether they are real or faked; and as generally he can't get the real ones he's always out to fake them'.[26] There would always be a tension between the two men because Brooks saw no wrong in faking a photograph, which offended Bean's ethics. At Gallipoli Brooks had faked a picture of a Turkish sniper camouflaged with branches, and another depicting the charge of the Royal Naval Division at the Dardanelles, which had become famous; it was in fact taken outside the battle zone on the Greek island of Imbros, just down the hill from the correspondents' camp. Bean was further frustrated by the fact that the British had allowed the Canadians to have their own official photographer but continued to block Bean's request.

Yet he did enjoy extraordinary journalistic access to Birdwood and the other senior Anzac Corps command staff, often working more as a de facto defence department press staffer; he was even asked by one officer to help sort aerial trench photographs and also spent a lot of time distributing his *Anzac Book* in the frontlines. His status as a defence employee meant his role was ambiguous: although he was given the privileges of an officer's rank without being an enlisted officer, the modest 'Captain' Bean particularly disliked the way the newspapers in Australia used his nominal rank in his articles and was very embarrassed when soldiers needlessly saluted him as he did his rounds:

> One doesn't like to appear to look for a salute … I hate it but you must look at them to see if they salute – and with a chap as sensitive and self-conscious as I am this makes walking up the street rather a thing to be dreaded. I have to make a rule of going through the village once each way on foot every day or I should shirk it altogether.[27]

Keith Murdoch continued playing politics behind the scenes and was trying to draw Bean into his intrigues. Billy Hughes had become prime minister in October 1915 and visited England in April 1916. Hughes was a keen supporter of Australia's involvement in the war and Murdoch, in collusion with press baron Lord Northcliffe, was even trying to get Hughes to stand for a seat in the British Parliament because 'he has the ear of the British people at the moment more than any other man'.[28] Bean was flattered that the prime minister greeted him like an old friend when he visited France and clearly he was as much a fan of Hughes as Murdoch.

Inside the Australian command, however, there was gloom about the British defeat at Loos and the continuing slaughter at Verdun. There was also devastatingly accurate German bombing of the Australian trenches and billets on a daily basis, killing many men before they even got into the fight. Everyone knew preparations were underway for a massive Allied offensive, but Brigadier General White rattled Bean when he privately admitted to serious doubts the offensive could succeed in the face of a seemingly formidable Germany army:

> I wonder whether we're going to win this war Bean. You know, I'm a bit doubtful of all this talk that's going on. They're manoeuvring as to who shall offer to enter into negotiations first – that's the meaning of it. We could win the war if we organised, I have no doubt of it. But I wonder if we are ready to do it. I don't know that we are.[29]

After that conversation, Bean wrote an article imploring Australians to show the same willpower in organising their economy and stretching out resources as the Germans were doing, feeling this effectively propagandist role was part of his job as the official correspondent, though it did not sit well with his other hat as a journalist. 'But,' he pondered, 'I don't know if the censor will let it through because it hints at what everyone here knows – that our great offensive may not necessarily succeed, if it indeed comes off.'[30] The censor did not block his article but only a couple of provincial Australian newspapers gave it a run, for pessimism did not sell papers. Bean never mentioned Brigadier General White's strikingly gloomy pessimism at this time in any of his news articles or the official history, and perhaps if Australian newspaper editors had known he was reflecting the views of a senior commander they might have published – but the censor again would no doubt have intervened. Prime Minister Billy Hughes was upbeat when he visited the frontlines in June, making clear to everyone, including Bean, his views on negotiating with the Germans: '[H]is one idea now is to beat Germany, hip and thigh, to fight her and organise against her ... He has no idea of compromise, which I am sure British statesmen have in the back of their heads.'[31]

By early June 1916, Bean was so sick of being mucked around by the British command that he even thought about resigning, especially because he was not being allowed to take his own photographs. The Australians were still very new to the Western Front and had not yet fought in any major offensive, but Bean was getting very concerned that the rigid British censorship was making his job impossible. 'I am very tempted to send in my resignation after this – help these fellows round in every way I can and then let the Government know that I cannot carry out the work in the manner to which I believe the Australian recorder ought to.'[32] He was furious when photographer Ernest Brooks faked a photograph showing a line of soldiers with bayonets fixed on the edge of a parapet with their commanding major, a ridiculously posed shot that Bean felt needlessly endangered their lives. He fumed in his diary, 'Brooks got his position because he was a friend of the King and Queen – their private photographer. And this is the sort of rubbish the Home Government sends us as its "Official Photographer", who may be trusted while [New Zealand official correspondent Malcolm Ross] and I may not be trusted.'[33]

No one but staff headquarters knew it at this time but a great Allied offensive was planned for July, and the British command ordered raiding parties to mount attacks on the German trenches to keep the enemy on edge. The AIF had moved into trench defences around Armentières during March and April 1916, learning the basics for survival: how to man trenches, direct artillery and snipe, and launch raids on the enemy just a few hundred metres opposite. After one such raid on 12 June, soldiers from the Australian 6th Battalion filed a report that showed an extreme ruthlessness in their treatment of a prisoner, bordering on a war crime. A badly injured German prisoner had resisted and was shot and wounded, but the Australians then clubbed him to death because he kept on crying out, jeopardising their covert raid. The killing of an unarmed prisoner disgusted Bean: 'There was some quite unnecessary boasting about the knocking of this poor chap on the head. It is not a great feat to hit a wounded man over the skull. He was sitting up crying said one man. The man who was bragging was a talkative English-born Australian but some of the others seemed quite to approve of his brag.'[34] Bean was haunted by the memory of a seized letter he had earlier read from the wife of a German soldier to her husband; he hoped the executed prisoner was not her beloved. The incident seems to be the first time in the entire war that Bean had recorded any moral qualms about the actions of Australian soldiers and, to his credit, he did mention it in his official history, '[l]est the historian be accused of failing to depict war as it is', albeit again in a detailed footnote.[35] He did, however, attempt to mitigate what had happened, writing that '[s]uch things happened in every army, and, possibly, on one side or the other, in almost every close battle'.[36]

Despite his private misgivings, in one news report on this raid he reassured his readers that the Australians were 'doing their daily work honestly and well', the article accompanied by an older photograph of the men in the raiding party when it was published.[37] General Birdwood confronted Bean about this, concerned that the report might not have gone through the censor. Bean was piqued at this suggestion because the photograph that offended Birdwood had in fact been taken in London, where there was generally no censorship. This exchange was very revealing about how Bean privately saw his official correspondent role as he acknowledges letting 'Birdie' read his notes on the raid, which contained the reference to the killing of an unarmed prisoner: 'my private notes which of course are quite different from anything I should think of publishing – and I think he was rather afraid that I might publish them'.[38] It is a measure of the relationship between the official correspondent and staff command that he was actually allowing the commanding general to read his private notes, something that today would be seen as crossing an unacceptable journalistic line.

The issue of whether a journalist should ever criticise was also a lively one. Just over a week later Bean discussed the role of journalists in war with Brigadier General White, at a time when Keith Murdoch (now based in London) was worried that the general disapproved of his Gallipoli letter, which had been scathing about the British command failures. White said he believed in press freedom:

> 'You know my opinion Bean,' said White. 'I think they ought to have been put on their trial for undertaking that expedition. I do honestly' and he grew red with warmth as he said it. 'Hamilton may not have been a success but we know that if he had had the help which these Generals here have – the ammunition and guns and so on – if they had backed him up as they back up other Generals, he would have got thro[ugh].'[39]

This was an astonishingly candid admission from one of the senior generals in the Australian command, and it was at least the second time that White had in confidence told Bean frankly how poorly he thought of the British command. But Bean never attempted to reflect that pessimism within the Australian command in his journalism, presumably at the very least because he knew the British censors would have blocked it. But he also did not report White's serious criticisms in his official history.

In late June, as the planned July offensive loomed, Bean received welcome news that all correspondents would be allowed to witness the opening bombardments and would also be allowed to interview men after the fight: 'it looks as if the War Office had decided that publicity could do no harm after the event'.[40] Bean noted with concern that the British and French papers were openly talking about the coming offensive, but he was full of anticipation at the imminent attack, 'the biggest battle that the Empire has ever been engaged in – the last great effort, very likely'.[41] In the final days before the offensive a heavy rain fell, clogging up the future battlefields of the Somme with sticky mud that dulled the effectiveness of the heavy Allied bombardments now supposed to be cutting the enemy's wire fortifications.

The night before the offensive was due to begin, at a hotel in Amiens where the press corps had been gathered, Bean met an English official named John Buchan, later to become a well-known novelist. Bean described Buchan as a 'natty little Oxford chap of the British civil servant type – I should have put him down as one of the highish officials of the Foreign Office (and indeed he is doing some sort of work there)'.[42] He was more right than he realised, for Buchan was actually working for the British propaganda bureau run by military intelligence. In 1915 he had also written *The Thirty-Nine Steps*, a spy thriller set just before the First World War that was crafted to shock the British public about the extent of Germany's militaristic intentions on England. As the horrific casualty toll reports rolled in from the Somme battle over the next few weeks, it was Buchan who made an astonishing admission to Bean and other press correspondents that Britain was prepared to sacrifice as many as half a million men in this massive offensive. In his diary, Bean noted the response from one of the press pack: 'As somebody said – that is alright for them but what about the half million?'[43]

Ten

A BLOODY HOLOCAUST

They'll get used to it.

Major General McCay's reported words after the Fromelles attack

Early on the morning of 1 July 1916, Charles Bean was woken by a frantic rapping on his billet door – it was the New Zealand official correspondent Malcolm Ross, excitedly announcing that the press officers were gathering the correspondents and were 'going to tell us something'. Bean immediately realised what this meant: 'Clearly the attack was on after all.'[1]

After days of relentless bombing of the German lines, the Allied advance was finally happening. It was to become one of the epic tragedies of the twentieth century, for before the day was out an incomprehensible number of soldiers would lose their lives in a hail of machine-gun and artillery fire. In just those first 24 hours of battle, 20,000 Allied soldiers would be killed in a mind-boggling total casualty toll of 57,470 men. By the end of the Battle of the Somme in November 1916, more than one million men from both sides would be either wounded or killed.

The Somme valley was an absurdly picturesque place to wage a war, the river Somme flowing in a generally westerly direction between the medieval town of Péronne and the city of Amiens, just a couple of hours' drive northwest of Paris. On each bank of the river the plains rise to rolling slopes of green-grassed chalk ridges, used by each side in 1916 to their defensive advantage. Germany's frontline crossed the Somme at a village called Curlu, a few kilometres west of Péronne, and it had also swallowed up numerous villages, tracking the Somme valley and surrounding rivers, before running north. Calling it a frontline was an understatement: the Germans had turned the villages into fortresses and the frontline was in fact three lines of trenches 180 metres apart, a formidable bulwark against any Allied attack.

At 6.30am on that first morning, the Allied guns let loose a final massive rapid-fire burst of shells, 'a perfect hurricane of sound'.[2] Along the frontlines men were told to check their rifles one more time, fix their bayonets, and then, at 7.30am, to the shrill peel of a whistle, it was up the ladders and over the top. In the next few minutes the first of the 750,000 Allied soldiers who would eventually fight in the battle stepped out into no-man's-land along an enormous 30-kilometre stretch of the Western Front. Bean and other correspondents had been collected from their billets and taken by British press officers to a position northeast of the British-held town of Albert along the road to Bapaume. They stood or sat on the parapet of a communications trench overlooking a plain festooned with a blaze of yellow mustard flowers. When the thunderous cacophony of the big guns finally settled they watched a line of infantrymen walking over the crest of a hill into the abyss, then running towards the German positions and finally, through the smoke and dust, falling.

The first time he stepped into no-man's-land was two days after the attack began, parting the wire of the old frontline and walking with a British press officer into the demolished ruins of the town of Fricourt. The Germans had been forced to retreat from their lines there and Bean gamely ventured through their old frontline trenches, noting the corpses of a German and four British troops who had died in one of the earlier failed attempts to seize the town. After his experience of combat in Gallipoli, Bean was able to control his feelings, but the British officer escorting him 'seemed very affected by this – he didn't like being near it'.[3] The Allies had won a tiny gain of less than two kilometres but at a terrible cost.

The Australians had not yet seen action in the Battle of the Somme and the Anzac Corps was eager to prove its mettle; Bean decided to attach himself to I Anzac Corps because it looked likely to be the first to see any fighting. But on 16 July he heard rumours that Major General McCay's 5th Division from II Anzac Corps was about to launch an attack further north near the village of Fromelles; it was McCay, of course, who had led the attack at Krithia in the Dardanelles, so Bean knew the commander well. He went up to McCay's headquarters the next day only to learn that the action was off, but on his return Bean noted that 'White was very anxious to know … whether it was merely postponed'.[4] The brigadier general was clearly concerned about what was being proposed there:

> I hate these unprepared shows Bean … and that is what it is. I am quite in favour of having a push at

> him up north but not just there. I think it would be quite a good thing to try and push where we thought we could go forward with a force sufficient to go forward and really do something. But I hate these unprepared little shows. What do we do? We may deceive the enemy for 2 days and after that he knows perfectly well it is not a big attack and that we are not in earnest there. We don't get anything that does us any good – the trenches are hard to keep and it would mean the breaking up of two divisions. It would cost 2 divisions. No I am all against these little half-baked attacks.[5]

As Bean later noted in the margin of his diary, White's concern was a remarkable forecast of what actually happened, for the action was indeed only postponed. Major General McCay and his 5th Division troops, together with the British 61st Division, had been given just a few days to prepare for a feint attack intended to draw German troops away from the main Allied advance 80 kilometres south at the Somme. The target assigned to McCay was a heavily fortified German position called the Sugar Loaf, but the ambitious hope was that the attack might even seize Fromelles itself, on the top of the Aubers Ridge behind the target.

What was about to unravel at Fromelles remains, one century on, Australia's greatest single military disaster, the subject even today of sometimes acrimonious debate and, indubitably, bitter regret about why the attack was ever allowed to go ahead. It is a measure of the strength of Charles Bean's fastidious attention to detail that much of what we know about the attack comes from his notes taken at the time, and from what he culled from Allied records. On or about 17 July, British commander General Haig sent a message re-endorsing the postponed attack, though adding a rider that it should only go ahead if the British First Army commander, General Sir Charles Monro, 'is satisfied that the conditions are favourable, and that the resources at his disposal, including ammunition, are adequate both for the preparation and the execution of the enterprise'.[6] As Bean's official history makes clear, Monro had actually wanted to cancel the attack but a rigid Haig – 'obviously determined by his principle of standing to a decision already given'[7] – had passed the buck to the local commanders.[8]

As commander of the Australian 15th Brigade that would be frontally assaulting the Sugar Loaf, a nervous Brigadier General Pompey Elliott realised early on it would be a slaughter. He wrote a letter to Charles Bean after the war describing how he and Major Howard from General Haig's staff had reconnoitred the battlefield before Fromelles while Elliott referred to a pamphlet on trench warfare he and other officers were given when they arrived in France. It advised that any advance over a no-man's-land of more than 200 yards (180 metres) should not be attempted, yet Fromelles was double that distance at the point where the 15th Brigade would have to cross. Elliott was well aware that when the Australians made it across the flat no-man's-land they would then have to breach, under heavy direct fire, the formidable two- to three-metre high and three-metre thick breastwork parapet defences that sat above the boggy ground and were also reinforced with dozens of concrete shelters. What he did not know was that the Germans also had deep dugout bomb shelters just behind the frontline in which the troops could shelter during any sustained bombardment. When Elliott asked his fellow officer for his honest opinion of the outcome at Fromelles, Major Howard had replied that he believed any attack would be 'a bloody holocaust'.[9] Despite these clear misgivings from within General Haig's own command, the commanding British general, Richard Haking, who had been assigned by Monro to plan the attack, decided to proceed.

To give mettle to his men, when the Allied bombardment of the German lines started Elliott assured his troops that 'you won't find a German in those trenches when you get there'.[10] But once the bombing was over the Germans rushed back into position from their deep dugout shelters, shredding the packed Allied trenches with airburst shrapnel shells even before they began the attack, for the Germans had a clear view of the Allied preparations for the attack from the Aubers Ridge behind the Sugar Loaf. As the British 61st Division advanced at 5.30pm on 19 July 1916, it was immediately cut to pieces by machine guns and artillery. When the Australians followed minutes later, they too were slashed down in swathes, particularly in their lower body from groin to knee; this meant hundreds of young men were grievously wounded in no-man's-land, unable to walk because their legs were severely wounded. Even after Lieutenant General Haking called off the attack just over two hours later, communications failures meant one battalion of the 15th Brigade did not know their attack had been cancelled. They made a forlorn but heroic charge of the formidable Sugar Loaf fortress that Bean later described as 'one of the bravest and most hopeless assaults ever undertaken by the Australian Imperial Force'.[11] In less than a day at Fromelles, Australia's 5th Division endured 5533 casualties, of which 1917 died. The British 61st Division was similarly devastated. The supposed Fromelles feint attack was a debacle, a shambolic failure of poor intelligence and weak logistical planning.

The first Bean heard about Fromelles was over breakfast the next morning, 20 July 1916, in his new billet at Contay, when one officer flippantly commented, 'The 5th Division had their little show last night.'[12] General Birdwood was clearly unaware the attack was going ahead having unwittingly told Bean just the previous evening that there was no need to rush up to see the II Anzac Corps action for another day. Hearing the news, the official correspondent decided to drive to Fromelles immediately; Brigadier General White lent Bean his staff car, telling him the last news they had heard was that the Australians were in the German trenches and holding on at all costs. But when Bean arrived at the 5th Division headquarters shortly afterwards the battle was all over, and he learned the last surviving Australians from the 14th Brigade had been forced to withdraw from the German trenches, only making it back across no-man's-land at around 9am just before Bean arrived. 'We've had an awfully rough passage,' he was told, in a classic understatement.[13] He was there as a 'very few distraught men, quite broken up and wild and almost beside themselves, came in from this part of no-mans-land this morning'.[14] The wounded could be seen crawling across the battlefield trying to take cover from the German machine guns; all of no-man's-land was strewn with bodies, some lay still and others were plaintively calling for help that could not yet come. 'As usual s-b [stretcher bearers] are very short and lots of wounded are left in no-man's-land. But the tale of missing is getting smaller. It's not quite the disaster which at first appeared. I should say we lost something between 4000 and 5000.'[15] But by any measure Fromelles was a disaster; perhaps Charles Bean was still thinking of John Buchan's admission that the British were prepared to sacrifice half a million men in the Battle of the Somme, but this was a huge catastrophe for Australia and Brigadier General Pompey Elliott, the 15th Brigade commander, knew it: 'When Elliott came out I felt almost as if I were in the presence of a man who had just lost his wife. He looked down and could hardly speak. He was clearly terribly depressed and overwrought. McCay was also I thought.'[16]

Bean wrote a cable which he rushed to Amiens for publication describing the attack and saying the losses were 'severe'; he hoped he could get this devastating news past the British censor, who had to vet the story before it could be telegraphed. His article, subtitled with an upbeat headline that Bean would never have used – 'Temporary success' – ran four days later in *The Sydney Morning Herald*.[17] He candidly told his readers that the Germans had been 'ready for the attack' and that the Australian and British attackers were 'driven out'. As usual, an astute Australian reader would know to read the final line of Bean's censored report, which chillingly ran: 'The losses amongst our troops engaged were severe.' Taking the rigid British censorship into account, Bean did well to get even that brief but telling story out, but he would have been appalled by many of the other stories on Fromelles that were run in Australian newspapers based on Reuters and English press reports. For Fromelles is a case study in the level of deception perpetrated during a war, the cover-up starting with the British military's own deceitful communiqué issued soon after the attack, which Bean made sure he ran in its damning entirety in his postwar *Official History of Australia in the War of 1914–1918*. There he wrote:

The severity of this reverse, though of course well known to the German Army and people, was concealed from the British public in the official communiqué:

'Yesterday evening, south of Armentieres, we carried out some important raids on a front of two miles in which Australian troops took part. About 14 German prisoners were captured.'[18]

Reuters, as usual, distinguished itself with the eyewash it allowed British propagandists to run in its name. Under a stirring headline that would have been written by the newspaper running the Reuters wire copy – 'In the thick of it. Australians in attack. Bayoneting the Bavarians. Germans demoralised' – readers were told that the Australians had struck a blow against the enemy, beating the Germans in what was described as a successful trench 'raid' and echoing the deceitful claims made in the British communiqué, which had sought to plant the misleading suggestion that it was always planned that the Australians would withdraw after their attack on the Sugar Loaf.[19] By contrast, *The Argus* ran Bean's article ending with the admission of severe losses and shrewdly added a story from the German press just below it that accurately reported the heavy losses:

A GERMAN CLAIM
The following official German communiqué was received in London on Friday night – 'An English attack in the Fromelles region yesterday by two strong divisions was repulsed. We made prisoner 481 men and counted 2000 bodies in front of our lines.'[20]

As Bean noted in his official history, the truth of what had really happened in Fromelles soon became known back in Australia, mainly because of soldiers' letters home and the grim telegrams sent to families. The revelation of this as yet unpublicised loss 'went far to shake the confidence of part of the public in the British official statements, which at first had been accepted as invariably true'.[21] The lies had started from the very first day of the Battle of the Somme; in one headline about that disastrous beginning, London readers were told 'The day goes well'.[22] In *The Sydney Morning Herald* a blatantly untrue claim was slavishly run that '[t]he British casualties were not heavy'.[23] Bean's anger over the lies told of Fromelles was a turning point in his growing disillusionment about not being able to give a truthful account to his Australian readers during the war. He was furious about the deceitful British military communiqué describing Fromelles as a successful series of 'trench raids', clearly a propaganda strategy by the British to cover up the retreat of two divisions from what was obviously an attack intended to seize the position: 'What is the good of deliberate lying like that? The Germans know it was an attack.'[24]

Even while he was still at Fromelles, Bean was confronted by the memory of Brigadier General White's grave reservations about the attack the previous night, privately querying: 'What is the result of it – What did White say? … We wanted to make the Germans think we were attacking there – so that he would hold his troops there. As a matter of fact we proved to him (what he would not know otherwise) that we intended nothing serious … he could now if he wanted withdraw half the men who are on that front. And we have put out of action a fine division.'[25] Back at the Contay headquarters, White told him that the attack had been postponed so the arrangements for the battle would be complete when it finally went ahead, but what was vexing Bean was that clearly the decision to attack at all was wrong in the circumstances. The British First Army was indulging in classic Orwellian doublespeak, telling the press that the Australians had done quite well and that they could have held on if the British 61st Division had done so. Bean angrily wrote in his diary: 'The 61st Division, they said, were rather second rate territorials. Why do they put second rate terriers in with our men on a job like this?'[26] The British spin doctors were also telling correspondents that 'the attack had succeeded in its object'; Bean furiously scrawled in his diary, 'That is not true – it is the opposite.'[27]

Tight censorship meant that during the war there was little more that Charles Bean could do to reveal the command failures at Fromelles, but postwar when he came to write his official history account of Fleurbaix, as it was also known, his attention to detail came to the fore. Running for hundreds of pages, his account of the battle is probably the only reason that Australians know the story of the tragedy of Fromelles today, because it could so easily have been forgotten; the Australian public's attention was soon to be distracted by the meat grinder of Pozières, where the nation would suffer even greater losses over several weeks. Bean pulled together his history of Fromelles in powerful detail, drawing from an array of sources including his own notes, sketches, letters, German historical accounts, and interviews with Australian officers right down to battalion level. His history sheeted home the blame for the disaster chiefly to Haig's British command headquarters for allowing the attack to go ahead.

But analysis of what Bean knew from his private notes and other sources raises the question of whether he deliberately softened his criticism of the Australian commanders who were also responsible for failures at Fromelles. After the war, Pompey Elliott accused Major General McCay of having been so delighted that his division was to be used in the Fromelles attack that he had allowed it to override his perception of the obvious inadequacies of the plan.[28] Elliott wrote that he would have protested if he had been in McCay's position, but he did acknowledge that a protest would not have done much good because the move was ordered from above, saying, 'McCay was terribly anxious that it shouldn't be stopped and made no mention of the difficulties facing us.'[29]

There was also criticism from some of McCay's own men because the general had refused the German offer of a truce so that both sides could recover their wounded in no-man's-land. In his defence, McCay suggested he had been forced to follow command headquarters' orders stipulating that such local truces were forbidden. But as historian Ross McMullin has pointed out, under military law McCay was perfectly entitled to authorise a local suspension of arms without superior approval.[30] Bean made no mention of this and he bent over backwards to exonerate McCay in his history, saying he was unfairly maligned, 'unpopular, but entirely innocent'.[31] The bitterness about McCay raged on well into the 1920s; one former sergeant wrote to Bean with his account of Fromelles, describing McCay walking along the duckboards afterwards, repeatedly saying of his shaken troops, 'They'll get used to it.'[32] It was a brutal and insensitive comment that said much about McCay's impetuous character, but Bean elected not to mention it in his official history; perhaps he found it difficult to criticise an Australian commander whom he had come to respect on the battlefield at Krithia as they both searched for his fallen officers among the wounded that night a year earlier. Charles Bean also arguably had a blind spot when it came to McCay's superiors, including his friends generals White and Birdwood, and it was they who Pompey Elliott targeted postwar under the pseudonym of 'Xenophon' in *The Bulletin* magazine. Both generals had grave reservations about the attack, so why had they allowed it to go ahead and what, if anything, had they said to Haig's commanders to try to stop it? Bean's handling of White's answer to this question is less than satisfactory; he chose to suggest in the official history that Haig's qualified order for the attack to proceed meant that it was a foregone conclusion it would go ahead, but Haig had clearly given his commander discretion to call it off.

During his official history research, Bean wrote to White asking if he could recall whether anything was said by he or Birdwood at the British headquarters command which 'might have put them on their guard' about the proposed attack – had they in fact spoken up or said anything at all?[33] White's reply appears to avoid the point of Bean's careful question, for rather than answering directly he said he could not say whether Birdwood's views or his had any effect on General Headquarters (GHQ) – he implied that they had, saying, 'It is quite probable.'[34] But, glaringly, the general's response did not explicitly confirm if anything was *actually* said, and indeed White appears to have left open in his reply whether the Australian commanders stayed silent, stating cryptically, 'We knew Haking's keenness for what we regarded as a most undesirable operation.'[35] Despite this obvious avoidance by White, Bean's official history went on to expressly state that Birdwood and White 'made no secret of their adverse opinion' at the British command headquarters.[36] Elliott too felt Bean had let White off the hook; after the official history account was published he wrote to Bean, saying: 'It does appear to me that you have strained your conscience in the endeavour to let the higher commands down as lightly as possible.'[37] In Elliott's view, Bean had allowed his admiration for White to cloud his judgment.

Intriguing too that nowhere in the official history does Bean acknowledge what Elliott told him, that he and an English officer from command headquarters had agreed before the battle that it would be 'a bloody holocaust',[38] and that Elliott had said he could never understand why the battle had been allowed to go ahead. Exactly what White and Birdwood said to Haig's command headquarters, if anything, is not clear, but Charles Bean should have pressed the question much more aggressively with White before definitively exonerating his friends in the Australian command. Bean's official history did criticise British Lieutenant General Richard Haking for his appalling failures in planning the attack, saying 'it is difficult to conceive that the operation, as planned, was ever likely to succeed'.[39] There is little doubt Haking, who continued on a distinguished career postwar, should have been court-martialled for his bungling at Fromelles.

While the real story of Fromelles was being suppressed in the press, the British military command began sanitising this disaster. Haking wrote a report on the battle that acknowledged the gallantry of the Australians but blamed their failure to gain the ground on their inadequate training.

He also criticised the British 61st Division for its lack of offensive spirit. In perhaps one of the most deluded claims ever made about the debacle at Fromelles, Haking wrote, 'I think the attack, although it failed, has done both divisions a great deal of good.'[40]

Eleven

WHY SHOULD YOU PEOPLE BACK HOME NOT KNOW?

It is horrible but why should you people back home not know?

LIEUTENANT ALEC RAWS

I always feel surprised when I get alive out of Pozieres – I don't pretend to be brave – I want very much to write the history of this war.

CHARLES BEAN

For weeks young Australians had been in and out of Vignacourt, enjoying wine, women and song in this rest village a short distance from the Somme frontlines. But as the village mayor lamented to Charles Bean in mid-June 1916, the Vignacourt townsfolk were increasingly saddened to see the same units now returning from the frontline a week or two later 'lacking a large proportion of the familiar jolly faces'.[1] Many of the Australians had visited the home of Louis and Antoinette Thuillier in Vignacourt to have their photographs taken before they went into battle; the Thuillier family's extraordinary cache of photographic glass plate negatives recording this defining moment in Australian history would lie hidden in a farmhouse attic for almost another century.[2] So many of those young Australians were to die or suffer terrible wounds in a nearby town whose name would soon become synonymous with the appalling suffering and cruelty of war, Pozières.

Charles Bean passed through Vignacourt on his way to the 1st Division headquarters at Albert on 21 July as it prepared for an attack on the village of Pozières just eight kilometres up the road. British forces had launched a series of attacks on the village from 13 to 17 July yet failed to make a breakthrough, so I Anzac Corps was marched in from Vignacourt and other surrounding rest villages to prepare to take Pozières. The Germans, expecting an attack, were lobbing artillery shells into the surrounding towns where they knew the Allies were gathering; even Charles Bean's billet was hit by shellfire. He had been hugely busy in the days after the disaster at Fromelles as he rushed to get an understanding of the coming Pozières attack. After watching the massive British curtain-raiser bombardment of the village, he walked through trenches towards a view of no-man's-land and was awe-struck to see for himself how the artillery fire had cut up the ground 'more frightfully than anything I had ever seen', as if dug by a 'titan'.[3] Pozières' buildings would be quite literally ground into brick dust in the coming weeks.

The Australian 1st Division troops had marched in along the Albert road to trenches just short of the Pozières front, the shattered red bricks and shredded trees of the desolated village visible just a few hundred metres ahead. Unburied corpses of men from both sides of the conflict lay scattered on either side of the road as they marched past. Underlining the gravity of the horrors they now realised they were about to be thrown into, a German gas attack forced the Australians to enter their positions wearing gasmasks. For all of them, their arrival at Pozières was a terrible jolt, a frightening descent into the abyss from the relatively comfortable training trenches at Armentières. What none of the infantrymen knew, as they huddled in their trenches, was that the 1st Division commander, British Lieutenant General Harold Walker, had stood up to his British commanders, including Lieutenant General Hubert Gough, resisting a reckless push for a rushed full-frontal assault on Pozières. He and Australian Major Thomas Blamey (who would be promoted to Colonel in November) instead planned a two-pronged attack on Pozières, using the 1st Brigade on the left and the 3rd Brigade on the right, the latter being the first unit ashore at Gallipoli. Everyone knew this would be an historic battle, and by the end of it there would be more Australian dead scattered across Pozières than anywhere else in the war.

At 12.30am on 23 July 1916, the Australians leapt from their trenches and began the attack, soon seizing the ruins of Pozières in brutal hand-to-hand fighting with the Germans. Bean had endured a harrowing night journey through shrapnel and gas attacks to get to Brigadier General Ewen Sinclair-MacLagan's 3rd Brigade headquarters at nearby Contalmaison where he could follow what was happening. Bean and the British soldier who had shown him the way were forced to don gasmasks in the darkness, making it almost impossible to see, so the two men had stumbled the last terrifying eighty metres to Sinclair-MacLagan's dugout in genuine fear for their lives, the musty aroma of the gas wafting through inside the command post. Bean's eyes were still stinging from the gas as he watched Scotsman Sinclair-

MacLagan trying to make sense of what was happening to his men behind the dust, smoke and cacophonous banging of artillery fire just outside. It is extraordinary just what the official correspondent was allowed to record in his diary notes, because if he had ever been captured as he roamed the trenches they would have provided his German captors with a meticulous insight into the Australian command and order of battle.

The Australians had seized Pozières but the British troops on the right and the left of them had not done so well, which meant the Australians were exposed on three sides where they had broken through the German lines. As Australian soldiers came out of the frontline to be relieved, Bean scrambled to jot down their excited and bloodthirsty talk as they stood around the glow of the mobile kitchen stoves: '"See them get into that fat Hun – my God – a trench full of them … by god the boys let 'em have it … I wanted to get at 'em with my fists – god what a time."'[4] The Australians proudly saw themselves as different men from the British 'Tommies', and so did Bean, who was clearly awed by them. But few men would be able to withstand what the Australians were now forced to endure as they held on to the devastated wreckage of the village of Pozières.

The Germans had orders never to give ground, and so they now mounted a furious counterattack on the Australians, whose only option was to dig in and hold on bitterly to what they had won. What the diggers had achieved was extraordinary; members of two Australian battalions had even chased the Germans as far as the distant ruined windmill that overlooked Pozières, but they were ordered back to the new Australian lines by their officers, dozens killed or wounded as they ran back through the

German shelling. Now the Germans ranged in on the Australians with their artillery and many men would be slowly driven mad by the incessant shelling, forced to watch mates being ground into a bloody pulp as they sheltered wherever they could. After four days of fighting, the 1st Division had lost 5285 officers and men, many of the grievously wounded dying where they lay because the desperate Germans were also shooting stretcher-bearers. When the 2nd Division entered the battle almost a week later on 29 July, the Germans anticipated the attack and another 3500 men became casualties. Bean wrote later that 'Pozieres set the standard by which enemy shell fire was ever afterwards measured in the AIF, subsequent experiences being described as "better or worse than Pozieres"'.[5] In six weeks of fighting the Australians would suffer more than 20,000 casualties.

Early in his coverage of the battle, Bean tempered the reality of the fighting in an overzealous effort to wave the flag back home and convey the undoubted pluck of the newly blooded Australian 2nd Division; readers of one of his articles were assured that their soldiers in Pozières had 'walked through [shell bursts] exactly as if they were going home to tea', a repeat of the overdone writing he had delivered at Krithia.[6] Pointedly, Bean had written this report before he visited the actual frontline – his attitude to the battle would dramatically change when he finally saw for himself the true horror of what was really going on. After the war, his British journalist colleague Philip Gibbs described Pozières as:

> the last word in frightfulness. The intensity of the shellfire under which [the Australians] lay shook them

if it did not kill them. Many of their wounded told me that it had broken their nerve. They would never fight again without a sense of horror … Pozieres is now an Australian graveyard, and the memorial that stands there is to the ghosts of that splendid youth which fell in heaps about that plateau and the slopes below.[7]

On 31 July 1916, eight days after the Australian attack had begun, Bean went up to Pozières, threading his way to the frontline through deserted trenches scattered with dozens of clumped Australian dead. At times he was under shellfire and no doubt terrified, but he knew that to give a truthful account of what was really happening at Pozières he had to see it for himself. As a non-combatant under no obligation to visit the battlefield it was an extremely brave action, and making his way there he realised he was alone in a deserted and desolate landscape scattered with horrifically maimed human remains: 'There were only blackened dead and occasionally bits of men – torn bits of limbs unrecognisable along it.'[8] As he got closer he walked alone through eerily quiet trenches where dead Australian soldiers were sitting up half-buried, with no apparent wounds other than bandaged heads, others lying half-buried in the dugouts where they had been hit. He finally came across living Australian soldiers crammed into a narrow frontline trench who pointed him in the direction of the 19th Battalion. Well aware that a machine gun or an artillery shell could blow him to pieces at any moment, Bean was forced to step out again into the moonlike landscape, desperately clambering along a hedge line to avoid alerting a sniper. He was shocked by the condition of the dreadfully tired men he found from the 19th Battalion: 'they had been in for seven days and were clearly at the end of their powers ... There they live and are slowly pounded to death.'[9] Getting back out of the lines was even harder; Bean was led the way by a friendly soldier, past the corpses of blackened men, sending his guide back when he finally recognised the path – 'I hope he got home safe, good chap.'[10] When the shaken official correspondent sat down later that night and composed his thoughts he bluntly admitted, 'I don't want to go through Pozières again.'[11]

Bean camped that night on the side of a road with an Australian chaplain who ran a tea and coffee stall for the passing troops. The chaplain was also burying the scattered corpses of Australians who had fallen along the road, anxious to ensure the strewn dead not be too obvious to the troops still marching into Pozières: 'It does not encourage new troops to see a sight like that. They simply turn them into the nearest shell hole and cover them up.'[12] Lying in his trench listening to the padre going through the effects of dead men to be sent home to their families, Bean's recorded thoughts sound lonely and shattered by the experience. He heard screams as a shell fell in a wood a short distance away, discovering later that it had killed six men and wounded twenty-three. Bean admitted to himself that he found this constant shelling very trying; he was jolted to his core by what he had seen and, more than any other battle until then, it coloured his historical account of the battle.

One of the most powerful descriptions of Pozières came from letters written by a Victorian lieutenant, John Alexander (Alec) Raws. A journalist with *The Argus* newspaper in Melbourne prewar, Raws was among the 2nd Division troops thrown into an ill-conceived attack on the German trenches on 28 July; his account of what he witnessed before he was killed in the fighting remains one of the most quoted pieces of Australian war journalism of that era. Raws did not pull his punches, and nor did he affect the calm sangfroid expected of officers of the era; it is surprising that his letters escaped the censor's pencil as much as they did. He wrote about how distressed he was by what he witnessed, writing that his tunic 'is rotten with other men's blood and partly splattered with a comrade's brains. It is horrible but why should you people back home not know? Several of my friends are raving mad. I met three officers out in no-man's-land the other night, all rambling and mad. Poor devils.'[13]

Raws' shockingly candid accounts represented another Pozières entirely to the one correspondents like Bean had guilelessly portrayed, with cheery Australian diggers walking unaffected through artillery. Raws' journalistic instinct to report what he had seen came out in a letter to his family saying, 'Much that I would tell you cannot be spoken. But I boil to see the war through in order, inter-alia, to do what I can to expose some things the Australian public never dreams of.'[14] He told how he had driven Australian soldiers forward with his revolver, reaching to pull up what he thought was a fallen comrade and finding he had severed a head from a decaying corpse. Shortly before he was killed in action, Raws wrote a bitterly angry letter to a brother back in Melbourne about the death of Goldy, his other brother, in the same battle:

> Before going into this next affair at the same dreadful spot, I want to tell you, so that it may be on record, that I honestly believe Goldy and many other officers were murdered on the night you know of, through

> the incompetence, callousness, and personal vanity of those high in authority. I realise the seriousness of what I say but I am so bitter and the facts are so palpable that it must be said.[15]

In the writing of his official history, Charles Bean came under strong pressure to omit much of the detail in Raws' letters because several staff officers thought them 'overpitched and hysterical and showing the Australian as a weaker man than he really was'.[16] Even his friend Lieutenant General White (appointed lieutenant general in April 1919) wanted it omitted from the manuscript: 'Do you think the extract from Raws' diary is essential to the painting? I am doubtful … Don't you think his terms are a little extravagant? Perhaps in your desire to paint faithfully all he suffered, you have shown him to be weaker stuff than he is.'[17] But after wide consultation Bean decided that Raws' account accurately reflected the experience of Pozières, pointedly noting that the staff officers who made the criticism (including White) were rarely, if ever, in the forward trenches and had no conception of the nature of the bombing there. He quoted Raws' descriptions extensively throughout his official history, even taking a tilt at the staff officers who had tried to gag him, saying the Pozières fighting 'was not much visited by officers of the higher staffs'.[18] This was Bean at his journalistic best, for he had personally witnessed the shocked faces of men under fire in the forward trenches and he used his own experience to explain Raws' description of men driven mad by the shelling: 'The strain eventually became so great that what is rightly known as courage – the will to persist – would not suffice, since, however keen this will, the machinery of a man's self-control might become deranged.'[19] What was notable about Bean's postwar account of Pozières was its acknowledgement the Australians had a breaking point and that they had reached it there. He criticised the commanders for sending men back into the lines so soon after they had come out of the trenches, observing it only resulted in some soldiers being determined to never go through anything like it ever again.

Pozières was a shock for Bean: no more the disingenuous accounts for his readers of plucky Australians shrugging off the shellfire. He observed that Pozières had created:

> [a] certain bitterness towards the higher command. Some of the more thoughtful soldiers wondered (and could not be blamed for wondering) whether any sufficient objective was being gained by this excessive strain and loss. The prevailing tactics – repeated shallow advances on narrow fronts – were dreaded and detested ... it is not surprising if the effect on some intelligent men was a bitter conviction that they were being uselessly sacrificed.[20]

Addressing Alec Raws' claims that the British commanders' decisions were tantamount to murder, Bean compromised and said it was evidence 'not of the literal truth of his words, but of something much amiss in the higher leadership'.[21] This was extraordinary criticism for an official history and it is a credit to Bean that he held his nerve against those who wanted to suppress it.

However, yet again Charles Bean was gentle on the Australian command, for postwar in the official history he chose not to acknowledge the damning private admission by then Brigadier General White that he had been certain beforehand that it was wrong for the 2nd Division to have attacked at Pozières, an attack which subsequently failed with the loss of 3500 men. White had told Bean shortly after the battle: 'I was sure things were not ready but everyone was so eager that I gave my consent – through weakness I suppose – and you know what followed.'[22] It was an astonishing admission of command failure that would almost certainly have been gagged by the censor during the war but ought to have been fully recorded in the official history. Instead Bean compromised with what he revealed of his friend's admission, that White had held misgivings but not detailing his frank admission of failure. Bean's final official history account softened the blow: 'the atmosphere was one of extreme optimism. At corps headquarters General White, though full of misgiving, for once allowed the confidence of others to bear down his own judgment ...'[23]

Bean was always careful to protect White, whom he idolised as one of the greatest Allied generals, and so when he did finally air a criticism of his friend in his official history he again used the technique of a footnote to record a potentially embarrassing admission. While the note does mention White's feeling after the war that he and General Birdwood should bear the blame for not having protested more strongly about the British command's strategy at Pozières, such a significant admission should have been given more prominence.[24] It was an honourable expression of regret by White, who also gave Bean a candid account of his attempts to raise his concerns about the Pozières attack with General Haig. He described a condescending Haig, clearly not understanding the full facts of the battle, dressing down the two Australian generals based on his confused understanding: 'You're not fighting Bashi-Bazouks now … This is serious scientific war and you are up against the most scientific and most military nation in Europe.'[25] In his official history conclusions on Pozières, Bean was gentle, acknowledging that White and Birdwood shared responsibility for the disaster, 'but in this, their first introduction to the great operations of the Western Front, neither had yet fully attained the self-confidence which afterwards marked their actions'.[26] On balance, it may not have told the full story, but for a military history of the day it was a groundbreaking admission of failure.

More than any other battle, Pozières saw Bean connecting with the appalling suffering of the Australian soldier in a way he had not done so before. His diary, often written in a shallow trench amidst the human debris of the war, recorded his empathy for the men who were daily poured into such trenches, 'as in some ghastly mincing machine'.

> They have to stay there while shell after huge shell descends with a shriek close beside them. Each one, an acute mental torture – each shrieking tearing crash bringing a promise to each man – instantaneous – I will tear you into ghastly wounds – I will rend your flesh and pulp your arm or a leg – fling you, half a gaping, quivering man and like these that you see smashed around you one by one to lie there rotting and blackening … Every man in the trench has that instant fear thrust tight upon his shoulders – I don't care how brave he is – with a crash that is a physical pain and a strain to withstand.[27]

It is a pity writing like this did not find its way into Bean's journalism; he was often at his descriptive best in his private diaries.

Bean had lost far too many officer friends in the bloody graveyard of Pozières; one of the thousands of men killed by shellfire was the second-in-command of the 24th Battalion, Charles Manning, whom Bean had befriended at Lone Pine. Another was Captain Charles Littler from the 52nd Battalion, a Tasmanian who had served with American forces in the Philippines and was known as the Duke of Anzac, because he was older than most and a wise head. He had run the beach at Anzac Cove on Gallipoli and was now dead on the Western Front. Always carrying a walking stick into battle, Bean now told his Australian readers how Captain Littler had led his men into battle at Mouquet Farm near Pozières before being struck down during the charge. As he lay dying he had told the men around him, 'I will reach that trench if the boys do.'[28] A sergeant had then picked up the captain's walking stick and rallied the men to take the trench ahead of them. Bean was dejected by the loss of so many extraordinary men to what he felt were poor decisions from the British command – such sacrifice, but all for what?

> So ends another expensive, petty, operation. It has cost a fair part of a good battalion … and it has accomplished about half what was hoped for … I could not help being very bitterly depressed as I came back this morning. With all the will in the world one cannot see a spark of the genius or imagination which one would like to see in the British plans. Have they a plan?[29]

He was also bitter about the British newspaper correspondents, whose accounts tended to talk up the heroic role of British units, no matter the facts, and either played down or totally ignored the contribution of the Australians. '[N]one of them come within shellfire – much less rifle fire,' he complained. 'Every one of them is free to come where I do if they want – and goodness knows I'm careful and nervous enough; but they don't and the consequence is I suppose that they don't actually know what we have been doing.'[30] Bean subsequently wrote in the margins of this diary note, saying his attack on the British correspondents was an exaggeration but, as he wrote a little further on, 'we have fought the greatest battle in our history – one of the greatest in theirs – but not a suspicion of it would you get from the English papers'.[31]

Many of Bean's earlier reports had been run in the British press but he now discovered that his articles were being blocked, apparently because they referred to him as the official correspondent and the British censors had taken the view that the only 'official' comments on the war would come from them. The British command likely also took the view that the Australians were getting far too much good press, and that this was generating jealousy. As Bean himself described it, he was then hit by a 'bombshell': it appeared some of the British journalists were complaining about the facilities being given to Bean, and an unnamed British politician (probably Lloyd George) had voiced that grievance to command headquarters.[32] Bean's diary is coy on just what the complaint was about, but it is likely his candid frontline reports were ruffling feathers because they showed how much access he was getting, notably the fact that he had watched an opening bombardment from within 80 yards of the German trenches. As he wryly noted, those aggrieved British correspondents enjoying a nightly soft bed in their Amiens hotel away from the dangers of the front were welcome to join him anytime; they rarely did. Eventually the British relented and Bean's articles were allowed to be published, but without his name on the by-line. No explanation was ever given for this absurd restriction. 'G.H.Q. has apparently chosen this time to insist that too much appreciation shall not be given to the Australians. It is a miserably foolish decision when my country is fighting the greatest battle in its history,' Bean wrote.[33] He increasingly felt that Australia's contribution to the war was unappreciated by most of the British press.

On 5 August 1916, the Australian 2nd Division captured the windmill site that sat at the peak of the Pozières ridge, the German-held town of Bapaume now visible in the distance. The 4th Division was brought in to relieve the 2nd and tasked with taking Mouquet Farm, in a valley further along the ridge. But the attack was ill conceived and based on poor intelligence: the Germans had built an extensive network of defensive fortifications under the demolished farm buildings and, as the Australians moved along the narrow ridge towards the farm, they were cut down by German artillery fire. For three weeks the 1st, 2nd and 4th Australian divisions would be thrown into the attack on Mouquet Farm in what would ultimately prove to be a forlorn attempt to dislodge the enemy from its hidden bunkers.

When Charles Bean ventured again into the frontlines around Pozières on 17 August, he was horrified by the carnage as he carefully picked his way through the Australian trenches under shrapnel fire: 'dead men's legs – a shoulder, now a half buried body stick out of the tumbled red soil – bodies in all sorts of decay; some eaten away to the skull; blackened with the dried black skin drawn back from their teeth, eyelids dried thick and flattened like those of a mummy'.[34] On this journey he came the closest he had ever come to death when he walked alone up the trench line and a sniper took a bead on him, firing several shots and forcing Bean to shelter in a shallow crater. With classic understatement he realised he was 'in a bit of a quandary'.[35] What weighed on his mind as he lay there trying to avoid being shot was that if he was hit there was no one around who could come to his rescue; the risks Bean took to be faithful to his craft were breathtaking and made the pettiness of the British censors all the more difficult to comprehend. Bean later described the sniper attack as 'the biggest fright I ever had, and one had lots'.[36]

After the horrors of Pozières it scarcely seemed possible for things to get any worse, but when Bean finally caught up with the attack on Mouquet Farm he was assailed by even more confronting images of death around the frontline 10th Battalion command post: 'one poor chap had had his tunic and shirt torn bare by some piece of shell and you looked down past the bare white skin of the chest almost to the backbone – his whole body had been ripped open – he was bent back almost double as if he had taken strychnine. I can't bear to think of these things.'[37] Bean was haunted by the waxen faces of the dead men still reclining in lifelike poses around the trenches, and he was struck by how the guide showing him around had a 'strained, almost hunted, look' about him from days of dodging shells and snipers.[38] This was a new type of war, where men could be killed in clusters by concussion from a bomb blast and suffer no visible injuries. The effectiveness of the German artillery barrages meant nowhere was safe; it was only a matter of time before a man was hit.

It was in the midst of all this horror that Bean stumbled upon his Tasmanian cousin Leo Butler, the son of his mother's brother Ted. Leo had only been on the Western Front for a month with the 12th Battalion and the advance on Mouquet Farm was his first experience of combat. 'I heard a cheery voice say "Hello Charlie". It was Leo Butler. I was immensely relieved to see him.'[39] A practising barrister and a keen cricketer, Leo was the apple of his father Ted's eye and Bean knew it had been a terrible wrench for the family to send Leo off to join his brother Angus who was already in the fight. The two men sat yarning in the bottom of the 12th Battalion dugout and Bean left elated that day that he had been able to connect with his cousin.

But three days later came terrible news: Bean's brother Jack came to tell him that Leo had been hit just hours after Bean's visit, his leg severed by shrapnel while in the support trenches waiting to come out of the lines. Leo was taken to a hospital at Warloy-Baillon where his left leg was amputated at the hip but, despite the best efforts of the doctors, he soon died from shock.

One of Leo's oldest mates from years of cricket games at their Sandy Bay home was a doctor in the hospital; he hardly recognised his dear friend when he came in, only identifying him from his name on the ticket tied to his body. Bean lamented, 'So Leo – the finest specimen of manhood in Hobart – the big genial kindly chap who always used to come and meet us at the boat when she arrived, and to see us off when she sailed – who was always in my mind a man of the open air – the tennis court, the cricket field –Leo is gone.'[40] Charles Bean had known so many soldiers who had died in this war but this time it was a terribly personal loss and he was devastated: 'It is too sad and dreadful for words.'[41]

Leo's brother Angus, a mining engineer, was an officer with a British battalion then billeted in the village of Beauval, 24 kilometres north of Amiens. Bean's desperate efforts to find and console him the night he heard of Leo's death is touching testament to just how terribly distressed he was about his cousin's passing. It was a frantic trip in the middle of the night, Bean borrowing Brigadier General White's car; his driver rushing along the darkened roads at great risk without headlights. He hastened past carousing Australian soldiers enjoying a final drunken night in the village before entraining for the Somme the next day. For once the normally abstemious Bean confessed, 'I don't blame them – I should have felt inclined to get drunk myself.'[42] He resorted to banging on random doors in the village in the hope of finding Angus's billet, rousing French locals who came to the door in their nightshirts and bare legs. He finally found his cousin in a darkened bedroom sobbing for the loss of his older brother. 'I knew, of course, that he would be hit,' Angus told Charles. 'I made up my mind to that; but I always hoped he would just be wounded – not this.'[43] It was 3.30am when Charles finally left Angus, a slow three-hour drive past numerous military roadblocks back to the Australian command headquarters at Contay, then out again the next day to do his job as official correspondent.

Bean wrote a beautifully descriptive account for Leo's parents, Ted and Amy Butler, of Leo's passing and the burial service. He also kept the moving letters received from his family in the diary recording Leo's death, 'because they show the way in which a chance scrap of iron flung at random on the hillside in front of Mouquet drives its course right through to the furthest end of the world'.[44] Watching Leo's coffin being buried in a French wheatfield, a sympathetic French farmer's wife weeping near him, Bean could not help wondering whether it was all worth it, whether there was anything gained in this war that justified such sacrifices: 'I don't feel sure of it.'[45] It was a fair question; for what was the point now? The Allied offensive at Pozières to capture Mouquet Farm with the ultimate objective of seizing the town of Thiepval had totally failed with the loss of almost two divisions, British General Gough callously blaming his commanding officers' lack of discipline and motivation for their not being able to capture the ground.[46] In early September 1916 the battered I Anzac Corps was finally relieved at Mouquet Farm, and later that same month, with an artillery barrage that was finally big enough to properly support the attack, the farm was eventually seized by Canadian troops. But for all the sacrifice of the thousands of men who had died in the attacks at Pozières and Mouquet Farm between July and September, the Allied lines had only been advanced just under a kilometre along an eight-kilometre front. Charles Bean had good reason to question whether it was all worth it.

When the time came to record the official history account of Pozières, Bean was at pains to honour the terrible cost suffered by the Australians during the twelve-day bombardment of the village. His moving description of the effects of shellshock was only possible because he had suffered the bombing with them: 'the patients sitting in front of Vadencourt Chateau waiting for attention to their flesh wounds, nearly every one was shaking like an aspen leaf – a sure sign of overstrain by shell-fire'.[47]

He also tackled the question many Australians asked during and after the war: 'was this great effort of our countrymen – so pregnant with trouble for our nation – directed by prudent and capable generalship? Was it guided along lines likely to render a return for which it was worth incurring these crushing casualties?'[48] The postwar British line was that this was an 'economic' war of attrition, a strategy of mounting constant rolling attacks to wear down the enemy. But Bean was having none of that dissembling, and his analysis of Pozières was scathing: 'To throw the several parts of an army corps, brigade after brigade, in a series of battering ram blows twenty times in succession against one of the strongest points in the enemy's defences, may certainly be described as "methodical" but the claim that it was economic is entirely unjustified.'[49]

By September, after weeks of gruelling work recording the savagery of the Battle of the Somme, Bean needed a break. But before he left he went back into the battlefield one more time to find two other cousins from Tasmania, Duncan and Arthur Maxwell, brothers he had known so well in his youth whom he knew had just been through the horrors of Mouquet Farm as officers with the 52nd Battalion. They had served under their revered commanding officer, the now dead 'Duke of Anzac', Captain Littler, in some of the fiercest fighting. Perhaps after Leo's death, and the ghastly suffering he had witnessed at Pozières, Bean needed the reassurance of that connection with family. Following an arduous and dangerous hike through muddy trenches and fields he finally tracked down the lofty brothers, both of them well over six feet tall – so tall in fact that there was a hole dug in their trench to allow the tallest of the two, the six-foot five-inch brother nicknamed 'Shorty', a lower position from which he could fire his rifle without being too conspicuous. Bean was relieved that both had survived despite the loss of many of their officers and half the battalion. 'I walked back with Arthur light of heart and not the least reason was that I was turning my back on Pozières for the last time.'[50] Mercifully both Duncan and Arthur Maxwell were to survive the war despite extensive combat service, each of them earning a Military Cross for their valour. On their return Arthur farmed and Duncan became a doctor and married Marion Bridges, daughter of the former Gallipoli commander General Bridges, in 1934.

The battle and the loss of Leo had taken a huge emotional and physical toll on Bean. He later told his parents: 'I have aged a lot in this war. Everyone says so, so not to be surprised when you see me. Everyone lives three years in one during the war.'[51] Today the site where the windmill of Pozières stood is a solemn memorial to the thousands of Australian men who died trying to win the ground it once occupied. The bleak Picardy landscape stretches out into the distance, Mouquet Farm visible on the horizon. The cratered moonscape of 1916 is now just a memory, but farmers still find grisly relics of the dead: white bones, coins, identity discs or perhaps even a cigarette case from a fallen soldier a century ago. It was Bean who made the windmill iconic in his attempt to give some meaning to the losses; his tribute to those who fell there is written on the memorial stone and is justifiably one of his most quoted passages:

> The Windmill site … with the old mound still there – marks a ridge more densely sown with Australian sacrifice than any other place on earth.[52]

Twelve

A DECEIT ON THE AUSTRALIAN PEOPLE

There is only one way out of this war for an infantryman, and that is on his back, either sick, wounded or dead.

CHARLES BEAN

Australia's metropolitan newspapers were sobering reading in the months from July through to September 1916. Day after day, long casualty lists named the dead and wounded boys who just a year or so earlier had left the country in their prime. Entire communities had lost the bulk of their menfolk and the heart-achingly young faces of the fallen featured for weeks after the bloody mess of Pozières. The realisation was setting in that this war was not some happy adventure, and patriotic fervour to enlist began to wane. At the peak of Gallipoli fever in July 1915, enlistments had rocketed to 36,575 for the month. But by the latter part of 1916 the combined Australian casualties from Gallipoli and the Western Front were topping 56,000 men, while enlistments had fallen to just 6000 a month. However Prime Minister Billy Hughes looked at it, enlistments were nowhere near enough to top up the five Australian divisions with fresh blood. Australia was a volunteer army but he now desperately wanted conscription – compulsory military service – to keep the numbers up for the Empire. England had gone with conscription in January 1916 and the New Zealanders followed in June. Now a massive propaganda campaign was under way to persuade Australia to support conscription in a national vote on 28 October, with the troops voting a week earlier.

While resting behind the lines in Belgium in early September, Bean started hearing the rumours that Australia's 3rd Division would have to be disbanded because of the dwindling enlistments, meaning that all the 3rd Division men would be allocated as reinforcements to Australia's remaining divisions. It was a move Bean strongly opposed because it would be 'like carving up a living tree'.[1] But it was all a political play, a confidence trick on the Australian public: the British Army wanted more meat for the grinder and it knew that threatening to disband General Monash's 3rd Division would bring matters to a head, perhaps pushing public opinion in Australia towards support for conscription. 'Mr Hughes is very anxious to have conscription adopted in Australia against the wishes of his party,' Bean wrote in his diary, 'and a tremendous argument would be "Look, recruiting is so bad that we have had to do away with the 3rd Australia Division" … Hughes is working hand in glove with Lloyd George, who is also a politician and therefore crooked.'[2]

Bean wrote at the time that Brigadier General White was angry about them using the claim that the 3rd Division faced disbandment to push for conscription; he had told Bean it was not a straight thing to do. But clearly both generals Birdwood and White had embraced the push for conscription and they endorsed a highly disingenuous cable sent to Australia in late August, which recommended a special draft of 20,000 extra infantry to bring the 3rd Division back up to strength in addition to the existing enlistments. They also supported a call for monthly enlistments to be raised to 16,500 per month for the five Australian divisions. This was a totally unnecessary demand, as Bean later acknowledged in his official history: 'This staggering demand, though ultimately found to be enormously in excess of the need, was sincerely made, and, as such, was accepted.'[3] Ever laudatory about both men, he repeated this claim in his later biography of White that both generals had made this demand in all sincerity, but it is more likely that the wily generals knew full what they were doing and allowed the requested numbers of reinforcements to be deliberately inflated to help boost the 'Yes' campaign back in Australia.[4] When Bean arrived in London a few days later, Keith Murdoch, by now very close to Hughes and heavily involved as a political player for him in London, admitted the breaking up of the 3rd Division was all a ploy to force the conscription vote. 'It is crooked, crooked, crooked,' Bean wrote. 'It is a deceit on the Australian people. And I believe they would see the need for conscription without it.'[5] He was wrong. The politicians knew what he clearly did not: that Australians were tiring of the fight.

Bean was now a long way from the unquestioning subservience to the Empire that he had learned at Clifton College. He complained privately about a decision by the British command requiring press correspondents to don the Sam Browne belts commonly worn by British officers, a relic of the day when all officers wore swords. Before his experiences with the British in Gallipoli and the Western

Front, Bean would probably have heeded this edict without complaint, but after seeing the British up close he was having none of it: 'Somehow the Sam Browne belt is to me all that is worst in the snobbishness of the British Army. It is the secret of the British Army system that officers should be as unlike to and different from their men as possible.' Bean was increasingly contemptuous of how the British class system permeated the way the British Army officer class treated their troops, 'a race of gentlemen who can command and a race of Tommies who are to receive commands and who wouldn't dream of disputing that order of things'.[6] Bean felt that in contrast an Australian officer did not want the social distinction that the Sam Browne belt brought, 'that his men follow him for what he knows and what he does, and sometimes for what he is, and not because he is of a superior social caste'.[7] Bean did not know it yet but much the same kind of transformation pervaded the Australian attitude to conscription; the British command was glibly assuming the Australians would vote as they were told they should, but it was in for a rude shock.

On the boat back to France after leave in London on 24 September 1916, Bean ran again into Keith Murdoch, who was by now deep in intrigue on Billy Hughes's behalf, planning for the imminent vote on conscription to be cast by all the troops on the Western Front. Bean felt that 95 per cent of the troops would support conscription but Murdoch, gifted with a shrewder political head, was not so sure; he had been talking to soldiers on leave in England who were strongly opposed to it. He told Bean Australian soldiers were against conscription because they had 'been fighting England's battles for her and we don't see why we should ask more of our people to come over here and fight them'.[8]

The feeling about Australia's huge losses at Pozières was strong and the Australians were sick of fighting – there were even claims that some men of the 4th Division had hooted at General Birdwood as he passed and called out 'Butcher'.[9] Bean recorded one incident that showed just how out of touch Birdy was with that feeling among his men after he stopped to chat to some resting Australian soldiers: 'Well fellows, having a good rest?' The Australians had answered that they were. 'That's right. You deserve it. Get all the rest you can,' Birdwood told them. 'And then you'll be able to come back soon and kill some more Germans.'[10] Bean noticed how the men's faces had immediately dropped and how Birdwood never let them see that he also noticed their response.

> But they have not got over Pozieres yet. This new force of ours is just realising – each man in the infantry individually, for the first time in most cases – that there is only one way out of this war for an infantryman, and that is on his back, either sick, wounded or dead ... There is no way out. They are looking down the long road straight to the end.[11]

Bean said the censor would never let such an admission be written in the newspapers for fear it would affect recruiting, and he was angry about some of the nonsense being printed in the Australian newspapers. One article lavished praise on the Australians for their prowess at Mouquet Farm with knives and revolvers, yet it was a complete invention, he said; the Australians used no knives and few revolvers in that fighting.[12] 'The truth is soldiers are not the fictions which war correspondents have made of them but ordinary human men,' Bean wrote, perhaps not appreciating the irony that some of his own earlier overzealous articles had glowingly endowed the Anzacs with the superhuman ability to walk through shellfire unscathed.[13] He commented that after what he had experienced of Pozières, for any soldier to choose to go back into battle was far more heroic. Desertion was a growing problem in the AIF; 300 men were absent without leave in September and how to discipline these infractions was a concern because, while the British shot deserters, Australia carried out no death sentences on its volunteer army. Bean was defensive of the Australians. He felt that most of them were AWOL while they were on rest out of the lines, whereas he had seen British soldiers deserting their posts during the Somme frontline fighting: 'You don't hear them discussing that.'[14]

In late September Bean undertook a tour of the Australian positions on the Western Front with the former Labor prime minister Andrew Fisher, now high commissioner in London. Fisher was on the Dardanelles Commission investigating the debacle at Gallipoli and, privy to the obvious failings there, he now confided to Bean that he was strongly opposed to conscription in Australia. Fisher was appalled by the horrendous conditions the troops had to endure on the frontlines and increasingly sceptical of the British push for conscription. 'He told me the thought of it sometimes took away his night's rest. He thought it would lead to bloodshed in Queensland. I should have said that this was a complete misjudgement,' Bean recorded.[15] Twelve shells fell around the party, one landing just 45 metres distant. Looking out of the car window at the desolated landscape, a clearly affected Fisher said to Bean and his colleagues, 'You might as well leave me in hell as leave me here.'[16]

During September Bean also took Murdoch into the ruins of Pozières to show him around the scene of Australia's greatest battle, the only remains of what had once been a village being splintered wood and crushed bricks edging huge craters. Around the windmill he noted a crater moonscape of red brown mud, 'the thin walls between the shell holes stuck up in front of you like a series of frail crumbling fences'.[17] In the bottom of another shell hole the pair discovered one of the new weapons used in the battle, a tank covered with a tarpaulin, stranded in the deep crater. The two men did not stay for long as being there without a military minder could get them arrested, but they must have looked a comical sight carrying relics from the battlefield, Bean with a portion of a broken piano keyboard and Murdoch lugging a shell-battered steel rail. When they stopped to chat with some Irish Guards, Bean was struck by 'the sort of restrained, subdued, air of men who know they have probably got to die … and who accept the fate'.[18]

As the grim autumnal rain set in, the thick mud made any sort of sustained attack impossible, especially using the heavy tanks, and the brief to all Australian commanders was to keep up frequent raids on the German trench positions. Bean did what he could to record the recollections of men who had fought at Pozières and Mouquet Farm, also taking British photographer Ernest Brooks around the battlefield to record the scene. Rain and shellfire had exposed the buried corpses of Australian soldiers from the 24th Battalion, intermingled with German dead.

The feeling about what Australians had endured there was still strong and bitter; General Birdwood had asked men of the 12th Battalion if they wanted to go back into battle and 'he got a straight NO from one end of the trenches to the other'.[19] For the first time, Bean realised that this was going to affect the vote on conscription: 'the men think they are being driven … and they will not give the word for others to be driven too'.[20] In mid-October, just before the conscription vote, Bean began hearing rumours that the Australians would be involved in another big 'push', back into the horrors of the Somme; the commanders hoping to influence the conscription vote could not have timed things worse. Then, as Bean was about to leave for England to visit the Royal Navy's Grand Fleet, Brigadier General White sent a message asking him not to go without talking to him first. Prime Minister Hughes had just cabled General Birdwood explaining that the public opposition to conscription in Australia was formidable.[21] Clearly panicking at the possibility of a 'no' vote, Hughes was now calling on Birdwood to send a message to Australians calling on them to support conscription, a highly inappropriate request by a politician to any serving general. White now asked Bean to approach Birdwood while he was in London and ask him to undertake this 'big step'. Bean knew it was quite improper for Hughes to ask this – 'I have a very great fear of anyone in Birdwood's position – a military servant of the State using his influence in a big question at the polls' – but he did it anyway.[22]

It was also a curious step for White as a serving brigadier general to ask a journalist to lobby his commander in this way, and it was extraordinary for Bean to be involving himself in such a campaign as a supposedly independent journalist, even by the standards of that time. It was revealing too that White took for granted Bean would do as he was bidden by his AIF employer. When he got to London and tracked down Birdwood, the general told him he was not prepared to send a message to the Australian people, but he did eventually agree to send a message to the troops, despite already rebuffing a similar request from Keith Murdoch and Lloyd George because he felt his opponents might accuse him of telling his soldiers how to vote (exactly what he would have been doing). This time the general compromised and agreed to write a message to the men, taken down by Bean, saying 'he wanted them to vote by their consciences and not to influence them in any way. But he added that he probably knew better than they did, the need for reinforcements'.[23] Birdwood repeated the claim in his message that a vote against conscription might mean units would have to be broken up, also pushing the line that a 'yes' vote would capture the shirkers back home in Australia.

It was the day before the poll when Bean finally had this message in hand, too late to circulate it, so Birdwood actually ordered a postponement of the vote to allow sending it to all the troops. 'I hope it does the business. For I am <u>sure</u> conscription is right,' Bean wrote.[24] The official correspondent had crossed a line of propriety that flew in the face of all notions of journalistic independence. Back in Australia, Billy Hughes was deploying all manner of dirty tricks to sway the vote, his *War Precautions Act* allowing the censorship of any report that might discourage recruitment. Mindful that part of the reason for Australia's substantial Irish Catholic population's objection to conscription was because of the violent British military clamp-down in the Easter Rising, Hughes even asked the British government to make a conciliatory gesture to them to secure more of the vote.[25] Australian newspapers were almost unanimously supportive of conscription, including *The Sydney Morning Herald*:

> Our one clear call is to vote 'yes' on Saturday because we dare not be afraid. Our duty by the Empire demands that we shall send every man we can spare to the Front and do it without quibbling or hesitation.[26]

But as it became clear that the soldiers' vote a week before the main one was likely to go against conscription, it was Keith Murdoch who made the extraordinary suggestion to Hughes that the AIF vote be hidden among the mass result for each state lest the soldiers' views sway the rest of the nation. As Les Carlyon has written, 'Here was something unusual; a journalist telling a politician to suppress a news story.'[27]

His foray into politicking over, Bean went on to his tour of the Allied naval fleet at Scapa Flow in Scotland, a puzzling move considering the highly newsworthy conscription vote was imminent on the Western Front. But nothing was going to stop this enthusiast from seeing the seat of British imperial naval power. He was flattered when Admiral John Jellicoe placed him at his right hand at a welcoming lunch, and he was delighted when the admiral bade him farewell at the end of an exciting day discussing his passion for battleships, saying, 'We have followed your work Captain Bean. You seem to have been closer to this war than most people.'[28] Bean was rapt that his naval knowledge had been recognised, and he was perhaps too much in thrall to his long-held passion for things naval because now a major story was unfolding back in the Somme without him.

The results of the conscription vote were already becoming clear from early voting and Bean lamented that Birdwood's message to the troops appeared to have had the reverse effect to that intended: many troops were saying 'no' to conscription, so everything now rested on the vote back in Australia. So blatant was the attempted fix by AIF commanders that, Bean recorded, it was even agreed any favourable Western Front poll results helpful to the vote back in Australia would be telegraphed home, whereas 'anything unfavourable will be suppressed'.[29] Bean did not show the same high dudgeon about this deceit on the Australian public as he had about the ploy of the proposed disbandment of the 3rd Division. Even while voting was continuing, several prominent Australians were, with British commander General Haig's support, sent across to France to address troops about the importance of voting for conscription, pushing the line that Australia would lose her high standing with Britain if the vote was knocked back; what the AIF and Bean failed to understand was that the troops no longer cared what Mother England thought of them. Pozières had made them Australians.

Meeting Keith Murdoch in London, Bean learned that early results showed the Western Front vote going narrowly in favour of conscription by a ten per cent majority, but that was not the resounding win the AIF and Billy Hughes had hoped for to sway the main national vote. In fact, most of the soldiers voting 'yes' to conscription were men in support roles, not on the frontlines, and when the actual fighting soldiers' votes were isolated it was clear they had voted overwhelmingly against conscription, an astonishing act of defiance against the clear wishes of their AIF commanders that was suppressed from news reports in Australia. It appears Bean either never wrote an article about the soldiers' opposition to conscription or was gagged by the censor, but it was certainly a significant story that should have been told. A week later in Australia, the final vote came out narrowly against conscription. The decision did not prove to be the disaster for the AIF that had been so grimly predicted and, following another failed vote just over a year later, Australia was to remain a volunteer army for the rest of the war.

Bean was concerned that Brigadier General White felt Bean had made a mess of his errand with Birdwood, and that directing the latter's message to the troops and not to the people of Australia had kindled public fears that Birdwood was attempting a 'dangerous influence' on the poll; Bean was defensive, saying Birdwood had a perfect right to tell the troops his opinion.[30] Troops interviewed by Bean explained why they believed Australians had voted against conscription: 'They wanted enough Australians left to maintain Australia's present character after the war. They did not want so many Australians killed off that the population of immigrants flowing in should alter the characteristics of the country'.[31] That was one explanation; another was simpler, that the soldiers were so bitter about what they were enduring that they had simply chosen to do the opposite of what their commanders wanted as an act of defiance.

The conscription debate was a low point in Bean's role as official correspondent, and there is no escaping the fact that although much of his reportage was painstaking throughout the war, he sometimes allowed himself to be compromised by blind loyalty to the AIF commanders he saw as friends. The official history makes no mention of Bean's conspicuous role in soliciting Birdwood's message to the troops. When the *Bulletin* magazine correspondent known as 'Xenophon' commented in 1929 on the publication of Bean's official history account of 1916, no one but the editor knew it was actually former Brigadier General Pompey Elliott, one of the senior AIF commanders, who was writing such a scabrous diatribe against Bean for his perceived bias:

> Bean, it must be remembered, was not appointed in the first place as official historian. His appointment, as he conceived it; was that of publicity agent for the AIF, its commanders and their staff … He represented Birdwood as the soul of Anzac and White as the divinely gifted staff officer whose lynx-eyed vigilance foresaw every difficulty, anticipated every obstacle … Later Bean was made Official Historian. And can he be expected now to show indignation? Can he choke over his own words? How can he pull aside the curtain and display the clay feet of those colossi that he has so painfully built up?[32]

Pompey Elliott was haunted by the memory of the men he wept for at Fromelles, and today we would probably acknowledge that he suffered from post-traumatic stress disorder. It is likely too that he was still bitter towards Bean after his Cairo exposés of Australian Boer War veteran excesses. Tragically, in March 1931, when he was just 52 years old, Elliott took his own life. He had publicly praised Bean's *Official History of Australia in the War* but there is no record to show that Charles Bean ever learned that Elliott was privately also one of his strongest critics.

At the beginning of November 1916, Bean visited the new Australian frontline positions where the Anzac Corps had been deployed around the towns of Flers and Gueudecourt. The cruel Somme mud soon made it clear how impossible it would be for the men to do little other than just hold on and try to survive in their trenches during the coming winter months. Even the local roads were falling apart and liquid mud was streaming down them, the military horses almost completely daubed with sludge up to their eyes. Bean found the trenches narrow and 'sticky as glue' as he and a military intelligence officer escort waded through the ooze up to their knees.[33] Conditions for the men were appalling: soldiers were forbidden from digging shelters out of the trench walls because this caused collapses, so some stomped on the spot, turning the floor of the trench to a sloppy mire. Bean's official history describes one soldier 'standing with his feet deep in the mud, his back against the trench wall, shaken by shivering fits from head to foot, but fast asleep'.[34] Trench foot, a form of frostbite, was common in the frontlines, soldiers losing their lower legs to gangrene as infection set into the wound. Bean later wrote that the series of unsuccessful operations undertaken by the Australians to the end of November were, because of the weather and the state of the ground, 'undoubtedly the most difficult in which the AIF was ever engaged'.[35]

On 5 November two Australian battalions attacked the German's so-called Bayonet Trench, which bulged into the Allied lines about half a kilometre north of Gueudecourt. Another attack also targeted German positions north of Flers called the Maze. Both failed, the Australians winning and then soon losing a small part of the Maze in a German counterattack. Despite these clear warning signs that attacks were a waste of both time and good soldiers in the appalling conditions, General Haig insisted the offensives continue, but they were constantly delayed by bad weather. However the gruesome casualty toll continued, and Bean added another two friends, both exemplary commanders, to the list of the dead. Lieutenant Colonel Owen Howell-Price, one of the youngest AIF battalion commanders whom Bean had befriended at Gallipoli, was shot through the head by a sniper, his last words 'Give my love to the battalion'. Then Brigadier General Duncan Glasfurd, who had been a staff officer with Brigadier General White and was commanding the 13th Brigade, was hit and mortally wounded by a shell; the awful conditions meant it had taken ten hours to get his stretcher out of the battlefield to a casualty clearing station. Bean was jolted by Glasfurd's death; they had been close friends ever since they had shared the boat journey out from Melbourne on the *Orvieto*.

The First Battle of the Somme was over by 19 November after almost four grinding months of killing. There was little to show for the loss of hundreds of thousands of men, the British lines now only about ten kilometres further advanced than they had been when the offensive began months earlier. Bean had British propaganda officer John Buchan's comments from the very first day of the battle back in July ringing in his ears, that the British Army was prepared to lose 500,000 casualties on the Somme. Bean acidly noted that half a million men had now been 'duly expended. The question arises how far that sacrifice was justified by the results.'[36]

Thirteen

UTTERLY SICK OF THE WAR

Boys, I can assure you that no-one regrets this disaster that has befallen your brigade more than I do.

General Birdwood to the 4th Brigade after First Bullecourt

Five weeks before Christmas 1916, Charles Bean noted a change in the normally cheery disposition of the Australian 5th Division troops he saw returning from the Somme frontline. He was shocked by 'the look of the men. Not demoralised in any degree – but grey – drawn faces – and very very grim. It is the first time I ever passed an Australian battalion without seeing a single smile on any man's face.'[1] A concerned padre observed that their blank faces would not look any different if they were dead.

The next morning was Bean's thirty-seventh birthday and he looked outside to discover thick snow had fallen during the night; he at least was in a warm billet while thousands of shivering Australian soldiers were holding the frontlines with no shelter from the sub-zero temperatures in one of the most brutal winters on record in the Picardy region. Apart from occasional raids, the bitter cold meant that there was little fighting happening, but the incessant barrage of artillery from both sides meant the gruesome toll of casualties mounted anyway. Bean had spent so much time out in the field he too was suffering from chilblains on his toes and fingers and could hardly walk at times. But he still forced himself into the trenches, spending these stagnant, sapping weeks for the Australians in the frontline gathering information and anecdotes on recent battles, his battered diaries recording a litany of horror stories about the weather's impact. One injured officer of the 2nd Division was stuck in mud in a shell hole for four days before he was found. Well-meaning soldiers then tried to tug him out of the hardened slime by fastening a rope around him, but they broke his back and the poor man died.[2]

There was some Australian good humour; one staff officer told Bean how he asked an Australian soldier why he drank the 'beastly' rum ration they were given. 'This,' said the man, staring at him comically. 'This? Why, if you'd give us each a bottle of rum and put Berlin out of bounds I believe we'd be there tomorrow.'[3] When the story was told to British AIF commander General Birdwood, he did not see the joke. Like most British officers he saw the Australian vice for drink as a serious concern and felt that making light would only encourage it.

Bean was keeping busy despite the conditions, having agreed to be editor of a new troop newspaper, *The Rising Sun*. He also finally got permission to bring a staff photographer into the battlefield to begin recording key locations and was assigned British photographer Herbert Baldwin, who arrived in late November. They soon went up to Mouquet Farm to take pictures of the desolate shell-cratered battlefield, one of the trenches still full of unearthed corpses of buried Germans and Australians. Bean was by now quite cavalier about the constant threat of German artillery fire as the watching enemy targeted them: 'The Germans put some beastly quick shrapnel shell over, quite close enough to kill us.'[4]

War artist Will Dyson, a famed newspaper cartoonist from Ballarat in civilian life, also arrived to begin drawing under Bean's instructions. Bean immediately commissioned him to capture the look of the men returning from the winter frontlines: 'Dyson has got hold of the weary detached way in which men come out of these trenches … he will produce a drawing, he tells me, which will give the idea of it. [Y]ou know – a line of men, all going slowly along, no step more than about three inches – every man utterly detached as if they were living in a world by themselves.'[5] Dyson wrote of the men in his subsequent drawing 'Coming out of the Somme' as 'those ghosts of young men … moving like chain gangs dragging invisible chains … men walking in their sleep … garbed like ragged adventurers of another age.'[6]

The war was also beginning to take its toll on the commanders, including Major General James McCay (appointed major general in May 1916), notorious for the futile attacks at Krithia and Fromelles. His health was flagging and there were questions too about his mental state; he had led a failed 2nd Division attack at Flers that cost 819 casualties. Now, as Bean confided to his diary, there was talk that McCay 'had no longer his old courage' and that his nerve had given way: 'It needs a young hard man really to stand a winter on the Somme.'[7] Two weeks later Birdwood removed McCay back to England on medical grounds.

There was huge resentment that the vote for conscription had been rebuffed and Bean spent a lot of time asking men and officers why the vote had gone so hard against. One officer suggested the men had mistakenly believed that if the 'no' vote meant there were insufficient reinforcements to prop up the division then they would be taken out of the frontline, but there they still were. A small number of men were carrying a disproportionately heavy burden. Bean wrote in his diary: 'Very sad, as White says, that the willing men have to come and bear all the brunt of it while the straw hatted holiday makers and coal strikers stay at home and enrich themselves.'[8] When John Monash's 3rd Division came across from training in England to enter the Somme frontlines at Armentières, the troops were ribbed everywhere they went for finally joining the war.

At 11pm on Christmas Eve 1916, Bean was writing in his billet when a rolling and continuous artillery barrage began on the frontlines nearby; some commander, German or British, had decided to welcome in Christmas and Bean was livid about it.

> I must say I hate and detest the sheer sacrilege of this. I am not a religious man – I don't know that I bear any allegiance to the Christian faith. But this day represents the birth of a very precious ideal into the world; and the observance of it is a sign of our the [sic] attachment of a good part of the human race to the highest ideals yet imported on the earth. We are supposed to be fighting for just those ideals against other ideas which we hold vile.[9]

He felt that the men from the 5th Division were in the toughest sector along the whole British front and that provoking a German retaliation on Christmas Day was yet another miscalculation by unthinking commanders who did not comprehend how fragile the men were. 'Some of them are utterly sick of the war and do not want to fight again – it is as bad as that – peace at any price rather than that misery.'[10] What especially infuriated him was that he knew Birdwood had ordered an artillery bombardment on the German trenches at 11am on Christmas Day, just as the Germans were sitting down to Christmas lunch. 'What does it mean. It means that while GHQ is having its comfortable Christmas festivities – while General Birdwood is making nice speeches to troops in the rear, the German is retaliating on our poor chaps up in the front.'[11] When Bean went out into the trenches he could not bring himself to wish the troops 'merry Christmas' because it would have made a mockery of them.

As if he did not already have enough on his plate, Bean was also working on a book that would be published in 1917 as *Letters From France*. It was largely a compilation of many of his unpublished notes and articles, but what it showed was that whereas his *Official History* and news articles were sometimes stultifying in their obsession with detail, he was capable of writing moving prose. It was as if, once liberated from the constraints he had imposed upon himself as the official correspondent, he could let loose a little: 'On our way back is a field pock-marked by a hundred ancient shell holes around a few deserted earth works. On some by gone afternoon it must have been wild raging reeking hell there for half an hour or so because somebody in this landscape put a red tick once against that long forgotten corner.'[12] Admirably, he chose to earn nothing from the book project, donating any profits to nursing blinded or maimed soldiers. For Bean the book was an opportunity to drive home his mantra with the people back home: Australians and Britons were colossally ignorant of the privations and struggle required to win the war. He was at his best when he did not have to tell a blow-by-blow account of a battle, as he felt he had to do in his history or a news article. His descriptive eye came to the fore with his pen portraits of individuals, such as an elderly German soldier taken prisoner who 'looked about him firmly enough, but with that open-eyed gaze of a wild animal which seemed to lack all comprehension. It was the face of a man almost witless. He wore the uniform of a German captain. He was one of the men who had been through the bombardment.'[13]

The suffering of the Australians on the Western Front had concentrated Charles Bean's mind on how to ensure that the Australian public knew what their soldiers had endured when the war was over, and it was around this time that the official correspondent first conceived the idea of a war memorial that would preserve the sacred relics and historical documents of the war. During one visit to London in January he talked with the high commissioner, Andrew Fisher, and AIF officials about his idea for the creation of an Australian War Records Section that would collect items for such a memorial during the war. Almost immediately he came up against the English censors. He was keen to preserve a photograph taken by Ernest Brooks in August featuring Australian stretcher-bearers returning from no-man's-land under a white flag with a wounded soldier; but he was now told the censors had actually torn up the print and broken the negative photographic plate because they 'haven't much time here for white flags – to tell the truth'.[14] Bean knew that the use of a white flag was often the only way of safely getting a wounded man and his stretcher-bearers back safe and alive, and the photograph was not advocating surrender at all as the censor inferred; instead it showed the heroism of the stretcher-bearers who constantly took the risk of being shot. Bean privately vented his spleen at the censor, the 'stupid, overfed, fat red-tabs, enjoying their cigars in front of the fire until they drowse and their heads drop over their newspaper – they have no use for the system which enables the poor wretch groaning in a shell hole 100 yards out in no-man's-land, with the ants eating his lips and eyes, and the flies stinging him, and the knowledge of death from thirst staring him straight in the face, to be brought in and tended. Of course they haven't. But I'd willingly sign a warrant to make them change places with the poor wretch out there and get some atom of imagination driven into the dull matter of their heavy brains.'[15] However all was not lost as Bean was eventually able to retrieve another print of the photograph elsewhere, but his zeal to collect a record of Australia's service was to frequently bring him into conflict with the censors and obstinate British bureaucrats over the next couple of years.

Back home in Australia the conscription vote had split the federal Labor Party, many of whose members felt betrayed by Billy Hughes's support for it. The prime minister, after much agonising, decided to form a coalition with the Liberals, who made it a condition of the coalition that any federal election be deferred until October 1918 or six months after the war, whichever came earlier. This forced Hughes to go to the polls because the Senate refused to support the extension of the term of the current Parliament, and an election was called for 5 May. It also meant that Hughes, needing to campaign, would not be able to attend the London Imperial War Conference in March. This infuriated Bean; always something of a political naïve, he was angry at what he saw as petty politicking back in

Australia and wrote an article criticising the 'infinitesimally small-minded politicians' who could not put party considerations aside to allow the country to be represented at the conference.[16] The gathering was important because it showed the new British Prime Minister Lloyd George believed the former colonies should have a say about the conduct of the war, effectively representing an Imperial War Cabinet comprising England and all her dominions. But Billy Hughes was fighting for his political life and many of his Labor colleagues were deeply suspicious of what such an imperial federation represented, not least because they feared it might be a backdoor way of imposing conscription on Australia: if Hughes went to London, would he 'win the war and damn Australia'?[17] It was a highly controversial move then for Charles Bean to write another story calling for Australia's politicians to drop their 'party quarrels' and 'personal differences', purporting to speak for the Anzacs when he wrote that there was a need for unity.[18] The AIF's official correspondent was risking the accusation that he was improperly meddling in legitimate political debate, and criticism of his politicking soon appeared in newspapers across the country:

> It is regrettable that Captain Bean should butt in with a special cablegram on the matter to express as he says 'how the party situation in Australia appears to such Australians as I know overseas'. Such indiscretions seem to me particularly unfortunate at this juncture because they appear to be merely an attempt to help the Prime Minister. It is sheer impertinence and a waste of good Commonwealth money to utilise the cable to let us know what Captain Bean thinks

> upon the matter. The next we will probably have from him is advice as to how we should run the Commonwealth in his absence.[19]

There were even calls for Parliament to address Bean's 'unwarrantable intrusion' in going beyond his permitted role as a Commonwealth employee by effectively promoting the conscription cause. Ironically, he also copped it from the pro-conscriptionists for not going harder; Bean was worried that the influential Sydney-based *Bulletin* magazine had 'gone against' him for daring to assume to speak for the troops on the necessity of Hughes coming to the Imperial War Conference.[20] A *Bulletin* story had also blamed Bean in part for the low levels of enlistment, suggesting his articles had been 'colourless and no waverer's pulse has been quickened by them'. It suggested that Australia needed another Ashmead-Bartlett, presumably to write the kind of jingoistic patter that would drive young men to sign up. It also echoed the concerns of many commentators across the country about Hughes's ambitions at the conference, suggesting he had 'gone quite mad on the subject of an organic imperialism and would tomorrow, if he could, pull the Commonwealth into entanglements and commitments that would change the whole face of her political life and upend the status of the Australian citizen. It would be a calamity for Australia.'[21]

One of Bean's former Supreme Court friends, Justice Ferguson, also sent Bean a copy of a letter he had written to the London *Times*, complaining there was not enough news back home about the Australian troops. Bean was hurt – 'I don't think he means it to hit at me, but it does' – not least because the Australian papers were choosing not to publish many of his articles.[22]

For months the Allies had been picking up rumours the Germans were planning a withdrawal from their positions on the Western Front, and on 23 February 1917 it finally happened. The Germans abandoned their trenches and moved their entire western army back many kilometres behind a new defensive position that would become known as the Hindenburg Line. As Major General White (appointed major general a month earlier, in January 1917) explained to Bean, it was a crafty move because it freed up German divisions to be deployed elsewhere. It was also an exhilarating time for the Allied troops, who thought this meant the beginning of the end of the war, and there were heavy losses on both sides as the Germans engaged in a fighting withdrawal, often leaving booby traps in the empty trenches, while the villages they had occupied were all flattened, everything of strategic value destroyed. On 17 March Bean got the news that the French town of Bapaume, seventeen kilometres northeast of Albert, had been taken by the Allies, and he went there two days later with photographer Herbert Baldwin. The Germans still had snipers targeting the Australians entering the town, but as Bean watched they soon fled once the 5th Brigade troops began returning fire. Some of the destroyed houses in the town had furniture and wood stacked up inside them, with tar poured over the pile; the Germans had clearly not had time to set fire to the buildings as they had intended. Bapaume had previously been behind the German frontlines, and what struck everyone was that now, just beyond the town, instead of the usual shell-hole pock-marked landscape, beautiful green fields stretched off into the distance. Bean noted graffiti near the German observation post overlooking this scene saying *Gott Strafe*

England (may God punish England).[23] Time and time again throughout the war Bean exposed himself to extraordinary danger, but on 26 March came another close shave when the dugout he and his batman, Arthur Bazley, shared for several days at Bapaume was destroyed by a massive delayed mine left by the Germans, killing two signallers. After the war, Bean told how the rescue party trying to find the two men discovered one of his precious diary notebooks buried in the wreckage. Bazley discreetly noted in his diary for that day that Bean 'looks a bit nervy tonight'.[24]

The German withdrawal to the massively fortified Hindenburg Line threw Allied plans for a major new 1917 Somme offensive into disarray. But on 9 April British General Edmund Allenby's Third Army launched what at first was a successful offensive, its Canadian Corps heroically seizing the hugely strategic position of Vimy Ridge with terrible losses, but there the attack eventually stalled. The pressure was now on the Australians to have their own crack at capturing the German-held town of Bullecourt 30 kilometres to the southeast, British General Gough saying to the Anzac Corps after the thrilling Canadian success: 'What are you going to do?'[25] White confided his scepticism to Bean about the rush to blood the Anzacs again, saying, 'Unless there's some worthy object to be gained we can't put a Division up to face very heavy losses in front of [the] wire.'[26] Gough's eventual attack plan was dauntingly ambitious, requiring four Australian battalions to advance over one and a half kilometres along a front of nearly three kilometres, attempting a breach of the dense barbed wire of the Hindenburg Line at a point overlooked on three sides by the Germans. White knew that any such attack was doomed unless the barbed wire – 30 metres thick in parts – was cleared by artillery before the infantry charged; past experience told him it would take eight days to clear the wire in front of Bullecourt. But Gough, anxious to match Allenby's success, now seized on a proposal from the commander of a tank battalion suggesting that instead of just relying on the usual artillery barrage, tanks could be concentrated in front of the advancing infantry and lead the soldiers through the wire.

Australian scouts were sent out to reconnoitre the frontline, and they soon noticed that previous artillery barrages had not yet cut the wire in many places; they came back warning that unless there was a strong artillery barrage the Bullecourt attack was doomed. The original idea of Bullecourt had been for the Australian force to link up with Allenby's Third Army troops after breaking through and then cut off the German forces, but now that Allenby's offensive had stalled, Birdwood queried Gough's commanders about the necessity of the Bullecourt attack. He was assured it still was and the attack was set for just before dawn on 10 April.

Early on that morning Bean was sitting in an old infantry post overlooking the Hindenburg frontline position between Bullecourt and Riencourt, where the Australians were to attack, his hands so bitterly cold he had trouble writing in his notebook. At 4.30am he scrawled down a record of the beginning of the artillery bombardment, and then it was difficult until daybreak to know how the attack was going. At that point the grim news came that the attack was a fiasco, the dozen tanks assigned to it failing to get to the launching position in time for the attack to take place in darkness, and it was too dangerous for them to attack in daylight. The Australians, who had lain in the snow forward of their trenches waiting for the tanks for hours, were ordered back.

Incredibly, even though the Germans were now well alerted, General Gough ordered the same attack for the following morning, 11 April, against strong protests from General Birdwood. 'Same time, same place, same plan,' Bean wrote sarcastically in his diary.[27] When the attack was launched, once again the eleven tanks deployed this time were delayed and only four tanks arrived in time to begin the advance. Even then, when the infantry moved across no-man's-land they overtook the lumbering tanks, which were soon easily knocked out by artillery and armour-piercing bullets, or simply trapped in the wire; the Germans eventually destroyed all of the tanks, and half of the crews were killed. Since the tanks were meant to be leading the attack there was no creeping artillery barrage to keep the Germans down, so now as the Australian infantrymen advanced they were flayed as they tried to cut through the wire, slaughtered by a massive onslaught of German artillery and machine-gun fire. 'The tanks failed utterly,' Bean wrote in despair.[28] In an extraordinary feat of arms the Australian infantry finally managed to breach part of the Hindenburg Line without the tanks, but they were eventually forced to withdraw after running out of ammunition and because they did not get the artillery support so desperately needed. Poor intelligence had led the generals to believe the Australian infantry had made it beyond the German frontlines, and because of that mistake they refused a supporting artillery bombardment that might well have saved the day. The Australian survivors who had fought so valiantly were forced into a humiliating retreat back to their own lines under withering German fire. First Bullecourt, as the battle became known, was a shambles – there were 3289 casualties, not quite as disastrous as Fromelles but still horrendous. As many as 1164 Australians were taken prisoner and not an inch of ground was gained.

But when Bean's initial account of the Battle of First Bullecourt, written on the day of the battle, was published in Australia, he made no mention of the unsuccessful attack the previous morning, playing down the appalling failure of the tanks and the scandalous lack of artillery support. Instead readers were told of the 'Australian division's grand attack', and that 'Clearly we have carried the whole of the Hindenburg Line in front of us'. Bean made Bullecourt sound like a major Australian victory because the men had breached the supposedly impregnable line: 'How it was done we cannot guess. It was almost beyond hoping for.' As was common in his reports where the AIF took a hammering, he buried the lead; shrewd readers who made their way to the very end of the story read the telltale admission that it was a 'most gallant and stubborn fight but our bombs were far fewer, and a stage was reached when the Germans broke in at other points along the trench, and we saw our men driven from it'. Even then, Australian readers were probably confused by his final assertion: 'One of the most wonderful fights that was ever fought had been won. And victory or defeat, it achieved one invaluable result – it broke the face of the Hindenburg line at a single blow.'[29] Not a mention of the catastrophic Australian losses, nor the reaction when Birdwood offered his congratulations to the troops who had broken through the Hindenburg Line for the first time. General Gough's biographer records how as Birdwood reassured them them that their losses had 'not been in vain': 'Officers – hard-faced, hard swearing, men – broke down ... filled with an icy contemptuous anger' towards the commanders.[30]

A week later Bean wrote another news story which was more candid about the fiasco, his readers told the West Australian regiment 'went into this fight gloriously and although only half of it came out it has won for itself a name which will not be forgotten', and that the Australians had 'achieved a magnificent retirement'.[31] How any retreat could be magnificent is something Bean did not explain, but at least readers of this second account could have divined that the Australians had been defeated with huge losses, and that the tanks and artillery had been little if any use at all. It took months for the real story of First Bullecourt to filter back to Australia and, ironically, it was an enemy communiqué that alerted the Perth *Sunday Times* at the beginning of July to what had really happened. In an extraordinarily sharp report that exposed the British military's blatant deceit in its public bulletins, the paper compared what the British said about the attack with what the Germans had reported, an analysis which then allowed it to understand the cryptic significance of Bean's heavily censored report. The British statement had acknowledged the Australian withdrawal but claimed that '[t]he enemy's attacking troops were effectively engaged by our artillery and suffered heavy losses', whereas the Germans truthfully reported 'an initial enemy success was nullified by a counter-attack', boasting the capture of 25 officers, 1000 men and 27 machine guns. The *Sunday Times* then noted Bean's comments about the lack of artillery at Bullecourt, saying: 'And now ... we have Bean's story of the tragedy for a tragedy it was. Bean is little more than a faithful recorder of facts but it is difficult to read his narrative with dry eyes.' In closing comments, that must have given the censor a fright, the paper rued that it did not have the privilege of being able to pass comment on the British imperial command, saying that after the war 'Australia will demand to know the whole truth about Bullecourt and the equally lamentable affair of Fleurbaix [Fromelles] to which it bears a sinister resemblance'.[32]

After the disaster of First Bullecourt, it scarcely seems possible to believe that any prudent commander could see strategic value in attempting such a flawed offensive again, but that is what happened a few weeks later when the Australians were ordered back into a near identical attack. This time, poor planning by the Australian staff meant that artillery bombardments prior to the infantry attack again failed to knock out the German defences, so early on that morning of 3 May 1917, when the Australian 5th Brigade advanced, the Germans were able to effectively wipe out the brigade's entire attack with machine-gun and shrapnel bursts, many Australians eventually turning and running. Some of the 5th Brigade had actually made it through into the enemy lines, but in his postwar history Bean blamed an officer who had 'lost his head' in the centre of the battle, suddenly screaming to his men, 'Pull out – retire – get back for your lives.'[33] The parallel attacking Australian 6th Brigade did capture some of the German trenches, but within a day half of the entire brigade was killed, wounded or missing. By 15 May, after twelve bitter days of fighting, the Germans decided Bullecourt was no longer worth losing men over and they pulled out of the devastated town.

The British crowed about this victory for weeks, Haig praising it as one of the great deeds of the war, but it was in truth a relatively minor gain for the 10,000 casualties that both the battles at Bullecourt had inflicted on Australia.

A laudatory article by Bean entitled 'Bravo Australia!', written while the battle still raged, was sent across the country, but he made no mention of the terrible losses.[34] He knew full well that terrible command failures had cost far too many lives, for on the same day he sent the article he had privately recorded that 'White is very angry with the way Gough has messed up this Corps.'[35] Bean also scoffed at 'Gough's miserably arranged offensive'.[36] Bean recorded how Major General White had made the astonishingly frank private admission to Malcolm Ross that, after Bullecourt, 'strong imperialist though he was, he would never again consent to an Australian force coming away without it having someone on the Army staff who could put its point of view definitely and clearly of right before the C in C [Commander-in-Chief]; who could examine and judge of how it was to be used, and have the right to state his opinion without the man he stated it to, however high in command, resenting it'.[37] White also confided to Bean that he believed Birdwood should have raised his concerns about the Bullecourt attack more strongly with higher command, that he had not put up 'sufficient of a fight, not being independent of the British Army but dependent on it. It doesn't matter twopence to White what they say or do to him but it does to Birdwood.'[38] These were very significant admissions that went to the heart of imperial British control of the AIF. Bean's notes also recorded an even more shocking allegation by White, that when Birdwood objected to the Bullecourt attack General Gough had lied to the AIF commander, claiming that Haig's chief of staff had told him that Haig wanted the offensive. White told Bean: 'As we left the room, I told Birdie that I didn't believe it. Gough is an Irishman and he wanted to do the attack. Unquestionably he was speaking to the Chief-of-Staff but I think he made it an excuse for this story – I think he lied. There is no question that Gough wanted us to make that attack. He was anxious to do something. He was up against Allenby.'[39]

This was very serious, suggesting that duplicity by Gough and weakness by Birdwood had cost thousands of Australian lives. White even privately admitted to Bean that he should have put his job on the line and challenged Gough over Bullecourt: 'Gen[eral] Birdwood made a strong stand against Gough that time over Bullecourt ... In the end he gave way on the ground that it was a direct order ... "I don't think I should have given way even then," said White. "I should have let him send me back to England first – and I don't think he would have gone on with it."'[40] But once again Bean elected to be selective in his criticism, ignoring the failures of the Australian command; when he came to write the official history account of Bullecourt after the war, he chose not to mention White's admission of his and Birdwood's failure, yet he was scathing about the British command under General Gough: 'Bullecourt, more than any other battle, shook the confidence of Australian soldiers in the capacity of the British command.'[41]

Some of Charles Bean's best descriptive writing can be found in his contemporaneous diary notes, and they reveal much about what he really thought of the day's events that he never put in his stories. So many of Bean's news stories and his official history became hopelessly bogged down in unnecessary detail. But on 15 May, the day Bullecourt fell, his diary recorded an excruciating description that he never included in any of his published writing. As the clean-up around the Bullecourt battlefield began, everyone was weighing the supposed victory there against the grim reality of Australia's dreadful losses. It was Bean who noticed how, as the water now slowly drained out of the battlefield from months of heavy winter snow, 'a great number of dead are brought to light, but always far more of ours than of the Germans'.[42] It said so much more than simple numbers.

Fourteen

A FINITE RESERVE OF COURAGE

It was at this time that Australian soldiers – in particular, the infantry – came to be known, together with the New Zealanders as 'The Diggers'.

CHARLES BEAN

Three times in the day before the start of the Battle of Messines, Charles Bean was very nearly killed. His car was targeted as he drove into the battle zone on the morning and again as he drove out in the afternoon; the Germans could pride themselves on their efficiency but, thankfully, not their accuracy. Then, just after midnight on 7 June 1917, he picked up New Zealand correspondent Malcolm Ross and a photographer from the New Zealand headquarters and was targeted again by the Germans, this time with gas shells, as they drove towards the Anzac jumping-off points southwest of Messines. The thick poisonous gas was permeating the car interior and they had to drive with their gasmask nozzles in their mouths; then, as they walked across the farmland to where they had chosen to watch the attack, more gas shells fell, 'pat, pat, pat, all around'.[1] When they took their masks off, Malcolm Ross was immediately sick. Just another day at the office for the war correspondents, the three men finally made it through the rear Australian trench positions to the hillside where they would watch the first blooding of General John Monash's Australian 3rd Division on the Western Front.

Messines sat at the bottom of the Allied attack zone, the Ypres Salient, which stretched up to Ploegsteert Wood just south of Ypres in the northern Flanders region of Belgium just across the French border. The Ypres Salient was seen as strategically important because it was a bulge in the enemy line that, if breached, would allow the Allies to target the Ruhr industrial heartland that produced much of Germany's supplies for the war and the rail transport that delivered those munitions. For over two weeks the German lines had been bombarded with artillery, and Australian tunnellers worked with British and Canadian miners to plant about half a million kilograms of explosive mines under the German trenches, including the now legendary Hill 60 mine. Messines Ridge was to be blown sky-high.

Bean and Ross watched from a hillside observation post close by when at 3.10am on 7 June 1917 the largest man-made explosion in history detonated, instantly killing as many as 10,000 enemy soldiers. The Allied troops, comprising twelve divisions including Monash's 3rd Division, quickly seized the German frontlines, taking the Messines Ridge, but the Australians suffered terrible losses from a gas attack before they even went into action. After eighteen fierce days of fighting the Allies accrued 26,000 casualties, 14,000 in the Australian and New Zealand forces alone. And despite the explosion, in raw numbers Germany actually suffered a lesser number, 23,000 casualties.

One of those who died at Messines was Lieutenant Phillip Schuler, the former Melbourne *Age* newspaper correspondent and close friend of Bean in Egypt and the Dardanelles. Schuler's father, Frederick, was a child immigrant to Australia from Germany in the 1860s and his son had distinguished himself as a correspondent at Gallipoli, exposing the lamentable care for the wounded taken off Anzac Cove after the landing. Arguably a much better and bolder writer than Charles Bean, Schuler's stories proved that it was sometimes possible to get a critical report past the censor if you pushed, one story revealing how wounded men had gone untended because medical staff had gone to the Alexandria horse races. Schuler was a fine journalist but on the Western Front he chose to join up to fight as an officer with Monash's 3rd Division and, to Bean's despair, on 23 June 1917 he was mortally wounded by an artillery shell during the Battle of Messines. When Bean had caught up with Schuler earlier that month he'd told him that after the war he intended to marry a Russian countess he had met in Egypt; now just a few weeks later he was dead.[2] Bean wrote a glowing obituary for Schuler, describing him as a 'brilliantly handsome, bright, attractive, generous youngster'. The noblest tribute he could pay to his friend was that his letters were truthful, 'and only those who knew what oceans of false stuff have been poured on to the world in this war can appreciate what that means'.[3] Among the personal effects returned to Phillip's father, Gottlieb, after his death was his beloved typewriter. It was Schuler who had nursed Bean when he was shot on Gallipoli and the two men enjoyed a close friendship and respect. Why Schuler chose to join up is a mystery, but perhaps a young man of such principle decided it was time to share the suffering of the troops that he had witnessed so many times as a journalist.

For General Monash the Battle of Messines was a vindication of his 3rd Division in its first fighting on the Western Front and a credit to his fastidious planning and attention to detail; the battle was hailed as a textbook modern military victory (albeit with huge Australian casualties). Bean's news story was effusive: 'There never was such a spectacle in warfare as the attack on Messines Ridge. One watched it as it were from an armchair looking across on to the stage.'[4] But, for reasons that were never fully explained, perhaps because he was not named in the article, General Monash privately savaged Bean's reporting in a letter to his wife as 'the apotheosis of banality. Not only is the language silly tosh, but his facts are, for the most part, quite wrong.'[5] This was to be just the beginning of an often acrimonious relationship between the official correspondent and the general.

When British 4th Division commander General Alexander Godley summonsed Bean to cover his review inspection of the 3rd Division shortly after the victory, Bean not only griped in his notes about Godley's arrogance – '"Come and report my speech"' – he also privately vented what was clearly the growing view of Monash in the AIF command, that he rarely visited the frontlines and that he and his commanding officers in the 3rd Division were 'a bit shy of fire in some cases and Monash is not the man to keep them up to it'.[6] It was an unfair slur on Monash, who was also often the victim of anti-Semitism from many in the AIF command.

The sort of infantry officer Bean idolised was his towering cousin Arthur Maxwell, whom he caught up with at the 52nd Battalion headquarters after Messines. Arthur had just escorted Lord Salisbury around the frontline, sniping the enemy to keep them down as the elderly British statesman crossed in the open, and on another occasion offering to help one soldier to bury his brother who had been killed in battle. To Bean, Arthur was the ideal of Australian manhood that he celebrated in his writing: a Tasmanian country gentleman, easy in a saddle, a crack shot and a born leader, apparently spoiling to take it to the Germans up the front. But while heroic soldier leaders like Arthur Maxwell were needed, it was the technocratic organisational skills of Monash that would soon help transform the AIF.

Bean clearly did not like Monash though, frequently criticising him in his private notes, and even when he wrote his postwar account of Messines in the *Official History of Australia in the War*, he pointedly took a swipe at him and all the 3rd Division's commanders for acquiescing to the theory – 'with which General Monash possibly agreed' – that the commander's duty in times of battle was to remain strictly at his headquarters.[7] He even backhandedly quoted Plutarch from the first century, that 'a good general should die of old age', while at the same time clearly suggesting that Monash was gun-shy.[8] There was a long enmity between Bean and Monash that had started at Gallipoli and continued well after the war, Bean still privately criticising him in 1930:

> Monash never saw a bayonet used in action and I don't think he so very often saw the inside of a front-line trench: and he knows practically nothing by personal experience of what went on there. I know far less about the actual fighting or the life of the front line than most ordinary privates in the infantry

> or gunners or engineers do, but I know fifty times as much as Monash did and I know that when he spouts about the front line he is just handing out the same old flamboyant stuff that he has read in the old war histories.'[9]

Bean's hostility was to colour his writing about Australia's greatest-ever general for years, but Bean did fulsomely praise Monash's organisational and logistics skills as a general, ranking him as the best in the Allied command.

Messines was seen as a great success but, again, it had only pushed the front forward a few kilometres at huge cost, and there was growing feeling in the ranks about the disproportionate losses suffered for much-trumpeted victories. Bean describes in his diary how he was told that French troops marching through one town en route to the front were yelling, 'A la hachette, A la hachette,' resentfully suggesting that they were lambs being led to the slaughter as part of the same Allied strategy of attrition against the Germans. There was even a frontline mutiny by French soldiers, Bean lamenting privately afterwards that the French 'don't seem to have the stick of other troops', and that the British and Australians would have to take the burden of the war from now.[10] But there were serious morale problems in the AIF, too; when the batman of one Australian captain was caught deserting in civilian clothes, he was just one of many Australians who walked away from the fight. As the Australian command did not shoot their deserters, a fleeing soldier knew he would instead be jailed throughout the war: 'It's what he wants – he doesn't get killed,' Bean diarised.[11] The desertion of hundreds of Australian troops was a story that remained untold by Bean and other correspondents throughout the war. So serious was the concern that Haig at one stage threatened the AIF command that he might withdraw the Australian troops from service if desertion continued to be the problem it was, and General Birdwood sent a memorandum to the defence department in Melbourne in mid-1917 arguing for the death penalty.[12] The politicians, who understood the sensitivities of shooting members of a volunteer army, ignored his plea.

In mid-June 1917, Bean was able to take some much needed leave back in England, transporting with him a pile of memorabilia for the Australian war relics collection, including a trench signboard from the battlefield at Pozières. The defence minister, Senator George Pearce, had recently approved Bean's proposal for an Australian War Records Section and a young lieutenant, John Treloar, who had worked with then Colonel Brudenell White at the Gallipoli 1st Division headquarters, was put in charge of coordinating it in London. Treloar had almost died of typhoid at Gallipoli and was not well enough to return to a combat role, but he threw himself into the preservation of the Australian military's archives and the eclectic collection of memorabilia gathered from battlefields by Bean and his staff.

Bean ended up getting a solid four-week rest in London, even taking time out to attend a cricket match at his old school Brentwood. While there he was amazed to hear an artillery bombardment begin on the frontlines far across the English Channel, intrigued that he could actually listen to the pulsing guns so far away in France or Belgium. While in England Bean also went up to Oxford, spending a weekend with John Masefield, the celebrated English poet he had met as a British correspondent on the Western Front, later to become England's Poet Laureate.

The Oxford campus was almost empty of students; many of the undergraduates who had rushed to fight were now dead, and Masefield was in a maudlin mood about the war. Just as Bean had done, Masefield's 1916 book *Gallipoli* on the failed Dardanelles operation mythologised the Allied struggle on the peninsula as a Homeric victory of British manhood against daunting odds. His book cloyingly told of a letter found on a fallen Turk that said: 'These British are the finest fighters in the World. We have chosen the wrong friends.'[13] Masefield portrayed the Australians as 'smiling and glorious young giants' who had dealt the Turks a staggering blow.[14] Publicly, Masefield was another safe pair of hands propagandising the British military's prowess, but he admitted to Bean that he now saw himself as a revolutionary, believing the Australians should be sent back to Australia at once because it was 'a tragedy to have the young race killed off' and '[h]e would let the old race die rather', also hoping that a revolution might happen in England.[15] Bean privately questioned his host's sentiments, doubting that the 'intellectual snobs' of English political society would ever desire anyone else to rule except 'us'.[16] Monarchist that he was, Bean was confronted by reports that crowds fired up by republican sentiment after the recent Russian Bolshevik revolution had jeered King George and thrown a boot at him on a recent visit to northern England.

Bean and Keith Murdoch also caught up to discuss the growing view in the Australian command that Australia would be a lot better off if all of its divisions were allowed to operate as one fighting force on the Western Front rather than having to rely on joint operations with often poorly commanded British units. It did not seem unusual to either man that two civilian journalists were so heavily involved in politicking about the Australian Imperial Force; General Gough's failures at Bullecourt had galvanised both men to far exceed their brief as journalists and to push for change in how the AIF was deployed. Murdoch even wanted Gough relieved of his command; when Murdoch had heard that General Gough would command the Australians at Bullecourt he'd told Bean, 'I suppose they'll be murdered again.'[17]

There was a strong push from Murdoch and other journalists for Bean to solicit British Prime Minister Lloyd George's help in not only bringing the AIF divisions together as a fighting force but to also agitate with the prime minister against the extreme censorship imposed upon all the correspondents by the British command, not least because it was stopping them from revealing the kind of failures behind the disaster at Bullecourt. To that end, Bean had hoped to be able to meet Lloyd George during his London visit but he ended up writing a letter to the prime minister instead, asking for his assistance in bringing the five Australian divisions together to be deployed in battle as an Australian army on the Western Front. The British commanders believed that all Allied units should be completely interchangeable, that they were all 'British', but Bean reflected the view of most in the AIF that the Australians had been let down at both Fromelles and Bullecourt by British regiments and commanders – and that Bullecourt in particular had been a 'real shock to the confidence of the troops'.[18] He pleaded in his letter for Lloyd George to intercede to allow the Australians to be used as one force on the Western Front and also asked that General Birdwood be given access to a direct representative of Australia in London rather than having to always go through the British GHQ. There was also talk of lobbying Billy Hughes directly back in Australia, but Bean was depressed by Murdoch's frank admission that Hughes needed to be convinced such a dramatic move was politically beneficial for him before he would support it. Back in France, he noted: 'It is awful to think of Australia's part in the war being directed as Hughes thinks it benefits him … It is like touching pitch getting into this dirty business. One breathes freely now one is back in France among clean-handed generous soldiers.'[19] Before he returned to France Bean farewelled Arthur Bazley, his long-time batman, who had become a close friend after their many months of hazardous adventures together. Bazley was taking up the offer of a promotion to sergeant to work in the newly created War Records Section and it was a huge wrench for Bean to have to say goodbye.

He returned to France just as General Gough was preparing for his next massive offensive on the Ypres sector, a frontal attack along thirteen kilometres aimed at sweeping the Germans from the strategic Passchendaele Ridge east of Ypres by the date set by General Haig, 8 August 1917. Knowing the attack was coming, the Germans had built scores of reinforced concrete defensive positions that could withstand most major artillery. On 30 July, Bean wrote solemnly that it was the eve of 'the great fight' and how, as the Germans achieved major gains against the Russians on the Eastern Front, there was high hope for the great blow the Allies were expected to deliver the next day: 'GHQ and the Army are intensely optimistic about this fight. They think the war will end this year.'[20]

The British had bombed the German lines for two solid weeks before the attack, lobbing a mind-boggling

4.3 million shells. But even with that unprecedented bombardment, the British attack soon stalled badly as General Plumer's Second Army was hammered by undamaged German artillery and then bogged down in the Ypres mud – it rained from the very first day of the attack on 31 July and continued for most of the next few weeks, turning the whole Ypres sector into a muddy bog. A despondent Bean wrote: 'It quite negatives the idea of God having a hand in the world's affairs. If a God exists he has certainly no influence on these happenings of nature … It is unthinkable that a good mind could favour Germany's cause against that of the liberal nations.'[21]

Once again, Bean's team had a close shave. As they entered Messines, clambering through a shell hole, his artist colleague Will Dyson felt a piece of shrapnel slice his cheek open; a few centimetres further and an artery might have been severed. He and Bean had just witnessed civilians evacuating their homes in the nearby town of Hazebrouck where they had stayed for the night; they were shocked and angry that the Germans had dropped a cruel new burning mustard gas – 'the dirty, pitiable, torture of non-combatants' – endangering innocents, women and children, and blinding many.[22]

As the big push turned badly for the British, the military censor inevitably tried to suppress the news; soon after this Third Battle of Ypres began, Bean arrived at the GHQ censor's office to find the press correspondents there 'nearly mutinous'.[23] The censor had banned them from naming any village or implying anything about the battle in their reports, nor were they allowed to make any comment in them. It was a blatant attempt to gag coverage of another failed attack. The censor eventually caved in to their protests about not being allowed to comment but he was still insistent that the correspondents were to say nothing other than what was in the British military communiqué, which was inevitably a whitewash as they never said anything adverse to the British cause. He was even refusing to send their letters of complaint about this censorship to the chief of staff. Bean recorded that 'one subject they are not allowed to mention is the new German gas, which, [correspondent Philip] Gibbs says, does blind its victims for life in some cases. This is horrible – it's far more merciful to kill.'[24] The Allies were using the same gas; it killed unwitting Germans even when they wore their gasmasks because it was absorbed through the skin. Bean heard from fellow correspondent Philip Gibbs that one British officer witnessed a German brigade's command staff lying dead with their gas helmets still on; it was not a detail he ever shared with his readers.

On 4 August 1917, Bean recorded the end of the third year of the war and the beginning of the fourth. There was no good news on the horizon, and the weather was making an advance against the Germans in Ypres impossible; Bean visited an Australian artillery battalion attached to a British unit and was alarmed to see one howitzer so bogged in the mud that only one wheel could be seen above it: 'The conditions are the worst the men have ever been in.'[25] Bean was told a story of how one 2nd Division artillery driver was sitting on a mule when it stepped into a shell hole and disappeared from sight; the soldier stood on its back to keep alive in the mud but struggled to breathe and lost consciousness before being rescued from the sucking slime by a colleague.[26] Bean was not able to verify the details of the story but he felt it reflected the truth of what he had seen.

During early August much of the Anzac Corps was being given a long-needed rest, although Australian artillery and tunnellers were seconded to assist British units and suffered heavy casualties. Bean was busy writing up recent battles, his eye increasingly on the postwar history he was now determined to write, and he also wrote to the defence minister pushing for action on the government's previously stated support for an Australian war museum. The war came to his village billet in Hazebrouck on 10 August, however, when German shells flattened a local prison next to General Birdwood's house and blew out the front window of the command headquarters mess. Bean's French landlady was convinced the Germans were targeting the Anzacs and she wanted him out, but he was determined not to budge.

In mid-August he got the good news from Major General White that the Australian government had wired the British command asking that all its troops be brought together under General Birdwood's AIF command, in part due to lobbying by Bean and Murdoch. But there was also less welcome news: the Australian Press Association had sought and won permission from Prime Minister Billy Hughes and the AIF to be allowed to have a correspondent on the Western Front. For Bean it was another slap in the face regarding his role as official correspondent, for the fact that the association felt the need to demand this implied he was not fulfilling what was expected of him by the Australian editors. He worried: 'If this means working in competition, it is a pity. Competition is best out of war correspondence.'[27] To add insult to injury, the British censor told him that an article he had written had been stopped from publication because it was political, and that no political telegram could be sent from GHQ. Bean had

Keith Murdoch on Gallipoli in early September 1915, photographed by Bean. This was just before Murdoch tried to carry the letter from Ashmead-Bartlett back to England.
(Australian War Memorial)

General Birdwood on Gallipoli in October 1915, photographed by Bean.
(Australian War Memorial)

Bean's batman, Arthur Bazley, outside their snow-covered Gallipoli dugout in November 1915.
(Australian War Memorial)

Graves in Shrapnel Gully cemetery, looking towards the Sap, November 1915. The men paid great attention to this and the other cemeteries during the last few days of the occupation. A fallen soldier's cap has been placed over the grave in the foreground.
(Australian War Memorial)

A game of cricket on Shell Green, photographed by Bean in December 1915. The game was intended to distract the Turks from the imminent departure of Allied troops. Major George Macarthur Onslow of the Light Horse is being caught out. Shells were passing overhead all the time the game was in progress. (Australian War Memorial)

A group portrait of staff officers at Mena Camp. Bean is standing top left. He later kept a framed copy of this photograph in his study. (Australian War Memorial)

August 1916, the Battle of the Somme: Australian stretcher bearers coming in under a white flag, passing the old cemetery of Pozières, having come from the line near Mouquet Farm. The white flag, usually made on the spot out of a handkerchief or white rag, was intended to stand in for a Red Cross flag. Parties carrying this flag were not usually fired on, at this time, by German snipers, although as can be seen behind the men, the use of the flag did not affect German artillery barrages. Photographed by Ernest Brooks. (Australian War Memorial)

A group portrait of war correspondents and press censors outside the British Press Headquarters in France in 1916, probably at Rollencourt Chateau. Bean is seated in the front row, far right. (Australian War Memorial)

Bean knee-deep in mud in Gird trench near Gueudecourt, France, during the winter of 1916–17. (Australian War Memorial)

Bean near Martinpuich, France, watching the Australian advance through a telescope. Photographed by Herbert Baldwin. (Australian War Memorial)

Bean with John Masefield, Alexis Aladin and Will Dyson (the official war artist), surveying the old battlefield at Pozières in late 1917 or early 1918. (Australian War Memorial)

This work is from Will Dyson's early battlefield observations. It shows exhausted Australian troops, draped in waterproof sheets, plodding through the rain and mud as they reach Montauban on the Somme. Titled 'Coming out of the Somme', it is referred to on page 263 of this book. (Australian War Memorial)

A classic Frank Hurley 'composite', showing Australian infantry wounded at a first-aid post near Zonnebeke Railway Station in October 1917. Bean was utterly opposed to the use of 'composite' photographs. (Australian War Memorial)

A view of scattered Australian graves along the old OG1 line on the battlefield of Pozières, September 1917. Twelve months before, the area was a scene of heavy fighting and devastation. When the fighting passed, the undergrowth flourished, softening the appearance of utter desolation.
(Australian War Memorial)

Bean photographed at Samer, Nord-Pas-de-Calais, December 1917.
(Australian War Memorial)

A French farmhouse used by the Australian official correspondents during the Australian Corps' defence of Amiens. Bean is fourth from left. (Australian War Memorial)

Bean with his cousins in April 1918. Left to right: Duncan Maxwell, Bean, Arthur Maxwell and Angus Butler. (Australian War Memorial)

Bean, fourth from left, with other members of the Australian Historical Mission and the Turkish historian Zeki Bey (second from left), picnicking on Hill 60, the scene of the last major assault of the battle for Gallipoli.
(Australian War Memorial)

Bean at work on the official history at 'Tuggranong'.
(C.E.W. Bean Private Collection, Australian War Memorial)

Bean and his long-time assistant, Arthur Bazley, at 'Tuggranong'. (Australian War Memorial)

'Tuggranong', December 1920: Bean (centre) and colleagues, waiting to transport the finished first volume of the official history to its publishers, Angus & Robertson, in Sydney. (C.E.W. Bean Private Collection, Australian War Memorial)

Bean's private wartime diaries piled high in about 1935. Arthur Bazley is at left. (Australian War Memorial)

Bean's marriage to Ethel Clara Young, or 'Effie', 24 January 1921. From left to right: Agnes Young (Effie's mother), William Young (Effie's brother), Barbara Bean (Monty's daughter), Charles, Effie, Mabel Young (Effie's youngest sister) and Jack Bean. (Courtesy of Anne Carroll and Edward Bean Le Couteur)

An early photograph of the new couple. (Courtesy of Anne Carroll and Edward Bean Le Couteur)

Charles and Effie's adopted daughter, Joyce, aged about eight.
(Courtesy of Anne Carroll and Edward Bean Le Couteur)

An aging Lucy Bean visiting from Hobart in about 1930. From left to right: Effie, Charles, Lucy, Jack and his wife, Isabelle. Joyce is seated in front.
(Courtesy of Anne Carroll and Edward Bean Le Couteur)

Charles and Effie during their 1951 trip to the UK and Europe, photographed in front of the Fifth Australian Division Memorial in Polygon Wood, Belgium.
(Courtesy of Anne Carroll and Edward Bean Le Couteur)

Bean showing the young Queen around the War Memorial, February 1954.
(Australian War Memorial)

Bean in his mid-seventies.
(Courtesy of Anne Carroll and Edward Bean Le Couteur)

Possibly Bean's final public appearance, speaking at the War Memorial on 24 May 1959. The occasion was the opening ceremony for the Hall of Memory.
(Australian War Memorial)

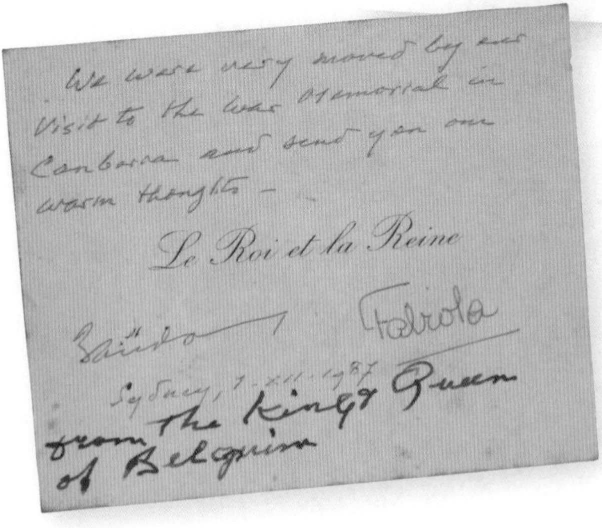

We were very moved by our visit to the War Memorial in Canberra and send you our warm thoughts –

Le Roi et la Reine

Baudouin Fabiola

Sydney, 7-XII-1987

from the King & Queen of Belgium

The card accompanying the flowers sent to Effie in 1987.
(Courtesy of Anne Carroll and Edward Bean Le Couteur)

suggested in his story that if Germany restored democracy it was not worth losing 10,000 Australian casualties to fight to keep Germany's former colony of New Guinea. After the flak he had received for his comments about the Imperial War Conference, the irony behind Bean's high dudgeon in response was that the censor had probably saved him from himself, because his comments would undoubtedly have drawn even more criticism in Australia. Increasingly, Bean seemed less interested in his journalistic role and much keener about his proposed history, where he felt he would be able to offer a much more candid assessment of the war.

One journalist who Bean admired was Henry Gullett, a Victorian newspaper journalist and former editor of *The Daily Telegraph*. Gullett had joined the AIF as a gunner in 1916 after a brief spell as an Australian correspondent on the Western Front before Bean's arrival from Gallipoli. Now Bean wanted him to cover the Australian forces in the Middle East for the official history, and to train him up he brought Gullett into the War Records Section to tour AIF units asking them to preserve their records. He liked and respected Gullett; he was an intellectual man with strong establishment connections. Together with artist Will Dyson they visited the crater where the massive mine had obliterated the Germans atop Hill 60. The area was under constant German shellfire, Bean calmly noting how bombs were falling every few minutes or so within a few hundred metres of where they were gathered. As they climbed, he was struck by the 'skeletons of old woods where the British line used to run', and when they reached the crest he understood why the Germans had fought so hard to hold it: the hill had given the Germans a crystal-clear view of all the Allied positions far below it.[28]

During their travels Gullett also gave Bean some sage advice about his journalism, telling him he wrote 'too much for the military critic – the men of the AIF, and such men as White; and not enough for the people'; Gullett confided he wrote his own articles with his sister Isobel in mind.[29] It was, in truth, a gentle criticism of Bean's journalism, whose obsession with often unnecessary detail and facts sometimes made his reporting colourless. Gullett also pressed him to start writing his official history as soon as possible, flatly advising Bean that although he was not indispensable as a war correspondent, he was indispensable as the official historian. The conversation clearly started Bean thinking about whether he wanted to still be a journalist. There were battalions he had not visited since Bullecourt and Messines, and he had only written two articles in the previous month, so busy had he been on research for the official history. 'It is obvious that the record work makes it impossible to do the correspondent work properly, and they both suffer,' he privately admitted.[30] He also rationalised that as the Australian Press Association's recent request for its own representative at the front meant that he was now in competition with any correspondents that might now be allowed to follow the AIF at war, 'this competition is exactly what the system of the official correspondent was intended to avoid'.[31] So Bean made a momentous decision: he discussed with White that he begin writing the official history fulltime and that his primary role would no longer be that of official correspondent. Major General White agreed with this proposal and Bean was asked to nominate a successor; Bean would base himself in London and only come across to France when there was 'anything on'.

There were personal reasons too for this decision. Bean was exhausted from his time on the Western Front; at that time the war looked likely to last at least another two years, and he doubted he had the stamina to do both jobs. The personal toll on him and those he loved was also mounting, as was made clear to him after catching up with Arthur Maxwell again, who had been ordered to recuperate at a II Anzac Corps officers' rest camp in the town of La Motte because he had suffered a nervous breakdown in the field. Arthur confessed to his cousin that he had gone 'quite off the handle' when one of his mates was hit by a shell, completely broken up and could not speak without crying.[32] His brother Duncan had raised it with the commanding general and Arthur had been ordered out of the line to rest. Arthur and so many keen young Australian officers like him had been kept at it so long that the strain had broken them. It was a lesson to Charles Bean that every man, including himself, had a breaking point; any soldier had only a finite reserve of courage.

There was so much he wanted to set in place for the official history and the proposed war museum. One of the new AIF photographers who Bean now also brought to the Western Front was the legendary Frank Hurley, a working-class boy from the Sydney suburb of Glebe who had run away from school as a young teenager, training as a photographer, then joining both the Douglas Mawson and Ernest Shackleton two-year polar expeditions to the Antarctic. On his return to England in mid-1917 he had joined up as an AIF photographer, and on one of their first forays together Charles Bean took him on another trip into the old German bunker below Hill 60. It was strewn with the decaying corpses of German soldiers, nothing new to Bean but shocking to Hurley, who described the scene in his diary: 'The exaggerated machinations of hell are here typified … oh the frightfulness of it all. To think that these fragments were once sweethearts, maybe, husbands or loved sons … Until my dying day I shall never forget this haunting glimpse down into the Mine crater on Hill 60.'[33]

Bean had argued the case with Haig's head of intelligence, Brigadier General John Charteris, that he should be allowed to gather photographs of key battlefield sites for a future history of the war, telling him that the Australians had been through Pozières, Bullecourt, Bapaume and Messines, and yet they still had precious few pictures that covered what a historian needed for such an account. He found himself arguing the reasoning behind the official history that he did not yet realise would absorb him for most of the next three decades of his life: 'I felt I was in a position in which scarcely any historian of a war had ever been – that of a man who will write about a war which he has seen all through, in which he has been in every important trench, and seen almost every important event.'[34] Eventually Charteris relented and agreed to Bean having a second official photographer who could begin taking the photographs he would need for his history; it was a major victory. Bean arranged for Frank Hurley and Hubert Wilkins to share the task and they now began methodically photographing sites across the frontlines.

Hubert Wilkins was an experienced journalist and photographer who had covered the 1912 fighting between the Turks and the Bulgarians in the Balkans, befriending Ashmead-Bartlett of Gallipoli fame at this time. As Frank Hurley had done in Antarctica, Wilkins had travelled with the Canadian Arctic Expedition, returning to Australia in May 1917 and enlisting almost immediately. Because he had flying experience he was commissioned as a 2nd Lieutenant in the Australian Flying Corps, but when he reached England in July and went for his medical he was knocked back on the grounds that his feet and legs were damaged due to frostbite and the long treks in the Arctic. The doctors also discovered he was colourblind.

With Major General White's support, Bean was assembling a cadre of talent to record the AIF's role in the war. In early September 1917 he brought two artists back from England, Fred Leist and Harold Septimus Power, to spend three months on the frontlines. Leist was an adventurous 'man-of-the-world' from Sydney's Surry Hills who had drawn for the Sydney *Bulletin* and London papers and had already created a name for himself as an artist exhibiting paintings at the London Royal Academy of Arts; he had a penchant for rendering handsome women in oils and used his portraiture skills to great effect in the trenches.[35] Harold Power was a New Zealander who migrated to Adelaide, eventually exhibiting in Paris and London. On their trip over to France together, Bean realised Harold was very different from his colleague; he was part deaf and 'a very shy gauche chap, intensely nervous mainly, I think, because of his deafness, a loveable man'.[36] He was delighted that Leist looked out for his friend, and the two men went on to produce a rich harvest of paintings from the Western Front, especially Power's portrayal of the horses suffering in the appalling conditions.

In mid-September Bean and Hubert Wilkins went back to the Pozières battlefield with two military trucks, filling them with relics they salvaged from the battlefield and taking photographs. They half-filled one lorry with rifles found in the trenches that had cost so many Australian lives, many still fitted with their fixed bayonets. The burial parties had already been through, leaving rows of white crosses where those men now lay. As they drove back they came down the slope of Vimy Ridge, which had cost so many Canadian lives weeks earlier, and saw the awful vista of the war spread out in front of them across the normally beautiful French countryside; shells were exploding in the distance and on the horizon was the rosy flare of a burning ammunition dump. For the war was churning on, and when Bean returned to the Hazebrouck AIF headquarters that night, Major General White took him aside and briefed him on the details of another massive attack due in just a few days on 20 September, the resumption of the Third Battle of Ypres. Eleven divisions were to be thrown against German positions that the Allies had failed to seize in August, and the 1st and 2nd divisions of Australia's I Anzac Corps would fight next to each other for the first time. The Australians would be right in the thick of the attacking army pushing east from the Menin Road just outside Ypres along a thirteen-kilometre front.

Three weeks before this great offensive began, the Australian Divisions were moved into a reserve area in Flanders where they could practise the attack. Soon after they arrived there was a minor riot near the British Army headquarters; an Australian soldier had been arrested for supposedly being drunk because he had the impertinence to ask a British sergeant of the military police for directions to the nearest brothel. His mates had stood their ground against the British policeman saying he was not drunk at all; a canny British officer settled things down with the Australians and all were eventually let go without charge. After the mud and the blood of Bullecourt and Messines, a confident sense of Australian self-identity was more obvious among the troops and, as Bean wrote in his official history, it was about this time that the Australian and New Zealand soldiers came to be known as 'diggers', a term that had its origins with Australian miners before the war but was most probably a reference to the endless digging done by the Australian infantrymen throughout the war.[37] Bean noted that the British soldiers resented being called 'Tommies' because of the patronising notion that lay behind it of a superior talking down to a working-class lad. The Australians had no such hang-ups; they were proud to be the diggers and now they were going into the fight of their lives together.

Fifteen

A GREAT BLOODY EXPERIMENT

If the dear ones at home could just see this there would be an alteration, but they are never told.

LETTER FOUND ON A DEAD GERMAN SOLDIER

Somewhere across the Allied frontline around the Flanders village of Westhoek, a distant German artillery officer was squinting through his binoculars, doing his best to try to kill Charles Bean and Hubert Wilkins. The correspondents were visiting the Australian frontline troops who were going over the top in just a couple of days for what would become known as the Battle of Menin Road; now they were playing a deadly game of chance, dashing from shell hole to shell hole to make it to the frontlines, a trail of thudding incendiary and shrapnel shells following their wake. They had darted through a British infantry position at Sanctuary Wood just before the Germans lobbed a massive artillery bombardment on the slope they had climbed. Then, as they neared a position dubbed Clapham Junction, shrapnel burst straight ahead of them and a huge shell flew over their heads. It exploded in a shell hole on one side of the route they were walking and they dived into another shell hole to avoid it. They had been spotted; probably taken for officers in their correspondents' garb. Sure enough, as they backtracked away from where the shell had fallen, yet another barrage hit the spot where they had just taken cover. They then clambered across a red-cratered plain through sections of a half-dug trench where they finally reached the view they sought, across the devastated remains of Westhoek village. Men from the Australian 22nd Battalion were holding the frontline and they had made 'little undercut pozzies' on the front side of their trench to shelter from the rain, their puttee-protected legs protruding from underneath waterproof sheets covering the man inside.[1] Bean noticed how sets of protruding legs were covered with blood-spattered waterproof sheets; it was the buzzing flies that told him that the men inside those holes were dead, victims of the relentless German shelling. An Australian officer – whom Bean noted to be a 'poor little startled boy, horrified by the sights and the shelling' – explained how the Germans did not even have to make a direct hit; they were aiming for the parados, the rear lip of the trench, and killing soldiers with the shock of the back blast. His battalion had lost 70 men in the 48 hours they had been holding the line, for just surviving the artillery was a cruel and ultimately futile gamble.

Although he was stepping away from his role as official correspondent, Charles Bean was staying for this major Australian trial in the Third Battle of Ypres to honour his promise to the Australian and New Zealand Press Association that he would help their new correspondent, Gordon Gilmour, learn the ropes as a frontline correspondent, despite the fact that the association posting was undermining his role. One of the AIF intelligence officers even suggested that having wire journalists like Gilmour and Keith Murdoch on the frontlines would make the role of official correspondent redundant, but Bean disagreed: 'The private interests of the papers are something which often cut right across the interests of the country – scoops, competition, magnification and exaggeration are out of all harmony with what is best for the country.'[2] By admitting this, Bean was effectively acknowledging that in his role as official correspondent he had been obliged to compromise his legitimate journalistic interests as a reporter for that of Australia's. It underlined the dilemma he had constantly felt in that dual role the previous three years of the war – that there were important stories he had chosen not to write.

The Germans were clearly expecting the Menin Road attack, and airmen reported seeing heavy concentrations of enemy troops in holding areas just outside the range of the Allied guns. At 11pm the night before the 20 September attack it was raining heavily, a huge concern because the valley the Australians had to move through was a marsh of massive water-filled shell holes, covered by German machine-gunners secured in concrete blockhouses. This time, though, it was not the impetuous General Gough in charge; commanding British General Herbert Plumer planned that the Allied infantry would attack one and a half kilometres into the German lines behind a creeping artillery barrage, backed up with tanks. Then when they made their new positions the troops would dig in under the protection of a massive artillery barrage to keep the Germans from counterattacking.

Bean's notes throughout the day and night capture the tense moments back at the forward headquarters as commanders tried to figure out what was happening. There were frantic messages that artillery was falling short and hitting Australians, that clusters of captured enemy were being sent back, and battalion commanders reporting their objectives had been seized – one message tellingly read: '9th Battalion reports that everything is alright except for fairly heavy casualties.'[3] Photographers Frank Hurley and Hubert Wilkins were right in the thick of it; Wilkins used a knocked-out British tank as a shooting platform for his camera until the tank came under fire again, the explosion shattering some of his equipment and precious photographic glass plate negatives. There are hints in Bean's diary of just how bloody the hand-to-hand fighting was: an Australian officer from the 10th Battalion had been killed and his men 'simply went mad and killed most of the Germans they found there'.[4] These were details he saved from his readers.

Three days into the fighting Bean walked to the new Australian frontlines in Polygon Wood with artist Fred Leist and the new Press Association correspondent Gordon Gilmour. When the Germans began shelling their route, Bean had a momentary panic as Leist and Gilmour behind him frantically signalled that they did not know what to do under the shellfire. But after they made it through on their wits, the war-hardened Charles Bean was actually pleased because it meant Leist could now portray a more active battlefield than most of the other AIF artists; it was a brutal lesson but Leist did indeed go on to paint some memorable pictures of the battle. By the standards of the time the Battle of Menin Road was seen as a success, but it ended five days later on 25 September with total Allied casualties at 20,255 – and of those, 5000 were Australians.

By the end of September the Australians had seized all of the now shredded Polygon Wood and so, following Plumer's step-by-step strategy, they now attacked the strategic Broodseinde Ridge, Bean methodically recording the battle's progress hour by hour from the forward headquarters. On 4 October 1917, as the Australians went over the top, they by chance ran into the Germans making their own assault, but the diggers drove the German attack back with a bayonet charge and by the next day the Australians had seized the ridge. It was a momentous achievement by the Anzacs. Hordes of captured German prisoners were brought back behind the Australian lines, including a demoralised battalion commander, who commented to Bean that the 'war was no longer a war but only a butchery. You don't hunt your enemy. You know where he sits and shell that area till he moves.'[5] Another captured officer was amused: 'Your men are funny. They rob while they fight,' referring to the ratting of souvenirs from German prisoners that was now a digger tradition.[6]

Bean realised that the new strategy of fighting with a limited objective that stayed within effective range of artillery barrage support was a 'weapon at last – at long last – which the Germans could not parry … For the first time, we only go so far as our guns can follow us.'[7] In his reports to Australian newspapers, Bean was upbeat: 'Many of us today feel an optimism which we have not before felt, realising that a means has at last been worked out of delivering on the Germans whenever it is desired, smashing blows which they cannot avoid or parry.'[8] Across in England the bells were rung in York Cathedral in celebration, Bean's colleague Philip Gibbs hailing Broodseinde as a great day for the Anzacs.

From the top of Broodseinde Ridge the Australians could see the German lines and, to the north, the German-held village of Passchendaele. In a short time the Australians had helped achieve a series of stunning victories; the question now for the Allied commanders was whether, as the rain again closed in, they should push on for Passchendaele. The bullish Haig insisted on pushing on, but Bean privately opined: 'I must say I suspect that they are making a great bloody experiment – a huge gamble and more than that; a deliberate attempt to see how it works. I think they are playing with the morale of their troops.'[9] He was terribly anxious in his diary notes about the decision to push on towards Passchendaele with the Australians so exhausted and in the worsening weather: 'They don't know the fight there was for the last ridge, these major-generals back there; they don't know how nearly the Broodseinde crest held us up. They don't realise how much and desperately hard it will be to fight down such opposition in the mud, rifles choked … men tired and slow … I shall be very surprised if this fight succeeds.'[10]

The wiser heads did not prevail and General Haig ordered the Anzacs to attack Passchendaele on 9 October, in the middle of a heavy rainstorm with gale force winds. Never before had Bean been so convinced that a coming battle would be a catastrophe for the Allies as he was at Passchendaele; it even put him at odds with his friend Major General White. He privately mocked White in his diary for using the British pronunciation for the so-called 'leap' strategy to take Passchendaele Ridge; White pronounced them as 'lepps', just like the upper-class British staff officers he had trained with in England. Bean clearly felt that in this battle White had allowed himself to again be swept along by the British desire for a big push, and his concerns were about to be proven right.

On the morning of 9 October 1917 it was bitterly cold and the Anzacs were flagging in the freezing conditions; Bean wrote how 200 men from the 6th Brigade had to be taken out of the line with trench feet just before the battle. It was fought in driving rain, men pulling themselves out of sucking mud well over their knees, and even though a small number of Australians made it as far as the wreckage of the Passchendaele church, the British troops beside them failed to provide the support they needed. The Australians were forced to retreat to their previous frontline, now a muddy swamp. The losses were appalling, Australia suffering 4000 casualties for no gain; the first day of the attack was an utter failure. A few days into the battle, Bean described the situation as a 'hopeless push. They are banking on a decline in the German morale.'[11] Keith Murdoch told him there was now huge anxiety up at the AIF headquarters, and that General Birdwood had suggested he'd wanted to postpone the original attack. But yet again it appears Birdwood allowed himself to be steamrolled by General Haig's impetuous and incomprehensible push for an advance, because, to everyone's incredulity, Haig now ordered a second attack on Passchendaele village and the ridge above it. Bean could not believe Haig was continuing on with the attack; by this stage men in the frontlines were 'sinking up to the thighs in the mud'.[12] The Australian brigades that would be going into the attack were heavily depleted because of the debilitating trench foot caused by the bitter cold and wet. It was an insane command decision. Bean had seen the condition of the Anzacs returning from the lines along the Menin Road after the first attack on Passchendaele: 'They were pale, white and drawn and detached and put one foot slowly in front of the other as I have not seen men do since the Somme Winter.'[13] Just as distressing was the sight of dead horses scattered alongside the duckboard tracks where they had fallen into the bog; 'they have most of them a small cloud of blood pink foam above the nostrils'.[14] He knew the imminent attack was doomed; it was so muddy that the British support troops had not been able to find the tape that had been laid to guide them to their frontline attack positions. The artillery shells that were supposed to be providing a supporting barrage were ineffective in the morass of mud across no-man's-land. In perhaps his angriest private comments at any time during the war, Bean wrote that the 'Army has no right to squander men in this fashion'.[15]

In fact Bean was so concerned he did later speak out to the AIF command, but it backfired terribly. In mid-October he ran into another of his cousins, Ken Maxwell, brother of Duncan and Arthur. Ken, an Australian officer who had been seconded to temporary command of the 6th Battalion of the British Manchesters Regiment, told Bean in confidence of a litany of catastrophic command failures inside the British 66th Division which was also in the battle: troops not knowing where they were meant to be going, rations not properly supplied, and the sheer impossibility of meeting the expectations of the commanders who clearly did not understand the appalling conditions. It was very astute criticism but it was also extremely dangerous for Ken to be talking out of turn. When Bean returned to headquarters he passed the information on to generals White and Birdwood, who insisted that the British be told – 'it's only right that they should hear what a man like Maxwell has to say,' Bean noted them saying.[16] Bean tried to insist that Ken's identity be kept confidential but

Birdwood credulously replied that he thought commanding British General Harrington would actually want to know of any staff failures. Of course the British took umbrage at this impertinence and Bean was summonsed to meet the general who commanded Ken's regiment and told that Maxwell's mooted promotion to permanent command of the battalion had now been put on hold because he had been 'speaking evil of the men and officers of the 66th Division'.[17] Outrageously, the general even insisted he would not approve the promotion until Ken denied what he had said; it was a very unsubtle bullying of Bean to keep his mouth shut in future. (Ken was subsequently awarded a Military Cross and made a commander of his battalion, so it appears the general did not follow through with his threat for long, if at all.)

The day before the next attack on Passchendaele was due to begin Bean and the other accredited correspondents met with General Haig, in part to discuss their concerns about excessive British censorship. Earlier in the year Bean had been delighted when his nemesis, British censor Lieutenant Colonel Hutton Wilson, was replaced, but things had not improved. Haig was nervously rubbing his hands as he greeted the correspondents in the drawing room of his chateau in the French village of Montreuil, 100 kilometres northwest of Amiens, well behind the frontline, seating them in gilt Louis XVI chairs to admire the sweeping views across the countryside. The ongoing problem had been that military censors were terrified of making a mistake, so their instinct was to ban almost any detail, including the name of a battalion or a village, for fear that publishing it might benefit the enemy. One British intelligence officer present at the correspondents' meeting even asked Haig how much could be written about the difficulties of fighting in the mud 'without cheering the Germans'.[18] But the commander-in-chief earnestly told the assembled correspondents that 'the simplest thing was they should tell the truth'. Bean no doubt rolled his eyes as he recorded this assurance from Haig, privately commenting that it revealed just how little the general had been consulted about censorship. Haig told them: 'It was simply the mud which defeated us on Tuesday. The men did splendidly to get through it as they did. But the Flanders mud, as you know, is not a new invention. It has a name in history – it has defeated other armies before this one … I certainly think you should explain the difficulty of the mud.'[19]

When the meeting was over, Haig asked Bean to stay alone, wanting to know if he thought a second planned conscription vote later in the year would pass in Australia. Bean told him that the Irish Roman Catholics and socialists were so well organised that conscription probably would not be supported in Australia, which disappointed Haig. The conversation then turned to the idea that Australia should have her own Australian Army command staff and Haig confided how much he admired General John Monash as a very capable and solid man. Bean felt this was overlooking his friend Major General White; he had already heard rumours from White that Haig was considering creating one corps comprising the five Australian divisions under the command of John Monash, with Birdwood nominally in administrative command of the entire AIF. Bean took it upon himself to advise the commander-in-chief of whom he thought should be put in charge: 'Yes sir – you know <u>we</u> look upon General White as the greatest soldier we have by a long way – we consider him the man whom Australia has produced in this war.'[20] He told Haig that White was the one man no Australian would be jealous of, that no one would begrudge him the promotion, for Bean privately begrudged any thought of Monash being given the command.

Knowing the attack was due in the morning, Bean hardly slept that night, as frantic as everyone else that it would rain during the night. At 3am on 12 October he woke Keith Murdoch, who had come across from London to follow the attack, with a cocoa and they set off into a misty rain, driving in darkness past long lines of horsemen carrying ammunition towards the front. By the time they got to Monash's 3rd Division headquarters at Ypres it was raining heavily. Bean grimly noted in his diary that the weather report warning of the rain had come through at 9pm the night before, 'so the battle could have been stopped. Of course now, it was far too late'.[21] He knew catastrophe was imminent. Just before the next 'jump' was to take place at 8.25am, he and Murdoch hurried up the Menin Road, making their way to the top of a ridge where they could look down on the advance towards Passchendaele. Just hours after Bean enjoyed his intimate tête-à-tête with General Haig, sitting in a Louis XVI chair in his French chateau far behind the lines, he and Keith Murdoch were now trampling down the mud in a sodden shell hole from which they could have some cover to safely watch the battle. The insights Bean was able to gather as a result are still breathtaking today; no journalist since has enjoyed such unhindered access to a commander-in-chief and then been able to roam a battlefield during an attack.

Through his telescope Bean could see the Australians winding their way past shell holes towards Passchendaele; one man appeared to be hit but Bean was then relieved to see him get up and continue. For Bean and Murdoch to be where they were on the battlefield was already a dangerous risk, but the two men now moved forward to another hill closer to Passchendaele to get a better view of the fighting. As they staggered across the battlefield where the Australians had just advanced they realised how difficult it must have been for the troops to negotiate this treacherous morass with full kit under fire. Bean watched as a British aircraft tried to crash-land a short distance away, somersaulting on its tail and finishing up on its back; the pilot was almost certainly killed but there were nearby soldiers rushing to help. When they finally made it to their new hill they had a perfect view of Passchendaele, including the ruins of the church. Keith Murdoch remembered that according to the battle plan, in just a few minutes, at 10.41am, there were meant to be Australians taking the church, but as they watched there was, ominously, no sign of the diggers. 'When you see no movement on a battlefield it means the tightest corner of all,' Bean wrote in his diary.[22] It was then that he and Murdoch realised the village was still full of German soldiers and, as they watched, they noticed three men running down the hill from Passchendaele 'as fast as they could. Sometimes they stopped for a moment and dropped into a shell hole. But they got up and ran on again…One's heart misgave one that they might be our men retiring'.[23] It became clear that the Australians were retreating, and as Murdoch and Bean despondently turned to head home they ran into a group of recently arrived staff officers who were clearly under the illusion that the men in the village were Australian. Bean used his telescope to show them the truth.

As Bean had predicted, the attack was a total disaster; in the mud the artillery had not worked effectively to cut wire or knock out the German guns. The Germans had also used a new poisonous gas that irritated the skin so badly that men were driven to remove their gasmasks, suffering blindness, blistered skin and shocking respiratory distress. The Australian 3rd Division made it to Passchendaele but they had been forced to retreat because the New Zealander and British units that were meant to be advancing beside them had been cut down in droves early in the attack by German artillery. It was a very bloody day in Passchendaele for the Australians: in the first 24 hours of the attack, 3199 men from the 3rd Division were killed, many men drowning in the mud or blown to pieces before they got anywhere near the village. In all there were 7000 casualties that first day. When Canadians finally took Passchendaele a month later, a mind-boggling half a million men from both sides had lost their lives in the three months of fighting for the village.

A few days later Bean's Australian readers received his first report of the Passchendaele debacle. Constrained by censorship, he could make no criticism of Haig or the AIF commanders who had assented to the insane attack, optimistically telling readers instead 'not to put too much weight to the fact that the last two [attacks] were not completely successful'.[24] He reassured them that the new attack strategies were working and that was why Germany's own correspondents were now writing that the fatherland was fighting for its very existence on the battlefield. Taking Haig's cue to tell the truth about the mud, Bean did mention it in another report, blaming the rain for forcing the Australians to be 'withdrawn from the most advanced positions'.[25] It was the sort of positive spin that was expected from the correspondents but little consolation for the 38,000

Australian families that were now receiving telegrams telling them their sons had been killed or seriously wounded.

After the war, Bean wrote more candidly in his official history that Haig's stubborn insistence on the two Passchendaele attacks meant the effect of the earlier successes was thrown away. He squarely laid the blame at Haig's feet, saying, 'as with the Somme offensive, it is incredible that he would have persisted without a most searching revision of his methods, or that the British Government would have allowed him to do so if the true incidence of the loss had been known'.[26] He was scathing of Haig for not considering how the mud limited the Allied artillery – 'it is unbelievable that he was aware of the ineffectiveness of the immense effort of his artillery' – but Bean's history makes no criticism of the AIF command for allowing the Passchendaele attack to continue when the odds were so clearly hopeless.[27]

When Wilkins and Bean went up into the Allied frontlines a few days after the battle to take some photographs, the soldiers were bitter, asking 'if these would be photographs of the "glorious Anzacs" … "I suppose the papers said it was another glorious victory of Haig's," one said'; after what they had been through, one could hardly blame the Anzacs for being cynical.[28] In every third or fourth shell hole at the old German frontline there were the scattered bodies of Germans; Bean's notes show he was struck by a 'good looking boy with rather close cropped reddish hair, lying on his back in the water of a shell hole, his head and trunk out of the water, his chest twisted round, and his tunic and his white shirt torn open and one hand, half-extended, half-closed, almost as if he slept. Only his eyes which were dull sunken white had changed since he died.'[29] A hundred yards further on he found the old Australian frontline where the body of a dead Anzac lay, cut in half at the waist. At one stage a German machine-gun opened up on them and Bean was forced to lie in a waterlogged shell hole as the bullets whipped around the side of the crater. 'It was a thing one was glad to have experienced,' the perpetually stoic Bean wrote later, 'for it showed in the most practical way the difficulties of our position.'[30] He was absolutely exhausted when, close to dusk, he and Wilkins finally made it back to their car near the Menin Gate.

Together with Keith Murdoch, Bean was very focused on a future Australian command of the AIF and the two men drafted a cable to send to Prime Minister Billy Hughes. They were worried that the loss of so many men in the Passchendaele offensive meant that at least one of the Australian divisions would have to be broken up unless conscription was approved. They advised Hughes that conscription was necessary to maintain the five Australian divisions and that it would be a good selling point in any conscription vote to see all these divisions in one corps under Australian command. 'But Monash for an Australian C in C [commander-in-chief] we cannot have. He is not the man,' Bean complained in his diary.[31] He wanted John Gellibrand or White to lead the AIF and he sank to anti-Semitism to justify his take against Monash: 'We do not want Australia represented by men mainly because of their ability, natural and in-born in Jews, to push themselves.'[32] Bean clearly believed he was doing the right thing but it was the beginning of what was to become an indefensible meddling campaign by both men against General Monash.

On 2 November 1917, Bean heard the good news that General Haig had approved the formation of a single

Australian Corps, and that the men of the 4th Division would be used as a reserve unit to be spread among the remaining four divisions. It meant the Australians would soon be fighting as a cohesive army under Australian control for the first time in the war. Even better news for the diggers, they were to be rested out of the frontlines during the winter months. 'Everyone is as pleased as punch,' Bean wrote in his diary. 'I think that little Hughes must have more real true live patriotism in him than we often credit him with.'[33] A few days later Bean was with the men of one battalion when they heard the news they would be part of the new Australian Corps; all were delighted, not least because, after the horrors of Passchendaele, there was a perception that an AIF under Australian command would not allow such appalling mistakes to be repeated. It represented a very real coming of age for the Australian Army, an acknowledgement that it had Australian officers who were more than capable of commanding their own soldiers. Bean's experiences with the English had also changed him completely; he was disdainful of 'the extraordinary British method of choosing men not by their capacity but by their "breeding" or tact or birth … White agrees that this system is the blight of all English institutions.'[34]

On 11 November, during a brief visit back to London, Charles Bean caught up with his brother Jack, now based there as medical officer with a venereal diseases hospital. Jack had come up with a quaint idea to attempt to curb the spread of venereal disease among the troops: soldiers were invited to enrol themselves in a legion of honour to 'protect the purity of our nation against disease and against drink' by abstaining and helping mates who were drunk.[35] Jack was fighting a lost battle but his heart was very much in the right place, and Charles admired his brother's good deeds. General Birdwood probably very prudently refused Jack's plea for him to overturn the army's decision to issue soldiers with condoms – 'French letters,' Bean wrote disapprovingly, which 'they poke under the nose of every boy going on leave'.[36] When Australian Anglican Archdeacon Ward, a former AIF chaplain, wrote to Birdwood supporting Jack's abstinence pledge campaign, one general incredulously asked: 'Is Ward mad … Doesn't he know this is a primitive instinct with men and you cannot stop it?'[37]

On his way back through Boulogne to the front Bean ran into war artist Will Dyson, learning to his horror that Dyson had been hit by a shell blast while doing a sketch on the battlefield at Passchendaele. His painting was destroyed by the blast but Dyson, mercifully, had suffered fairly minor cuts and sprains. Dyson's main worry was that he might be sent to hospital against his will because he wanted to get his work done and return to London. Like all of the artists he was doing this war service for no salary, and he needed to get back to England to make enough money to survive. There was an extraordinary dedication among the men working with Bean in the War Records Section. Revealingly, Charles Bean was forced to recant the innate Church of England prejudice of that era against Roman Catholics because many of the men working on the collection of war relics for the museum were Catholic; they were 'quite contrary to one's preconceived notion of the R.C. in Australia', Bean wrote in his diary. 'There one had an idea of them as tending to laziness.'[38]

As Bean's team of war relics gatherers stalked the battlefields looking for the best items to send back for

Australia's future museum, there was also a reaction from Britain: he was told by the powerful Anglo-Canadian press baron Lord Beaverbrook, owner of the London *Daily Express* and *Evening Standard* newspapers, that the British governors-general of both Australia and Canada had written complaining that the most unique and irreplaceable trophies should be kept only by the war museum in London. Beaverbrook, similarly enthusiastic to see Canada's role in the war honoured by his fellow Canadians, not surprisingly told Bean he intended to fight this tooth and nail. Bean also discovered that the Canadian had made an offer to photographer Frank Hurley, recognising his talent, asking him to work for the Canadians, and was trying to take control of a proposed military exhibition of pictures covering the whole Allied front as well. Beaverbrook particularly liked Hurley's composite pictures where he wove two or more photographic negatives into one image, a technique that Bean regarded with great irritation as a 'faked' image. Bean was infuriated by the prospect of any such composite images being used to represent the AIF and insisted on having control over what images would be used. Bean's relationship with Hurley would continue to be strained throughout the war; Hurley felt it was his responsibility to present as powerful and evocative a portrayal of the war as possible, and if that meant weaving images together that he had gathered on the battlefield then he saw nothing wrong with that.

By the end of November 1917 Charles Bean was a very weary man and, judging by his private thoughts, probably a little depressed. His thirty-eighth birthday had come and gone and he had been away at war for more than three years. He was missing his family terribly, especially his mother, and feeling painfully homesick. After all the horrific scenes that

Charles had witnessed, especially in the last few months at Passchendaele, he took great comfort thinking of his parents back in Australia in their new house at Sandy Bay, Tasmania, tending her garden and building up a circle of admirers whom she attracted 'like some sweet goddess'.[39] But outside his billet he knew men were still dying in this dreadful war, and as the year was drawing to a close the grim news came that the leader of the Russian Bolshevik revolution, Vladimir Lenin, had ordered Russian troops to withdraw as allies from the war against Germany. There were also worrying reports of German successes in Italy and disturbing calls in the newspapers from one English lord for a negotiated peace with Germany. Bean grimly opined in his diary that while many in the ruling classes of England were not that keen on fighting for democracy, the Australians and most of the British were 'for democracy at all costs'. He felt the English were 'afraid of disturbing the masses more than the German might before right'.[40]

Despite Haig's disingenuous promise to the press correspondents that they should just tell the truth, the absurdly restrictive British censorship was continuing, and there was beginning to be more than a whiff that the British Army was using its censorship powers to gag publication of some impressive Australian actions. Bean had written an article about the Australians at Pozières, for instance, only to learn that the entire story had been prohibited by the head of British military intelligence, General Charteris, who had insisted on cutting all the battalion numbers out of the story. British Major Neville Lytton, who was nominally the British GHQ censor, had gone into bat for Bean, reminding Charteris of Haig's stated support for greater openness; 'I think I am the person best able to interpret what General

Haig said,' Charteris had stubbornly replied.[41] He had been sitting beside Haig when the commander-in-chief assured the correspondents that such absurd restrictions would be stopped. It later emerged that it was also Charteris who had earlier insisted on destroying the photographic glass plate negative of the stretcher-bearers bringing in wounded men under a white flag. Bean was no doubt pleased when later in December Charteris was recalled to England; he felt that Charteris's misguided optimism was his biggest defect, that 'it infected everyone who went to GHQ. Haig, Asquith, all of them, were all saying the Germans couldn't last.'[42]

The campaigning against General Monash also continued. In early December Bean heard that Monash had originally won command of the Australian 3rd Division after raising his concerns about a British officer being put in command. Clearly, Bean and the AIF officers he was talking to all supported an Australian rather than a British commander, but they and Bean distrusted Monash's self-promotion. Charles Bean again condemned Monash's supposed 'Jewish capacity for worming silently into favour without seeming to take any steps towards it, although many are beginning to suspect that he does take steps'.[43]

Bean's replacement as official correspondent was also confirmed: Frederic Cutlack, an English-born South Australian who had worked on London newspapers as a journalist before the war. He and Bean got on well, probably because they shared a passion for the Australian navy; Cutlack had covered HMAS *Australia*'s maiden voyage in 1913. As Bean had also done, Cutlack was studying for the London bar when war broke out, joining up with a British artillery regiment then transferring to the AIF as an intelligence officer. Fred Cutlack had been adventurous in his youth, bicycling through Germany living on his wits and very little money, tutoring English to wealthy German families. One of his tasks was to start a new magazine for the AIF troops called *Aussie*, the name suggested because the troops had started calling themselves 'Aussies' for the first time. It was also decided Cutlack would be called the 'assistant official war correspondent'.

Imminent also was the last day of the latest referendum vote on conscription along the Western Front on 12 December 1917. Bean was privately optimistic that the vote would pass – 'I have very little doubt that it will go through' – but he was out of touch with the strength of feeling against the conscription vote.[44] The vote in Australia was held on 20 December, the referendum asking voters to support the continuation of voluntary enlistment but that any shortfall on recruits would be met by reinforcements drawn by ballot from all men aged between 20 and 44 who were either single, widowers or divorcees. Once again Hughes misused the Australian media censorship laws to bludgeon a pro-conscription result, one Catholic newspaper punitively fined for trying to print an article describing the proposed ballot as a 'Lottery of Death'.[45] To Bean's shock and despair, the campaign opposing conscription saw the referendum narrowly defeated. 'One is most depressed about it,' Bean noted when he heard the result; it would mean the break-up of the 4th Division.[46] Australia's frontline soldiers had again voted strongly against conscription and Bean felt the main reason was because they were suspicious of just what conscription would mean, perhaps even the implementation of the death sentence on all AIF soldiers for deserting. Ultimately, he privately acknowledged, the troops were tired and disillusioned with war; they felt they were being exploited and overused in the heavy fighting and 'they are disinclined to force anyone into it if he doesn't want to come.'[47]

In the days before Christmas 1917, all this grim news made Bean more despondent than he had been at any time during the war. He had just learned that two old friends from Bathurst had died in the recent fighting, both in September's battle for Polygon Wood. One was killed just before the 'hop off'; the other had time to bury his mate and then he too was killed in an artillery barrage. News came in too that Maurice Maxwell, another of his cousins from the Tasmanian end of the family, had suffered a terrible wound to his thigh in battle and was now seriously ill in hospital with an infection. Then came more shocking news that his very close friend and fellow correspondent New Zealander Malcolm Ross had lost his son Noel, who had been discharged from the New Zealand Expeditionary Force after suffering paralysis from a shell blast on Gallipoli. Noel had recovered and made himself a highly successful career writing for *The Times* and other English papers. Just before he was due to be married he had died from typhoid, weakened by his earlier wartime injury. Bean was clearly devastated by this news, coming as it did in a year where he could now list a lengthy toll of fine men he had counted as friends who had died in the fighting. The last straw for Bean was a *Daily Mail* account of a bayonet charge in Jerusalem during the fighting between British troops and the Turkish Ottoman Army on the Mount of Olives, a sacred place in the Christian Bible. 'If only the full meaning of that short sentence or two impressed itself upon the world there would be no more fighting. The war would stop. It couldn't go on,' he lamented.[48] Even to an avowed non-believer like Bean it seemed a shocking sacrilege to have a bayonet charge in a place of such religious significance.

He spent Christmas Day dinner with General Gellibrand and his staff at Péronne, all enjoying four bottles of champagne Bean had bought in Amiens. It was snowing heavily outside and Bean noticed that the sentries had also enjoyed a drink or two and were clearly very unsteady on their feet. When Bean brought in 1918 a week later with the Australian 56th Battalion that had fought in Ypres with huge losses, he was struck by its warm-hearted soldiers who 'live so close to death' but were still imbued with a 'pathetic generosity'.[49] He privately admitted to himself how probably only two or three of the men in the mess he had just visited would survive the year, aside from the commanding colonel and his headquarters staff. With hundreds of thousands of fresh German soldiers coming in from the now peaceful Russian Eastern Front, Bean was bitterly pessimistic about the diggers: 'For the Australian force here, the outlook is not rosy – Australian defeat a certainty. Australia may manage to reinforce it by conscription yet. But if she doesn't I do not think more than 3 divisions will return to Australia.'[50]

It was very hard to feel festive after a year like 1917, by far the worst year of the war: nearly 77,000 Australians had been either killed or wounded, and those who were still alive were exhausted. Now that the Bolsheviks were out of the fight, the ledger was more in Germany's favour than for the Allies.

Sixteen

A LACK OF VIRILITY

Generals without brains and an army without physique.

Charles Bean on the British Army, 12 April 1918

'I'm not going,' the prisoner said, standing on parade in front of 500 other Australian soldiers. Having already served time in military prison at the Salisbury Plains AIF training camp in southern England, this refusal was a serious challenge to the commander, Colonel Billy Watson, a former 24th Battalion commander now briefed to return reluctant soldiers to combat. The issue had become a huge one now that another failed conscription referendum meant reinforcements from Australia would continue at a slow trickle.

'You are going,' Colonel Watson told him. The reluctant soldier replied, 'You'll have to bloody well drag me there. If I go, I'll go in an ambulance.'[1] In all likelihood the soldier was one of the many Australian troops who had already had a bitter taste of frontline fighting in France and Belgium and had decided it was better to sit the war out in a military jail than run the statistically high risk of being severely wounded or killed in the trenches. So, in a harsh display for the 500 assembled men watching on, the colonel had the prisoner tied by his wrists to a military ambulance that was then driven slowly along the parade ground road, this soldier dragged painfully behind. He soon begged for mercy, to the great amusement of his assembled colleagues, and not surprisingly agreed to go back to fighting the war. When Bean visited the Salisbury Plains military prison where this incident had taken place in mid-January 1918, Colonel Watson told him the shirker had unsurprisingly complained about the brutality of his treatment all the way to the top of the army, but General Birdwood strongly supported the colonel's decision. That was how reluctant soldiers were forced to the front in 1918.

Charles Bean was visiting the enormous AIF training camp in his new role as official historian for the AIF, touring as many units as he was able to build up a picture of the Australian commitment in Europe. He also used the visit to catch up with his doctor brother Jack Bean, still working at a nearby military hospital specialising in venereal diseases. Jack, he soon learned, had made himself unpopular with the jailers at the Salisbury Plains prison, who had banned his visits because of a supposedly unsettling influence on the prisoners, encouraging a 'recital of grievances'.[2] Jack was a man of increasingly controversial and libertarian views that made many in the top brass uncomfortable. He had embraced theosophy, a religious philosophy derived from Indian mysticism that had drawn him into supporting colonial India's call for independence from British rule. On 1 January 1918, the head of the AIF in London, Brigadier General Tom Griffiths, wrote a grave private letter to Charles Bean disclosing that a recent War Office intelligence branch raid found Jack's name among the membership of the Young India League, and that investigations had revealed he was also a member of the Home Rule for India League. Clearly under the impression from British intelligence that the league was a seditious organisation, Griffiths kindly offered to have Jack Bean quietly sent home sick, 'away from the influences that are bearing upon him here'.[3] But Charles Bean was furious at the insinuation that his brother might be involved in seditious activity and wrote back to Griffiths, arguing that being a member of a group with high ideals for justice in India was in no way at odds with Britain's war aims. 'He wouldn't dream of doing anything disloyal to his side. These damned police would make a conspiracy out of anything,' Bean wrote in his diary.[4] He eventually showed Griffiths some of the league's literature and pointed out that a British member of Parliament was also in the league, 'but no police touch him'. Griffiths had huge respect for Jack, a much-liked man in the AIF, and – the allegations proving baseless – he was left alone.

Rather than be embarrassed by his brother's principled support of soldiers afflicted with venereal disease or locked up in prisons, or his support for the aspiring Indian nationalists, Charles was in fact protective of Jack, so much so that he even contemplated the possibility that Jack might one day have to fight on the other side for Indian emancipation from Britain: '… it would be the sorest trial to oppose his country but he would do so, whatever it cost him.'[5] He was fiercely proud of his brother and not swayed at all by criticism from the stuffy military brass: 'He is the grandest man I know.' Jack's views were encouraging Charles's own tolerance and challenging his previously very fixed beliefs about British imperialism, race and religion.

For much of the first part of 1918 Charles Bean was enjoying being back in London, working on his official history research out of a tiny office in the AIF's central London headquarters on Horseferry Road. With much of the Western Front blanketed in snow and ice, things were very quiet on the frontlines across the Channel; Bean recorded how the feeling was 'very electric. Because of the quietness, everyone expects an attack.'[6] War correspondents were being encouraged to write openly about the likelihood of an impending German offensive to let the Germans know the Allies were ready for them. Meanwhile, Bean and John Treloar were fighting a bureaucratic war of their own against a determined push from the British military for its Imperial War Museum to have the pick of all of the war relics – 'trophies', as Bean called them. The Australian government had meekly agreed to this imperious British demand without consultation with Bean or Treloar's fledgling War Relics Section; now, together with a similarly outraged Canadian media magnate Lord Beaverbrook, they were fighting to have the British government's decision reversed. The AIF units along the frontline were all enjoying the diversion of collecting such trophies for the future Australian museum and, on a visit to France a few days later, soldiers from the 3rd Battalion proudly showed Bean a fake tree used by German artillery observers. Retrieved from Oosttaverne Wood, it was a camouflaged tube of iron with a seat near the top for the German observer to spy across the Australian lines. It even had the signature of an Australian Victoria Cross recipient, Sergeant John Hamilton, scribbled on the side. 'We must get it to Australia at all costs,' Bean wrote, noting too that the men of the 3rd Battalion were 'out for souvenirs for all they are worth'.[7] One probably apocryphal story doing the rounds in the battalion had it that General Birdwood caught a soldier just about to steal the flag from the front of his car. 'Here, you mustn't take that,' Birdwood had told the soldier. 'Oh, we'll have it someday yet General,' the soldier cheerily replied.[8] It was a fun story that suggested how much mischief the trophy collecting caused, but Birdwood could not remember the incident when Bean asked him about it.

The British government's response to the growing power and influence of Canadian media baron Lord Beaverbrook, Bean's powerful ally in the trophy war, was to make him the Minister of Information in the British cabinet, probably deciding it wanted Beaverbrook inside the cabinet rather than out of it to control his sway. British-born AIF Major General Neville Howse VC, director of the Australian Army Medical Corps, confided to Bean that he had been told Beaverbrook was an 'unmitigated rogue', but Bean admired the outspoken lord's can-do attitude, although he was worried the peer's previous support for faking photographs would clash with 'our Australian standards of truthfulness'.[9] Beaverbrook gave him a wink and a nod that he was trying to get the Imperial War Museum under his ministerial control and that, if he did, he would help Australia all he could on the war trophies issue.

In mid-February Bean was invited to tour the United States Army lines in France, enjoying the company of some high-spirited British Women's Army Auxiliary Corps officers on the train to Paris. It was still a refreshing sight to see women in military uniform and the joke was shared that their WAAC acronym stood for 'Warned Against All Colonials'. 'The women (and the men too) of England will never be content to go back to the same narrow limits of life after their travellings in this war,' Bean dryly observed.[10] The official correspondent was cutting loose a little with his new assistant official correspondent, Fred Cutlack, enjoying a visit to the dancing girls at the Folies Bergère music hall in Paris and delighting in the multinational crowd in the café at the interval: 'I suppose the world will never see it again,' he wistfully lamented.[11] He was intensely proud of the Australians he saw there, 'marked amongst all the rest by their easy, frank, natural manners; their confident walk, their free unrestrained enjoyment'.[12] A young Australian soldier he met outside the Notre Dame cathedral the next day told him he was tired of the war, but being able to visit England and France had given him an education. The Queensland mate with him had once visited Sydney, sleeping in the Domain, and now they were both off to the Riviera for eight days' leave.[13] It would have been an impossible dream for most young Australian men before the war, and this opportunity to visit England and France as a soldier was a lure the recruiting pamphlets of the day had exploited to encourage men to sign up.

When Bean and Cutlack finally made it to the American GHQ at Chaumont the following day, Fred Cutlack was more than a little seedy from the excesses of the night before and had to have a lie-down during their visit. Bean, however, was typically energetic, scrupulously recording the minutest detail brought to his attention by his minders with avid fascination. He took an instant liking to the Americans, who reminded him of the Australian 1st Division troops he had met in the desert at Mena and behind the lines at Gallipoli. The Americans had only entered the war in April 1917, after the reports of Belgian atrocities and the sinking of the passenger liner RMS *Lusitania* had finally swung public opinion against a previously strong sentiment for neutrality. One of the American staff officers, a Major Williams, had been a military attaché to Turkey during the 1915 fighting at Anzac Cove and had often gone down through the Turkish trenches to an observation post to watch them exchanging artillery fire with the Australians.

Bean suggested to Major General White that the American press correspondents should also be allowed to visit the AIF frontline positions, not least because after the war Australia would need the sympathy of America in the Pacific 'to the fullest extent to which it is possible to obtain it'.[14] He was already thinking ahead to the implications for Australia after the war, as it looked as though the war would end with a League of Nations, any nation not abiding by the league's decision finding itself ostracised by every other member nation. At this stage Bean still passionately defended the White Australia policy and naïvely believed the Americans could be enlisted to support Australia's embargo on the 'oriental races'.[15]

When Bean returned to London in late February, his entire War Records Section was moving into new offices opposite the main AIF headquarters. It had darkrooms in the basement and two floors of offices for himself, Captain Treloar[16] and the other staff now engaged in collecting exhibits for an Australian museum. His battle with the British government still raged over its plans for their Imperial War Museum to be '<u>the one</u> great representative collection of the British Empire'.[17] Bean felt an Australian museum would mean a great deal more to Australians than a British equivalent, and that it would be an institution that would equal anything in the world. He deftly played the press back in Australia, writing a strong cable that aroused public indignation at the idea of the British getting the pick of the war trophies. This drew a denial from the defence minister that Australia had ever agreed to the British request and forced Prime Minister Hughes into making a statement that he wanted all the Australian trophies to go to an Australian museum, 'the troops having earned this right by their gallantry and sacrifice'.[18] The British committee soon backed down; Bean's lobbying had helped win the day.

A couple of weeks later Bean enjoyed a pleasant night at the opera on Drury Lane with Captain James Herbertson, a British officer who served on General Birdwood's Anzac headquarters intelligence staff. As they were leaving, Herbertson took Bean aside and told him he had heard at the War Office that a German attack was imminent and expected to come in three places: against the British Army at Cambrai and Armentières and the French at Alsace.

Two days later on 21 March 1918, the Germans began a massive bombardment along the Allied frontlines, launching their infantry offensive just a few hours later. Bean, still in London, found it curious that few people there understood that this was the beginning of what he and his colleagues saw as the great battle for survival. 'I cannot say how relieved I felt at the coming of this news,' Bean exulted.[19] He believed the German commanders were overconfident in their belief that they could win the war this year with a massive offensive; they would very likely retake Bapaume close to their frontlines, but that would be the end of it. 'This is the best thing that could happen to us. Our men will be hammered – but at least they will lose less in defence than in attack.'[20] But this time Bean was not on the ground, because Fred Cutlack was there as his assistant, and his diaries reflect an unwarranted optimism that the British forces would be able to hold the Germans back. The British

Fifth Army, under General Gough of Bullecourt infamy, was very soon overwhelmed by the highly effective German artillery and troop numbers. In fact, by the evening of the first day of the offensive, the Germans had already broken through the British lines and the entire Fifth Army was forced into an ignominious retreat towards the Somme, yet another of Gough's battle plans going awry.

Two days into the battle Bean arrived in France, reaching the AIF headquarters at the Château de Bertangles, eight kilometres north of Amiens, at 11pm; news had still not reached the Australian command of the catastrophic British position. It was only the next day, Sunday, 24 March, that Major General White told Bean for the first time how anxious he was about the situation. When Bean made his way down to Amiens along the crowded roads full of panicked civilians and stern soldiers, it was clear from conversation with correspondents Philip Gibbs and Herbert Russell that they did not appreciate the gravity of the German advance. It was Bean who led them into the Amiens Allied headquarters press office and only then did they all learn just how serious things were. The Germans had retaken many of the old hard-won Somme battlefields and had even been seen in the southeast corner of Delville Wood, northeast of the town of Longueval in the Somme valley, well within the old Allied lines. Contrary to Allied expectations, the Germans had sidestepped the French Army and thrown their entire attack against the English positions; the sense of crisis in the Allied headquarters was intense. 'I hope the Germans don't arrive here and wake us in the morning,' Bean anxiously penned.[21] White told him how the Germans had even sent over a phoney deserter who had tricked the Allies into launching a bombardment on the German lines on 13 March; all that had done was allow the Germans to target the British artillery when they finally did launch their offensive.

The next day Bean and other press correspondents began their move towards the scene of the fighting; he was thrilled to meet lorry after lorry full of Australian 3rd Division troops who were being moved in to support the British defence. Two Australian divisions had been left to hold the frontline at Messines. Bean was terribly worried about photographer Hubert Wilkins, fearing the Germans might have captured him as they swept through Bapaume. Next day, Tuesday, 26 March, came the shocking news that the whole British line had been pushed back some 50 kilometres by the German advance, but one piece of good news was that Wilkins had managed to stay out of the Germans' clutches; he had stuck with Australian tunnellers working on defences at Pozières and then been forced to join the retreat as the British Fifth Army fled in the face of the determined offensive. As Bean lamented, it meant the Australian 1st and 2nd Division memorial at Pozières was now in German hands. That same day, a crisis meeting of the French and British command at the Hôtel de Ville in Doullens, 30 kilometres north of Amiens, resolved that Amiens must be defended at all costs. Some of the correspondents who had stayed in Amiens told how their hotel had already been hit by long-range German shellfire and the town was now deserted. Bean was staggered at the speed of the German advance; just a few days earlier he had promised Captain John Treloar in London that on this day he would catch up with him at the opera *Carmen* and now, instead, here he was watching the Allied armies in their fight for survival on the Western Front.

These were hectic and panicked days; a lack of adequate communications meant no one really knew where the Germans were and the intense rumour mill about enemy movements imparted a sense of foreboding doom. In the midst of it all, Charles Bean was determined to cover this moment in history and stocked up his car courtesy of a friendly soldier at a supplies warehouse in Doullens, who happened to be one of the 4th Division soldiers who had contributed to *The Anzac Book*. He and Fred Cutlack and their driver found General Monash's 3rd Division at Franvillers, twenty kilometres northeast of Amiens, where Bean encountered Monash 'as lucid as usual', clearly on top of things.[22] Then, as war correspondents do, Bean headed for trouble, setting out further northeast along the Amiens to Albert road to see where the Germans were. As luck would have it he chanced upon Angus Butler, his Tasmanian cousin serving with a British tunnelling regiment, whom he had not seen since the terrible night when they shared their grief over the death of Leo Butler at Mouquet Farm. Angus gave Charles a firsthand account of the rush of the initial German advance; Angus recalled that both sides were so tired that they would stroll at a distance from one another, trailing their arms, and then somebody would take a shot and there would be an exchange of fire.

Bean had billeted with a French woman in the nearby town of Heilly during Australia's first winter on the Western Front and he dropped in at her home to see if she was still there. Shells were falling on the village as she delightedly opened the door to greet him; the Germans were five kilometres away at Morlancourt. He knew that if she stayed during the German advance her home would be obliterated by shellfire so he very kindly returned later in the night and moved her and her sister to Vignacourt, the rest town to the west of the fighting, and then on to a train to Paris, only returning to where he was staying with the 4th Division at 3am. It had been a trying night but a quintessentially selfless act by Charles Bean.

Bean and Fred Cutlack were working well together in their first battle as official and assistant correspondents; while Bean caught up with his diary entries, Cutlack toured the divisions to find out what was going on. The Australian divisions were preoccupied with filling the holes in the breached British Army lines, and for the next few days the Australians and a British division fended off repeated German attacks. The shambolic nature of the battlefield meant it was very easy for Bean to roam and he wandered from unit to unit recording and photographing what he saw. In one town he found a boy from country Victoria helping round up a French farmer's cattle startled by nearby falling artillery, and on the edge of the town he discovered a crashed German aeroplane with the burned body of the dead pilot beside it. Many of the French civilians he met were reluctant to leave their homes because they feared their homes would be looted. What struck the correspondents was that wherever they went, the staff officers of the various British units seemed to have broken down in the panic; he wrote how the men blamed Haig, but 'of course the Australian officers blame [British General] Gough whom they have never liked since Pozieres'.[23]

Throughout April 1918 the Germans went all out to try to capture the major transport and industrial hub of Amiens, moving first on the Somme village of Villers-Bretonneux twenty kilometres to the east of the city. Taking that town would give them a clear line of sight to Amiens;

it offered an excellent position from which to fire artillery onto the crucial railway station in the centre of the city. On 30 March the Germans launched a massive attack on Villers-Bretonneux with eight divisions of troops; the Germans were held off as they advanced by the Australians from Monash's 3rd Division, but the British 14th Division infantry fighting alongside them was panicked into an embarrassing retreat to a position just short of the town. From their billet Bean and Wilkins could hear the frenzied artillery fire, and on 4 April they set off up the road in their 'little tin car' towards Villers-Bretonneux to find out what was happening. Australia's 9th Brigade troops had been ordered to help the British 31st Division hold the town and, at huge cost, they had stopped the German advance where they were. Bean's diary shows he was initially sceptical of claims that the British infantry had fled their positions without a fight, but in his postwar official history, much to the irritation of the British military, Bean wrote that 'it is undeniable that during and after their race to the Amiens front the Australian divisions were witnesses of many incidents that impressed them with a lack of virility in a certain proportion of the British troops'.[24]

Australian 9th Brigade troops had proudly marched into the battle past fleeing British troops who breathlessly told them the Germans were advancing with 'overwhelming strength'. It was another story the British military tried to gag; Bean ensured his official history later recorded that when rumours of this British timidity began to surface during the German advance, the British War Office telegraphed the Australian government demanding that there be no reference in the papers to 'these scurrilous and unfair allusions to the conduct of United Kingdom troops'.[25] Press reports at the time were so strictly censored that there was no chance of such devastating revelations ever being published during the war. However Bean did go to great pains to also acknowledge incidents of great heroism in the British ranks, including a charge by a horse cavalry regiment of British Lancers who helped the Australians stand their ground. In another stirring account of breathtaking bravery, he noted how a senior British officer arrived at one Australian post facing German positions at Vieux-Berquin, addressing a Lieutenant McGinn:

> 'Boy, is this your post?' said the senior to McGinn.
>
> 'Yes, Sir'.
>
> 'Are you going to make a fight of it?'
>
> 'Yes, Sir'.
>
> 'Well, give me your rifle – I'm one of your men.'
>
> And taking a proffered rifle, he jumped into the post. He proved to be the colonel of the 1st Lancashire Fusiliers and his companions were his adjutant and intelligence officer. He was bitterly disappointed with his troops who, he said, for the first time in the regiment's history, had retired from a position which they were ordered to hold. As soon as dusk fell he went out into the village and, finding it unoccupied, collected a number of his men and led them to hold it.
>
> 'You can report,' he said to McGinn, 'that the 1st Lancashire Fusiliers held the village to the last'.
>
> All night the Australians could hear fierce machine-gun fire in that direction.[26]

Bean's account of the Australian defence of Villers-Bretonneux is a fine illustration of the painstaking way he went about collecting the smallest details of a battle to build up an understanding of what actually happened. As he went around interviewing soldiers and their officers, he even found the time to challenge some Australian soldiers who were also retreating in front of the German advance, suggesting they wait until an Australian officer told them where to go; they obediently did as Bean told them to do and sat down, exhausted: 'Their rifles were choked with mud but every single Australian carried a rifle.'[27] Just as he was talking to the soldiers a 5.9-inch shell landed just a few metres from where they were standing, injuring one man; another close shave for Bean. Watching the mass retreat, Bean wrote later that he had thought right then that the situation was so hopeless that Villers-Bretonneux would fall, but the one thing that cheered him was that at least the Australians would still obey an officer's orders and return to the fight if they were told what to do. While the British were panicked and spiritless, Bean only noted one Australian who was frightened: 'He had foam at the corners of his lips and shocked eyes … he had been through a very bad time.'[28] Absurdly, in the midst of all this confusion, Bean was also terribly worried about the Australian battlefield relics he had stored up at Bailleul, now in the face of the advancing Germans. He was relieved when an AIF staff officer, Colonel Butler, agreed to go there to get British help to move them to safety.

The only way Bean could accurately find out what was really happening during this panicky time was not by speaking to AIF headquarters, whose information was often old, but to walk into the fighting and test the water. So it was that he and Fred Cutlack calmly walked into Villers-Bretonneux under heavy shellfire, cannily avoiding the main roads by following the bicycle tracks of a messenger to find their way to Australian Lieutenant Colonel Leslie Morshead's battalion headquarters in a bombed-out villa. There he took down a briefing from a weary Morshead, two days of beard stubble on his face, describing how the Australians had held off the Germans. As Bean wandered the empty streets of Villers-Bretonneux he found a solitary elderly French woman who had been left behind, doing what he could for her. 'The idea of a stray fragment catching that poor old thing – of her spending the night amidst the shell flashes is terrible.'[29] He was scathing in his impressions of the British command's planning, especially how the exhausted Australian troops were enduring days of marching to get into position while British troops retreated beside them. He felt the British were 'plastering up their tottering fabric with colonial troops'.[30] He wrote that 'though there are fine men amongst the British, the majority of them are not fit to face the Germans'.[31] After hearing of the heavy losses of thousands of young Australians in the defence of Villers-Bretonneux, a sober Bean commented in his diary: 'Our Australians have been holding nearly half the British battle line. I wonder if the British people will ever realise this.'[32]

There are often painfully moving personal stories of sacrifice that, for whatever reason, Bean never told in his newspaper stories or the *Official History of Australia in the War*. One of those he gathered in April during the Battle of Dernancourt, in the defence of Amiens, was that of a young lieutenant, Irvine Barton, who had started the war in the Light Horse and then transferred to the 52nd Battalion. The son of a Queensland farmer, Barton was a handsome and heroic young man who, while recovering in hospital after a gas attack, fell in love with the young British nurse looking after him, who turned out to be the daughter of a countess; the couple was smitten with each other and wanted to marry. As Bean's notes tell the story, her mother had consented to them being engaged, not wanting to stand in the way of their happiness, but was apparently more than a little worried about what the absent count would have to say about it. Barton, who was an exemplary soldier and had won a Military Cross for conspicuous gallantry earlier in the year, had warned his nurse lover that life on a farm in Queensland would be a lot different from the life of English aristocracy. But fate was to deal a cruel blow. Barton returned to his unit from hospital to find his company had rushed into battle without him, and he was assured there was 'no disgrace in being left out'.[33] But he had protested so strongly that he was allowed to join his comrades and sent up to the frontline. 'He was very sure (for some reason) this day that he was going to be killed.'[34] Sadly, during the fighting that same day a bullet hit him above the knee, travelling through his body to his abdomen, severing an artery in his leg on the way. Lieutenant Barton was never to marry his betrothed – he died of his wounds, one of so many exemplary Australians who were to die defending Amiens in these desperate weeks.

In the middle of this fierce fighting in the defence of Amiens, an article appeared in the London *Times* announcing that the British Army would no longer select its top generals based on seniority but on merit. For Bean, who was daily witnessing the failures of British senior command, the decision was laughable. 'It has needed the British Army to be halfway to Boulogne before they did that.' He contemptuously noted that if the British Army had also excluded officers selected for their social qualifications then 'they would have covered [two-thirds] of the trouble'.[35]

Along with so many educated men and women of the era, his experience in this war was awakening socialist sensibilities in Charles Bean. He felt the root cause of the British failure was the class system: 'the exploitation of the whole country for the benefit of a class, a system quietly assumed by the "upper class" and accepted by the lower class so that the upper class does not have to employ brains or ability … except tact or manners in order to occupy all the positions of command; and the lower class has to exist without any hope of right or betterment in whatever hovels or slums this "system" allows for its workers.'[36]

On 11 April 1918, General Haig issued his now legendary backs-to-the-wall order to all Allied troops. 'Words fail me to express the admiration which I feel for the splendid resistance offered by all ranks of our Army,' wrote Haig with no intended irony. He must have known that many of his men in the British Fourth Army had run from the enemy, but now he told them that '[e]very position must be held to the last man'.[37] So much of that responsibility was to now fall on men of the AIF.

Seventeen

THE GREATEST INDIVIDUAL FEAT OF THE WAR

Kill every bloody German you see, we don't want any prisoners, and God bless you.

Captain 'Billy' Harburn, 51st Battalion, AIF, 24 April 1918

The Australians had noticed a curiously dramatic change in the British troops now being sent to join them in the battle for Villers-Bretonneux: they were suddenly getting younger. Charles Bean noted his own diary entry in his official history that the Australians told him: 'For two days, companies of infantry have been passing us on the roads, companies of children, English children; pink-faced, round-cheeked children, flushed under the weight of their unaccustomed packs with their steel helmets on the back of their heads and the strap hanging loosely on their rounded baby chins.'[1]

In breach of the undertakings Lloyd George had given to his Parliament, the British government had reduced the age at which soldiers were now drafted to France, and many of the youngsters now being called into the panicked defence of Amiens were under nineteen years old.

Bean was appalled by this and made a point of recording in his official history how 60 per cent of the boys in one battalion now being sent into battle were under nineteen and, until the week before, had never fired a shot.[2] Such was the desperation as the Germans rolled towards Villers-Bretonneux, their shells already landing in the strategic prize of Amiens, visible from the heights around the village. A second German attack on Villers-Bretonneux was inevitable and just before dawn on 24 April 1918 it began. The Germans had previously rained artillery fire and gas shells along the entire Allied frontline between Villers-Bretonneux and the nearby village of Hangard Wood for a week, and when they finally advanced with new tanks and a huge high explosive barrage, the British 8th Division buckled. By 10.30am Charles Bean was standing in the AIF forward headquarters to hear the grim news that Villers-Bretonneux had fallen.

Brigadier General Pompey Elliott's Australian 15th Brigade was in the thick of the counterattack to retake the town. Elliott was not having any more nonsense with fleeing British troops and he issued an extraordinarily brutal order on his men to enforce military law if necessary: 'All British troops to be rallied and re-formed, as our troops march through them, by selected officers, and on any hesitation to be shot.'[3] He was eventually ordered to withdraw his inflammatory edict and Bean called Elliott's original order a 'gross error of judgment', but it reflected the feeling at the time among the AIF about British timidity in the face of the German offensive.[4] Bean's colleague Fred Cutlack even heard suggestions that the British 8th Division had withheld some of their own troops from the counterattack at Villers-Bretonneux because the British 'thought the Australians could do it'.[5] Of course, none of these concerns could ever have been reported during the war.

It was ruthless fighting; two-thirds of the Australian 5th Division, the 13th and 15th brigades, was ordered to seize back the village. The commanding Australian generals, William Glasgow and Pompey Elliott, were told at first to mount a frontal assault in daylight, but this time (there can be no doubt Elliott still held bitter memories of the command failures at Fromelles) the AIF had the confidence to challenge that British command and a night attack was finally agreed on. It was still seen as suicidal; just before the attack started at 10pm, a gloomy Charles Bean did not believe they had a chance. But the Australian attack in fact went stunningly well and the two brigades soon swept the Germans out of Villers-Bretonneux in a pincer movement. The Germans were also in Monument Wood, just to the south of the village, and Australians from the 9th Brigade were told to force them out as well. Bean's official history gives some of the flavour of the bloody desperation of the fighting, including how an Australian captain, in apparent defiance of the laws of war, had given the order to his troops for no prisoners to be taken because he did not know what to do with them.[6] Without any criticism, Bean recorded that the officer had told his men: 'The Monument is your goal and nothing is to stop your getting there. Kill every bloody German you see, we don't want any prisoners, and God bless you.'[7] In an extraordinary feat of arms the Australians did take Monument Wood, and by 29 April the German commanders realised their massive offensive was stalled: Villers-Bretonneux was securely back in Allied hands and Amiens was saved. British Brigadier General George Grogan was to later describe the Australian counterattack as 'perhaps the greatest individual feat of the war', but it was at a cost: among the killed or wounded were 2500 Australians.

Bean's powerful official account of the AIF's crucial role in the Battle of Villers-Bretonneux, and the defence of Amiens, secured its legendary place in Australian military history, and a century on the town is still the focus of Australia's Western Front commemorations of the war. What set Bean's description apart from other military histories of the time was that he acknowledged the triumph and daring of individual soldiers, including one account of how Sergeant Stanley McDougall of the 47th Battalion had earned his Victoria Cross at Dernancourt, northeast of Villers-Bretonneux. McDougall had held off a strong German attack with a Lewis machine gun and Bean's official history described Stan's reckless heroism in forensic detail, with a storyteller's eye for the narrative:

> … McDougall heard, from the mist 50–100 yards ahead of him, the sound of bayonet scabbards flapping on the thighs of marching troops. He at once called to the two resting men. Lieutenant Reid, hearing the voice, shouted:
>
> 'Is that you, Mac?'
>
> 'Yes,' was the reply, 'come up here quick. I think they are coming at us.'
>
> Reid ran up the bank. 'By jove, they are!' he exclaimed …
>
> [McDougall] was well ahead of his party – three of four of whom were quickly killed or wounded – when two German light machine-gun teams started to cross the embankment seven yards away. McDougall, with his gun across his chest, at the 'port',

> switched its fire straight into them like water from a hose, blew away half the head of the nearest man and shot down all the rest.[8]

Where historical accuracy demanded it, Bean did not shrink from describing the savagery and ugliness of war, but he was always wary of gloating or triumphalism. His historian's sobriety restrained him from reporting in his history what McDougall said to his sergeant immediately after the battle, though Bean's unpublished private notes record the VC recipient bloodthirstily saying, 'The best day's fighting we ever had, wasn't it Laurie?'[9] Yet McDougall's laconic relish said so much about the confidence of the Anzacs by this stage of the war.

In the wake of the battle there was now considerable speculation behind the scenes about whether General Birdwood would step aside as commander of the Anzacs and who would replace him: General White or General Monash? Fred Cutlack and Will Dyson shrewdly picked Monash as the likely successor, a choice that irked Bean, who still saw Monash as a showman. He recorded Will Dyson saying Monash: 'has the crude, advertising, pushing genius which must succeed'.[10] Bean's colleagues descended to the anti-Semitism common in the era to justify their dislike of Monash, Will Dyson saying Monash would end up winning the key Australian Corps command: 'he must get there all the time, on account of the qualities of his race; the Jew will always get there'.[11]

Bean was rarely the everyman in his dealings with the soldiers whose battles he told; his attitudes were driven very much by the prejudices of the educated officers with whom he most commonly associated, and there was a huge social and class gulf that coloured his writing. His official history and journalism most commonly names the officers in an action, and less often the non-commissioned officers and private soldiers whose heroism was often the key to success in a battle (unless they did something especially heroic, such as Stan McDougall). Bean was receptive to the criticism he copped from one old Sydney friend, Edwin Brissenden, who took the official correspondent on about never having taken the time to write up 'the life of the soldier'.[12] Brissenden was an intriguing character; a Sydney barrister before the war, he had joined up as a private and would end it as a lieutenant colonel. Bean had the humility to admit that his friend's criticism was fair, that he had indeed treated the common soldier shyly in his writing. (It's likely he was still smarting from the flak he drew at the Mena camp in Egypt in 1915 when he had criticised the wasters in the ranks), but now he resolved to spend time with men from the 21st Battalion camped at Querrieu, getting Wilkins to take their photograph and Dyson to draw them. Bean's notes show that he was always transparently uncomfortable and slightly wary of these men, much more comfortable speaking to the officers. He was fascinated with their physicality and crudity: 'The language in the yard is such that you would think there was going to be a knifing every two minutes. "Aaaah – you, you lazy bastard", "Go to buggery, to hell wid yer" ... The most ferocious oaths are flung between passing men.'[13] Tragically, some of these same men would soon be killed by Australian artillery falling short at the Battle of Ville-sur-Ancre a few weeks later.

Captain Bean also suffered a crisis in his own war relics unit command that underlined the sacrifice and risks taken by the enlisted men working under him. It had always been a dangerous occupation for he and his colleagues to roam the frontlines as correspondents or to be a member of the salvage teams working on Bean's war relics collection units, but now their luck ran out. A trench mortar bomb killed one member of his war relics salvage team, Corporal Ernie Bailey, while he was trying to clear it of explosive. Summonsed by frantic staff, Bean rushed to the salvage yard to see Bailey's shattered body lying amidst the debris of the explosion. Ernie had been scraping out the TNT explosive with a chisel and appeared to have struck a spark on the side of the bomb casing. Bailey was buried in the nearby Vignacourt war cemetery and Bean went to great lengths to console his wife, Emily, that the future Australian war museum would one day be a great monument to his work.

Now began an episode of court intrigue that was to be Charles Bean's biggest mistake. In mid-May 1918, General Birdwood confided to Bean that he would be leaving the Anzac command to head the British Fifth Army, and that he had recommended General Monash to head the entire Australian Corps as field commander in France and Belgium, and for Major General White to join Birdwood as his chief of staff. This should not have come as any surprise after Monash's demonstrated successes in battle, but Bean was shocked by this proposal, not least because White was a close friend and also one of his best journalistic sources inside the AIF command. He was convinced White was the best man for the corps command and Bean now took it upon himself to lobby on White's behalf because he believed 'Monash would leave no stone unturned and no underground channel untried' to win the role.[14] He resolved to travel to England with Fred Cutlack immediately to see Keith Murdoch because he knew the by now very powerful

London-based journalist had considerable sway with Prime Minister Billy Hughes. This was a serious misjudgment by Bean, for he knew soon after he got to London that Monash's appointment was already a done deal; it had been approved by the Australian cabinet a few days earlier. Moreover, he was trying to be a player in a key command decision by the Australian government, something totally outside his brief as a correspondent. While he waited for Murdoch to return from a trip to Scotland, Bean drafted a memorandum setting out why he believed White was the man for the job, asserting that 'the universal opinion of the force is that General White is the best commander of operations in the AIF'.[15] This was not the case at all, for many officers supported Monash. One fear in the ranks was that if Birdwood went then Major General McCay, notorious in the AIF for both the disastrous Krithia and Fromelles attacks, might get the AIF command.[16] So now, damning Monash with faint praise, Bean suggested in his memorandum that Monash be given that secondary administrative AIF job while pushing for White to be given the operational Australian Corps command.

Murdoch took some convincing; when he finally arrived back in London he was initially very sceptical about White, partly because he had discovered that White was hindering his efforts to be allowed access to the Somme frontline AIF headquarters as a press correspondent. But Bean turned Murdoch around and convinced him to telegraph Billy Hughes, pushing for no action to be taken until the prime minister arrived on an imminent visit to England. Incredibly, this in turn swung Hughes to urge the appointment be delayed until he reached London – it was preposterous that two journalists had successfully meddled in the most important command appointment in the Australian military while the Allies now had their backs to the wall.

In early June Bean was back in London to view an impressive military exhibition of Australian war photographs taken by his official photographers. He angrily diarised that there was 'too much of [Frank] Hurley in it – his name is on every picture with few exceptions – including some that Wilkins took; and what should be a fine monument to the sacrifice of Australians in France is rather an advertisement for Hurley'.[17] Hurley was indeed a shameless self-promoter, and both artist Fred Leist and Australian government publicist Henry Smart took him on about his appalling behaviour, leading Bean to resolve that Hurley would not have management of the exhibition when it toured Australia. Bean was also working on a catalogue of the pictures so that soldiers could order images of their own units at war.

He also caught up with Keith Murdoch and discovered that because the Monash appointment had been confirmed by the Australian government in Hughes's absence, General Monash could not be replaced or removed from the new Australian Corps field command role without his agreement. For the ardently nationalistic Murdoch, his complaint with the change was that the Australian government's new proposed restructure would leave the British General Birdwood with administrative command of the entire AIF as well as his new command of the British Fifth Army. But Bean's concern was more to see Major General White given the fighting command, yet the truth was there was no grassroots support for White at all in the AIF; Bean was operating completely beyond his brief in an emotional pitch for his friend, despite the fact that White had never even held a field command and that Monash had demonstrated great ability in modern battle strategy.

One of Birdwood's staff officers, Colonel Thomas Dodds, even had it out with Bean, challenging him over an article written by Murdoch suggesting that the force 'universally' wanted Monash in the administrative AIF role and White in the key corps command role. Dodds said that Keith Murdoch, and by inference also Bean, was an 'irresponsible pressman' for pushing such 'a lie'.[18] But Bean, blind in his loyalty to White, remained convinced that Monash had secretly schemed for the job. Major General White seemed embarrassed by Bean's lobbying on his behalf and was in fact fiercely loyal to General Birdwood.

All this scheming against Monash was a huge distraction for the general himself at a time when he and other commanders were planning how to turn the German advance. Monash's biographer, Geoffrey Serle, vouchsafed: 'There might easily have been much harm: the Australian high commanders were distracted during some of the most vital days of the war. It is perhaps the outstanding case of sheer irresponsibility by pressmen in Australian history.'[19] Monash also told his wife that he believed the attack was anti-Semitic: 'It is a great nuisance to have to fight a pogrom of this nature in the midst of all one's other anxieties.'[20]

It was possibly only when Bean dropped in at his headquarters on 11 June 1918 that Monash understood how much Bean was part of the campaign against him, though perhaps not even then realising that it was actually Bean who had originally kindled Murdoch's opposition; for Bean admitted to the general that he thought Murdoch was right.[21] Monash described Murdoch's opposition to his taking over the corps as 'very cruel' and explained that the commander-in-chief General Haig had told him that even if the Australian Corps was not vacant then he wanted him to have another corps command in the British Army.[22] He flatly told Bean that he would rather return to Australia than take the secondary administrative AIF role, which would have him based in London. The irony in all of this was that White was so appalled by Murdoch and Bean's scheming against Birdwood that he would probably have refused the Australian Corps command job even if he was offered it. Bean desperately wrote to White suggesting that 'our men are not so safe under General Monash as under you. You know that no one will safeguard them against a reckless waste – or useless waste – of life in impracticable or unnecessary stunts, or will get so much effect out of them in a good stunt – as you can or would.'[23] But there was no evidence that Monash was a reckless commander at all, and White's response to this campaign was to write to General Monash reassuring him that 'if the conspirators in this matter do happen to be General White's friends, they are not acting at the suggestion or with the approval of General White'.[24] The whole campaign was a seriously deluded misjudgment by both Bean and Murdoch.

When Prime Minister Billy Hughes arrived in London that month the jockeying continued. Monash stood his ground, refusing to budge from the Australian Corps command job, not least because he knew he was the best man for the job. In the end Hughes offered Birdwood the fulltime AIF command, expecting he would not want to take it, but Birdwood did accept, and he ended up staying in the role until the end of the war. During this period of political haggling, Bean spent time at the Regents Park mansion the British government had lent Hughes for his stay, watching as Hughes briefed the great Fleet Street newspapers. The prime minister knew his comments were weighted with the gravity that came from the sacrifice of so many young Australian lives across the Channel, for Australia had made a disproportionate contribution for the British Empire in this war. Hughes' zeal to see Australia's role acknowledged reminded Bean of the one thing that vexed him most about the British military's propaganda department: it repeatedly sent out communiqués that failed to report the role of Australian troops in the recent fighting. Now this passionate politician was hammering the British press with the stories of Australian heroism. It cemented Bean's own strong sense of mission, that his official history should 'make known some day … what the Australians have done in this time'.[25] Billy Hughes was also signalling the stirring of a more aggressive Australian nationalism, the end of an era where the Australian government obediently accepted London's edicts.

Bean continued to have issues with Monash for many years after the war. Perhaps with an eye to future histories, he left an undated 'Confidential and personal only' document among his research notes, which he probably wrote around 1930 when he was communicating with Monash for his official history research about the merits of British officers who served in the AIF. He clearly felt unrepentant even then for challenging Monash's command appointment: 'I am not sure that Murdoch and I were not wrong in trying to get these changes in the AIF command … What guided me was that Monash's chief motive was ambition and that the lives of his troops and the greater interests of his side were not his paramount cares.'[26] But, as the decades went by, Bean softened his harsh judgment of Monash; nearly forty years after he first wrote the comments in his diary accusing Monash of scheming for the command job, he added a comment in the margin recanting: 'I do not now believe this to be true.'[27] In his book *Two Men I Knew* he also claimed that his and Murdoch's meddling did no harm, but the reality was that Lieutenant General Monash had to fight to keep his job while also planning one of the set-piece battles of the war, the Battle of Hamel. During his visit in early July 1918, Hughes spent time touring the frontline preparations for the battle, including an extremely impressive briefing by Monash, who had memorised every aspect of his battle plan and knew all the details of the units that would be engaged in it. What swung Hughes to a favourable impression of Monash was the praise the general got from his own men, as Bean recollected later in his diary: 'Hughes was seriously shaken. He said to Murdoch just before he left: "Well – I haven't met a single one of them that thinks as you do. They all say the same thing – You tell me there are men who think the other way – Where are they?" Murdoch told him that of course the men he had seen all thought the other way, because it had been arranged that they should be the ones to meet him. However, when Hughes drove off … we all felt pretty blue. I did at any rate.'[28]

Hughes gave a rousing speech to the Australian soldiers about to go into battle at Hamel, Bean watching as the prime minister then lay full length on the ground chewing a stalk of grass while another speaker continued. 'He seemed wrapped up in the men and was gazing into their faces all the time. I suppose that he was thinking to himself: within thirty-six hours these men will be out there advancing under the bursting shells, going straight into the thresh of the machine guns.'[29] Monash's performance at Hamel was to very soon dispel any doubts about his suitability for the fighting command job.

Eighteen

THE BLACK DAY OF THE GERMAN ARMY

We have suffered a severe defeat.

GERMAN COMMANDER ERICH LUDENDORFF TO THE KAISER, 10 AUGUST 1918

It took just 93 minutes for General John Monash's surprise attack to defeat the Germans at Hamel on 4 July 1918 – three minutes longer than he had precisely estimated the attack would last. What had previously taken weeks on the Somme using conventional battlefield tactics took a little over an hour and a half using a series of new methods, conceived by the general and his staff in exhaustive planning meetings. The very attributes for which Monash had been undermined by Charles Bean and Keith Murdoch in weeks of political intrigue now proved his mettle at Hamel.

The evening before the attack Bean had dinner with Keith Murdoch and wire correspondent Gordon Gilmour and, while it was still light, the three men set out to the forward lines to watch the battle unfold. Just before 3.10am it began, a concentrated artillery bombardment and machine-gun barrage to keep the Germans down as 7500 Australian and American infantry followed the creeping shells towards the German lines. (The 4 July – US Independence Day – attack date was a deliberate gesture by Monash to his American ally.) Sixty new British Mark V tanks were also used; they were stronger and more reliable, and, unlike Bullecourt, this time the infantry had been trained to work with them and knew which tank to follow. Tanks were also deployed to carry ammunition up with the infantry, a huge logistical leap, and radio communications were also used effectively for one of the first times in the war. In another innovation, aircraft were used to resupply.

The village of Le Hamel sat on a ridge northeast of Villers-Bretonneux, and the heights it occupied allowed the Germans to overlook the Australian positions. The combination of tactics used to seize it back – comprising air power, artillery, infantry and tanks – was revolutionary, a light-year leap from Haig's plodding strategy of bloody attrition that had ground the Somme fighting into years of stalemate. Bean's photographer colleague Hubert Wilkins, bold as always, followed the attacking Australians straight into the frontline German trenches, watching as the Germans bolted, running for their lives. Bean noticed how one German officer taken prisoner would not lift his head from his hands – 'he seemed full of the realisation of his disgrace'.[1]

In the wake of Hamel, Bean was asked by the British Ministry of Information – essentially its propaganda arm – to write what it clearly hoped would be a hagiographic piece on the high regard which Australian and British troops had for each other. This put Bean in a real dilemma: 'I cannot do this without an explanation of the true position.

It is useless at this stage to attempt to cram into Australian troops that the English divisions beside them are as good as they … I am not going to attempt to persuade the Australian that the British soldier is as good as he is.'[2] Sure enough, what he wrote ruffled the feathers of the censors and a few days later he was summonsed for a lunch with the head of British GHQ's publicity and censorship section, Major General Guy Dawnay. Bean was perceived as far too powerful by now for the British to expect him to meekly accept their demand, so this was an opportunity for him to voice Australian frustration at the lack of British recognition for her sacrifice, and Charles Bean went into battle very sure of his principled position. It was an interesting clash of the old British officer culture and the independently minded Australian, the official correspondent's head still ringing with Prime Minister Hughes's pride about Australia's extraordinary military prowess on the battlefield. Dawnay struck Bean as a 'spoilt-boy, dogmatic English University type', and when Dawnay started taking issue with the claims in Bean's article that the Australians were increasingly being used as shock troops to take awkward or difficult positions, Bean stood his ground. 'I mentioned Villers-Bretonneux and Hazebrouck – and of course Dawnay could not say very much. He agreed with me that they were shock troops … He added that at the present he considered that the Australians and the Canadians were the best troops the British had. But he very strongly objected to the idea that the Scottish troops were any better than the English.'[3] Bean was rightly infuriated when Dawnay made the outrageously ignorant comment that the Australians had had no part in the fighting during the German offensive on Amiens. When he took the general to task on this, Dawnay backed down and promised to reflect this in future ministry communiqués; no one knew better than Bean just how much blood Australians had spilled defending Amiens as British troops turned and ran. Yet, despite what Bean knew about the timidity of many British troops at that time, he also graciously agreed to help write a pamphlet that would counteract German propaganda saying the British could not fight at all. He had witnessed enough individual acts of heroism by British soldiers to know they could fight if properly led.

When General Monash presented medals a few days later to the Australians who had distinguished themselves at Hamel, Bean noted what the photographer told him about the general's eye for self-promotion: 'When the old chap was taking the salute in front of Querrieu Chateau, he kept one eye cocked on the camera; and when it was clearly preparing to open fire, he made his salute one of overpowering dignity.'[4]

Towards the end of July Bean's friend and colleague British press correspondent Herbert Russell received the dreadful news that his son Sidney[5] had been killed while serving with the Australian 1st Division at Merris. Russell was beside himself with grief and it was the kindly Charles Bean who took the time to travel to the battlefield where his son had died to gather information. Bean's efforts to piece together the story and record this young man's bravery reflected his growing sense of mission to honour the valour of the Australians throughout the war. Herbert's son had immigrated to Australia at fifteen and worked on a farm on the north coast of New South Wales. He earned a Military Medal for rescuing wounded men at Pozières and was very likely to have been awarded a Military Cross after recent fighting. Russell's colleagues commented: 'You know, he must have been pretty good to get a Military Medal and a Military Cross amongst the Australians. That means something.'[6] It was little consolation to Herbert Russell but it was the only way that anyone could deal with such a loss that was, by now, so dreadfully routine.

Bean's efforts to record every aspect of Australia's involvement in the war were extraordinarily zealous. His salvage team painstakingly removed an entire room and its contents from a bombed-out house in Villers-Bretonneux. He also visited the new Australian frontlines just beyond Le Hamel before an attack by the 53rd Battalion and the 8th Brigade; the plan was to get the uniforms and kit of one man from each unit who had distinguished himself in the fighting and preserve everything he carried exactly as he stood. The two men were selected and photographed in their full kit, muddied and bloodied from the night before; everything they wore was retrieved from them and carefully packed for the planned Australian war museum.

At 5pm on 7 August 1918, General Monash, flushed with the success of Hamel, confided in Bean that the Australians would be part of a massive offensive out of Amiens, north of the Somme, the next day. It was to be the first time also that the Canadians would go into battle beside their Australian Corps allies. Bean and Wilkins had already heard the rumours and had even reconnoitred a spot from where they would be able to watch the attack. Soon after dark they and fellow correspondent Henry Gullett made their way through Amiens towards the launching point, passing lines of cavalry readying for the battle. As they drove through the village of Vaux there was a strong whiff of poisonous phosgene gas, and Bean's diary casually mentions how Gullett very nearly died during the journey, the gas actually causing permanent damage to his heart. Bean never admits being scared at times like this, but it is difficult to conceive that any man could witness so much violence and death and not be permanently affected.

As at Hamel, the Battle of Amiens used tanks, but this time it was an entire corps of 552 tanks, the largest tank battle of the war at that time. Air power was again employed, with the Allies having a huge number of planes in the air. It was also the first time that all five Australian divisions had fought together in the one battle, and under Monash's command. The weather was also on the Allies' side, a thick mist covering the infantry's advance behind the creeping artillery barrage that began at 4.20am. Bean walked through the frontlines following the advancing troops, 'And then, as the mist cleared, we beheld a sight that I shall never forget': the Germans were overwhelmed and retreating.[7] The British supply wagons, guns and troops advanced in an uninterrupted line towards the east over the ground the Germans had surrendered, and by ten in the morning the Australians had seized their objective at Harbonnières. By the end of the day every objective was seized; the battle was a rout. The Allied casualties totalled 22,200 dead, wounded or missing, including 6500 Australians, but the Allies had captured thirteen kilometres of ground across a thirteen-and-a-half-kilometre front, while the Germans had suffered 27,000 casualties. Bean watched incredulous as 200 German prisoners quick-marched out of the battle zone led by just one Australian soldier; nearby there was a similar line of 300 prisoners. He found himself looking into the horizon at an avenue of trees on the Péronne to Albert road that he had not seen since before the German offensive: 'It was like coming home, the sight of those trees again.'[8] Close to Harbonnières, Bean laid sight on what would become perhaps his biggest trophy of the war for the future museum, a massive eleven-inch field gun mounted on a railway platform, complete with stacks of 320-kilogram shells; it had the range to easily drop shells on Amiens. To become affectionately known as 'Little Bertha', the railway gun was originally mounted on the battleship SMS *Hessen* and now sits at the Australian War Memorial in Canberra. It was a day of astonishing sights and achievements; by the time Bean made it back to his tent that night he was dog-tired, having roamed the battlefield for hours.

Bean begrudgingly gave General John Monash credit he probably did not deserve for the success at Amiens, Monash having falsely claimed to Keith Murdoch that it was his pushing after Hamel that persuaded the Allied command to make the attack; it was the very sort of self-promotion that Bean found so distasteful. 'So it was John Monash's battle and he has certainly made a great name for himself in it,' Bean wrote.[9] But Monash's boast was an exaggeration: Bean later learned that generals White and Birdwood had actually planned the Amiens offensive at British General Rawlinson's suggestion. Amiens was certainly a stunning Allied victory and Germany's greatest defeat, German General Erich Ludendorff acknowledging 8 August 1918 as the 'black day of the German Army in this war'.[10]

Three days after the battle, Bean and Gordon Gilmour arrived at the Australian Corps headquarters to find the Château de Bertangles garden being filled with captured guns, howitzers, machine guns and field mortars. They learned John Monash was to be knighted by the King the next day and he had organised the trophies as a prize photograph for the event. It incensed Bean and Keith Murdoch, who felt it an unnecessary distraction from the ongoing offensive. 'The whole thing seems to me – to some of us – a damned waste of time and energy at a moment like this.'[11] Bean was furious when Hubert Wilkins, who had been out photographing the frontlines all day, was ordered to be at the chateau early next morning to photograph the event. He was disdainful of the knighthood ceremony, angry that the King did not acknowledge the diggers, and he privately mocked Monash's eagerness: 'John was tapped on the left shoulder and got up before the King had time to tap him on the right – so I suppose he is only half a Knight.'[12] When the photographic prints arrived a couple of days later, Monash gave the pictures to Murdoch, claiming Bean had arranged for them to be taken and that he had not known anything about them. 'The old poser,' Bean wrote in his diary. 'Well there are many like him and he's a most capable man.'[13]

Despite British chief censor General Guy Dawnay's assurances to Bean that the Australian role in the war would be properly acknowledged in communiqués, the Battle of Amiens was again written up by the British Army's propaganda unit as a feat of British arms in which the Australians and Canadians merely had a 'share'.[14] This angered Bean and Keith Murdoch, who saw the bitterness it generated among the diggers, but Major General White bluntly told them that the British 'had to have a success' and that it was important to rebut the effective German propaganda legitimately attacking the British fighting ability. With British censors controlling what Bean and Murdoch could write for the duration of the war, this was a serious issue for the two newsmen, who wanted to get the truth out to the Australian public about their soldiers' achievements. But White told them it was a sacrifice the Australians had to make. Ironically, General Monash later that month took Bean to task for the lack of acknowledgement of the Australian role in the papers, not fully understanding that as usual British censorship was stopping him from telling the story he wanted to tell. To add insult to injury, 'Little Bertha', the captured German railway gun, was put on display on the Champ de Mars in Paris, with an inscription on the side reading 'Captured by the British Fourth Army'.[15] An earlier inscription by the Australians who actually did capture it had been painted over.

For much of the rest of August the Allied offensive slowly pushed the Germans back. On 25 August Bean was back in newly liberated Albert and the push was on to get the Germans out of Pozières. Following troops marching along the road towards Pozières, Bean was moved to come across the memorial crosses of Australians from the 1st Division and 8th Battalion who had died in 1916; now in front of them were German graves, a sad legacy of the recent occupation. For days Bean and his colleagues literally roamed the battlefield, setting out on daily jaunts to see what they could find, often coming across abandoned German positions still strewn with uniforms, weapons and kit. On one occasion they found a wounded German officer in a trench, semi-conscious from a serious head wound; they could do little for him and notified the stretcher-bearers, who told Bean that there were still ten wounded Allied soldiers on the battlefield whom they were also trying to save. They promised to go back for the German when they could.

At dawn on Saturday, 31 August, in an extraordinarily bold attack, Australian 2nd Division troops of the 5th Brigade took the strategic heights of Mont St Quentin overlooking Péronne, whooping and yelling as they attacked to exaggerate their small number. Bean scrambled to get there to cover the battle as the Germans counterattacked. He arrived just after the 6th Brigade went in again in support and found himself under heavy shellfire as he bunny-hopped from cover to cover to get forward: 'It was like musical chairs – trying to get opposite a good-looking grassy shell hole before the distant bang of the gun gave us about 2 seconds warning.'[16] Bean was impressed to hear later that night that his extraordinarily courageous photographer Hubert Wilkins had been with the 6th Brigade as they attacked, photographing the men going over the top and then following the second wave of assault troops. By the night of 3 September the Australians had captured Péronne below Mont St Quentin, pushing the Germans into a retreat behind their Hindenburg Line fortifications. It was a huge achievement by the Australians; at the end of it all, for the loss of 3000 casualties, they had pushed back five German divisions.

But Bean's relations with Monash were not going as well. Not surprisingly, since learning of the official correspondent's campaign against him, Monash was freezing him out. When a group of Australian newspaper editors and owners visited the frontlines soon after the victory at Péronne, Bean was not invited by Monash to join them at the lunch. It was a weighty and influential group, including *The Sydney Morning Herald*'s James Fairfax, the Melbourne *Age*'s Geoffrey Syme, and the editor of *The Bulletin* magazine. Bean was effectively under Monash's command as official correspondent, not the free agent that Keith Murdoch was, and he envied Murdoch's willingness to take Monash on. In contrast, Bean realised Monash had less respect for him and his journalism, that the commander saw the official correspondent's role as essentially that of a public relations booster for Monash and the AIF: 'he is very dissatisfied with the publicity he is getting, and has always been a man who would have liked to have his own publicity in his own hands. I often think he would like to get rid of me if he could – of course he would; I often think that he will try, but Keith doubts it,' Bean diarised.[17]

Monash's issue with Bean was probably also to do with the uncomfortable truth that many of the visiting newspapermen had decided long ago not to publish most of Bean's news stories in their papers. Bean's journalism often lacked fire and it also suffered, possibly, because by this stage of the war he was utterly exhausted. He had grown increasingly uncomfortable too with the expectation of both general and editors that the traditional job of the war correspondent was to talk up the daring deeds of 'our boys', which Bean was only prepared to do within the bounds of accuracy. On one occasion Monash tore a strip off Bean for reporting that Australian artillery held their fire on German transports fleeing along the road south of Péronne; the reason this happened was because the careful Australian officers could not believe they were German troops and were fearful of bombing their own side. Monash clearly thought Bean should not have reported this at all, even though it was a truthful account. He accused Bean of a lack of imagination, and Bean privately rejoined in his diary that what Monash really wanted was 'to see the fighting written up with a lavish hand – not too much accuracy, as he himself told both me and Murdoch – in the fashion of some of the old war correspondents. "What a pity that we haven't an Ashmead-Bartlett," he said once to Murdoch.'[18]

Monash did have a point; for example, Bean's newspaper coverage of the brilliant capture of Mont St Quentin was underwhelming. While the French papers were enthusing about the magnificent exploit, Bean was dull, trying to find similarities between this latest battle and the storming of Anzac Cove in 1915: 'The country at that angle is more like Gallipoli than any the Australians have seen in France. The swift rush [up] Mont St Quentin reminded all who saw the position of that first swift rush up the hills by Ari Burnu which brought the Australian soldier into fame.'[19] To draw yet again on a strategic defeat like Gallipoli was a curious angle for Bean's story; Mont St Quentin was a key turning point in the war and his coverage did not reflect that. Moreover, his photographer and sketch artist had actually gone into battle with the diggers and their images could have been used to great effect in newspaper coverage back home; Charles Bean did squander an opportunity to play the victory at Mont St Quentin in his news reports for all it genuinely deserved. (It is also possible the British censor had culled his prose of any fulsome praise for the Australian achievement.) By contrast, Bean's excellent account of the battle in his *Anzac to Amiens* book was full of the colour missing from his wartime reportage:

> Their number was few, most Australian battalions at this time having only 3000 men available for action … The company leaders therefore decided that the best chance lay in making a noise as they attacked, 'yelling', as Captain E.T. Manefield urged, 'like a lot of bushrangers'. At 5am on August 31st, as the grey sky began to show behind the Mount, which was dimly visible across a gentle dip, the Australian

field artillery laid its fire … The cheering platoons at once ran into crowds of Germans, who seemed bewildered and quickly surrendered. They were from one of the best divisions in the German Army, the 2nd Guard, which had just been sent up to relieve the over-strained garrison. 'It all happened like lightning,' says the history of the Guard Alexander Regiment, 'and before we had fired a shot we were taken unawares.' The Australians charged on and, by the time they reached the main trench-line in the dip, the face of the Mount ahead of them was covered with Germans fleeing over both shoulders of the hill. The Australians swept up the slopes and over the summit, routing the German supports and reserves there … And General Rawlinson, as he shaved that morning, received the astonishing news that the Mount had been captured.[20]

It should be acknowledged that Bean's efforts in his newspaper reports to praise the fighting prowess of Australian troops were being constantly suppressed by the British censors. At the same time that Monash was unfairly criticising Bean for not lauding the work of the Australians, Bean was taking on British censor General Guy Dawnay yet again, complaining about the lack of credit for fighting done by Australians and Canadians in Allied communiqués. Dawnay sent a patronising response saying that the use of the word 'British' in their communiqués included all the Allies. 'I do not for a minute believe his explanation, though he may,' Bean wrote.[21]

When the visiting Australian newspapermen met Monash, the general tried to block Bean and Keith

Murdoch from showing them more than Monash had planned. But they were able to take them to a view of recaptured Péronne and the opposite side of the Somme where the Germans were now entrenched; it added a touch of grit that, as James Fairfax watched on, Hubert Wilkins came under sniper fire photographing from the top of the viewing trench.

Australian Prime Minister Billy Hughes was fiercely proud of the diggers and keen to show them off; in mid-September Bean joined him from England for a tour of the frontlines with another group of some of the most eminent newspaper owners and editors in Britain. There was increasingly strong feeling from Hughes that the Australians should not be thrown into every operation, and that the Americans and Royal Flying Corps should be used more to keep the potential Australian losses down. Bean went ahead of the prime minister to France and ended up drawing Monash's ire because he took the general on (probably unfairly, as it turned out) for not being sufficiently supportive of this visit of the influential British newsmen. Relations between the two men were clearly strained; Bean did not like Monash and Monash did not like him, but they had to get on, so they patched up their differences and Monash did brief Bean on his attack plans.

By mid-September 1918 the Germans were right back where they had started at the beginning of their spring offensive, and there was the realisation that the Allies would eventually prevail in the war, especially with America's support. To do that though, the Allies now had to breach and overrun the Hindenburg Line, the formidable defensive positions to which the Germans had now withdrawn.

Nineteen

PUT A LITTLE MORE GLORY INTO IT

You generally tell by the gait whether he is Australian or not. If he looks as though he owned the universe, he certainly is.

CHARLES BEAN, WATCHING AIF TROOPS ON THE BATTLEFIELD, 7 OCTOBER 1918

When Charles Bean walked into the Australian 4th Division headquarters near the French town of Cartigny on 18 September 1918, his familiar face was a welcome sight to the division's commander, Major General Sinclair-MacLagan. He hailed Bean as an 'old bird of ill-omen. I knew you would be here; you always are when anything's doing.'[1]

The official correspondent was there to witness the preliminary attack by the Allies on the first part of the Hindenburg Line, this daunting task – yet again – falling in part to the Australians. As Bean left the headquarters to move closer to the battle he noticed two sham tanks, intended to draw enemy fire. One had a shell hole right through it, so the ruse had clearly worked, allowing the Allies in turn to target the location of the German guns.

The Battle of Épehy was to be a great victory; the diggers had only eight real tanks but they managed to break through part of the Hindenburg Line and take 4300 prisoners. But it was again at the cost of 1000 casualties, and Bean learned he had lost yet another friend in the conflict, Captain Walter Rewi Hallahan, a New Zealand–born soldier who had won the Military Medal and the Military Cross. Hallahan exemplified the best of the Anzacs. He had served with distinction in Gallipoli and fought in many of Australia's greatest battles, Pozières, Mouquet Farm and Ypres, often bumping into Bean along the way. Hallahan was due to go back to Australia on leave but, because he was single, he had given way to married officers. Bean was saddened by Hallahan's death but, in his driven way, he solemnly recorded the event in his diary and never admitted to being stricken by grief at the loss of any soldier; perhaps he knew that if he did so he would inevitably have been overwhelmed and not able to do his job.

War artist Will Dyson told Bean that when he got a cup of tea from a YMCA stall after the battle, the diggers there were talking about Bean's dispatches:

> 'Some of them said: "I reckon he does the right thing in sending them the dinkum story" and were arguing pretty vigorously in favour of this. Others said: "That might be all very well for the historian but they reckoned the war correspondent ought to put a little more glory into it."'[2]

The next day General John Monash trustingly gave Bean a briefing on his plans to breach the rest of the Hindenburg Line while also flagging that the Australians would not be back in action for a week or so, so Bean took a break to do some work in London. Monash's candour was a welcome sign that the Australian Corps commander was again taking Bean into his confidence. There was more welcome news when Bean read the GHQ communiqués on the latest fighting; as he had demanded of British censor General Guy Dawnay, the communiqué now acknowledged exactly which division had distinguished itself. Bean was gratified: 'It is not a small thing for us to have our real share of credit for whatever is done by Australians in the war'.[3]

It was the Allied defeat of the Germans along the Hindenburg Line that would finally break Germany's resolve, six million men from twelve armies attacking on a front running from Verdun almost all the way back to the English Channel. On 26 September the French and Americans attacked between Verdun and Rheims, the largest battle in American military history, involving 1.2 million United States soldiers. This was the beginning of the Hundred Days Offensive, which would eventually end the war.

The following evening Charles Bean was catching up on some sleep at the war correspondents' camp at Barleux, east of Amiens, when he heard the 'tramp, tramp, tramp' of infantry soldiers moving up through the town towards the fight. The Australians were at the middle of a huge second-phase attack, comprising French, Belgian, American and British troops, that began on 29 September along a 40-mile front from St-Quentin on the river Somme north to Douai. Two American divisions had also been placed under Monash's operational command because his own Australian divisions were so depleted from the recent battles. The diggers were to attack the most formidable German defences between St-Quentin and Cambrai, masses of barbed wire, pillboxes, concrete fortifications, underground bunkers and the three-metre-deep water of the St-Quentin canal.

The day before the Australian attack, Bean was showing an eminent party of British visitors around the frontlines, including Sir Arthur Conan Doyle, creator of Sherlock Holmes and historian of the Boer War. The two writers were to become lifelong friends. As they visited an old battlefield at Péronne, soldiers were frantically saluting Conan Doyle because the uniform he was wearing, that of a lord lieutenant of an English county, was as colourful and glorious as that of a field marshal. Bean later wrote in his diary, 'The old chap was so abashed, in spite of his experience in public life, that he hardly dared lift his eyes from the ground when any soldiers were passing – a fact which attracted me to him at once.'[4]

General Monash's attack plan called for American troops to take the 5.5-kilometre long St-Quentin canal tunnel, which would allow Australian and British troops to cross at different points. On 27 September 1918, as Bean showed Conan Doyle around Péronne, the Americans launched their preliminary attack, and when Bean finally caught up with General Monash the evening before the Australians were due to follow, the Australian commander was close to despair. Monash frankly told him that he did not think the 'unprepared and untrained' Americans would achieve their objective. 'It struck all of us that John was hedging against a possible defeat, in which case he would be able to throw the blame on to the Americans,' Bean wrote.[5]

Early in the battle things did go very badly for the Americans, who were held up by a determined German counterattack, and when Bean saw Monash on 30 September the commander complained, 'Well, you see what

I expected might happen has happened. The Americans sold us a pup … They're simply unspeakable.'[6] The situation was grim but not irretrievable and, in a revised plan, it fell to two AIF reserve brigades to attack along the Hindenburg trench system to capture the town of Bony and the northern end of the tunnel. As usual, photographer Hubert Wilkins was up the front in the American lines and he later told Bean how he entered one American trench to find its soldiers sheltering at the bottom, oblivious to a German officer and two of his men who were actually right outside the trench dropping bombs on top of them. It was the battle-hardened Wilkins who suggested the Americans shoot at their attackers; they had thought they were being shelled and were taking cover, such was their inexperience.

In his postwar *Official History of Australia in the War of 1914–1918*, Bean strongly rejected Monash's self-serving attempts to blame the Americans for the initial setback in the battle, saying 'never indeed was criticism more unjust'.[7] He blamed the Allied commanders, including Monash, for not considering more the Americans' inexperience and their lack of officers, and then he went further, saying: 'Monash often lacked knowledge of what had happened in battle.'[8] (Monash had died in 1931 before this volume of the history was published.) For Bean, it was an opportunity to correct the record after Monash's vain efforts to control his own press coverage during and after the war; Bean wrote that Monash's battle plan 'broke down largely through his underestimation of the human element'.[9]

As soon as he could, Bean went in to see for himself the St-Quentin canal tunnel system the Germans had used in their fortified lines and, while there, soldiers told him to take a look at the 'corpse factory' they'd discovered within it, rumours of such macabre production mills for soap and other products being one of the most common atrocity stories of the war. In one room full of dead German soldiers they had found two large coppers sitting on dead embers, and in one of the coppers was the body of a mangled dead German. To many soldiers this was definitive evidence of the very worst kind of atrocities that encouraged many of them to join up for the war.

> The fact that this man was in the copper and the others lying dead in the place, and that two or three tins of fat were lying in the room, had given rise to the story that this was at last a German Corpse Factory which had been discovered in actual operation when the Hindenburg tunnel was seized. No story is too wild for some people to believe it and this had been related to the war correspondents.[10]

But Bean was careful with his facts and he pieced together what had really happened: a six-inch shell had pierced the underground chamber and blown the soldier's body into the copper. One similarly sceptical digger quipped, 'If this is the way they do it – one man at a time – all I can say is that it must be a bloody long job!'[11]

By 3 October the Australians had broken right through the Hindenburg Line. Two days later the Australian 6th Brigade was also sent in to capture the town of Montbrehain right behind the fortifications; it was a gruesome and hard fight and they suffered 430 casualties in what was the last battle of the war for the AIF. A captured German said 'they were sick of the war and had they known Australians were attacking they would not have fought at all'.[12] Bean hailed the Montbrehain victory as one of the most brilliant Australian infantry attacks of the war, but he questioned the cost, especially when Prime Minister Billy Hughes had asked for Australian troops to be preserved as much as possible after so many long years of attrition. Bean later lamented that the attack seemed in defiance of Billy Hughes' request that Australian casualties be kept to a minimum at this late stage of the war. 'It is difficult to feel it was wisely undertaken; it seemed, rather, devised to make some use of these troops before withdrawing them in accordance with the Prime Minister's demand.'[13] The action had cost Australia some 30 officers and 400 men. Many of the best NCOs and men were now dead, yet, as Bean pointed out, the attack had not captured any enemy battery or broken the line. He wrote: 'At such cost at this stage of the war, Australian troops could have achieved far-reaching results in any general attack.'[14]

It was apt that Bean was in and about the Hindenburg Line in those final days of fighting. He had been there from the very first shot in Gallipoli and now he was here at the culmination of four hard and bloody years of war. With rumours of an armistice in the air, it was clear the end of the war was imminent. Charles Bean was exhausted, shattered beyond fatigue, and he now realised this battle presaged the end of everything he had known for the last four years of his life.

> No more hurried car drives in the morning up to some place just within the limits of occasional shell-fire … No more wondering whether it would be wise to go one hilltop further. No more picking out a convenient shell-hole and settling into it with the

> telescope on the ledge of upturned earth and settling to find out where the men really are. Taking the skyline first, one follows it along and the telescope halts suddenly on a small figure moving along it. By the heavy ankles you guess it is a German. Then, halfway down the green slope below him, you see a figure wandering from one little scooped-out shell-hole to another as if he were dropping round for a cup of tea. That is one of our men. You generally tell by the gait whether he is Australian or not. If he looks like he owned the universe, he certainly is.[15]

As he crossed the English Channel to farewell his brother Jack, who was heading back to Australia on leave, Charles Bean realised he could not think properly and that his memory was suffering; the official correspondent needed a holiday. But, typically, he spent a lot of his time in London worrying about the war relics and plans for the war museum he was now beginning to conceive. Then he headed across to Paris to see Keith Murdoch and Prime Minister Billy Hughes, there for a War Cabinet meeting. The Germans were seeking peace but, after so many lies from the German High Command, the Allies were sceptical.

On 15 October 1918, Bean left Paris by train for a two-week break in Cannes, spending most of it sleeping and reading. While he was there he realised that it was four years since he had left Australia on the *Orvieto*. Aside from the physical fatigue he was suffering, it is likely, from the tone of Bean's diary notes, that he was also emotionally fragile, battered by the weeks, months and years of conflict; as Cyril Brudenell White later acknowledged, Bean had possibly witnessed more battles firsthand than any other member of the AIF. There were also the looming adjustments of civilian life, posing more practical concerns. He had booked a sleeping berth on the train back to Paris from Cannes but was horrified to see it would cost him 92 francs, so he changed to a cheaper couchette sleeper seat for 33 francs instead. 'Think what you could do with 92 francs, the presents you could buy, theatres, teas – a whole week's wage to many people!'[16]

While resting in Cannes, Bean also began writing what eventually became *In Your Hands, Australians*, an easy-to-read book pitched at the youth of Australia, encouraging them to take up the legacy of the AIF and work for their country rather than for themselves. Brimming with idealism, Bean told his young readers they had been left a legacy by the men who had fallen. 'They gave it into your hands Australians, when the bullet took them … Australia lies in your hands now where those men dying laid her … it is the simple, splendid truth.'[17]

It says so much about Charles Bean that when he did finally board the train back to Paris, he took pity on a young French girl sitting in the cold corridor of the train and selflessly gave her his couchette seat. 'I changed places with her and camped in the passage and was pleased to find that after the hardening of these campaigns, it was no great hardship … I believe one could sleep anywhere now.'[18] When he made it back to Paris, Bean still did not properly relax, craving a glass of wine but choosing to deny himself alcohol until the war was over. In between writing his book, Bean took time out to sit at a café on a beautiful Parisian sunny day, marvelling how just a few months ago the possibility of peace had seemed so remote. Thinking back to the extraordinary Australian feat at the Battle of Amiens, still so recent an event, he wrote: 'it was very largely that dashing offensive on August 8 that changed the whole course of affairs!'[19]

While negotiations continued for an armistice between the Allies and a defeated Germany, Bean threw himself into the battle and battalion histories that he had not yet completed. He was also rushing to finish *In Your Hands, Australians* before the diggers returned to Australia. White had assured him it would be the 'bible' of a proposed new public education scheme and Bean let his own passion for remembering the sacrifice of the men who had fallen fire his sometimes overzealous prose:

> … they wanted Australia to be the kind of place which we think ideal to live in. They wanted to make her a great and good country – yes the greatest and best country in the world. That is what Australia was to them. That is why they fought … Many a man lying out there at Pozieres or in the low scrub at Gallipoli, with his poor tired senses barely working through the fever of his brain has thought in his last moments: 'Well – well, it's over; but in Australia they will be proud of this' … If there is to come about what they fought for, then you must do it. Otherwise they will have died in vain … You will put up a memorial to them – a memorial which will enclose forever the sacred relics of their fighting and the treasured, precious pictures of their sacrifice. A history of it will be written to crystallise for all time the greatest incident in Australian history – the first revelation of the Australian character.[20]

Bean was in Lille on 11 November 1918 when the Armistice was declared:

> One could not realise it. No more gun flashes; no more flares. Tonight the streets would be bright – the towns would be lit; the cars would take the black painted eyelids off their headlights … the business of the world for the last four years was finished. We had won – beyond all hope, everything exactly as the most optimistic democrat would have planned it … I couldn't realise it and I am sure the people of Lille couldn't.[21]

Across the entire Western Front, villages were breaking out their wine cellars and civilians and soldiers were carousing, cheering and dancing in the streets; the Armistice was the perfect excuse for a party after so many years of misery. But Charles Bean, as tightly disciplined as always, chose to go back to Fromelles, the scene of Australia's biggest single military disaster in 1916 where he had witnessed Pompey Elliott in tears after losing 5533 men in a night. Bean wanted to see Fromelles before it changed. As he was walking along the battlefield near a water channel close to the old German wire, a route that would have meant certain death just a day earlier, Bean found a cluster of Australian water bottles, so many it could not have been chance that left them there. For this was the spot where the wounded boys, hit mainly in the groin and legs by close-range heavy machine-gun fire during the battle, had forlornly tried to stay alive. 'The poor chaps must have crawled here wounded, at night, for water,' Bean wrote. '… We found the old No man's land simply full of our dead.'[22] For he discovered unburied skulls, bones and torn Australian uniforms and kit lying where they had fallen over two years earlier, the bones of an Australian officer and his men 90 metres from the German 'Sugar Loaf' feature that had been the battle's objective. Amid the celebration of the Armistice, this was a distressing reminder of the awful cost Australia had sustained. In truth, Bean probably found it difficult to celebrate Armistice because he knew better than almost any other man the immensity of the suffering that had brought the Allies to this day; it was right that he was there, and it says so much about him that he was.

Crossing to London the next day, Bean felt a thrill to be back on the ocean without having to worry about submarines and war. He walked through London in a daze, amazed to see the streets lit up and thrilled to see some girls doing a jig with troops and civilians in Trafalgar Square. Bean just stood and watched. 'The feeling is bewildering: one doesn't get used to peace in a day; and the old remaining anxiety and strain of war is still at the back of one's brain and will remain there till the world is itself again.'[23]

Bean soon returned to France to finish his notes on battalion histories and interviews with soldiers, fastidiously updating the research on which he had fallen behind since the frantic fighting began on 8 August. He was also planning a return visit to Gallipoli early in 1919 and wanted to have his European work done by Christmas. Bean had been away from Australia, his parents and extended family for more than four years. The natural inclination would have been to go home as soon as possible, and that is certainly what his parents expected. Edwin and Lucy Bean were attending a public meeting about the Western Front when the end of the war was announced with a volley of cannon fire in Hobart harbour; there had already been several false alarms so Edwin was sceptical:

Suddenly, about 9pm, 'bang', a pause, 'bang', a pause, 'bang', a pause. Then even I began to waver. Then spread a rumour that it was a bogus salvo. But the crowd shouted louder, the bangs clashed, the big drums boomed. Men jumped on to the hustings and waved arms and hats and yelled … Inside the Mayor's courtroom sat the Premier and the various dignitaries, waiting, waiting for the message which did not come … As we stood chatting about midnight, a fresh outburst of distant cheering was heard, the sirens of the ships began to sound, and we said 'Ah, there is the news at last' – and so it was as we found next day … the house is now ready for you and Jack when you return, which we hope may now be not a distant event …[24]

Twenty

THEY GAVE THEIR SHINING YOUTH

... it seemed to me that the finest memorial of these men was that they lay where they lay ...

Charles Bean on his return to Gallipoli, 1919

At the very end of it all, Charles Bean went back to where it all began. By the end of the war he had toured most of the Western Front battlefields but he had never had the chance to roam Gallipoli, having left Anzac Cove in 1915 as he entered it – under the constant threats of shellfire and bullets. He knew that before he returned to Australia, if he wanted to give his readers a full account of the fighting on Gallipoli then he would need to return and see it in peacetime. He even admitted to a certain 'homesickness' for the place, and so he obtained government permission for a special historical mission to return to work out what really happened in the various battles and skirmishes.

Historian Ken Inglis's book on Australian memorials, *Sacred Places*, sees Bean's life after the war as being dedicated to the creation of two monuments, his *Official History of Australia in the War of 1914–1918* and the Australian War

Memorial.[1] It was inevitable that Australia's baptism of fire in the land once the home of ancient Troy and immortalised by Homer's *Iliad* would become perhaps the most resonant myth that Bean now seized upon to memorialise the Anzacs. The Australians had distinguished themselves in many more battles since Gallipoli, but the elegiac story of that ultimately futile struggle on the Dardanelles peninsula had, by the end of the war, achieved a mythical status that played to a generation schooled in the Greek classics. Writers like novelist Compton Mackenzie, who served on General Ian Hamilton's staff at Gallipoli, wrote books soon after the war casting the Australians in a Homeric vein that may feel absurdly excessive to a modern audience:

> Their beauty, for it really was heroic, should have been celebrated in hexameters, not headlines … There was not one of these glorious young men I saw that day who might not himself have been Ajax or Diomed, Hector or Achilles. Their almost complete nudity, their tallness and majestic simplicity of line, their rose-brown flesh burnt by the sun and purged of all grossness by the ordeal through which they were passing, all these united to create something as near to absolute beauty as I shall ever hope to see in this world.[2]

When Bean finally came to write an account of Gallipoli 29 years after his 1919 visit, it was no whimsy that he chose to end it with an abridged version of words found on a memorial to Athenian soldiers who had fallen in the Dardanelles 2355 years earlier: 'They gave their shining youth, and raised thereby valour's own monument which cannot die'.[3] Bean was drawn to the stories of fifth century BC Athens because they fit his mythologising of the Anzacs: just as in ancient Athens, the Australia they were fighting to defend was a new democracy with similarly high-minded ideals. Ken Inglis's study also describes the official history as 'An Australian Iliad', saying Bean's work was unlike any other military history in texture and tone:

> He had an unparalleled intimacy over four years with the experience of men and war and he wrote of his subjects with reverence, convinced that 'the only memorial which could be worthy of them was the bare and uncoloured story of their part in the war'.[4]

Bean's Gallipoli mission left Southampton on 19 January 1919, eight Australians in all including his devoted assistant, Arthur Bazley. When they reached Rome, Bazley had to remain behind: like so many people across Europe and the United Kingdom, he had contracted the influenza that was to become a global pandemic, eventually killing somewhere between 50 and 100 million people worldwide; Bazley, mercifully, survived. Bean and his team arrived at Gallipoli in early February. The former Turkish officer and historian Zeki Bey, who had fought against the Australians in the campaign, kindly helped Bean investigate the key events at Gallipoli, Bean interviewing the Turk in their only common language, French. It was a unique opportunity for Bean to meticulously put together the story of the battles fought there from both the Australian and the enemy side. In one example, the official correspondent remembered how Pompey Elliott had told him that after one 1915 battle he had 'blazed with his revolver' against the enemy when the Turks broke into the Australian mine tunnel near the so-called German Officers' Trench. Four years on, Zeki Bey was able to tell Bean how he had picked up two of those revolver bullets and gave one to Enver Pasha, a senior Turkish military commander.[5]

Bean also wrote a report on what to do about all the graves of Australian soldiers on Gallipoli; recognising that the site should be preserved as 'one great cemetery' and correctly divining its future enormous national significance.[6] Visiting the site of the famous charge at The Nek, he discovered the bones of the Light Horsemen exactly where they had fallen: 'it seemed to me that the finest memorial of these men was that they lay where they lay, marking the lines of that astonishing struggle. We did not know whose relics these were but we could ascertain the names of all men missed in that area.'[7] He also returned to the scene of Colonel McCay's disastrous charge on Krithia at Cape Helles, roaming a plain still strewn with Australian remains and kits, including the bronze rising sun badges Australian soldiers wore on their tunics, poignantly scattered among tattered rags and bones lying among the grass.

His visit to Gallipoli completed, Charles Bean finally returned to Australia in April 1919 on board the *Kildonan Castle*. He spent some of the long journey developing and refining his ideas about the proposed war museum, suggesting in a memorandum to the government that a temporary travelling exhibition be put together as soon as possible to generate enthusiasm for it. When he arrived in Australia, after clearing a lengthy quarantine because of the flu pandemic, Bean went straight to Hobart to see his family. It was an emotional reunion after four years away.

Bean discovered he was much sought after as a speaker and he made numerous presentations to rapt audiences about the battles he had witnessed. By mid-July 1919 he had returned to Sydney and was guest of honour at a lunch hosted by the Institute of Journalists. New South Wales Premier William Holman gave the welcoming address, having seen Bean in action on the Western Front: 'No single writer … had shown a greater grasp of the problems and a clearer understanding of the war situation than Mr Bean.'[8]

Bean told the gathering about the dangers of big cities. He said that one of the most important things the Australians had learned during the war was that 'life in big cities, especially the cities of the old world, was ruinous to the population … the big cities in which the people had grown up had altered their physical and mental outlook for years. No Australian who had gone about with his eyes open had come back with any other impression.'[9] Bean also praised the British journalists who covered the war, reserving highest praise for Sir Arthur Conan Doyle, who he had met when he visited the Western Front for *The Times* of London.

Already Bean was having a huge influence on how the Anzac role in the conflict would be memorialised, especially the idea that Australia's nationhood was grounded in her prowess during the war. By government invitation he wrote a special address to be read out in schools during the handing out of souvenir peace medals: 'Australia rides safely in harbour today, a new nation. Five years ago the world barely knew her. Today the men who went to fight for her have placed her high in the world's regard … the great world has recognised her right to mould her future as she pleases.'[10]

Bean's most immediate priority was to find somewhere to locate himself and his staff to write the official history. After years of the censors meddling with his news copy, Bean was also pleased to obtain an unprecedented written agreement from the government guaranteeing that his Australian official history would be uncensored.[11]

In October 1919, Bean and his staff moved into a rambling old homestead called 'Tuggranong' (later, as a Canberra suburb, it was spelt 'Tuggeranong') on the banks of the Murrumbidgee River about fourteen kilometres from Canberra (which became the seat of government and national capital in 1927). The government had taken over the homestead during the war as a place to house the administrative staff of a proposed arsenal that had been planned to be built nearby, but the plan was dropped and the building had remained vacant. For Bean, with his passion for the benefits of country air and open space, it was an ideal place to work. He had at least eight staff at any one time, including his assistant, Arthur Bazley. The ever-spendthrift Bean, mindful that the official history was government-funded, used furniture retrieved from the old German prisoners-of-war camp at Molonglo to furnish the house, filling the homestead rooms with his copious files and hundreds of diaries and notebooks. But even these rooms did not provide enough space; there was also a large collection of newspapers Bean had kept throughout the war – *The Times* and many Australian publications – which were stored in the property's old stone woolshed.

In an extraordinary exercise in self-discipline after so many years of hardship in war, Bean wasted no time to sit down and begin writing. His monastic location, a half-hour drive from the still unbuilt federal capital and eight kilometres from the next station, meant he was able to focus on crafting his history in splendid isolation. Bean originally expected he would be finished the entire history by the mid-1920s: 'I had been dreaming of completion in five years and, in that belief, continued as during the war, to work late each night and throughout the weekends.'[12] This must have been demanding for his small staff, including Arthur Bazley, who had married and brought his wife to the homestead.

Bean saw Australia's experience in the First World War as a test of the country's intrinsic character:

> The first question for my fellow-historians and myself was: how did the Australian people – and the Australian character, if there is one – come through the universally recognised test of this, their first great war? Second was the question: what did the Australian people and their forces achieve in the total effort of their side in the struggle? Third: what was the true nature of that struggle and test so far as Australians took part in it? How well or ill did our constitution and our preparation serve us in it? What were their strengths and weaknesses? And what guidance can our people or others obtain from this experience for future emergencies?[13]

Working from the official records, GHQ memoranda, the records of flanking Allied armies and corps, the Australian Corps records, as well as his own numerous diaries and notebooks with his largely contemporaneous notes from the conflict, Bean crafted his own unique technique for retelling Australia's role in the entire war. There were huge holes in the official records of fighting until about the middle of 1917, so Bean relied enormously on his own diaries and notes. It is hard to fathom now that Bean often had nothing else other than his own primary source material to work with. At the beginning of his work he could not go to a library to look up books and papers already written on the subject, other than the newspaper reports of the time; he was indeed starting from scratch. With this in mind, he decided that the only safe course was to at least glance at every document on any file that might reasonably be expected to contain relevant material, an immense task requiring what turned out to be many years of analysis and writing. Bean used a system of colour coding in his notes: red for British and Australian operations, red stripes for American, blue for French and green for German. He had realised that his personal notebooks and diaries would one day be of enormous historical significance, and his invaluable archive of material is still available today at the Australian War Memorial he helped conceive, much of it online. It is to Bean's credit that he does not appear to have sought to censor any of his private diary comments made during the war, especially those that reflected adversely on him. He did insist that when they were made available to future historians and other readers by the Australian War Memorial, each diary should carry a printed warning:

> These diaries represent only what at the moment of making them I believed to be true. The diaries were jotted down almost daily with the object of recording what was then in the writer's mind. Often he wrote them when very tired and half asleep; also, not infrequently, what he believed to be true was not

> so ... These records therefore should be used with great caution ...

To write his Australian official history, Bean needed the cooperation of the British military's imperial command in London, and this brought him into close contact with the indomitable British official historian, Brigadier General Sir James Edward Edmonds, who was also working on his own 28-volume history of Britain's role in the war. Edmonds had trained in his youth at Britain's Staff College, Camberley, with Allied commander General Sir Douglas Haig and he was not a man who brooked criticism of the British Army lightly. In a 1931 paper he wrote to guide his own staff working on British military histories, he dictated that 'historians ... should avoid all but implied criticisms on operations and should be wary of being "wise after the event"'.[14] He felt that there should be no criticism at all of sister services or their operations, and any comments or views offered by them should be 'accepted without fail'. Edmonds was very much an old-school historian who clearly saw his role differently from Bean, although he approvingly cited Bean's personal accounts of how he compiled his own history.[15] Edmonds especially would not tolerate any suggestion that the disastrous Battle of the Somme was a defeat for England, despite the calamitous 485,000 casualties the British suffered, dismissively spluttering his indignation at how an unidentified 'naval historian without sufficient data or knowledge, or being in a position to know' had dared to suggest just that.[16]

To his credit, Bean stood his ground when Edmonds criticised his analysis of the Battle of the Somme, his final take insisting the battle was not the British victory the propagandists in the army had spent most of the war telling him and the rest of the media. He wrote: 'Far from the German loss being the greater, the British Army was being worn down – numerically – more than twice as fast, and the loss is not to be measured by bare numbers … The battle marked a definite step towards the winning of the war. But the cost was dangerously high … It is inconceivable that Haig would have persisted in his offensive on the Somme had he realised, even approximately, how much lighter than his own was his enemy's loss.'[17] He suggested that Haig was grossly and tragically mistaken in his belief that the Somme wore down the Germans more; it probably ruffled Edmonds' feathers, but he had enough respect for Bean to know he was across his brief. Edmonds also demanded to know whom the British official was who had told Bean that the Allied offensive on the Somme 'could be maintained until the British had lost 500,000 men'.[18] Bean told him it was British author and wartime intelligence officer John Buchan and, just in case Edmonds tried to dispute the claim, he pointed out he had made a full note in his diary. It was Bean's fastidious note-taking that gave him the argument.

Bean also clashed with General Hubert Gough, the former commander of the British Fifth Army, who accused the official historian of reporting 'camp gossip' with his postwar analysis of Pozières and Bullecourt. Bean's history suggested that Gough was temperamentally inclined to make hasty, ill-considered attacks without proper reconnaissance. He sent the page proofs of his criticisms to Gough, who exploded and fired back that Bean was 'animated by a strong personal dislike to myself'.[19] Historian Eric Andrews has suggested that Bean ignored major failures by White and Birdwood at Bullecourt: 'Anzac command itself was almost as culpable as the British for the disasters at Bullecourt, though Bean avoided facing the fact,' Andrews has opined.[20]

Edmonds took on Bean fairly when he criticised him for tending to suggest in his official history that the Australians were as consistently good throughout the war as they were in the extraordinary battles they won in 1918.[21] Eric Andrews says Bean ignored Edmonds' point that the Australians '[i]n 1916 were "distinctly amateurs, in 1918 they were finished artists, not only in fighting but also in staff work"'.[22]

Bean and his staff were tireless in tracking down every last circumstance of an operation. The Australian War Memorial holds hundreds of documents that demonstrate Bean's meticulous devotion to detail; he would seek out individual returned soldiers who took part in a particular operation at a particular hour just to find out whether they went to the right or the left after leaving a trench. It was this obsessive attention to facts that forced Bean to the realisation that he would never finish the task within five years as he had hoped. So rather than change the fastidious way he wrote his history, he decided to pace himself and allow for some rest and recreation for both himself and his staff. In the warmer months they established a routine of playing tennis before dinner and also formed a couple of cricket teams with their neighbours from the nearby properties. There were social gatherings and picnics and tennis parties on weekends. Bean told a friend: 'We have bought a few horses, a cow and some sheep and have acquired a tin Lizzie [a Ford Model T motorcar], a billiard table and a pianola. The Government supplied a tennis court … so it is not such a bad time.'[23]

The introduction of a bit of fun forced the shy and probably lonely 40-year-old Bean into mixed company, and so he met a young nurse from Queanbeyan, Ethel Clara Young, known as 'Effie'. The family story goes that Effie attended one of the homestead tennis parties on a stiflingly hot day, but Effie arrived with a parasol and remained looking cool while everyone else sweltered. Bean family lore also says the official historian was smitten, although he probably did not admit that to anyone at the time. Effie was acting matron at the Queanbeyan hospital when Charles's chronic sinus problems developed into a serious infection during the winter of 1920, so he was forced to spend several weeks in the care of Matron Young. And so Bean surprised his friends, family and probably himself by falling for the 26-year-old Effie Young; fifteen years his junior, Bean nicknamed her 'Nipper'. Both Bean and his brother Jack held nurses in high regard. Jack had written glowingly of the qualities that make a good nurse: 'tact, wisdom, broad sympathy, self denial, self control … in Australia, there is no single class of men or women who give themselves so unstintingly, so continuously, so unrequitedly, so unobtrusively to the good of the world as the great nursing sisterhood'.[24]

By October 1920, when he was visiting his parents in Hobart, Bean had asked Sister Effie Young to marry him and she was considering his proposal. He must have felt fairly certain of her intentions as, while he was away, he wrote to her thus: 'My Dear Nipper … You're going to marry me in the end.'[25] The same letter shows that by the end of that year he had also finished the first draft of volume one of his official history (which told the story of Anzac on Gallipoli through to May 1915), because he told Effie he had sent a copy to his father to be proofread. 'He picked out one or two flaws in the grammar,' Bean admitted to his beloved. The ageing Edwin was not well by then and Charles was anxious his father should live to see the first volume published.

Effie accepted Bean's proposal and there was much excitement in the family about his impending marriage. Lucy Bean had longed to see her eldest happily settled. It seems he did have at least one love interest before the war as a letter from younger brother Monty to Edwin Bean in 1906 refers to 'Chas' being lovesick: 'Poor old Chas he seems to be in the last stages of the disease of love, he has got it badly. I hope she has the sense to accept the best offer she will ever have.'[26] A later reply from Edwin at that time makes reference to the 'bride-elect' but it clearly came to nothing, possibly because at the time Bean did not feel he had the means to support a marriage and family. Bean had also joked with his mother several times during the war, whenever his letters mentioned women, that none of them was yet a future wife. When the news of his engagement to Effie arrived, Edwin Bean was thrilled that his 40-year-old son was about to marry and wrote a charming note to her: 'I don't wonder at his falling in love with you as I almost fell in love with your photograph when it was shown to me … Charlie is one of the noblest and most unselfish fellows in the world'.[27]

A few days later, Bean wrote to Effie from Hobart telling her that 'the news of our engagement has improved old Pater's health'.[28] Bean himself seemed utterly besotted and wrote an excited letter to Effie's mother, Agnes Young, about his future wife: 'Effie has all the qualities I most admire – the qualities which my own mother has and as I have always admired my mother above every other woman, I fell in love with Effie very nearly at first sight … I shall be just as much in love with her when I die.'[29] Charles and Effie were married on 24 January 1921 at St Andrew's Cathedral in Sydney. Monty had earlier ribbed his older brother about the initial time of 8am chosen for the wedding – 'My dear old Chas – what on earth is the matter with you?' – joking that the dean would probably attend the service in his pyjamas and the wedding 'breakfast' would be porridge. He implored the humble Charles not to 'carry your wish to avoid the public gaze to an absurdity'.[30]

The newly married couple drove to the Blue Mountains and stayed at Jenolan Caves for their honeymoon. Afterwards they returned to Sydney for a few days and then drove down to the south coast and inland to Cooma before arriving at 'Tuggranong' on 9 February 1921. Charles and Effie had already organised their 'rooms' at the homestead and Bean went straight back to work on the official history. The first volume was already in production and would be published on Armistice Day, 11 November 1921. Sadly, Bean's father, Edwin, would not see his son's achievement in its published form. He had been ill for some time, too ill to travel to the wedding and meet Effie, but in mid-August 1921 his health seriously deteriorated. Charles was later proud that his father had still been able to coach some local school boys preparing for a performance of Shakespeare's *Twelfth Night* as late as 11 August, but on 16 August Lucy Bean had wired the three brothers suggesting they come to Hobart urgently. Bean sailed from Sydney immediately but the 71-year-old Edwin died on 19 August while Charles was still making the crossing to Tasmania. The *Sunday Times* in Sydney invited Charles Bean to write a tribute to his father and it appeared under the headline 'Edwin Bean – Great Headmaster'.[31] Bean credited his father with: a selfless commitment to his country, his school and his friends and family.

Married life did not change Charles's workload and he was constantly busy, involving himself with the ongoing plans for the war museum, writing the official history, contributing newspaper articles and letters and speaking at various events. It seems he rarely turned down a request – on Empire Day in May 1924, for example, he attended a school fete at Yarralumla and gave a talk to the children, telling them the origin of the Union Jack and then the story of posthumous Victoria Cross winners British officers Teignmouth Melvill and Nevill Coghill, who had died heroically in the Zulu War forlornly trying to save the colours of their regiment.[32]

Meanwhile, all was not well with Bean's health. For some years he had been suffering kidney disease but had put off any treatment because of his workload. Indeed, he had been unable to play his beloved game of cricket in the competitions between the neighbours at 'Tuggranong' throughout 1923 because of his health. During a visit to a Sydney specialist in mid-1924, Bean was told he could no longer ignore the problem and that an operation was necessary; at this time in Australia, the removal of a kidney was not a common procedure and surgeons in London had more expertise in the area. Volume two of his official history was almost finished and Bean had secured another five years on the government contract. He had always promised to take his young wife to England, so the trip was settled. Bean was delighted to find out that, without him asking, his former AIF staff officer colleagues, generals Howse and White, had secured government funding to pay for his passage. Charles and Effie also sold their Dodge car to help pay for the trip, and Bean worked frenetically to finish volume two before they set sail; he stayed up all night on 8 July 1924 and delivered the final manuscript to the publisher on the way to the boat the next day. They set sail for the United States and England on the *Ventura*, his first return visit to Europe since the war.

Bustling 1920s America rankled with Bean's then antiquated notions of white superiority; he was not impressed with 'the mixture of races' being admitted into the country. This was also the era of prohibition and he was struck by how there was one law for the rich and one for the poor: 'the rich can always get liquor if they want it'.[33] Bean was thankful to finally board the liner *Homeric* for the trip from the United States to England, remarking in his travel diary that it was a relief to be on a ship where the British flag was not banned, as custom dictated it was on land in America at the time: 'Nothing but American flags seem to be tolerated in that most jingoistic of all countries. In America you may only fly your own flag provided you fly the American over it. I don't care a dump for flying flags but one has a strong antipathy to the narrow attitude of the American public in the matter.'[34]

Bean's private diaries during this trip often used the term 'Jew' or 'Jewish' in a pejorative way to describe someone in a less than flattering light. On board the *Homeric*, he wrote about meeting a 'rather Jewish looking young man' but discovers that he was actually German and not Jewish at all. He asked Bean, 'How are you towards Germans in Australia?' Bean replied, 'Not yet very cordial.' The German also asked,

'Will they give us back our colonies?' and Bean said, 'No, I don't think so, they are too important to us from the point of view of keeping the Asiatics out.'[35] This German had fought in the war, including the Battle of Passchendaele in October 1917. He told Bean he did not want to fight in another war and had taken out naturalisation papers in America.

Arriving in England and then catching the train to London, it brought out the old Anglophile in Bean to see the English homes and gardens: 'It gives one the impression that there is more family life and more healthy interest in the home than in America. Anyway, it is far more like our country and we felt as though we were back there.' It was an exciting time for the couple; Effie was seeing England for the first time, but her excitement must have been tempered by concern for her husband. The medical specialists they visited in London confirmed the need to remove a kidney and a date was set for the operation. They made a quick trip to Brentwood School northeast of London to tour the Bean Library (named for Edwin) and to Oxford, as well as a visit to some of Effie's relatives in Bedford. Just before his operation, Bean set himself the task of writing down details of his early life: this became his 'Account for Effie'.[36] Penned during his time at King's College Hospital, it begins: 'I promised to write you sweetheart, a little account of my old life before you knew me.'

Charles Bean knew the operation he was about to undergo was dangerous, and he likely wrote the account in such detail not just for Effie but also for posterity in case he did not survive. It ends a bit like a will, Bean instructing that if Effie survived him she should go through all his papers and give them to 'my mother, Brentwood school, Clifton, Bathurst, Baz, Jack and Tig and others … My manuscript and notes can be sold'. He ended, touchingly, with: 'Sweetheart keep all that you wish, if you go first, I'll do the same for you.' Bean survived the operation and, after some months recuperating, he was well enough for a brief trip to the Continent where he took Effie to Amiens and the battlefield at Pozières. There was also time for a quick visit to Geneva and Paris before embarking for Australia from Marseille.

The Beans returned home early in 1925 and initially went to the 'Tuggranong' property. However, doctors warned Bean that the climate there was not suitable for him so it was decided that the official history headquarters would move to Sydney, acquiring rooms at Victoria Barracks army base in the inner Sydney suburb of Paddington. Bean set to work on volume three and the couple moved to the northern suburbs of Sydney, which would become their permanent home (in various houses) and the centre of their social and family life.

Both Bean and Effie adored children; in his 'Account for Effie', Bean described the trip to England in 1889 when he was still just a boy, travelling on the P&O steamer *Valetta*. He had loved playing with the other children on board, telling Effie that even as a boy, he had an affinity for children and could often be found nursing or caring for some of the very young ones on board. Effie came from a family of eight children; her father was a police sergeant but he had died when the youngest child was just three weeks old, so Agnes Young had struggled valiantly to provide for the large family. Agnes at this time still ran a boarding house at Tumbarumba in the Snowy Mountains, and during their visits there Charles and Effie became very close to a young relative, a child called Joyce. The little girl would often come to stay with Charles and Effie and they, unable to have children of their own, grew to love her as their own daughter. This eventually became a permanent arrangement with a formal adoption – Bean wrote in the little family diary with delight that 'Joyce came to us before Christmas 1928 and has stayed with us as our little girl ever since'.[37]

Bean was surrounded by strong women across a lifetime, from his mother to Effie and her extended family, who lived in Sydney and also the central west of New South Wales. Having been alone for a great part of his younger adult life, Bean revelled in the company and social life of the large family he had married into. There were outings, picnics, camping trips and seaside holidays, with Charles and Effie always joined by relatives and friends. Effie anchored Bean and gave him the strength and support to continue in his work. She also loved to arrange social occasions and delighted in meeting and hosting a variety of people. Bean was the 'quiet observer' who took enormous pleasure in seeing his much adored wife in this role. According to their niece Phyllis Bauer, Effie brought the fun out in Bean; she was a complete extrovert.[38]

Charles had always had a strong and idealistic interest in children's education; he and Effie generously paid for and guided the education of many of their nieces and nephews. The family diary is full of details about which schools they attended and how they fared academically. Phyllis Bauer remembers that 'Chas' would often turn mundane household chores into a chance to educate young relatives; washing up after dinner, for example, would be an opportunity to recite details of the alimentary canal or test their history knowledge. He never lost his love of history and encouraged Joyce and his nieces and nephews in their studies. According to Phyllis, he was always generous with his time and the young relatives would often visit the Sydney home or call him asking for assistance with schoolwork, which was always given with patience and enthusiasm.

Joyce eventually attended Abbotsleigh, a private girls school in the northern Sydney suburb of Wahroonga. In those days there were two classes of train travel from their home in Lindfield to Abbotsleigh, first and standard class, and the school had a policy that all the girls had to travel first class. This offended Bean's sense of egalitarianism and, as the family tells it, he told the school that his daughter would be travelling standard class. As a compromise, Charles agreed to go with Joyce as an escort in standard class, sitting beside her and using his small suitcase as a desk to work on.

As well as the official history, Bean was also hard at work on his other monument, the development of what would become known as the Australian War Memorial. It was hardly an easy passage. Even though the Australian government had in 1917 agreed to the setting up of an Australian War Museum Committee, once the war was over, the reality in 1919 was that there was a strong anti-war sentiment among some politicians as well as many other priorities. There was opposition to an Australian War Memorial from within the Labor Party, and this echoed a strong feeling among the general public, which was opposed to the glorification of war. There was also a sense that the country had to move forward and get on with it and not dwell on the awful immediate past. As well, the federal government had a huge financial burden: added to the cost of the war itself and repatriation, there was the ongoing commitment to soldiers' pensions, widows' pensions, the soldier settlement policy and other retraining programs. Nonetheless, a temporary exhibition of relics for the proposed museum travelled to Melbourne in 1922 and Sydney in 1925; these were very popular and attracted favourable reviews. In late 1923, a site was reserved for the memorial building at the foot of Mount Ainslie in Canberra and then in 1924 cabinet approved a budget of 250,000 pounds for the project. Finally, in September 1925, the Australian War Memorial became a legal entity with an act of Parliament.

The project was still fraught with difficulty and delay – a competition for the architectural design of the museum stalled when no single design measured up. It was decided to invite two of the entrants, John Crust and Emil Sodersten, to collaborate on the project, but this did not always run smoothly. One of the design difficulties was Bean's determination that enough space be provided for the names and details of every soldier who died in the Great War, a solemn bronze roll of honour in the open-air cloisters surrounding the commemorative area, which is now such a special part of the memorial.

It was a very proud moment for Charles Bean when he finally stood on the dais with the official party for the formal opening of the Australian War Memorial on 11 November 1941. It was by now two years into the Second World War, and Bean was there not just because he was on the war memorial's board but especially because of his long and tireless efforts to establish it. Ever humble, it seems he had ensured his efforts were not formally acknowledged during the proceedings. In his history of the Australian War Memorial, *Here is their Spirit*, historian Michael McKernan explains why this might have happened: 'He was a reserved man and, possibly in deference to his wishes, no-one made mention that day of his work or that of [the AWM's first director, Lieutenant Colonel John] Treloar. It was left to an admirer, unknown to Bean, to pay him the tribute he so thoroughly deserved: "You must feel proud indeed, this day, to view what you have striven for so long, as an accomplished fact."'[39]

Across Australia there are also many other solemn war memorials in towns and cities that carry inscriptions penned by Charles Bean; for Tamworth's memorial, for example, he drew on the words he had seen on the ancient Greek memorial for their fallen Athenian warriors in the Dardanelles: 'They gave their shining youth and built thereby valour's own monument that shall not die.' Bean also regularly accepted invitations to attend Anzac Day dawn services and Armistice Day ceremonies. In the personal family diary of his life begun by Lucy Bean, he recorded that for Armistice Day 1934, he drove with Effie and Joyce to Cootamundra and spoke at the local Returned Sailors and Soldiers Imperial League (RSL) dinner; a trip from Sydney to Cootamundra by car in those days would have been no easy journey. They stayed with Charles's cousin Duncan Maxwell, with whom he had become so close during the war.

During a speech to the state council of the RSL in early February 1931, Bean attempted to counter the public backlash from those who were arguing against both war memorials and the official history:

> I am aware that there exist good people in Australia and elsewhere who would wish to obliterate

> all memory of the Great War, cut it out of our consciousness if that were possible, in the belief that reading the history of war tends to the making of it. One respects those people but the sheltered innocence which they desire is not attainable, and would not be desirable if it could be obtained … We should be leaving men to plan their future without knowledge of the most important episode in their immediate past.[40]

Despite all his other commitments, Charles Bean was also a prolific letter writer to newspapers, often on the subject of war and the AIF, but not always. A cricket tragic, he was incensed by the use of the bodyline bowling tactics during the acrimonious Test between Britain and Australia in late 1932 and early 1933. He was so angry that he wrote to *The Times* in London joining the debate, which had even likened the use of these tactics to the use of poison gas in wartime. He also contributed to the spate of reactive letters and articles both in Australia and in England.

Bean also advised the New South Wales state government on physical education in schools and campaigned about the lack of planning in towns and cities and the need to provide for parkland and recreational areas. Building on his theories about the benefits of country life and open spaces, he founded the Parks and Playgrounds Movement of New South Wales in 1930 and served as secretary for many years. He wrote a pamphlet for the movement detailing the history of public spaces going back to the ancient Greeks, urging the state government and councils to set aside land to preserve open areas for recreation and leisure: 'Spots of particular beauty, and lookout points from which grand views can be obtained, need to be sought out, listed and bought before private enterprise realises their value and spoils them with tea-houses and service stations.'[41] Charles Bean's campaigning had a significant influence on how our cities and towns look today.

Before the First World War, Bean's ideas about human nature were grounded in unenlightened notions of Anglo-Saxon racial superiority as well as his belief in the influence of the Australian environment, especially the country and outback, in forming a national character. But, as Stephen Ellis has written, in this period between the First and Second World Wars, Bean's prejudiced ideas were being gradually replaced by his belief that it was a healthy environment that had the most impact on character. 'His efforts in the town planning and fitness movements were aimed at preserving the standards which produced the AIF,' Ellis said. 'These standards did not refer simply to physical fitness but also to such qualities as initiative and inventiveness, social equality and loyalty to one's friends and nation, self-effacing sportsmanship and dislike of irrelevant control and restraint.'[42] As it was for many Australians of his generation, it would be the shock of Adolf Hitler's barbaric racism and anti-Semitism in the coming Second World War that dispelled forever Charles Bean's notions of white Australian racial superiority.

Twenty-one

NOTHING CAN ALTER NOW

We failed, failed wretchedly.

Charles Bean, 1943

During the 1930s, as speculation intensified about the intentions of Adolf Hitler and his increasingly militant new German republic, Charles Bean penned a letter to *The Sydney Morning Herald* in response to other writers who were concerned about Germany's intentions towards its former colonies in the Pacific. He argued, as so many others did who were in favour of appeasement at this time, that Hitler should be given a chance: 'I believe that young Germany can be trusted, as Hitler says, to maintain as firmly as any other nation a treaty negotiated by it as an equal … and only if we are prepared to give that trust – which we once implicitly undertook to give but never yet have given – can we hope for peace and all that it means for the daily happiness of us all.'[1] He did strongly refute Nazi claims reported in the press that no Jews served in the German army in the First World War, describing that as 'ludicrously untrue'.[2]

His idealistic views on appeasement had led Bean to earlier persuade the Australian War Memorial (AWM) board that the nameplate of the German raider vessel *Emden* should be returned to Germany; it had been souvenired by the navy and was held at the AWM as a war relic. Bean felt that it should go back to Germany, in recognition of the chivalry of the *Emden* captain and 'the magnificent fight put up by him and his crew. This and similar expressions do much to ease the feelings of ex-enemies visiting the Memorial and to emphasise its spirit.'[3] The nameplate was eventually handed over to German President Paul von Hindenburg at a ceremony in Berlin in 1933. News reports at the time say the former field marshall was touched, but the idealistic gesture behind the nameplate presentation was overshadowed that same year by the rise of Nazi Germany. President von Hindenburg capitulated to the Nazis and issued decrees suspending all German civil liberties, appointing Adolf Hitler as Germany's chancellor; quaint notions of Teutonic chivalry went out the window as the era of the 'Führer' and fascist Nazism dawned. The following year von Hindenburg died and Hitler made himself an absolute dictator. But after all the horrific suffering he had witnessed in the First World War, Bean was not yet prepared to contemplate there might need to be a second confrontation with German militancy. In 1936 he asked: 'are we prepared to say that the only solution lies in our being ready to fight a Great War?'[4]

Central to Bean's attitude towards Nazi Germany was his belief that the Allies had broken a pledge they had given to Germany to secure peace in the First World War, promising they would treat Germany leniently if the Kaiser was replaced with a democratic German republic. Bean believed that the Allied refusal to change the harsh terms of the Versailles treaty drove the German nation to Hitler.

As Stephen Ellis has written, 'He believed, like many others, that Germany only desired to regain her position in the world and this desire was a perfectly reasonable one.'[5] When Hitler invaded Czechoslovakia in 1939, six days later Bean finally recognised negotiation with Hitler was futile and publicly acknowledged his appeasement views had been wrong. 'Useful negotiation with the German people is impossible until it has a leader in whose faith other nations can trust. … Hitler's assurances having proved untrue, his intentions can be judged only by his actions. And from these it is to be inferred that he will strike wherever his notion of German interest renders it advisable, entirely regardless of rights hitherto recognised in civilised society. His appeal to those rights has been proved to be only camouflage – he will probably appeal to them again in the hope of deceiving not other nations but his own.'[6]

When the Second World War broke out in September 1939, the 60-year-old Bean was actually offered the job of chief wartime press censor but he declined, saying his 'capacity is much more positive than negative'.[7] He was still working on his final official history volume for the previous war and editing those being authored by others. But Keith Murdoch (now Sir Keith) was appointed director-general of information and in July 1940 he persuaded Bean to join him for nine weeks to help oversee the management of press liaison with the military. It was like old times because his revered friend Lieutenant General Sir Cyril Brudenell White had been called back into duty from his country farm to become the Chief of the General Staff. Bean the former journalist stressed in this advisory role the importance of a free press and freedom of speech. Although he condoned some censorship in wartime, he felt it should be strictly 'limited to preventing useful information from reaching the enemy'. In a dig at the censorship he endured in the First World War, he condemned 'the withholding of news from our own people on the ground that it may weaken their morale'.[8]

Lieutenant General White was now 63 and had made it clear that he wanted to return to his beloved farm in rural Victoria as soon as his services were no longer needed. Tragically, less than six months into his new job, White, perhaps Bean's greatest friend, was dead. On 13 August 1940, just a few weeks after Bean had come down from Sydney to join White in Melbourne to advise on press liaison, White was travelling by plane from Melbourne to Canberra with three federal cabinet ministers and other departmental staff. In what has become known as the Fairbairn disaster, the Hudson plane crashed and exploded into flames on approach to the airport in Canberra. All ten people on board were killed instantly. Another of Bean's closest friends also died in the crash – Sir Henry Gullett, Bean's old official war correspondent colleague, now a politician and senior federal government cabinet minister. Bean was devastated; White and Gullett were two of his closest friends. Bean had flown directly from Melbourne to Sydney on that morning and it is part of the family folklore that he was at one stage intending to be on the same plane. Bean arrived at the Department of Information in Sydney to hear the devastating news about the loss of his close friends and so many key government officials. 'At first, in that office, the information about White was uncertain. When presently, after hoping against hope, I learnt the truth, for me a light went out. He was the greatest man I have known. In no other was genius so quickly and so clearly evident.'[9]

White had proofread all five of Bean's previous volumes of the *Official History of Australia in the War of 1914–1918*, but the final sixth volume was not published until August 1941, 23 years after the end of the war. The official history series was well received, albeit overshadowed by yet another calamitous world war. Bean admitted in a newspaper interview that, now that he had finished, 'one feels a bit lost … Though we may make a few additions later on, the story of the first AIF has now been written.'[10]

The thrill of finishing his official history was marred just two months later by the death of Bean's beloved mother, Lucy. Throughout the years after her husband's death, Lucy Bean was a regular visitor to the Beans' Sydney home. Charles himself would also travel to Hobart and often assisted in getting his mother the medical treatment she needed as she grew older; almost 90, she had been ailing for some time. In an added blow for Bean, his mother died in the early hours of 18 November 1941, Bean's sixty-second birthday. Lucy Bean's ashes were interred alongside the graves of Edwin and firstborn baby Madeline in Hobart's Sandy Bay cemetery.

In early 1942, the Department of Information began running short broadcasts on ABC radio in the evenings entitled 'The Jap as he really is'. Bean saw these as crude racist propaganda, his past prejudices against Asians now behind him, and he wrote a series of letters to *The Sydney Morning Herald* strongly objecting to what he regarded as a 'hate' campaign 'disastrously below the dignity of a civilised people'.[11] *The Herald* editorialised against the broadcasts but the then minister, Senator William Ashley, initially refused to back down, describing Bean and others as unrealistic: 'I believe that we must be realistic and face the facts. The war is not a game of chess. We are not going to win it with the technicalities of debate but by getting down to cold hard facts. Does anyone suggest that the Japanese should be depicted as nice genteel people to be received with open arms?'[12] The broadcasts were eventually shelved, the minister maintaining that they had run their course anyway.

In 1943 Bean published his *War Aims of a Plain Australian.*[13] Nearly 25 years earlier his idealistic *In Your Hands, Australia* had told readers that there was a long peace ahead but now, so soon, the world was again at war. He subtitled *War Aims* as 'An effort to stimulate thought towards grasping *this* time the chances we missed after World War I'. The initial tone of this new book was one of resignation and disappointment, Bean writing in the preface: 'We failed, failed wretchedly.' He lamented that Australia was again in crisis, writing that there had been a 'deadness of vision' in Australia between the two wars: 'deadness in political, social and religious efforts; when our labour parties forsook their fine ideals to busy themselves with lotteries, dog races and similar trash, and our "National" parties forgot the development of this great land in their hurry to liquidate the public industries their predecessors had established'. He also attacked 'the narrowness and lack of vision that bound our education system'.[14] Bean appeared to feel that no one had listened to the views he espoused in the earlier manifesto on town planning, education, fitness and health. He longed for 'a land where every boy and girl has a chance; a chance not to struggle through life on a basic wage; but to develop to any greatness of which they are capable'.[15] He also made an argument for socialism: 'The system which gives most social as well as economic equality is the socialist system.'[16]

Like so many others of his generation, Bean had also fallen for Stalin's lies about communist Russia, lauding the country's economic achievements, even praising collective ownership: 'Onlookers feel that they are seeing how a people will fight for a country that it really owns – for factories, farms and houses, and a method of life that belongs to every man, woman and child in the nation, and for a cause that they intensely believe in.'[17] He also used this book to decry the English social structure, declaring 'it is too pyramidal; the apex of highly refined life is maintained there by altogether too large a base of under-privileged humanity – a mass of ordinary folk'.[18] He returned to the familiar theme of the fear of invasion from the north, urging an increase in both the birthrate and immigration: 'Every Australian knows in his heart that if the Australian nation is not increased to at least several times its present numbers, it will probably within this generation, almost certainly within this century, lose its continent to its more populous neighbours.'[19]

The wartime prime minister, John Curtin, also asked Bean to head up a War Archives Committee to ensure that there would be no inadvertent destruction of important documents as had occurred during the previous war. Bean personally interviewed the heads and deputy heads or other senior responsible officers of some 35 federal departments to discuss the committee's proposals for preserving documents. He took the long view on the need to preserve records and documents for posterity as well as for future students and historians, and it was Bean's vision that would ultimately lead to the creation of the National Archives of Australia. In February 1943, Bean recommended a system of presumptive preservation of government records that dictates how Australia's archive operates today: 'No records (except for those held under an obligation to destroy them if so directed) shall be destroyed except under the signature of the appropriate archival authority confirmed by the War Archives Committee.'[20] Because of Bean, the general motto became 'When in doubt, preserve'. It revolutionised archive retention in Australia and influenced many other countries around the world.

Bean also lobbied the federal government on the need for the early appointment of an official historian for the Second World War. He was not immediately successful, however, as there was some opposition to the idea on the grounds that preserving the records would be sufficient. As well, some politicians, notably the Labor government's attorney-general and future leader, Dr Herbert Evatt, were not enamoured of Bean's official history and the time it took to complete it; Doc Evatt had lost two brothers in the First World War and he was intensely suspicious of anything that might be perceived as glorifying the horror of the war. Bean's view eventually prevailed and Gavin Long was appointed as the Second World War official historian. This pleased Bean as Long was an old boy of All Saints' in Bathurst and the son of his clerical friend Bishop Long.

The Second World War changed Charles Bean dramatically, overturning his long-held and indubitably racist idea of white superiority that, while offensive to most people these days, was a fairly mainstream view in his youth. As he grew older, his passionate belief in the superiority of the English race transformed to an acceptance that this culture, with its class system and resistance to change, was seriously flawed. The same can be said for his anti-Semitic views: by the early 1940s, in fact, Charles Bean was actively championing the plan for a Jewish refuge in Australia. In the late 1930s, the Jewish Freeland League was searching for an underpopulated area of the world where displaced Eastern European Jews could settle. One of the league's founders, Dr Isaac Steinberg, visited Australia in 1939 to scout for a large tract of land – about seven million acres – in the Kimberley region of Western Australia, the Freelanders willing to accept co-existence with people of a friendly nation. The idea won endorsement in both Western Australia and South Australia and Bean devoted several pages in *War Aims of a Plain Australian* to arguing for support of the plan on the basis that Australia needed to increase its population: 'who doubts that this continent could hold three times as many people as its present seven million …?'[21] Bean argued that Australia had a duty to help the displaced people of eastern Europe: 'If there is any sincerity in our professions of what we are fighting for (God help us if there isn't) I don't see how we can decently refuse these courageous people the chance to "have a go" and to become the good Australians they want to be.'[22]

After the war, he had a much more personal reason to abandon any perceived anti-Jewish sentiment when one of the Bean's much-loved nieces, Phyllis, fell in love with a young Austrian. Gaston Bauer and his family had Jewish background. The family had converted to Protestant Lutherans in the late 1800s but because of their ancestry, they left Vienna as soon as the Germans invaded, ending up in Sydney. Phyllis met Gaston when she was just seventeen and took him to meet the Beans after the war:

> Now they knew that Gaston was from Europe, we walked from Roseville station to Eton Road and … Effie flung open the door and said, 'My darling,' and embraced him and he and Chas chattered away in

German, and Gaston says to this day that it was when he felt that he was an Australian because it was the first Australian home he had been in.[23]

Gaston Bauer graduated in medicine from Sydney University in 1946, winning the university medal. He went on to become a leading cardiologist working in both Australia and overseas. In later years, Gaston told family members that Charles Bean was one of the greatest influences on his life.

Bean's appointment as official historian for the First World War formally ended in February 1942, but there was still much to keep Bean busy: his advisory work during the Second World War, writing, speeches, and the entertaining of visitors at their home. Family members recall many politicians calling on Charles and Effie; Billy Hughes was a regular, but there was also 'at least one' other prime minister, most probably John Curtin. There is also reference in the family diary to a famous acting couple: 'We entertain Sir La[u]rence and Lady Olivier probably in June.'[24] Bean was always drawn to those who shared his passion for education and some of his closest friends were the headmasters of schools, including Philip 'Pip' Le Couteur, headmaster of Sydney's Newington College. On a family holiday to the south coast, Joyce became friendly with Le Couteur's son Ted, and they later married. Bean and Effie were soon delighted to have two grandchildren – Edward born in 1941 and Anne in 1944.

Bean also kept writing – there was *Anzac to Amiens* (a condensed version of the *Official History*) in 1946, *Gallipoli Mission* in 1948 and then in 1950 a book on Australian independent boys schools with the title *Here, My Son* (taken from the Newbolt poem about Clifton). He also visited Broken Hill in mid-1948 in order to revise and update *The Dreadnought of the Darling*, republished in 1956. Bean had chairman roles with the Australian Broadcasting Commission's promotions appeal board and the AWM, and he was also vice-president of the United Nations Association of New South Wales. The president of this association was Richard Boyer, but on at least two occasions Bean took over as host, chairing a large reception for the deputy leader of the House of Commons, Anthony Eden, in February 1949, and another when Dr Evatt returned from his presidency of the United Nations.

Charles and Effie had longed to make a return visit to both the United Kingdom and Europe ever since their 1924 visit and promised themselves they would do so once the official history was completed. In 1949, Phyllis married Gaston Bauer and they went to live in London, their move spurring on Charles and Effie's plans. They sailed for England in March 1951 when Charles was 71 years old. In his diary of this trip, Bean wrote that he still had so much more to do, 'biographies of White, Monash, Gellibrand, Elliott, Bridges and Colonel Butler'. But, having always prided himself on his strong memory, Bean was privately concerned that this was now waning. The voyage was a nostalgic trip for the ageing Bean; sailing through the Suez Canal, he saw traces of the old redoubt posts and wire entanglements from the First World War, but Bean was the only one on board who knew what they were. From the deck he pointed out to Effie where he was camped and in hospital in 1916. He stayed on deck long after Effie went below for the evening, watching and no doubt remembering.

In England, he and Effie stayed near Phyllis and Gaston in Chiswick and visited Brentwood, where Bean was the guest of honour at a luncheon and at the school prize-giving ceremony. On a trip back to the Western Front, Bean carefully pinpointed and then photographed the exact place where his cousin Leo Butler was struck near Mouquet Farm. He and Effie visited various war memorials in France and also made a quick trip to Germany and Austria.

One of Charles Bean's guiding principles with the Australian War Memorial and his official history was that neither should glorify war or boast about victory. In 1952, back in Australia, as AWM chairman, Bean found himself caught up in unwelcome controversy concerning a display of instruments of torture used by the Japanese against Australian prisoners in the Second World War. Visitors could also view tokens of surrender, including the table on which the surrender documents had been signed and swords handed in by Japanese generals. Bean felt this exhibit breached his principles, pointing out that visiting families of Australians who had been prisoners of the Japanese might find the torture instruments distressing. Because of these concerns the display was removed in October 1952. This removal might have gone unnoticed but for the fact that some visitors had already seen the display and that early in 1953, for the first time since the war, Australia was due to host a Japanese delegation, including the Japanese ambassador. The AWM was on the official tour itinerary and in the federal Parliament in late March, a Liberal politician accused the memorial of removing the display so as not to offend the Japanese. The accusation was unfair, although the timing of the removal was unfortunate, and it served to fan anti-Japanese feeling in the community. There was an angry public reaction after newspapers reported on the issue, headlines referring to the hiding of 'Jap relics' to protect the feelings of the delegation.

'Fancy any one in this country worrying about the feelings of a representative of a nation which committed the foulest atrocities possible against Australian servicemen,' declared the Thirty Niners Association.[25] A spokesman for the British Ex-Servicemen's Association also angrily declared: 'The memory of our comrades who died in the fight against the Japanese has been shamed by the Memorial Trustees.'[26] Bean was very distressed by the reaction and the accusations. As chairman of the AWM board, he was forced to issue a media statement clarifying the position and stressing that the removal of the items from display had nothing to do with the visit of the Japanese ambassador: 'From the first it has been a principle not to exhibit trophies, that is to say tokens of victory, but to make the exhibition one of relics of the sacrifice, courage and devotion in the trials of war … This policy has always been fundamental and the result of steady adherence to it has been that there is no record of any one of the millions that has visited the memorial having received the impression that it is an institution glorifying war.'[27] In the end, public and political pressure forced the AWM board to reconsider and the surrender items were eventually returned to display, but not the instruments of torture. Bean had underestimated the depth of postwar feeling about the crimes committed by Japanese soldiers, but the event at least prompted Bean to write a detailed 'principles document' for the AWM so there could be no confusion in the future.

In 1954, a very proud Charles Bean guided the young Queen Elizabeth II on a tour of the Australian War Memorial. Bean still held a deep affection for the monarchy and was extremely honoured to be the new Queen's guide. As he rehearsed and prepared for the Royal visit, Bean confessed to his family that he was quite nervous, but said he conquered his nerves by viewing the young Queen as though she was one of his much-loved nieces, who were about the same age.

By the end of the 1950s Bean was almost 80 and his health was suffering. He would have dearly loved to attend the fourth centenary celebrations for Brentwood School but, in a letter to the school, he explained that for both financial and health reasons, he and Effie were unable to travel. He also wrote of his failing memory: 'I have given up practically all public work. I find that my memory is too unreliable for it.'[28] Bean's last book, *Two Men I Knew*, his biography of generals White and Bridges, was published in 1957. In early May 1959, Bean went to Canberra to accept an honorary Doctor of Laws from the Australian National University. Sir Keith Hancock described him as '[a] man and a scholar of self-effacing modesty.'[29] While he appreciated the honour, Bean's health was failing and he recorded in the family diary that 'the dinner was a great strain for me'.[30]

Shortly after this, he and Effie were in Canberra again for the much delayed opening of the Hall of Memory at the Australian War Memorial. Bean made a short speech and this was quite probably his final public appearance. He wrote in the little family diary that it was an 'exquisite day'. A few months later, Bean relinquished his positions on the Commonwealth Archives Committee and as chair of the AWM board. In an editorial reflecting on his work in September 1959, *The Canberra Times* touchingly wrote that Bean had actually achieved three memorials: the Australian War Memorial building, the written history, and 'the memorial of the spirit which more than any other person, Dr Bean has built, for no-one has better expressed, nurtured and preserved that spirit which is the legacy of all the sacrifice and valour of battle and the motivating force in the endeavours that are worthiest in this land ... Dr C.E.W. Bean is one of those shining examples of what a journalist can be, do and inspire. His example is a memorial that will long outspan his years.'[31]

Bean was withdrawing from public life but he still could not let go of the Great War. He had plans for a biography of Australian Major General Sir John Gellibrand and he also had an idea for another book, tentatively called *The Unofficial History of the War*. However, age had caught up with him, as he explained in a letter to Arthur Bazley in January 1960 apologising for his lack of correspondence: 'Through my own foolishness in tackling writing and other tasks about the time when I gave up my two chairmanships ... my memory broke down: and trying to carry on correspondence then and afterwards did not improve matters. Gaston [Bauer] advised me to give up all work in the study for a good spell, and I largely did so.'[32]

Bean's final entries in the little family diary record that he had been informed by Prime Minister Menzies that his honorarium was to increase from ten to twenty-five pounds and that, after his death, Effie would receive twenty pounds per week: 'this was unasked for and entirely unexpected and a great relief'. Bean also wrote 'Baz [Arthur Bazley] will write my biography'. From 1961 onwards, Bean was in and out of hospital. He suffered a series of heart attacks in 1963 and it was feared his death was imminent. Arthur Bazley never did write a biography of Bean but he did prepare a draft obituary, and he also lobbied for Bean to receive a state funeral when the time came.

Bean was admitted permanently to the Concord Repatriation Hospital in 1964. Effie visited him regularly as did members of the extended family. Old friends also called in but he often didn't know them. The managing director of Fairfax and Sons, Angus McLachlan, would visit most Monday evenings. As McLachlan later wrote, 'Even in his last years when old age brought its weakness his serenity of spirit remained with him. Graciousness, modesty and a wonderful purity of heart never forsook him even when the tired body failed him.'[33]

Charles Edwin Woodrow Bean died on 30 August 1968; he was 88 years old. He had outlived his younger brother, Monty, who died in 1964, while Jack Bean died in 1969. A memorial service (but not the hoped-for state funeral) was held at St Andrew's Cathedral in Sydney on 2 September. In his address, Angus McLachlan told mourners that Bean was a modest man who became a legend in his own lifetime: 'In him there were none of the contradictions, the conflicting values that dwell in so many men. There were no hidden vanities lurking behind the modest exterior.'

Bean refused a knighthood on several occasions and it was his humility that many of his friends remembered most; the associate editor of *The Sydney Morning Herald*, Guy Harriott, himself a correspondent during the Second World War, wrote an obituary saying Bean had always put public service before self and had never sought public recognition or honours. He said that he would be 'sincerely mourned by a wider circle of his countrymen than any other Australian of his generation, a generation of whose finest hour, he was the chronicler, of whose virtues he was the epitome and of whose meaner spirits he was the conscience'.[34]

McLachlan predicted that Bean would live on 'in his books and in the proud tradition of nationhood that he did so much to create and inspire'. But in truth Charles Bean has not really lived on in the nation's memory, despite the fundamental role he played in crafting the Anzac myth. His significant contribution in tracing not only the history of Australia's role in the First World War but also the qualities of Australia's national character has been overlooked, and it was sometimes forgotten even while he was still alive. Certainly his place in history has been long underplayed.

For Effie, more than fifteen years Bean's junior, his passing left a huge hole; she had devoted her life to Charles and now he was gone. As she grew old and infirm, Effie went to a nursing home on Sydney's northern peninsula, a move that the family says she wasn't entirely happy about. One day, Effie rang Joyce and told her that she had just received some flowers from the King of Belgium. Joyce was a little disbelieving so went to see her mother. However, when Joyce arrived, sure enough, there were the flowers and a card from the King and Queen of Belgium. The royal couple had visited the War Memorial in Canberra and seen the work of C.E.W. Bean. They inquired further about him and were told that although he had died, his wife was still alive – they had asked for the details and then sent the flowers; the Belgians and the French will never forget what the Australians did for them a century ago. Effie lived for 23 years after Charles, dying in 1991 at the age of 97.

Charles Bean has been most commonly lauded for his role as a journalist, but although he went to the First World War as the official war correspondent, he grew acutely uncomfortable with the often ludicrous constraints of self-serving British wartime censorship. He developed disdain for the expectations of editors and the military alike that it was a journalist's job to spice his copy with fabricated accounts of drum-beating derring-do by 'our boys' that sanitised the horror of war. Although Bean did try occasionally to be an Ashmead-Bartlett, stretching the truth by portraying the diggers as unconcerned by flying bullets, he could never have submitted the gross canard that *Daily Mail* journalist William Beach Thomas wrote after the disastrous first day of the Somme, that 'the very attitudes of the dead, fallen eagerly forwards, have a look of expectant hope. You would say that they died with the light of victory in their eyes.'[35]

Bean was unable to peddle the falsehoods and mawkish bunkum spouted by so many other correspondents because, unlike most of his journalistic contemporaries, he was almost always there on the spot to witness the grim reality of the blood and the mud. Bean was obsessed with the simple truth, the fundamental journalistic tenet that the facts should tell the story, and this sometimes made his copy dull – replete with unnecessary detail. What Charles Bean realised as he roamed the hills of Gallipoli and the battlefields of the Western Front was that he was witnessing the emergence of a distinctive, proud and resilient Australian national character, and this was what he devoted himself to recording in his official history and to commemorating in the Australia War Memorial. Sometimes it made him blind to the failings of the AIF and its commanders that he so revered, but one thing that can be said about Bean is that he got it right most of the time, which was a huge improvement on the output of most correspondents of the era. His legacy is an unparalleled historical account of one of the most defining events in Australian history.

Bean had intended to write an unofficial history of the First World War and was adamant that all his diaries, folders and notes should eventually be publicly available, insisting the qualification note be placed on them stressing that it was the truth as he knew it to be at the time, recognising that he sometimes got things wrong. He knew that his version of the 'truth' would shift and change over time and that, by opening his private papers up to unhindered future analysis, some of his own shortcomings and prejudices during the fog of war might one day be revealed. The scrupulously precise historian in him always relished candid verisimilitude.

Most Australians may not know it but it is the self-effacing Charles Bean, more than anyone, who moulded the memory of the Anzacs and Australia's very sense of itself as a country. As he wrote at the end of his official history: 'When the A.I.F. first sailed it left there a nation that did not yet know itself. Even the 1st Australian Division entered its first battle not knowing what manner of men Australians were. The people of the six States which formed the Commonwealth were much divided. Many an Australian had no confidence in the capacity of his people for any big enterprise … It is in disaster that human character is most clearly exhibited, and though she had known fire, drought, and flood Australia had never seen the one trial that, despite civilised progress, all humanity still recognises – the test of a great war …Australians watched the name of their country rise high in the esteem of the world's oldest and greatest nations. Every Australian bears that name proudly abroad to-day; and by the daily doings, great and small, which these pages have narrated, the Australian nation came to know itself.'[36]

Bean ended the historical account that took nearly a quarter of his life with an epitaph that is as apt for him as it was for the men whose sacrifice he so passionately sought to commemorate:

What these men did nothing can alter now. The good and the bad, the greatness and smallness of their story will stand. Whatever of glory it contains nothing now can lessen. It rises, as it will always rise, above the mists of ages, a monument to great-hearted men; and for their nation a possession for ever.[37]

ACKNOWLEDGEMENTS

I am extremely grateful to Bean's grandchildren, Edward Bean Le Couteur and Anne Carroll, and to Anne's husband, Ian Carroll, for their warm hospitality, their sage editing advice, and for their sharing of family memories, photographs and stories. Thanks also to the charming Phyllis Bauer, CEWB's niece, who sadly passed away just before publication. Special gratitude also to historian Dr Michael McKernan, former deputy director of the Australian War Memorial, for proofreading the manuscript and for offering such valuable and good-humoured advice.

Fulsome thanks once again to Katie Stackhouse, Shona Martyn and James Kellow from my publishers HarperCollins. Thanks also to Simone Ford for her painstakingly careful editing. Gratitude always to my agent Lyn Tranter, from Australian Literary Management (and her husband John), for helping and guiding me with good humour through a fourth book. I also want to warmly acknowledge the kind advice and assistance of Ashley Ekins, head of Military History at the Australian War Memorial.

This book was made possible with the assistance of the many helpful staff of the Australian War Memorial, the New South Wales State Library, the National Archives of

Australia, the National Library of Australia, the National Library of New Zealand, the British National Archives, and the Liddell Hart Centre for Military Archives at King's College London. The National Library of Australia's archived database of digitised newspapers – Trove.nla.gov.au – has been indispensable, as has the Australian War Memorial's digitised Bean diaries and notebooks and official history, and also the National Archives' First World War service files. I acknowledge the kind assistance of Dr C.S. Knighton, archivist at Clifton College, Bristol, Dr Stacey Harmer, archivist at Brentwood School in Essex, Julie Daley, archivist at Abbotsleigh in Sydney, and Dr Richard Scully, senior lecturer in modern European history at the University of New England (for his help in locating and providing the Stephen Ellis thesis). I also want to acknowledge the research done by the Honourable Justice Geoff Lindsay of the Supreme Court of New South Wales in detailing Bean's early life and his time as a barrister in Sydney.

Finally, I could not have done this biography without the extraordinary research job carried out once again by my wife, Kerrie Douglass. Her careful diligence and thorough investigation into the minutiae of C.E.W. Bean helped bring this great Australian to life. She also proved an excellent copy editor and style and grammar adviser (the second best grammar expert I know). And bless our wonderful daughters, Lucy and Millie, for tolerating their parents incessantly discussing Charles Bean and the First World War.

BIBLIOGRAPHY

Australian War Memorial

The diaries, notebooks and folders of C.E.W. Bean can be found online at: http://www.awm.gov.au/collection/RCDIG1066752/.

The Official History of Australia in the War 1914–1918 can also be found on the AWM website online at: http://www.awm.gov.au/histories/first_world_war/

The personal papers of C.E.W. Bean including *The Tasker Letter* and *Account for Effie*, accessible through the AWM Research Centre.

National Archives of Australia

Personnel dossiers from the First World War are available online at: http://www.naa.gov.au/collection/explore/defence/service-records/army-wwi.aspx.

C.E.W. Bean books

Two Men I knew, William Bridges and Brudenell White, Angus and Robertson, 1957

Letters from France, Cassell and Company Limited, 1917 and Gutenberg.org E-book

On the Wool Track, Alston Rivers, London, 1910

The Dreadnought of the Darling, Alston Rivers, London, 1911

Gallipoli Mission, Australian War Memorial, 1948.

In Your Hands Australia, Cassell and Company Ltd, London and Melbourne, 1919.

War Aims of a Plain Australian, Angus and Robertson, 1943
Here my Son – A History of Independent Boys Schools in Australia, Angus and Robertson, 1950
Anzac to Amiens – A shorter History of the Australian Fighting Services in the Great War, Australian War Memorial, 1946.
What to know in Egypt – A Guide for Australasian soldiers, Société Orientale de Publicité, Australian National Library, 1915
With The Flagship In The South, Printed by T. Werner Laurie, London, 1909
Flagships Three, Alston Rivers, London, 1913
The Anzac Book (1916) London, AWM & UNSW Press 2010 Edition
Personal Diary (diary of Charles Bean, by Lucy Bean and C.E.W. Bean, courtesy of Anne Carroll and Edward Bean Le Couteur)

C.E.W. Bean papers

'Australia's Federal Archives: John Curtin's Initiative', C.E.W. Bean – Reprinted for *Historical Studies*, November 1947, Melbourne University Press, State Library of NSW
'Sidelights of the War on Australian Character', by C.E.W. Bean, Royal Historical Society, vol. XIII, 1927, Part IV (read before the Society, 31 May 1927)
'The Technique of a Contemporary War Historian', by C.E.W. Bean, *Historical Studies*, Australia and New Zealand, vol. 2, Nov 1942, Number 6
'Furphy, War Historian' – speech delivered by C.E.W. Bean to the Australian English Association, 21 June 1937 (from a booklet in the National Library – Australian English Association, offprint Number 29, from the *Union Recorder*, 16 September 1937).
'The Writing of the Australian Official History of the Great War – Sources, Methods and some Conclusions', speech by C.E.W. Bean to the Royal Australian Historical Society 22 February 1938. The speech was subsequently published in the Society's Journal – volume 24, Part 2, pages 86–112.
'The Old AIF and the New', by C.E.W. Bean, M.A. D.Litt. *Through Australian Eyes*, Pamphlets on World Affairs, No. 4, Angus and Robertson, Sydney, 1940
'Parks and Playgrounds, Why their importance is growing', Dr C.E.W. Bean, State Library of NSW

Other books

Kevin Fewster (ed), *Frontline Gallipoli – C.E.W. Bean's diary from the trenches*, Allen & Unwin, Sydney, 1983

Dudley McCarthy, *Gallipoli To The Somme*, Leo Cooper Secker & Warburg, London, 1983

Walter Reid, *Architect of Victory: Douglas Haig*, Birlinn Ltd, Edinburgh, 2006

Anthony MacDougall, *Australians at War: A Pictorial History*, The Five Mile Press, 1991

Denis Winter, *Making the Legend – The War Writings of C.E.W. Bean*, Queensland University Press, 1992

Peter Hart, *The Somme. The Darkest Hour. On The Western Front*, Pegasus Books, 2008

John Crawford (ed.), *No Better Death – The Great War diaries and letters of William G. Malone*, Reed Publishing, 2005

Niall Ferguson, *The Pity of War*, Basic Books UK, 1998

J. Laffin, *Australians at War: Western Front 1917–1918*, Time Life Books, Sydney, 1988

Ken Inglis, *Sacred Places, War Memorials in The Australian Landscape*, Melbourne University Press, 2008

Michael McKernan, *Here is Their Spirit: A history of the Australian war memorial 1917–1990,* University of Queensland Press, 1991.

Malcolm Andrews, *Hubert Who? – War Hero. Polar Explorer. Spy. The Incredible Life of unsung adventurer, Hubert Wilkins*, ABC Books and Harper Collins, 2011

Christopher Wray, *Sir James Whiteside McCay – A Turbulent Life*, Oxford University Press, 2002

Ross McMullin, *Pompey Elliott*, Scribe Publications, Melbourne 2002

Ross McMullin, *Will Dyson – Cartoonist, Etcher and Australia's finest war artist*, Angus and Robertson, 1984

Peter Stanley, *Bad Characters – Sex, Crime, Mutiny, Murder and the AIF*, Pier 9, Murdoch Books, 2010

Alasdair McGregor, *Frank Hurley – A Photographer's Life*, Viking by Penguin Books, 2004

Nola Anderson, *Australian War Memorial, Treasures from a Century of Collecting*, AWM and Murdoch Books, 2012

W F Mandle, *Going it Alone, Australia's National Identity in the Twentieth Century*, Penguin Books, 1980

Geoffrey Serle, *John Monash – a Biography*, Melbourne University Press, 1982
Roland Perry, *Monash – The Outsider who won a War*, Random House, 2004
Fred and Elizabeth Brenchley, *Myth Maker – Ellis Ashmead-Bartlett. The Englishman who sparked Australia's Gallipoli Legend*, John Wiley and Sons Australia Ltd, 2005
Scott Bennett, *Pozières,* Scribe Publishing, 2011
Fay Anderson and Richard Trembath, *Witnesses to War, The History of Australian Conflict Reporting*, Melbourne University Press, 2011
Les Carlyon, *The Great War*, Picador, 2006
Joan Beaumont, *Broken Nation. Australians in the Great War*, Allen & Unwin Sydney, 2013
John F. Williams, *Anzacs, The Media And The Great War*, UNSW Press, 1999
Eric Andrews, *The Anzac Illusion*, Cambridge University Press, 1993
Robin Prior, *Gallipoli The End of the Myth*, Yale University Press, 2009
John Horne and Alan Kramer, *German Atrocities, 1914: A History of Denial*, Yale University Press, 2001
Jeremy Paxman, *Great Britain's Great War*, Viking – Penguin, 2013
Ross Coulthart, *The Lost Diggers*, Harper Collins Australia, 2012
Michael Caulfield, *The Unknown Anzacs*, Hachette Australia, 2013
Philip Gibbs, *The Battles Of The Somme*, G.H. Doran, 1917
Philip Gibbs, *Now It Can Be Told*, Garden City Publishing UK, 1920
Paul Moorcraft and Philip Taylor, *Shooting The Messenger – The Political Impact Of War Reporting*, Potomac Books Inc, Washington DC, 2008
Philip Knightley, *The First Casualty – From the Crimea to Vietnam: The War Correspondent as Hero, Propagandist and Myth Maker*, Harcourt Brace Jovanovich, 1975
Sergeant-Major Edward Cotton, *A Voice From Waterloo: A History Of The Battle Fought On 18th June 1815* (First published circa 1848) Mont St-Jean, Belgium

Other Papers and Articles

Gallipoli News cuttings, Newspaper cuttings giving accounts of the Gallipoli Campaign, Mitchell Library Q940.425/4
'CEW Bean –- A Study of his Life and Work', thesis by Stephen Ellis, University of New England, Armidale, 1969

'C.E.W. Bean Australian Historian', Professor Ken Inglis, John Murtagh Macrossan Lecture. University of Qld Press, 1969

'Be substantially great in thy self: Getting to Know C.E.W. Bean; Barrister, Judge's Associate, Moral Philosopher', by Geoff Lindsay SC, 2011

'A Praise that Never Ages, The Australian War Memorial and the "national" interpretation of the First World War, 1922–35', thesis by Craig Melrose, The University of Queensland, 2004

'The Story of the Story of Anzac', thesis by M Ball, University of Tasmania, 2001

'Champion of Anzac: General Sir Brudenell White, the First Australian Imperial Force and the emergence of the Australian military culture 1914–18'; thesis by John Bentley, University of Wollongong, 2003

'No Straw Man: C.E.W. Bean and some critics', John Barrett, *Australian Historical Studies*, 23, no. 89, April 1988: pp. 102–14

'The Anzac Book and the Anzac Legend: C. E. W. Bean as editor and image-maker', D.A. Kent, *Historical Studies,* 21, no. 81, 1985, pp. 376–90

'"Steadfast until death?" C. E. W. Bean and the representation of Australian military manhood', Alistair Thomson, *Australian Historical Studies,* 23, no. 93, 1989, pp. 462–78

'The Vilest Libel of the War? Imperial Politics and the Official Histories of Gallipoli' by Alistair Thomson, *Australian Historical Studies*, Oct 1993, vol. 25, no. 101, pp. 628–636

'Lessons in Leadership – The Life of Sir John Monash', by Rolfe Hartley. A presentation to the Engineers Australia Sydney Division, CELM, March 2013

'The Entente Ideal', Pamphlet from The Entente Club, written for the *Australian Trained Nurses' Association Gazette*, December 1919, Dame Mary Gilmore Collection, Courtesy of the Mitchell Library, NSW State Library

Oral History – Interviews with Phyllis Bauer, Anne Carroll and Edward Bean Le Couteur, 7 August 2013

NOTES

Introduction

1 Christopher Wray, *Sir James Whiteside McCay: A turbulent life*, Oxford University Press, Melbourne, 2002, p. 25.
2 C.E.W. Bean, *Official History of Australia in the War of 1914–1918*, [Hereafter '*Official History*'], vol. 1, Australian War Memorial, Canberra, 1941, 'The Story of Anzac from the outbreak of war to the end of the first phase of the Gallipoli campaign, May 4 1915' 11th edition. All cited references to the official history in this book are available online on the AWM's website at: http://www.awm.gov.au/histories/first_world_war/.
3 Charles Bean, diary, 8 May 1915, AWM38 3DRL606/7/1, Australian War Memorial, Canberra, p. 50. [hereafter 'Bean Diary']. All cited references to Bean's diaries and notebooks in this book are available online on the AWM's website at: http://www.awm.gov.au/collection/RCDIG1066752/.
4 ibid.
5 ibid.
6 ibid., p. 51. Another account also in *Official History*, op. cit., vol. 2 'The Story of Anzac from 4 May 1915 to the evacuation of the Gallipoli Peninsula' 11th edition, Australian War Memorial Canberra, 1941, p. 27.
7 Bean, diary, ibid., p. 53.
8 Geoffrey Serle, 'McCay, Sir James Whiteside (1864–1930)', *Australian Dictionary of Biography*, http://adb.anu.edu.au/

biography/mccay-sir-james-whiteside-7312, accessed online 7 June 2014.

9 Charles Bean, 'The Peninsular War, Fighting on Gallipoli, Assault on Krithia', *The Adelaide Advertiser*, 4 August 1915, p. 12.

10 *Official History*, op. cit., vol. 2, p. 19.

11 ibid., p. 3.

12 ibid., p. 19.

13 ibid., p. 19.

14 Speech by Senator John Faulkner, Minister for Defence, 2010 C.E.W. Bean Foundation dinner address, National Press Club, Canberra.

15 Philip Gibbs, *The Battles of the Somme*, G.H. Doran, London, 1917, p. 21.

16 Paul Moorcraft and Philip Taylor, *Shooting the Messenger: The political impact of war reporting*, Potomac Books Inc., Washington DC, 2008, p. 42.

17 Phillip Knightley, *The First Casualty: The war correspondent as hero, propagandist and myth-maker from the Crimea to Iraq*, Harcourt Brace Jovanovich, London & NY, 1975, p. 109.

18 Bean, diary, op. cit., pp. 57, 59.

19 Charles Bean, 'Australians at Cape Helles. A Historic Charge. The Battle of Krithia', *Maitland Weekly Mercury*, 14 August 1915, p. 14.

20 Bean, diary, op. cit., p. 58.

21 Cited in John Williams, *Anzacs, the Media and the Great War*, UNSW Press, Sydney 1999, p. 84.

22 Cited in footnote 20 of Chris Baker, 'Was the Australian *Official History* more truthful than the British?', *The Long Long Trail – The British Army in the Great War of 1914–1918*, http://www.1914–1918.net/bat15E_Fromelles.html, accessed online 7 June 2014.

23 *Official History*, op. cit., vol. 2, pp. 42.

24 ibid., p. 42.

25 Charles Bean, 'An Australian Charge. Glorious Achievement', *Kalgoorlie Western Argus*, 8 June 1915, p. 1.

26 Bean, diary, op. cit., 24 April 1915, AWM38 3DRL606/5/1, p. 13.

27 C.E.W. Bean, *Anzac to Amiens: A shorter history of the Australian fighting services in the Great War*, Australian War Memorial, Canberra, 1946, p. 181.

28 Manning Clark, *A History of Australia*, vol. 5, Melbourne University Press, Carlton South, Victoria, 1997, p. 426. The full quote reads: 'Australia's day of glory made her a prisoner of her past, rather than the architect of a new future for humanity.'

29 Martin Ball, *The Story of the Story of Anzac*, unpublished thesis – University of Tasmania, Hobart, 2001, p. 239.

Chapter One

1 Cited in Robert A. Huttenback, *The British Imperial Experience*, Harper & Row, New York, 1966, pp. 91–2.

2 Charles Bean, 'Account for Effie', written on the reverse-side pages of Bean's 'Diary 2 – Our trip to England', 1924, AWM PR00283, series 1/2, Australian War Memorial, Canberra, unpaginated. This handwritten account was also incompletely transcribed in a typewritten version in the papers of Arthur Bazley, AWM 3DRL/3520, folder 10a of 143, Australian War Memorial, Canberra.

3 Edwin Bean, travel diary, 1885 AWM PR00283, series 1/1, Australian War Memorial, Canberra.

4 'Vitai Lampada', accessed online, *First World Waronline – a multimedia history of World War One*, http://www.firstworldwar.com/poetsandprose/newbolt.htm .

5 Lucy Bean, diary, 'Charlie Bean', undated – sourced from Bean private family collection.

6 Letter from Jack Bean to Arthur Bazley, *CEW Bean Influences and Significant Circumstances, 1957*, AWM 3DRL 3520 10c, Australian War Memorial, Canberra, (no page number).

7 Letter from Jack Bean to Arthur Bazley, ibid.

8 Bean, 'Account for Effie', op. cit.

9 Arthur Jose, *The Growth of the Empire: A handbook to the history of greater Britain*, 2nd edition, Angus & Robertson, New York, 1907.

10 Charles Bean, *In Your Hands, Australians*, Cassell & Co. Ltd, London, 1919, pp. 90–2, cited in Geoff Lindsay, *Be Substantially Great in Thyself: Getting to know C.E.W. Bean, barrister, judge's associate, moral philosopher*, accessed online 7 June 2014. Forbes Society papers, http://www.forbessociety.org.au/wordpress/wp-content/uploads/2013/03/bean.pdf.

11 Lucy Bean, diary, op. cit.

12 Bean, 'Account for Effie', op. cit.

Chapter Two

1 Edward Cotton, *A Voice from Waterloo: A history of the battle fought on the 18th June 1815*, Keissling & Co, Mont-St-Jean, Belgium, 1894.
2 ibid., p. 282.
3 ibid., p. 202.
4 H.T. Siborne, *Waterloo Letters*, Cassell, London, 1891. Bean's careful study of this book is noted by Denis Winter in *Making the Legend: The war writings of C.E.W. Bean*, University of Queensland Press, St Lucia, Qld, 1992, p. 4.
5 Charles Bean, 'Account for Effie', 1924, AWM PR00283, series 1/2, Australian War Memorial, Canberra.
6 ibid.
7 UK Parliament School Commission Inquiry, *Special Reports of Assistant Commissioners*, vol. 8, Eastern Division, UK Parliament, 1869, p. 14.
8 'Clifton Chapel', Henry Newbolt, *Clifton Chapel and Other School Poems*, John Murray, London, 1908, p. 5.
9 ibid. This is a translation from the Latin closing line of the poem: 'Qui ante diem periit: Sed miles, sed pro patria.'
10 Charles Bean, 'What England Means to Me', manuscript for an address to the Women's League of Empire, Sydney, March 1934. Cited in Ken Inglis, *C.E.W. Bean, Australian Historian*, University of Queensland Press, Brisbane, 1969, p. 4.
11 Letter from Charles Bean to Henry McKean Tasker, editor of *The Bathurstian*, 18 October 1930, p. 6, AWM 38 3DRL/6673.
12 C.S. Knighton (ed.), *Clifton College: Foundation to evacuation*, Bristol Record Society in conjunction with Clifton College, Bristol, 2012, pp. 158–9.
13 Cited in Dudley McCarthy, *Gallipoli To The Somme*, Leo Cooper Secker & Warburg, London, 1983, p. 37.
14 ibid.
15 Bean, 'Account for Effie', op. cit.
16 ibid.
17 Letter from Bean to Tasker, op. cit.
18 Letter from Edwin Bean to Charles Bean, 14 February 1900, AWM Bean Archive 3DRL6673/897, Australian War Memorial, Canberra.
19 *The Pall Mall Gazette*, 20 October 1901.
20 Bean, 'Account for Effie', op. cit.

21 Letter from Bean to Tasker, op. cit.
22 Bean, 'Account for Effie', op. cit.
23 Charles Bean, 'The approaching sea fight. Its place in naval history. Why it will be worth watching', *Daily Telegraph*, 13 April 1905, p. 5.
24 Bean, 'Account for Effie', op. cit.
25 Letter from Bean to Tasker, op. cit., p. 10.
26 Bean, 'Account for Effie', op. cit.
27 ibid.
28 Charles Bean, 'The Real Significance of The "White Australia" Question', London *Spectator*, 13 July 1907, p. 13.
29 Letter from Bean to Tasker, op. cit., p. 12.
30 Bean, 'Account for Effie', op. cit.
31 ibid.
32 ibid.
33 ibid.
34 ibid.
35 Charles Bean, *With the Flagship in the South*, printed by T. Werner Laurie, London, 1909, dedication page. First published in Australian Edition, 1909, by William Brooks.
36 ibid., p. 1.
37 Charles Bean, *On the Wool Track*, Alston Rivers, London, 1910.
38 Bean, 'Account for Effie', op. cit.
39 Charles Bean, *On the Wool Track*, John Lane Company, New York, 1910, Preface p. viii.
40 ibid., pp. 137–8.
41 ibid., p. 138.
42 ibid., p. 99.
43 Charles Bean, *The Dreadnought of the Darling*, Alston Rivers, London, 1911.
44 ibid., p. 317.
45 ibid., p. 312.
46 C.E.W. Bean, *Flagships Three*, Alston Rivers, London, 1913, p. 207.
47 ibid., p. 208.
48 Cited in Inglis, op. cit., p. 31.
49 Charles Bean 'The Last Great Passing by One Who Was There', *The Sydney Morning Herald*, 14 May 1910, p. 14.

Chapter Three

1 Phillip Knightley, *The First Casualty: The war correspondent as hero, propagandist and myth-maker from the Crimea to Iraq*, Harcourt Brace Jovanovich, London & New York, 1975, p. 82.
2 John Horne and Alan Kramer, *German Atrocities, 1914: A History of Denial*, Yale University Press, New Haven & London, 2001.
3 'War scenes – German atrocities, revolting tale, suffering Belgians', *The Sydney Morning Herald*, 15 October 1914, (no by-line) p. 8.
4 Arthur Ponsonby, *Falsehood in Wartime*, Institute for Historical Review, Costa Mesa – California, 1980, p. 157.
5 Charles Bean, 'Account for Effie', 1924, AWM PR00283, series 1/2, Australian War Memorial, Canberra.
6 Kevin Fewster, *Frontline Gallipoli: C.E.W. Bean's diary from the trenches*. Allen & Unwin, Sydney, 1983, p. 10.
7 Sir Henry Luce, 'Life in London and thereabout', *The Sydney Morning Herald*, 10 October 1914, p. 7.
8 Denis Winter, *Making the Legend: The war writings of C.E.W. Bean*, University of Queensland Press, St Lucia, Qld, 1992, p. 7.
9 Knightley, op. cit., p. 42.
10 Walter Reid, *Architect of Victory: Douglas Haig*, Birlinn Ltd, Edinburgh, 2006, p. 78.
11 Knightley, op. cit., pp. 55–6.
12 *Defence of the Realm Act*, supplement to the *London Gazette*, 1 September 1914.
13 C.E.W. Bean, *Official History of Australia in the War of 1914–1918*, Australian War Memorial, Canberra, first edition 1942, vol. 6 'The Australian Imperial Force in France during the Allied Offensive 1918', p. 196.
14 Letter from Charles Bean to the general staff officer, 1st Australian Division, 27 June 1915, AWM/3DRL6673/270, Australian War Memorial, Canberra.
15 'Last man and last shilling', *The Canberra Times*, (no by-line), 25 October 1928, p. 1.
16 Bean, 'Account for Effie', op. cit.
17 Charles Bean, diary, 28 October 1914, AWM38 3DRL606/1/1, Australian War Memorial, Canberra,p. 1.
18 ibid., 1 November 1914, p. 6.
19 ibid., 2 November 1914, p. 6.

20 ibid., 9 November 1914, p. 20.
21 ibid., 12 November 1914, p. 33. (Bean reports Captain Silver saying *Emden* must have passed within 20 miles of the convoy when she crossed its bows in the night.)
22 Bean, diary, op. cit., 9 November 1914, p. 20.
23 ibid., pp. 24–5.
24 ibid., p. 26.
25 ibid., 15 November 1914, p. 44.
26 ibid., 27 November 1914, pp. 97–8.
27 ibid., 30 November 1914, p. 106.
28 ibid., 3 December 1914, p. 117.
29 ibid., p. 127.
30 Charles Bean, 'What to Know in Egypt – A Guide for Australasian Soldiers', Société Orientale de Publicite, Cairo, 1915 p. 14
31 ibid., p. 16.
32 Bean, diary, op. cit., 1 January 1915, AWM38 3DRL606/2/1, p. 3.
33 ibid., pp. 5–6.
34 ibid., p. 5.
35 ibid., p. 4.
36 Charles Bean, 'Australia's Fair Fame, Wasters In The Force, Some Not Fit To Be Soldiers', *Adelaide Advertiser*, 22 January 1915, p. 6.
37 ibid.
38 ibid.
39 ibid.
40 Ross McMullin, *Pompey Elliott*, Scribe Publications, Melbourne, 2002, p. 104.
41 'Our Soldiers', Letter from Pompey Elliott to Cr J.F. Henderson, *Essendon Gazette*, 29 April 1915, p. 9.
42 Cited in McMullin, op. cit., p. 104.
43 Sergeant Frank E. Westbrook poem, 1st AIF Mena, *Portland Observer and Normanby Advertiser*, Victoria, 19 April 1915, p. 3.
44 Charles Bean, 'Troops in Egypt. Unjustified criticisms', *The Argus*, 1 March 1915, p. 9.
45 Sergeant Frank Westbrook poem, *Flemington Spectator*, Victoria, 29 April 1915, p. 83.
46 Bean, diary, op. cit., 4 March 1915, p. 104.
47 ibid., pp. 102–3.

48 C.E.W. Bean, *Two Men I Knew: William Bridges and Brudenell White, founders of the AIF*, Angus & Robertson, Sydney, 1957, p. 43.
49 'Defaming Australia. Captain Bean Taken to Task'. Letter from Fred Newling, published in *The Singleton Argus*, 24 April 1915, p. 8.
50 Bean, diary, op. cit., 4–5 March 1915, p. 104.
51 ibid., 9–30 January 1915, pp. 48–9.
52 ibid., pp. 49–50.

Chapter Four

1 Haig diary entry from 18 January 1916, cited in Peter Hart, *The Somme: The darkest hour on the Western Front*, Pegasus Books, New York, 2008, p. 31.
2 C.E.W. Bean, *Official History of Australia in the War of 1914–1918*, Australian War Memorial, Canberra, vol. 1, 'The Story of Anzac from the outbreak of war to the end of the first phase of the Gallipoli campaign May 4 1915', 11th edition 1941, p. 174.
3 Robin Prior, *Gallipoli The End Of The Myth*, Yale University Press, Sydney, NSW, 2009, p. 22.
4 ibid., p. 58.
5 Bean, diary, 8 February 1915, AWM38 3DRL606/2/1, Australian War Memorial, Canberra, p. 82.
6 ibid., p. 83.
7 ibid., 13 February 1915, p. 91.
8 ibid., p. 93.
9 ibid., 14 March 1915, pp. 114–15.
10 ibid., 16–18 March 1915, p. 117.
11 Bean, diary, 30–31 March 1915, AWM38 3DRL606/3/1, p. 10.
12 ibid., 1 April 1915, p. 22.
13 ibid., 2 April 1915, p. 23.
14 ibid., p. 24.
15 ibid., p. 26.
16 *Official History*, op. cit., vol. 1, p. 215.
17 Bean, diary, op. cit., 3 April 1915, p. 30.
18 ibid., p. 31.
19 ibid., p. 37.
20 ibid., 8 April 1915, p. 44.
21 ibid., 8 April 1915, p. 46 [numbering in Bean's handwriting, not the diary pagination].

22 ibid., 10 April 1915, p. 52.
23 ibid., pp. 55–6.
24 ibid., 19 April 1915, p. 78.
25 ibid., p. 91 [written (inverted) on facing page from Bean's p. 79].
26 Bean, diary, 23 April 1915, AWM38 3DRL606/5/1, p. 6.
27 ibid., p. 8.
28 ibid., p. 12.
29 ibid., 24 April 1915, pp. 11–12.
30 ibid., 25 April 1915, pp. 13–14.
31 ibid., 25 April 1915, p. 18.
32 ibid., p. 19.
33 ibid., p. 19–20.
34 ibid., p. 21.
35 ibid., p. 22.
36 *Official History*, op. cit., vol. 1, p. 280.
37 Bean, diary, op. cit., p. 26.
38 *Official History*, op. cit., p. 256.
39 Bean, diary, op. cit., p. 28.
40 Charles Bean, notebook no. 28, 25 April 1915, AWM 3DRL/606/28/1, Australian War Memorial, Canberra (not paginated, but 24 pages into online digitised folder).
41 Bean, diary, op. cit., p. 34.
42 Bean, diary, 25 April 1915 AWM38 3DRL/606/4/1, Australian War Memorial, p. 18.
43 Bean, diary, op. cit., undated February–March 1916, AWM38, 3DRL606/40/1, p. 24.
44 Bean, diary, 25 April 1915, AWM38, 3DRL/606/5/1, p. 40.
45 C.E.W. Bean, 'How the Australians fought. Imperishable fame', *The Sydney Morning Herald*, 15 May 1915, p. 14.
46 ibid.
47 'Mr Ashmead-Bartlett's story', *The Sydney Morning Herald*, 8 May 1915, p. 13.
48 Phillip Knightley, *The First Casualty*, op. cit., p. 101.
49 Bean, diary, op. cit., p. 37.
50 ibid., facing page to p. 40.
51 Alistair Thomson, '"The vilest libel of the war"? Imperial politics and the official histories of Gallipoli', *Australian Historical Studies*, vol. 25, no. 101, October 1993, pp. 628–36.
52 ibid., p. 630.
53 ibid.

54 ibid., p. 631.
55 Bean, diary, op. cit., 26 April 1915, AWM38 3DRL/606/5/1, p. 42.
56 ibid., p. 43.
57 ibid., facing page to p. 44.
58 ibid., pp. 45–6.
59 ibid., p. 47.
60 ibid., 27 April 1915, p. 48.
61 ibid., undated/unnumbered two pages on from p. 50.
62 ibid., 26 April 1915, unnumbered four pages on from p. 49.
63 Bean, diary, op.cit., 28 April 1915, AWM38 DRL/606/6/1, p. 2.
64 *Official History*, op. cit., p. 471.
65 John Crawford (ed.), *No Better Death: The Great War diaries and letters of William G. Malone*, Reed Publishing, Auckland, 2005, p. 164; extract dated 27 April 1915.
66 ibid., p. 164.
67 ibid., p. 165.
68 ibid., p. 166.
69 *Official History*, op. cit., p. 502.
70 Crawford, op. cit., p. 166.
71 ibid.
72 Diary of Lieutenant Colonel W.G. Malone, National Library of New Zealand, Papers of W.G. Malone MS Group 0056, p. 106.
73 *Official History*, op. cit., pp. 515–16.
74 Christopher Pugsley, *Gallipoli: The New Zealand Story*, Reed Publishing, Auckland, 1998, p. 283.

Chapter Five

1 Devon Heritage website – George Raymond Dallas Moor VC of Braunton, http://www.devonheritage.org/Places/Braunton/GeorgeRaymondDallasMoorVC.htm, accessed online, 12 June 2014.
2 C.T. Atkinson, *The Royal Hampshire Regiment, 1914–1918*, University Press Glasgow, 1952, p. 87.
3 Militarian – Military History Forum, http://www.militarian.com/threads/george-raymond-dallas-moor-vc-mc-bar.8224/, accessed online, 12 June 2014.
4 Charles Bean, diary, 5 May 1915, AWM38 3DRL606/7/1, Australian War Memorial, Canberra, p. 23.

5 ibid., 5 May 1915, p. 24.
6 C.E.W. Bean, *Official History of Australia in the War of 1914–1918*, [hereafter *Official History*] Australian War Memorial, Canberra, 1941, vol. 2, op. cit., p. 2.
7 ibid.
8 ibid., p. 3.
9 Les Carlyon, *The Great War*, Picador Pan McMillan, Sydney, 2006, p. 27.
10 *Official History*, op. cit., p. 23.
11 Bean, diary, op. cit., p. 48.
12 ibid., pp. 48–9.
13 Charles Bean, 'In the Dardanelles, Australian Infantry, another famous charge', *The Sydney Morning Herald*, 28 May 1915, p. 10.
14 Bean, diary, op. cit., p. 50.
15 Charles Bean, 'The Peninsular War. Fighting on Gallipoli. Assault on Krithia', *Adelaide Advertiser*, 4 August 1915, p. 12.
16 Charles Bean, 'An Australian charge. Glorious achievement', *Kalgoorlie Miner*, 31 May 1915, p. 2.
17 Cited in Christopher Wray, *Sir James Whiteside McCay: A turbulent life*, Oxford University Press, Melbourne, 2002, p. 135.
18 *Official History*, op. cit., p. 30.
19 Bean, diary, op. cit., 8 May 1915. AWM38 3DRL606/7/1 p. 55.
20 ibid., p. 56.
21 ibid., p. 59.
22 ibid., p. 63.
23 ibid., p. 50.
24 ibid., p. 63.
25 'Captain Bean. Soldier's Praise', *The Sydney Morning Herald*, 30 July 1915, p. 8.
26 'The attack on Krithia – a gallant charge', *The Age*, as reprinted with attribution to *The Age* in *The Dominion* Wellington, New Zealand, 26 May 1915, p. 6. Also appeared in South Australia: 'Taking of Krithia. Gallant Australian Charge. Commanding Officers' bravery', *The Register*, Adelaide, 21 June 1915, p. 8. (no by-line).
27 Bean, diary, op. cit., 12 May 1915, AWM38 3DRL606/7a/1, in pp. 25–6 of transcribed shorthand notes.

Chapter Six

1 It should be acknowledged that while this is Kemal's version of this quote, it has been contradicted by Turkish historians who cite his actual order as being slightly different.

2 Charles Bean, diary, 17 May 1915, AWM38 3DRL606/8/1, Australian War Memorial, Canberra, pp. 6–7.

3 ibid., p. 5.

4 ibid., pp. 5–6.

5 ibid., p. 8.

6 ibid., p. 13.

7 ibid.

8 ibid., pp. 17–18. (Bean's emphasis).

9 ibid., 17–18 May 1915, p. 19.

10 C.E.W. Bean, *Official History of Australia in the War of 1914–1918*, [herefater *Official History*] Australian War Memorial, Canberra, vol. 2, op. cit., p. 138, footnote 10.

11 Bean, diary, op. cit., 20 May 1915, p. 41.

12 ibid., 19 May 1915, p. 25.

13 Letter from Private S. Leserve [Service number 10056, enlisted 12 Sept 1914] to his parents at Norton St, Leichhardt, *The Sydney Morning Herald*, undated (1915); part of a collection of newspaper cuttings giving accounts of the Gallipoli campaign, Q940.425/4, Mitchell Library, Sydney.

14 'Turkish fiends exposed. Captain Bean's defence refuted. Overwhelming evidence of enemy's barbarous methods', *Sunday Times* (Sydney), 13 June 1915, p. 4.

15 Reuters, 'Gallipoli. Australians' Part. A Great Feat. The Landing Rushes.', *Singleton Argus*, 5 June 1915, p. 8.

16 Phillip Knightley, *The First Casualty*, ibid., p. 84.

17 ibid., p. 85.

18 Mitchell Library newspaper cuttings collection, op. cit.

19 Major Oliver Hogue died of influenza in London in 1919. 'Trooper Bluegum Dead', *The Port Macquarie News and Hastings River Advocate*, 15 March 1919, p. 4.

20 Letter from Trooper Bluegum, Mitchell Library newspaper cuttings collection, undated, ibid.

21 Bean, diary, op. cit., p. 25.

22 Charles Bean, 'The Australians trench warfare … baseless atrocity stories', *The Sydney Morning Herald*, 8 June 1915, p. 7.

23 Charles Bean, 'The peninsula war: Australian soldiers … Turkish atrocities', *The Advertiser*, 23 July 1915, p. 9.

24 Charles Bean, 'The Australian Army: The reported Turkish atrocities. Warning to the public', *The Mercury* (Hobart), 30 June 1915, p. 5.
25 Charles Bean, 'Captain Bean's reports: Why they are late. Desire for accuracy', *The Argus*, 7 July 1915, p. 9.
26 'Turkish fiends exposed. Captain Bean's defence refuted. Overwhelming evidence of enemy's barbarous methods', *Sunday Times* (Sydney), 13 June 1915, p. 4.
27 ibid.
28 Charles Bean, 'Gallipoli. Australians Win Undying Fame. The 3rd Brigade. How They Scaled The Heights', *Tamworth Daily Observer*, NSW, 15 May 1915, p. 3. Also in *Commonwealth of Australia Gazette*, no. 39, 17 May 1915.
29 C.E.W. Bean, 'Furphy – war historian', speech to the Australian-English Association, published in *The Union Recorder*, booklet 29, National Library of Australia, 16 September 1937, p. 1.
30 Charles Bean, *Gallipoli Mission*, Australian War Memorial, Canberra, 1948, p. 145.
31 *Official History*, op. cit., vol. 1, pp. 470–1.
32 Charles Bean, 'Gallipoli. Fight in the hills. The first day. Men that went beyond', *The Sydney Morning Herald*, 18 June 1915, p. 10.
33 'Historian's task ending', *The Sydney Morning Herald*, 30 August 1941, p. 12 (no by-line).
34 ibid.
35 Charles Bean, 'The Australians. The manner of man he is. Some of the true stories', *Swan Hill Guardian* and *Lake Boga Advocate*, 30 December 1915, p. 4.
36 Bean, diary, op. cit., 20 May 1915, p. 42.
37 Charles Bean, 'Stretcher bearers. Their magnificent work. The man with the donkey', *Maitland Mercury*, 21 July 1915, p. 7.
38 Ernest Buley, *Glorious Deeds of Australasians in the Great War*, Andrew Melrose, London, 1915.
39 Cited in Mark Baker, 'Taken for a ride?', *The Age*, 7 March 2013, accessed online, 14 June 2014, http://www.smh.com.au/national/taken-for-a-ride-20130306-2flf1.html.
40 Charles Bean, 'Shells. One can hear them. As Australians know them', *The Mercury* (Hobart), 10 September 1915, p. 5.
41 Cited in a thesis by Stephen Ellis, 'C.E.W. Bean: A study of his life and works', University of New England, 1969, p. 28.

42 C.E.W. Bean, 'Ashmead-Bartlett: Most brilliant of war correspondents', 9 May 1931, *The Sydney Morning Herald*, p. 17.
43 Bean, diary, op. cit., 22 May 1915, p. 59.
44 Bean, diary, ibid., 27 July 1915, AWM38 3DRL606/10/1, p. 73.
45 Charles Bean, 'Position of the assistant correspondent AIF and duties of the Australian War Correspondent', 12 December 1917, Bean papers, folder 268, Australian War Memorial, Canberra.
46 'War correspondent's declaration', as quoted in Transcripts of Keith Murdoch at the Dardanelles Commission, 5 February 1917, papers of Sir Keith Murdoch, MS2823, Series 2, Folder 3, National Library of Australia, Canberra.
47 Fred and Elizabeth Brenchley, *Myth Maker: Ellis Ashmead-Bartlett, the Englishman who sparked Australia's Gallipoli legend*, John Wiley and Sons, Brisbane, 2005, p. 47.
48 ibid., p. 106.
49 ibid., p. 97.
50 ibid., p. 98.
51 ibid., p. 99.
52 C.E.W. Bean, 'Obituary: Ashmead-Bartlett', *The Sydney Morning Herald*, 16 May 1931, p. 12.
53 Bean, diary, op. cit., 3 October 1915, AWM38 3DRL606/17/1, p. 65.
54 Bean, diary, ibid., 20 June 1915, AWM38 3DRL606/9/1, p. 38.
55 Bean, diary, ibid., 22 June 1915, p. 51 (inverted page opposite p. 31).
56 Charles Bean, 'Memorandum to GSO Australian 1st Division', attachment in Bean, diary, ibid., 27 June 1915, at p. 13.
57 Bean, 'Obituary: Ashmead-Bartlett', op. cit.
58 Ellis Ashmead-Bartlett, diary, 18 July 1915, Ellis Ashmead-Bartlett papers, 1915–17, item 01 (call number A1583), Mitchell Library, State Library of New South Wales, Sydney.
59 Bean, diary, op. cit., 6 July 1915, AWM38 3DRL606/10/1, pp. 32–3.
60 Bean, diary, op. cit., 7 July 1915, ibid., p. 34.
61 Ashmead-Bartlett diary, op. cit.

Chapter Seven

1 C.E.W. Bean, *Official History of Australia in the War of 1914–1918*, [hereafter *Official History*], Australian War Memorial, Canberra, 1941, vol. 2, op. cit., p. 503.

2 ibid., p. 507.
3 'The Capture of Lone Pine. Sir Ian Hamilton's Tribute', *The Sydney Mail* (a weekly edition of *The Sydney Morning Herald*), 15 September 1915, p. 62 (no byline).
4 Cited in John Hamilton, *Goodbye Cobber, God Bless You*, Pan Macmillan, Sydney, 2004, p. 11.
5 *Official History*, op. cit., p. 614.
6 ibid., pp. 616–17.
7 Charles Bean, 'The Anzac battle. Brilliant attacks by colonials. Heroic Light Horsemen', 27 August 1915, *The Mercury* (Hobart), p. 5.
8 *Official History*, op. cit., p. 631.
9 ibid., p. 618.
10 ibid., p. 631–2.
11 Charles Bean, diary, 9 August 1915, AWM38 3DRL606/11/1, Australian War Memorial, Canberra, pp. 41–2.
12 Charles Bean, 'Australian soldiers. Sir Ian Hamilton's tribute. Deeds will live in history', *The Argus*, 20 September 1915, p. 7.
13 *Official History*, op. cit., p. 767.
14 Bean, diary, 29 August 1915, AWM38 3DRL606/10/1, p. 111.

Chapter Eight

1 Charles Bean, diary, 4 October 1915, AWM38 3DRL606/17/1, Australian War Memorial, Canberra, p. 73.
2 Letter from Keith Murdoch to Prime Minister Andrew Fisher, 23 September 1915, papers of Sir Keith Murdoch, MS 2823, series 2, folder 1, National Library of Australia, Canberra.
3 ibid.
4 Bean, diary, op. cit., 29 September 1915, AWM38 3DRL606/17/1, opposite page to p. 34.
5 ibid., 28 September 1915, p. 36.
6 ibid., p. 37.
7 ibid., pp. 38–9.
8 ibid., 26 September 1915, pp. 26–8.
9 ibid., pp. 29–30, 34.
10 ibid., 28 September 1915, p. 40.
11 ibid., 11 November 1915, AWM38 3DRL606/20/1, p. 18.
12 ibid., 30 September 1915, AWM38 3DRL606/17/1, p. 41.
13 ibid., pp. 41–3.
14 *The Bulletin*, 7 October 1915, p. 26 (no by-line).
15 Bean, diary, op. cit., 1 October 1915, pp. 44–5.

16 ibid., pp. 46–7
17 ibid., p. 47.
18 ibid., 17 October 1915, AWM 38 3DRL606/18/1, p. 32.
19 ibid., p. 34.
20 ibid., pp. 35–6.
21 ibid., 2 November 1915, AWM38 3DRL606/19/1, p. 43.
22 ibid., p. 44.
23 C.E.W. Bean, *Two Men I Knew: William Bridges and Brudenell White, founders of the AIF*, Angus & Robertson, Sydney, 1957, p. 118.
24 Bean, diary, op. cit., 12 November 1915, AWM38 3DRL606/20/1, pp. 34–5.
25 ibid., 18 November 1915, p. 67.
26 ibid.
27 Captain Bean, 'Australians at Anzac. Message from the King', *Gippsland Mercury*, 17 December 1915, p. 4.
28 Charles Bean – Editor, *The Anzac Book*, (first published by Cassell, London, 1916); Australian War Memorial and UNSW Press edition, 2010.
29 Bean, diary, op. cit., 29 November 1915, AWM38 3DRL606/21/1, p. 12.
30 ibid., 16 December 1915, AWM38 3DRL606/22/1, p. 8.
31 ibid., 26 December 1915, AWM38 3DRL606/24/1, p. 31.
32 Charles Bean, 'Anzac Evacuation. How it was accomplished. Rearguard of "Die-Hards".' Melbourne *Argus*, 17 January 1916, p. 10.
33 C.E.W. Bean, *Official History of Australia in the War of 1914–1918*, Australian War Memorial, Canberra, 1941, vol. 2, op. cit., p. 908.
34 ibid., p. 909.
35 Charles Bean, *Anzac to Amiens: A shorter history of the Australian fighting services in the Great War*, Australian War Memorial, Canberra, 1946, p. 181.

Chapter Nine

1 Charles Bean, diary, 16 January 1915, AWM38 3DRL606/36/1, Australian War Memorial, Canberra, p. 27.
2 Bean, diary, 31 January 1915, AWM38 3DRL606/37/1, p. 35.
3 ibid., pp. 39–40.
4 ibid., 20 January 1915, AWM38 3DRL606/36/1, p. 37.
5 Charles Bean, 'Captain Bean visit to the Western Front. The great struggle', *The Mercury* (Hobart), 24 January 1916, p. 5.

6 MacGregor Knox, *To the Threshold of Power, 1922/33: Origins and dynamics of the fascist and national socialist dictatorships*, Cambridge University Press, Cambridge, 2007, p. 153.
7 Bean, diary, op. cit., 31 January 1916, AWM38 3DRL606/36/1, p. 59.
8 ibid., pp. 59–60.
9 ibid., p. 64.
10 ibid., p. 68 (Bean's emphasis).
11 C.E.W. Bean, *Official History of Australia in the War of 1914–1918*, [hereafter *Official History*] Australian War Memorial, Canberra, 1941, vol. 3 'The Australian Imperial Force in France 1916', 12th edition 1941, p. 6.
12 ibid., p. 6, footnote 12.
13 Bean, diary, op. cit., 6 January 1916, AWM38 3DRL606/37/1, pp. 63–4.
14 *Official History*, op. cit., p. 21.
15 Bean, diary, op. cit., dated February to March 1916, AWM38 3DRL606/40/1, pp. 16–17.
16 ibid., 17 February 1916, AWM38 3DRL606/37/1, p. 82.
17 ibid., dated February to March 1916, AWM38 3DRL606/40/1, p. 13.
18 ibid., 2 April 1915, AWM38 3DRL606/41/1, pp. 71–2.
19 ibid., p. 75.
20 Bethune order, 'Captain Frank Bethune MC. Fight To The Death', accessed online, 14 June 2014, http://www.anzacday.org.au/justsoldiers/bethune.pdf.
21 Bean, diary, op. cit., p. 76.
22 ibid., 8 April 1916, AWM38 3DRL606/42/1, p. 20.
23 ibid., pp. 38–9.
24 ibid., 11 April 1916, pp. 48–9.
25 ibid., 17 May 1916, AWM38 3DRL606/44/1, p. 17.
26 ibid., 1 June 1916, p. 67. (Bean's emphasis).
27 ibid., 13 May 1916, pp. 14–15.
28 ibid., 1 June 1916, p. 48.
29 ibid., 24 May 1916, p. 30.
30 ibid., p. 32.
31 ibid., 1 June 1916, p. 44.
32 ibid., pp. 70–1.
33 ibid., 3 June 1916, AWM38 3DRL606/45/1, pp. 15–16.

34 Appendage to Bean diary, ibid., 12 June 1916, at p. 100, 'Notes on raid made by 6th Batt AIF on night of Monday June 12th 1916'.
35 *Official History*, vol. 3, op. cit., p. 248, footnote 10.
36 ibid.
37 Charles Bean, 'In the limelight', undated newspaper clipping appended to Bean, diary, op. cit., p. 103a.
38 Bean, diary, op. cit., p. 109.
39 ibid., 16 June 1916, AWM38 3DRL606/47/1, p. 4.
40 ibid., 24 June 1916, p. 60.
41 ibid., 28 June 1916, p. 88–9.
42 ibid., 30 June 1916, AWM38 3DRL606/48/1, p. 36.
43 ibid., p. 57.

Chapter Ten

1 Charles Bean, diary, 1 July 1916, AWM38 3DRL606/48/1, Australian War Memorial, Canberra, p. 48.
2 Major Walter Vignoles, 10th Battalion, Lincolnshire Regiment, as quoted in Peter Hart, *The Somme*, Pegasus Books, New York, 2010, p. 111.
3 Bean, diary, op. cit., 3 July 1916, AWM38 3DRL606/49/1, p. 22.
4 ibid., 17 July 1916, p. 61.
5 ibid.
6 Haig message to Gen Monro, *Official History*, vol. 3, op. cit., p. 349.
7 Bean comment, *Official History*, vol. 3, op. cit., p. 350.
8 *Official History*, vol. 3, op. cit., p. 349.
9 Letter from Pompey Elliott to Charles Bean, 17 August 1926, AWM38 3DRL606/Folder243a, Australian War Memorial, Canberra.
10 Cited in Carlyon, op. cit., p. 61.
11 *Official History*, vol. 3, op. cit., p. 394.
12 Bean, diary, op. cit., 20 July 1916, AWM38 3DRL606/52/1, p. 10.
13 ibid., p. 11.
14 ibid., p. 17.
15 ibid.
16 ibid., p. 20.
17 Charles Bean, 'Australians Attack Trenches Temporary Success. Take Two Hundred Prisoners', *The Sydney Morning Herald*, 24 July 1916, p. 9.

18 *Official History*, op. cit., p. 446.
19 'In the thick of it. Australians in attack. Bayoneting the Bavarians. Germans demoralised', *The Bathurst Times*, 24 July 1916, p. 2 (no by-line).
20 *German communiqué*, 24 July 1916, *The Argus*, p. 7.
21 *Official History*, op. cit.
22 Cited in Harro Grabolle, *Verdun and the Somme*, Akademiai Kiado, Budapest, 2004, p. 114.
23 'British offensive, several villages captured, over 5000 prisoners', *The Sydney Morning Herald*, 3 July 1916, p. 9 (no by-line).
24 Bean, diary, op. cit., pp. 22–3.
25 ibid., p. 25.
26 ibid., p. 25–6. Bean's emphasis.
27 ibid.
28 Ross McMullin, *Pompey Elliott*, Scribe Publications, Melbourne, 2002, pp. 207–8.
29 ibid.
30 ibid.
31 *Official History*, op. cit., p. 446.
32 Letter from former Sergeant W. (Aussie) Miles to Charles Bean, 30 July 1929, AWM38 3DRL606/243a/1, Australian War Memorial, Canberra.
33 Letter from Charles Bean to Cyril Brudenell White, 27 May 1926, Folder AWM38 3DRL606/243a/1, Australian War Memorial, Canberra.
34 Letter from Cyril Brudenell White to Charles Bean, 1 June 1926, Folder AWM38 3DRL606/243a/1, Australian War Memorial, Canberra.
35 ibid.
36 *Official History*, op. cit., p. 346.
37 McMullin, ibid., p. 306.
38 Bean never mentions the 'bloody holocaust' quote but does acknowledge Elliott's and Howard's reservations during their no-man's-land visit at footnote 139, *Official History*, op. cit., p. 443.
39 *Official History*, op. cit., p. 444.
40 Cited in Carlyon, op. cit., p. 96.

Chapter Eleven

1 C.E.W. Bean, *Official History of Australia in the War of 1914–1918*, [hereafter *Official History*] Australian War Memorial, Canberra, vol. 3, op. cit., p. 451.

2 Ross Coulthart, *The Lost Diggers*, HarperCollins, Sydney, 2012.
3 Charles Bean, diary, 22 July 1916, AWM38 3DRL606/52/1, Australian War Memorial, Canberra, p. 41.
4 Bean, diary, 25–26 July 1916, AWM38 3DRL606/53/1, Australian War Memorial, Canberra, pp. 37–8.
5 *Official History*, op. cit., p. 869.
6 Charles Bean, 'The Australians. Battlefield pictures', *The Sydney Morning Herald*, 28 July 1916, p. 7.
7 Philip Gibbs, *Now it Can be Told*, 1920. First published by Harper & Brothers, New York, accessed online as Project Gutenberg Ebook, 15 June 2014, http://www.gutenberg.org/ebooks/3317, chapter 18, p. 842.
8 Bean, diary, op. cit., 31 July 1916, AWM38 3DRL606/54//1, p. 40.
9 ibid., p. 44.
10 ibid., p. 46.
11 ibid., p. 47.
12 ibid., 1 August 1916, p. 48.
13 Transcript of letter from Lieutenant J.A. Raws to Norman Bayles, MLA, 4 August 1916, Bean folder 1916–33, AWM38 3DRL606/244/1, Australian War Memorial, Canberra, p. 22.
14 Transcript of letter from Lieutenant J.A. Raws to his brother William Lennon Raws & family, 12 August 1916, Bean folder, ibid., p. 24.
15 Transcript of letter from Lieutenant J.A. Raws to his brother William Lennon Raws & family, 19 August 1916, Bean folder, ibid., p. 34.
16 Letter from Charles Bean to Captain L.G. Short, MC, 21 March 1928, Bean folder, ibid.
17 Letter from Cyril Brudenell White to Bean, 19 September 1927, cited in Denis Winter, *Making the Legend: The war writings of C.E.W. Bean*, University of Queensland Press, St Lucia, Qld, 1992, p. 157.
18 *Official History*, op. cit., p. 657.
19 ibid., p. 658.
20 ibid., p. 871–2.
21 ibid., p. 872.
22 Bean, diary, op. cit., 4 August 1916, p. 118.
23 *Official History*, op. cit., p. 619.

24 ibid., p. 877, footnote 32, which reads: 'This accords with General White's own judgment, placed on record by him after the war.' Bean's undated notes of his conversation with White are at Bean folder 1916–33, op. cit.
25 'Australia's New War Chief. Pages Of History Turned Back', *The Mercury*, Hobart, 26 May 1940, p. 3(no by-line).
26 *Official History*, op. cit., p. 877.
27 Bean, diary, op. cit., p. 110.
28 Charles Bean, 'Captain Littler – Mouquet Farm incident', *The North Western Advocate and the Emu Bay Times* (Tasmania), 13 October 1917, p. 2.
29 Bean, diary, op. cit., 9/10 August 1916, p. 168.
30 ibid., p. 195.
31 ibid., p. 197.
32 Bean later implies it was Lloyd George in Bean, diary, 29/30 August 1916, AWM38 3DRL606/57/1, p. 19.
33 Bean, diary, op. cit., 20 August 1916, AWM38 3DRL606/55/1, p. 83.
34 ibid., 17 August 1916, p. 32.
35 ibid., p. 37.
36 Cited in Winter, op. cit., p. 10.
37 Bean, diary, op. cit., 20 August 1916, p. 109.
38 ibid., p. 115.
39 ibid., 22 August 1916, p. 138.
40 ibid., 24 August 1916, AWM38 3DRL606/56/1, pp. 30–1.
41 ibid., p. 28.
42 ibid., p. 37.
43 ibid., p. 52.
44 Note appended to the end of Bean diary, op. cit., undated, AWM38 3DRL606/55/1.
45 Bean, diary, ibid., 24 August 1916, AWM38 3DRL606/56/1, p. 34.
46 Scott Bennett, Pozières: *The Anzac story*, Scribe, Carlton North, Victoria, 2011, p. 271.
47 *Official History*, vol. 3, op. cit., pp. 723–4.
48 ibid., p. 872.
49 ibid., p. 873
50 Bean, diary, op. cit., 5 September 1916, AWM38 3DRL606/58/1, p. 40.
51 Letter from Charles Bean to his parents, 21 June 1917, cited in Winter, op. cit., p. 11.

52 C.E.W. Bean, *Anzac to Amiens: A shorter history of the Australian fighting services in the Great War*, Australian War Memorial, Canberra, 1946, p. 264.

Chapter Twelve

1 Charles Bean, diary, 8 September 1916, AWM38 3DRL606/59/1, Australian War Memorial, Canberra, p. 11.
2 ibid., p. 12.
3 C.E.W. Bean, *Official History of Australia in the War of 1914–1918*, [hereafter *Official History*] Australian War Memorial, Canberra, vol. 3, op. cit., p. 868.
4 C.E.W. Bean, *Two Men I Knew: William Bridges and Brudenell White, founders of the AIF*, Angus & Robertson, 1957, Sydney, p. 144.
5 Bean, diary, 11 September 1916, op. cit., p. 19.
6 ibid., p. 24.
7 ibid., p. 26.
8 ibid., 24 September 1916, AWM38 3DRL606/60/1, p. 2.
9 ibid., p. 2. Bean reports the 'Butcher' story and describes it as a 'wild story' and as 'a lie' but comments in his diary that it is 'an indication of a certain feeling at the moment'.
10 ibid., p. 5.
11 ibid., pp. 7–8.
12 'Stand by Anzacs. Magnificent achievement. Success Crowns Effort. Fight with Knives and Revolvers', *The Argus*, 9 August 1916, p. 9, appended in Bean, diary, ibid., p. 16.
13 Bean, diary, ibid., undated, p. 16.
14 ibid., p. 73.
15 ibid., p. 35.
16 ibid., p. 33.
17 ibid., pp. 39–40.
18 ibid., p. 58.
19 ibid., 12 October 1916, p. 130.
20 ibid., p. 131.
21 ibid., 15 October 1916, AWM 38 3DRL606/61/1, p. 15.
22 ibid., p. 16.
23 ibid., p. 24.
24 ibid., p. 27 (Bean's emphasis).
25 Les Carlyon, *The Great War*, Picador Pan McMillan, Sydney, 2006, p. 259.

26 'One Clear Call', *The Sydney Morning Herald*, 25 October 1916, (no by-line), p. 10.
27 Carlyon, op. cit., p. 261.
28 Bean, diary, op. cit., 19 October 1916, p. 61.
29 ibid., 22 October 1916, AWM38 3DRL606/62/1, p. 17.
30 ibid., 25 October 1916, AWM38 3DRL606/63/1, p. 5.
31 ibid., pp. 8–9.
32 Cited in a thesis by Stephen Ellis, 'C.E.W. Bean: A study of his life and works', University of New England, 1969, p. 80.
33 Bean, diary, op. cit., 1 November 1916, AWM38 3DRL606/63/1, p. 74.
34 *Official History*, vol. 3, op. cit., p. 919.
35 ibid., p. 940.
36 ibid., p. 943.

Chapter Thirteen

1 Charles Bean, diary, 17 November 1916, AWM38 3DRL606/66/1, Australian War Memorial, Canberra, p. 48.
2 ibid., 17 December 1916, AWM38 3DRL606/68/1, p. 43.
3 ibid., 28 November 1916, AWM38 3DRL606/67/1, p. 54.
4 ibid., 27 November 1916, p. 5.
5 ibid., 16 December 1916, AWM38 3DRL606/68/1, pp. 18–19.
6 Ross McMullin, *Will Dyson: Cartoonist, etcher and Australia's finest war artist*, 1984, Angus & Robertson, Sydney, p. 150.
7 Bean, diary, op. cit., 3 December 1916, AWM38 3DRL606/67/1, p. 73.
8 ibid., 28 November 1916, p. 29.
9 ibid., 24 December 1916, AWM38 3DRL606/68/1, p. 56.
10 ibid., pp. 57–58.
11 ibid., pp. 59–60.
12 C.E.W. Bean, *Letters from France*, Cassell, London, 1917, p. 38, accessed via www.gutenberg.org.
13 ibid., p. 30.
14 Bean, diary, op. cit., 17 January 1916, AWM38 3DRL606/69/1, p. 41.
15 ibid., pp. 42–3 (Bean's emphasis).
16 Bean article in *The Sydney Morning Herald*, 26 January 1916, cited in Dudley McCarthy, *Gallipoli to the Somme*, Leo Cooper Secker & Warburg, London, 1983.

17 Neville Meaney, *Australia and World Crisis 1914–1923*, Sydney University Press, Sydney, 2009, pp. 186–9.
18 Charles Bean, 'Party quarrels. Opinion among the Anzacs. Need for unity', *Maitland Daily Mercury*, 26 February 1917, p. 6.
19 'Proposed National Government Treated With Contempt', *Daily Herald* (Adelaide), 3 February 1917, p. 5 (no by-line).
20 Bean, diary, op. cit., 14 May 1917, AWM38 3DRL606/78/1, p. 48.
21 'Plain English', *The Bulletin*, 15 March 1917 (no by-line).
22 Bean, diary, op. cit., 4 March 1917, AWM38 3DRL606/73/1, pp. 9–10.
23 ibid., 17–19 March 1917, AWM38 3DRL606/74/1, p. 2.
24 Arthur Bazley, diary, 26 March 1917, AWM 2DRL 215, Australian War Memorial, Canberra.
25 Bean, diary, op. cit., 9 April 1917, AWM38 3DRL606/75/1, p. 11.
26 ibid.
27 ibid., 11 April 1917, pp. 114, 116.
28 ibid., p. 116.
29 Charles Bean, 'The Hindenburg Line. Australian division's grand attack', *The Register* (South Australia), 16 June 1917 (by-lined as written 11 April), p. 8.
30 Joan Beaumont, *Broken Nation: Australians in the Great War*, Allen & Unwin, Sydney, 2013, pp. 290–1. 'Icy contemptuous anger' attributed to General Gough's biographer Anthony Farrar-Hockley, *Goughie: The life of General Sir Hubert Gough*, Hart-Davis, MacGibbon, London, 1975, p. 206.
31 Charles Bean, 'Australians in France. The Hindenburg Line. Splendid infantry. Assault without guns', *The Advertiser*, 25 June 1917, p. 6.
32 'The First Battle of Bullecourt', *The Sunday Times*, 1 July 1917, p. 8 (no by-line).
33 C.E.W. Bean, *Official History of Australia in the War of 1914–1918*, [hereafter *Official History*] Australian War Memorial, Canberra, vol. 4, 'The Australian Imperial Force in France 1917', 11th edition 1941, p. 435.
34 Charles Bean, 'Bullecourt. The second battle. Bravo Australia!', *The World's News* (Sydney), 7 July 1917 (sent 6 May), p. 17.
35 Bean, diary, op. cit., 6 May 1917, AWM38 3DRL606/78/1, p. 7–8.
36 ibid., p. 17.

37 ibid., p. 19–20.
38 ibid., p. 20.
39 ibid., May–June 1918, AWM38 3DRL606/113/1, pp. 23–5.
40 ibid., pp. 22–3.
41 *Official History*, vol. 4, op. cit., p. 544.
42 Bean, diary, op. cit., 15 May 1917, AWM38 3DRL606/78/1, p. 55.

Chapter Fourteen

1 Charles Bean, diary, 6 June 1917, AWM38 3DRL606/81/1, Australian War Memorial, Canberra, p. 11.
2 ibid., 2 June 1917, AWM38 3DRL606/80/1, p. 43.
3 Charles Bean, 'Lieutenant Phillip Schuler', 13 September 1917, *Bendigonian*, p. 10.
4 Charles Bean, 'Messines Ridge. The great attack. Exactly as it appeared', *The Morning Bulletin* (Rockhampton), 21 August 1917, pp. 7–8.
5 Geoffrey Serle, *John Monash: A biography*, Melbourne University Press, Carlton, Victoria, 1982, p. 292.
6 Bean, diary, op. cit., 15 June 1917, pp. 62, 66–7.
7 C.E.W. Bean, *Official History of Australia in the War of 1914–1918*, [hereafter *Official History*] Australian War Memorial, Canberra, vol. 4, op. cit., pp. 656–7.
8 ibid., footnote 50, p. 657.
9 Letter from Charles Bean to Gavin Long, 30 June 1930, as cited in Denis Winter, *Making the Legend: The war writings of C.E.W. Bean*, University of Queensland Press, St Lucia, Queensland, 1992, p. 213.
10 Bean, diary, op. cit., 17 June 1917, pp. 83–4.
11 ibid., p. 87.
12 ibid., 4 August 1917, AWM38 3DRL606/84/1, p. 42.
13 John Masefield, *Gallipoli*, S.B. Gundy, Toronto, 1916, p. 84.
14 ibid., p. 112.
15 Bean, diary, op. cit., 18 July 1917, AWM38 3DRL606/82/1, p. 30.
16 ibid., p. 29.
17 ibid., p. 9.
18 Letter from Charles Bean to Lloyd George, 15 July 1917, appended inside Bean, diary, ibid., p. 1.
19 Bean, diary, ibid., 18 July 1917, p. 16.
20 ibid., 30 July 1917, AWM38 3DRL606/83/1, pp. 1, 9.

21 ibid., 3 August 1917, AWM38 3DRL606/84/1, pp. 14–15.
22 ibid., 31 July 1917, AWM38 3DRL606/83/1, p. 40.
23 ibid., p. 56.
24 ibid., p. 58.
25 ibid., 4 August 1917, AWM38 3DRL606/84/1, p. 18.
26 ibid., 15 August 1917, AWM38 3DRL606/86/1, pp. 44–5.
27 ibid., 14 August 1917, AWM38 3DRL606/86/1, p. 42.
28 ibid., 16 August 1917, p. 52.
29 ibid., 23 August 1917, AWM38 3DRL606/87/1, p. 58.
30 ibid., 7 September 1917, AWM38 3DRL606/88/1, p. 39.
31 ibid., p. 40.
32 ibid., 25 August 1917, AWM38 3DRL606/87/1, pp. 62–3.
33 Alasdair McGregor, *Frank Hurley: A photographer's life*, Penguin, Hawthorn, 2004, p. 161.
34 Bean, diary, op. cit., 20 August 1917, AWM38 3DRL606/86/1, p. 74.
35 ibid., 3 September, AWM38 3DRL606/88/1, p. 34.
36 ibid.
37 *Official History*, op. cit., vol. 4, p. 732.

Chapter Fifteen

1 Charles Bean, diary, 18 September 1917, AWM38 3DRL606/88/1, Australian War Memorial, Canberra, p. 51.
2 ibid., 19 September 1917, p. 55.
3 ibid., 20 September 1917, p. 68.
4 ibid., 22 September 1917, p. 92.
5 ibid., 4 October 1917, AWM38 3DRL606/89/1, pp. 18–19.
6 ibid., p. 16.
7 ibid., 10 October 1917, pp. 38–9.
8 Charles Bean, 'Haig's success. All gains held. Great artillery duel', *The Argus* (Melbourne), 8 October 1917, p. 7.
9 Bean, diary, op. cit., pp. 29–30.
10 ibid., pp. 30–2.
11 ibid., 12 October 1917, p. 49.
12 ibid., p. 53.
13 ibid., p. 60.
14 ibid., p. 83.
15 ibid., p. 85.
16 ibid., p. 100.
17 ibid., p. 102.
18 ibid., 11 October 1917, AWM38 3DRL606/90/1, p. 6.

19 ibid., pp. 7–8.
20 ibid., pp. 12–13 Bean's emphasis.
21 ibid., 14 October 1917, p. 30.
22 ibid., p. 53.
23 ibid., pp. 62–3.
24 Charles Bean, 'Germans fighting for existence', *The West Australian*, 20 October 1917, p. 7.
25 Charles Bean, 'The Anzacs' difficulties. Fighting the winter', *The West Australian*, 16 October 1917, p. 5.
26 C.E.W. Bean, *Official History of Australia in the War of 1914–1918*, [hereafter *Official History*] Australian War Memorial, Canberra, vol. 4, op. cit., pp. 943–4.
27 ibid., p. 908.
28 Bean, diary, op. cit., 15 October 1917, p. 98.
29 ibid., 18 October 1917, AWM38 3DRL606/91/1, p. 25.
30 ibid., p. 44.
31 ibid., 19 October 1917, p. 65.
32 ibid., p. 66.
33 ibid., 2 November 1917, AWM38 3DRL606/92/1, p. 38.
34 ibid., 16 November 1917, AWM38 3DRL606/94/1, p. 14.
35 ibid., 11 November 1917, AWM38 3DRL606/93/1, p. 34.
36 ibid., 27 November 1917, AWM38 3DRL606/94/1, p. 43.
37 ibid., p. 45.
38 ibid., 15 November 1917, p. 7.
39 ibid., 22 November 1917, p. 36.
40 ibid., 1 December 1917, p. 51.
41 ibid., 3 December 1917, p. 57.
42 ibid., 23 December 1917, AWM38 3DRL606/95/1, p. 29.
43 ibid., 3 December 1917, AWM38 3DRL606/94/1, pp. 56–7.
44 ibid., 12 December 1917, AWM38 3DRL606/95/1, p. 4.
45 Ernest Scott, *Official History*, op. cit., vol. 11, 'Australia during the war', 7th edition, 1941, p. 424.
46 Bean, diary, op. cit., 22 December, p. 27.
47 ibid., 30 December 1917, p. 51.
48 ibid., 16 December 1917, p. 11.
49 ibid., 31 December 1917, p. 52.
50 ibid., 11 January 1918, p. 57.

Chapter Sixteen

1 Charles Bean, diary, 13 January 1918, AWM38 3DRL606/96/1, Australian War Memorial, Canberra, p. 19.

2 ibid., 13 January 1918, AWM38 3DRL606/96/1, p. 2
3 Letter from Tom Griffiths to Charles Bean, 1 January 1918, appended inside Bean, diary, ibid., AWM38 3DRL606/95/1, p. 47.
4 Bean, diary, ibid. 1 January 1918, p. 48. (on reverse page)
5 ibid., 13 January 1918, AWM38 3DRL606/96/1, p. 11.
6 ibid., 5 February 1918, AWM38 3DRL606/98/1, pp. 6–7 Bean's emphasis.
7 ibid., 11 February 1918, pp. 31–2.
8 ibid., p. 33.
9 ibid., 12 February 1918, AWM38 3DRL606/99/1, pp. 7, 8.
10 ibid., 16 February 1918, AWM38 3DRL606/100/1, p. 30.
11 ibid., p. 32.
12 ibid., p. 36.
13 ibid., pp. 40–2.
14 ibid., 24 February 1918, AWM38 3DRL606/101/1, p. 37.
15 ibid.
16 Capt. Treloar was promoted to Major in late 1918.
17 ibid., 26 February 1918, p. 44 Bean's emphasis.
18 ibid., p. 45.
19 ibid., 21 March 1918, AWM38 3DRL606/102/1, p. 15.
20 ibid., p. 17.
21 ibid., 24 March 1918, p. 42.
22 ibid., 27 March 1918, AWM38 3DRL606/103/1, p. 17.
23 ibid., 1 April 1918, AWM38 3DRL606/104/1, p. 64.
24 C.E.W. Bean, *Official History of Australia in the War of 1914–1918*, Australian War Memorial, Canberra, vol. 5, 'The Australian Imperial Force in France during the main German offensive 1918', 8th edition 1941, p. 236.
25 ibid., p. 237.
26 ibid., pp. 460–1.
27 Bean, diary, op. cit., 4 April 1918, AWM38 3DRL606/105/1, p. 26.
28 ibid., p. 33.
29 ibid., 5 April 1918, p. 58.
30 ibid., p. 61.
31 ibid., 12 April 1918, AWM38 3DRL606/106/1, pp. 46–47.
32 ibid., 8 April 1918, pp. 24–5.
33 ibid., 10 April 1918, pp. 34–5.
34 ibid., p. 36.
35 ibid., 12 April 1918, p. 42.

36 ibid., pp. 49–50.
37 Field Marshall Sir Douglas Haig, 'Special order of the day', Tuesday, 11 April 1918, accessed online, 19 June 2014 at FirstWorldWar.com, a multimedia history of World War One: http://www.firstworldwar.com/source/backstothewall.htm.

Chapter Seventeen

1 C.E.W. Bean, *Official History of Australia in the War of 1914–1918*, [hereafter *Official History*] Australian War Memorial, Canberra, vol. 5, op. cit., p. 540.
2 ibid.
3 ibid., p. 549.
4 ibid., p. 550.
5 Charles Bean, diary, 27 April 1918, AWM38 3DRL606/108/1, p. 64.
6 *Official History*, vol. 5, op. cit., p. 591.
7 ibid., p. 580.
8 ibid., pp. 194–5.
9 Cited in Denis Winter, *Making the Legend: The war writings of C.E.W. Bean*, University of Queensland Press, St Lucia, Queensland, 1992, p. 199.
10 Bean, diary, 4 May 1918, AWM38 3DRL606/109/1, p. 29.
11 ibid., 17 May 1918, AWM38 3DRL606/111/1, p. 20 (Bean's emphasis to Dyson's words).
12 ibid., 8 May 1918, AWM38 3DRL606/109/1, p. 42.
13 ibid., pp. 85–6.
14 ibid., 17 May 1918, AWM38 3DRL606/111/1, p. 22.
15 ibid., note appended to Bean diary, 'Changes in AIF command, confidential notes', p. 27.
16 ibid., 20 May 1918, p. 32. 'Murdoch pointed out the difficulty wh[ich] I found later had struck everyone else … Birdwood, no doubt Griffiths, White, all said the same: if the GOC-ship of the AIF is divorced from the Corps McCay will get it.'
17 Bean, diary, ibid., 5–7 June 1918, AWM38 3DRL606/114/1, p. 1.
18 Cited in Bean diary, ibid., 1 June 1918, AWM38 3DRL606/113/1, p. 49.
19 Geoffrey Serle, *John Monash: A biography*, Melbourne University Press, Carlton, Victoria, 1982, pp. 322–8.
20 ibid., p. 325.

21 Bean, diary, ibid., 11 June 1918, AWM38 3DRL606/114/1, p. 89.
22 ibid.,.
23 Cited in Serle, op. cit., p. 324.
24 ibid., p. 326.
25 Bean, diary, op. cit., 16 June 1918, AWM38 3DRL606/115/1, pp. 20–1.
26 Charles Bean, 'Historical note: Birdwood and command of AIF', undated, folder at AWM38 3DRL606/262/1, Australian War Memorial, Canberra, final page.
27 Serle, op. cit., p. 323.
28 Bean, diary, op. cit., 2 July 1918, AWM38 3DRL606/116/1, p. 12.
29 ibid.

Chapter Eighteen

1 Charles Bean, diary, 10 July 1918, AWM38 3DRL606/116/1, Australian War Memorial, Canberra, p. 24.
2 ibid., 14 July 1918, p. 26.
3 ibid., 19 July 1918, p. 27A.
4 ibid., 21 July 1918, p. 29.
5 Lieutenant Sidney Henry Russell MM, 9th Batt AIF, KIA 20 July 1918. Also detailed by C.E.W. Bean in *Official History*, op. cit., vol. 6, 'The AIF Offensive in France 1918', first edition, 1942, p. 423.
6 Bean, diary, op. cit., 27 July 1918, p. 34.
7 ibid., 8 August 1918, p. 54.
8 ibid., p. 59.
9 ibid., 11 August 1918, p. 74.
10 *Official History*, vol. 6, op. cit., p. 614.
11 ibid., p. 78.
12 ibid., 12 August 1918, p. 79.
13 ibid., 17 August 1918, p. 82
14 ibid., 18 August 1918, p. 83.
15 John F. Williams, *Anzacs, the Media and the Great War*, UNSW Press, Sydney, 1999, p. 229.
16 Bean, diary, op. cit., 1 September 1918, p. 112.
17 ibid., 2 September 1918, p. 115.
18 ibid., 6 September 1918, p. 119.
19 Charles Bean, 'Our own men. The latest battle. A reminder of Gallipoli', *Daily Herald* (Adelaide), 7 September 1918, p. 5.

20 Charles Bean, *Anzac to Amiens: A shorter history of the Australian fighting services in the Great War*, Australian War Memorial, Canberra, 1946, pp. 478–82.
21 Bean, diary, op. cit., 7 September 1918, p. 120.

Chapter Nineteen

1 Charles Bean, diary, 18 September 1918, AWM38 3DRL606/116/1, Australian War Memorial, Canberra, p. 126.
2 ibid., p. 135.
3 ibid., 22 September, p. 138.
4 ibid., 27 September 1918, AWM38 3DRL606/117/1, p. 5.
5 ibid., 28 September 1918, p. 5.
6 ibid., 30 September 1918, p. 13.
7 C.E.W. Bean, *Official History of Australia in the War of 1914–1918*, [hereafter *Official History*] Australian War Memorial, Canberra, vol. 6, op. cit., p. 993.
8 ibid., p. 994.
9 ibid., p. 995.
10 Bean, diary, op. cit., 1 October 1918, p. 18.
11 ibid.
12 *Official History*, op. cit., p. 1036.
13 ibid., p. 1043.
14 ibid.
15 Letter from Charles Bean to his parents, 7 October 1918, cited in Denis Winter, *Making the Legend: The war writings of C.E.W. Bean*, University of Queensland Press, St Lucia, Queensland, 1992, p. 227.
16 Bean, diary, op. cit., 23 October 1918, p. 60.
17 Charles Bean, *In Your Hands, Australians*, Cassell & Co. Ltd, London, 1919, p. 7.
18 Bean, diary, op. cit., 29 October 1918, p. 63.
19 ibid.
20 Bean, *In Your Hands, Australians*, op. cit., pp. 9–10.
21 Bean, diary, op. cit., 11 November 1918, p. 74.
22 ibid., p. 76.
23 ibid., 12 November 1918, p. 80.
24 Letter from Edwin Bean to Charles Bean, 14 November 1918, AWM38 3DRL7447 items 11–16, Australian War Memorial, Canberra.

Chapter Twenty

1 Ken Inglis (assisted by Jan Brazier), *Sacred Places: War memorials in the Australian landscape*, Melbourne University Press, Carlton, Victoria, 2008.
2 Compton Mackenzie, *Gallipoli Memories*, Cassell, London, 1929, pp. 80–2.
3 Charles Bean, *Gallipoli Mission*, Australian War Memorial, Canberra, 1948, p. 390.
4 Inglis, op. cit., p. 79.
5 Charles Bean, 'Our war history', *The Bulletin*, 27 May 1942, p. 2.
6 Bean, *Gallipoli Mission*, op. cit., pp. 68–9.
7 ibid., p. 68.
8 'War correspondent entertained. Some reminiscences of France', *The Sydney Morning Herald*, 11 July 1919, p. 9 (no by-line).
9 ibid.
10 Charles Bean, 'Address for Commonwealth Peace Celebrations Committee', *The Sydney Morning Herald*, 19 July 1919, p. 11.
11 Charles Bean, speech to the Royal Australian Historical Society, 22 February 1938, reproduced in *Journal of the Royal Australian Historical Society*, vol. 24, part II, pp. 86–112.
12 ibid., p. 89.
13 ibid., p. 91.
14 Sir James Edmonds, 'Experience gained in compiling the official military histories of 1914–1918', part 3, p. 9, Miscellaneous Papers – Edmonds VII/11, Liddell Hart Centre for Military Archives, King's College London.
15 ibid., p. 2.
16 ibid., p. 9.
17 C.E.W. Bean, *Official History of Australia in the War of 1914–1918*, [hereafter *Official History*] Australian War Memorial, Canberra, vol. 3, op. cit., pp. 945–6.
18 Letter from Charles Bean to Sir James Edmonds, 28 August 1928, Miscellaneous Papers – Edmonds VI/2, op. cit.
19 Les Carlyon, *The Great War*, Picador Pan McMillan, Sydney, 2006, p. 353.
20 Eric Andrews, *The Anzac Illusion*, Cambridge University Press, Melbourne, 1993, p. 101.
21 Letters from John Edmonds to Charles Bean, 7 February and 8 August 1928, Bean papers, AWM 3DRL7953/34, Australian War Memorial, Canberra.

22 Andrews, op. cit., p. 147.
23 Letter from Charles Bean to Borthwick, 18 January 1920, AWM 3DRL 7447/24 to 25 part 1, Australian War Memorial, Canberra.
24 Jack Bean, 'The Entente ideal', pamphlet from The Entente Club, written for the *Australian Trained Nurses' Association Gazette*, December 1919, Dame Mary Gilmore Collection, Mitchell Library, New South Wales State Library, Sydney.
25 Letter from Charles Bean to Effie Young, October 1920, AWM PR00283, series 2, wallet 1, Australian War Memorial, Canberra.
26 Letter from Monty Bean to Edwin Bean, 5 February 1906, ibid.
27 Letter from Edwin Bean to Effie Young, 8 November 1920, ibid.
28 Letter from Charles Bean to Effie Young, 16 November 1920, ibid.
29 Letter from Charles Bean to Agnes Young, November 1920, ibid.
30 Letter from Monty Bean to Charles Bean, 8 January 1921, AWM 3DRL 7447/ 24 to 25, part 1, Australian War Memorial, Canberra.
31 C.E.W. Bean, 'Edwin Bean. Great Headmaster', *Sunday Times* (Sydney), 3 September 1922, p. 13.
32 Lucy Bean, diary, 'Charlie Bean', courtesy of Bean's family.
33 Charles Bean, travel diary 1, 1924, AWM PR00283, series 1, wallet 1, Australian War Memorial, Canberra.
34 ibid.
35 Charles Bean, travel diary 2, 1924, ibid.
36 Charles Bean, 'Account for Effie', written on the reverse-side pages of Bean's 'Diary 2 – Our trip to England', 1924, AWM PR00283, series 1/2, Australian War Memorial., Canberra.
37 Charles Bean in Lucy Bean diary, op. cit., p. 22.
38 Interview with Phyllis Bauer by the author, 2014.
39 Michael McKernan, *Here is their Spirit: A history of the Australian War Memorial*, University of Queensland Press in association with the Australian War Memorial, St Lucia, Queensland, 1991, p. 10.
40 'Dr C.E.W. Bean. Entertained by Returned Soldiers. Value of War History', *The Sydney Morning Herald*, 4 February 1931, p. 12 (no by-line).

41 Charles Bean, 'Parks and playgrounds: Why their importance is growing', undated, p. 3, State Library of New South Wales, Sydney.
42 Unpublished thesis by Stephen Ellis, 'C.E.W. Bean: A study of his life and works', University of New England, 1969, p. 144.

Chapter Twenty-one

1 Charles Bean, Letter to the Editor, (untitled), *The Sydney Morning Herald*, 11 April 1936, p. 6.
2 Charles Bean Letter to the Editor, 'German Jews in the War', *The Sydney Morning Herald*, 21 April 1933, p. 8.
3 Charles Bean in Lucy Bean diary, 'Charlie Bean', courtesy of Bean family.
4 Charles Bean Letter to the Editor, 'The German Colonies', *The Sydney Morning Herald*, 7 April 1936, p. 9.
5 Stephen Ellis, 'C.E.W. Bean: A Study of his life and works', University of New England (unpublished thesis), p. 114.
6 Charles Bean, Letter to the Editor, 'Recantation. Germany's Bad Faith. End of Appeasement', *The Sydney Morning Herald*, 21 March 1939, p. 10.
7 Charles Bean in Lucy Bean diary, op. cit., p. 34.
8 C.E.W. Bean, *War Aims of a Plain Australian*, Angus & Robertson, Sydney, 1943, pp. 32–3.
9 C.E.W. Bean, *Two Men I Knew: William Bridges and Brudenell White, founders of the AIF*, Angus & Robertson, 1957, Sydney, p. 222.
10 Staff correspondent, 'First A.I.F. "Most Democratic Army". Historian's Task Ending', *The Sydney Morning Herald*, 30 August 1941, p. 12.
11 Charles Bean, Letter to the Editor, 'The Information "blurb"', *The Sydney Morning Herald*, 27 March 1942, p. 3.
12 '"Hate" Talks Defended. Statement by Minister', *The Sydney Morning Herald*, 1 April 1942, p. 6.
13 Bean, *War Aims*, op. cit.
14 ibid., p. 8.
15 ibid., p. 19.
16 ibid., p. 43.
17 ibid., p. 44.
18 ibid., p. 88.
19 ibid., p. 134.

20 C.E.W. Bean, *Australia's Federal Archives: John Curtin's initiative*, Melbourne University Press, Melbourne, 1947, p. 9.
21 Bean, *War Aims*, op. cit., p. 138.
22 ibid., p. 140.
23 Interview with Phyllis Bauer by the author, 7 August 2013.
24 Charles Bean in Lucy Bean diary, op. cit., p. 43.
25 'Hiding' of Jap War Relics Stirs Soldiers', *The Sydney Morning Herald*, 27 March 1953, p. 5 (no by-line).
26 ibid.
27 'Removal of War Relics. Dr Bean explains policy', *The Sydney Morning Herald*, 28 March 1953, p. 3.
28 Letter from Charles Bean to Ralph Allison, principal of Brentwood School, December 1957, courtesy of Brentwood School, London.
29 Cited in Arthur Bazley's C.E.W. Bean obituary, 'Charles Bean. Chronicler of Australia at War', *Canberra Times*, 31 August 1968, p. 2.
30 Charles Bean in Lucy Bean diary, op. cit.
31 'The Memorial of Example', *The Canberra Times*, 26 September 1959, p. 2.
32 Letter from Charles Bean to Arthur Bazley, 7 June 1960, AWM 3DRL 3520 10c, Australian War Memorial, Canberra.
33 Address by Angus McLachlan at Charles Bean's memorial service, St Andrew's Cathedral, Sydney, 2 September 1968, National Archives series M1129, barcode 31640017, Canberra.
34 Guy Harriott, 'Great War Historian', *The Sydney Morning Herald*, 31 August 1968, p. 2.
35 Cited in Jeremy Paxman, *Great Britain's Great War*, Penguin Viking, London, 2013, p. 186.
36 C.E.W. Bean, *Official History of Australia in the War of 1914–1918*, 1st edition, Australian War Memorial, Canberra, 1942, vol. 6, 'The Australian Imperial Force during the Allied offensive in France 1918', pp. 1094–5.
37 ibid., p. 1096.

INDEX

M